Where the New World Is

SERIES EDITOR

Riché Richardson, Cornell University

FOUNDING EDITOR

Jon Smith, Simon Fraser University

ADVISORY BOARD

Houston A. Baker Jr., Vanderbilt University

Leigh Anne Duck, The University of Mississippi

Jennifer Greeson, The University of Virginia

Trudier Harris, The University of Alabama

John T. Matthews, Boston University

Tara McPherson, The University of Southern California

Claudia Milian, Duke University

Where the New World Is

LITERATURE ABOUT THE U.S. SOUTH
AT GLOBAL SCALES

Martyn Bone

The University of
Georgia Press
ATHENS

Paperback edition, 2020
© 2018 by the University of Georgia Press
Athens, Georgia 30602
www.ugapress.org
All rights reserved
Set in 10/13 Kepler Std Regular by Kaelin Chappell Broaddus

Most University of Georgia Press titles are
available from popular e-book vendors.

Printed digitally

Library of Congress Cataloging-in-Publication Data

Names: Bone, Martyn, 1974– author.
Title: Where the new world is : literature about the U.S. South at global scales / Martyn Bone.
Other titles: Literature about the U.S. South at global scales
Description: Athens : The University of Georgia Press, 2018. | Series: The new Southern studies | Includes bibliographical references and index.
Identifiers: LCCN 2017032683 | ISBN 9780820351865 (hardcover : alk. paper) | ISBN 9780820351858 (ebook) LED
Subjects: LCSH: Globalization in literature. | American fiction—Southern States—History and criticism. | American fiction—20th century—History and criticism. | American fiction—21st century—History and criticism. | Emigration and immigration in literature. | Cultural pluralism in literature. | Southern States—In literature.
Classification: LCC PS374.G58 B66 2018 | DDC 813/.540935875—dc23
LC record available at https://lccn.loc.gov/2017032683

ISBN 9780820357874 (paperback : alk. paper)

To Samuel, Rosa, and Isaac

CONTENTS

PREFACE ix

INTRODUCTION The Transnational Turn in the South 1

CHAPTER ONE The Extended South of Black Folk: Intraregional and Transnational Migrant Labor in the Writing of Zora Neale Hurston 28

CHAPTER TWO Transnational/Intertextual Migrations and U.S. Southern, Danish, and English "Folk" Identities in Nella Larsen's Fiction 53

CHAPTER THREE Downsouth, Upsouth, Global South: Migration and the "New World" in John Oliver Killens's Writing 78

CHAPTER FOUR The North–South Axis of Race, Class, and Migration in Russell Banks's Fiction 106

CHAPTER FIVE Workings of the Spirit, Spirit of the Workers: Migration, Labor, and the Extended Caribbean in Erna Brodber's *Louisiana* 135

CHAPTER SIX Neoslavery, Immigrant Labor, and Casino Capitalism in Cynthia Shearer's *The Celestial Jukebox* 155

CHAPTER SEVEN Southern Transpacific: Narratives of Asian Immigration, 1965–2015 176

EPILOGUE Transnational American Studies with "the South": Morrison, Matthiessen, Eggers, and Lalami 196

NOTES 215

WORKS CITED 249

INDEX 269

PREFACE

In the epilogue to *The Postsouthern Sense of Place in Contemporary Fiction* (2005), I called for contemporary southern literary studies to go "against the Agrarian grain" that for decades dominated the field and to take "the transnational turn" ascendant in American studies. In the final paragraph, I stated my belief "that writers will emerge from the region's new transnational populations to rewrite 'the South' again in unexpected and exciting ways."[1] In *Where the New World Is: Literature about the U.S. South at Global Scales*, I consider how contemporary fiction—from 1980 to 2014, most of it by or about immigrants—has resituated the U.S. South globally, and how earlier twentieth-century writing already had done so in ways that traditional southern literary studies tended to ignore.

In the years since I finished that first book and began working on this one, southern literary studies has been radically reconstructed. At the time of writing, it is fifteen years since Houston Baker and Dana Nelson issued their clarion call in *American Literature* for a "new Southern studies."[2] That call generated and gave a collective name to a substantial body of scholarship, some of which I discuss in the introduction that follows, and which includes the books that preceded this one in the University of Georgia Press's New Southern Studies series. In the wake of the new southern studies, my more modest proposal to go "against the Agrarian grain" seems rather quaint: Jon Smith has remarked that "still grappling with the Agrarians" was something that "mainstream American studies would not even bother doing."[3] Yet as Smith notes elsewhere, self-consciously "sexy, militant," and "radical-chic" American studies has also failed to take seriously other versions of the South. In *Finding Purple America: The South and the Future of American Cultural Studies* (2013), Smith charges that "an American studies that continues to rely on such a convenient southern exceptionalism"—an image of the South as nothing more than "the staid, backward Other to a nation and a field continually rebranded as energetic, future-oriented, young, and passionate"—"is, surely, no American studies at all."[4] One might demur that the South has been somewhat less marginalized in American studies outside the United States—for example in Britain, where I was trained. Still, I conceived *Where the New World Is* as a contribution to transnational American studies, as much as to a (then) germinal new southern studies.

Given that this book takes various transnational turns—south of the U.S. South to the Caribbean, across the (black) Atlantic, and into the South Pacific—

it is worth addressing the "newness" of that orientation. After all, if the new southern studies dates to the salad days of the twenty-first century, American studies' "transnational turn," with its focus on what Robert Gross once sunnily summarized as "a world of fluid borders, where goods, ideas, and people flow constantly across once-sovereign space," began during the mid-1990s.[5] Since then, leftist scholars like Joel Pfister have stressed that a "usable" transnational American studies must attend more critically to "the migrations of capital, corporations, commodities, laborers, technologies, mass culture, ideologies, and resistance movements across borders." Pfister insists that "globalization is our social reality, the 'context' for the movement of capital, labor, resistance, culture, and ideas," and calls for a kind of combined Marxist-transnationalist "focus on capitalism and labor."[6] Elsewhere, though, a certain fatigue with transnationalism has emerged, indexed by Graham Thompson's remark in a roundtable on Fredric Jameson's *The Antinomies of Realism* (2013) that "the much-vaunted transnational turn" is beginning to sound "old and redundant."[7] Another British scholar, Christopher Lloyd, claims in *Rooting Memory, Rooting Place* (2015) that transnationalism is now "dominating" (new) southern studies and takes his stand for a doubly "rooted" regionalism against that alleged dominance. But as I believe this book demonstrates, there is still much to be said and done to reassess the U.S. South, and literature about the U.S. South, from an array of transnational perspectives. For starters (and as I will argue more thoroughly in the introduction), Baker and Nelson's initial model for the "new southern studies" was almost entirely concerned with the relationship between region and nation. Furthermore, to the degree that (new) southern studies has ever been "under the sway" of transnationalism, its orientation has been overwhelmingly hemispheric, linking the U.S. South to the Caribbean and Latin America.[8] *Where the New World Is*, then, seeks not only to resituate the South transnationally but to do so at various global scales: hemispheric, transatlantic, and transpacific.

In my first book, I drew on the critical spatial theories of thinkers like Jameson, Edward Soja, and David Harvey to apply a "simultaneously historical and geographical materialism" in my analysis of how, from the early 1960s to the late 1990s, (post)southern literary texts depicted the capitalist reproduction—or creative destruction—of "place" in the U.S. South.[9] In *Where the New World Is*, I recommit myself to historical-geographical materialism, not least to illuminate my subthematic focus on forms of migration and labor. This approach also dovetails with Paul Giles's call in *The Global Remapping of American Literature* (2011) to "reconsider American literature specifically in the context of geographical materialism," and the new southern studies' increasing emphasis on the relationship between economic globalization, immigration, and the South's long history of labor exploitation.[10] However, in taking hemispheric, transatlantic, and transpacific turns, I also utilize theories of "scale" that originated in human geography, have been adapted to literary studies, but appear only occasionally in the new southern studies. In many of the literary texts discussed across the seven chapters and epilogue of this book, "the South" no longer seems to suffice: as a scale at which characters might cognitively map their being in the world, this most (in)famous "region" sometimes seems to have been rendered redundant by the material and mental shifts engendered by economic globalization and transnational migration. Having said that, *Where the New World Is* also attends to ways in which an apparently "globalized" U.S. South yet remains imbricated with a range of other scales, from the local to the national.

In the first six chapters, I focus on six writers—Zora Neale Hurston, Nella Larsen, John Oliver Killens, Russell Banks, Erna Brodber, and Cynthia Shearer—who between the 1920s and the early twenty-first century resituated the U.S. South at global scales. All these writers, like the contemporary Asian American immigrant authors I discuss in chapter 7—Monique Truong, Lan Cao, and Ha Jin—emphasize in varying ways the role of migration in reconfiguring the region transnationally. Most of the newer novels—by Banks and Shearer as well as Truong, Cao, and Jin—focus on the current era of economic globalization, which has generated considerable immigration to the U.S. South. However, part of the project of this book is to explore how earlier black authors—Hurston, Larsen, and Killens—were already rewriting the U.S. South at intraregional, national, and transnational scales, and across a temporal range spanning from slavery and Reconstruction to the Civil Rights movement and postcolonial revolution. The chapter devoted to Brodber details how one nonsouthern, non-American writer from the wider black diaspora riffed on Hurston by remapping the region as part of what Immanuel Wallerstein terms the "extended Caribbean."[11] But there are also clear historical-geographic continuities between the representation of Caribbean migration to Florida in Hurston's writing and, in a later period, the fiction of a white male northern U.S. author like Banks. In the epilogue, I briefly discuss how four more authors regarded as important contemporary *American* authors—Toni Morrison, Peter Matthiessen, Dave Eggers, and Laila Lalami—also represent the region transnationally and transhistorically, from (in Lalami's case) the beginnings of settler colonialism in the so-called New World to (in Eggers's nonfiction) the "Third World-ing" of New Orleans after Hurricane Katrina. In doing so, these authors may reveal to southernists and Americanists alike that literature about (rather than from) the South is not simply or reductively "regional." Indeed, reading these writers' work regionally *and* globally can help us imagine the futures of both southern studies *and* American studies. Though only two of the authors featured in this book were born in the U.S. South (Hurston and Killens), a commonality between all of them is their emphasis, however eclectically expressed, on migration to and from the region, across and between various regional, national, and transnational borders. Many of the novels and stories under discussion also excavate the labor exploitation that has recurred in shape-shifting fashion from the Old South to today's globalized South.

In the introduction, I begin by providing some historical and geographical context for contemporary debates about the "globalization" of the U.S. South. I emphasize ways in which the region has always—even before it became what we call the "U.S. South"—been inextricably bound up with transnational trends and processes, especially the forced migration of African slavery. However, the centrality of slave labor to the socioeconomic structuring of antebellum southern society, followed by postbellum forms of neoslave labor relations (sharecropping, convict labor), precluded—notwithstanding notable exceptions—the growth of voluntary migration into the region. Hence there are sound reasons why, in the literature of the Southern Renaissance, foreigners and immigrants usually figure as exotic individual aliens entering inward-looking rural or small-town locales. In the second section of the introduction, I consider how post-1965 immigration on a mass scale, tightly connected with capitalist globalization, has transformed the demographics of the U.S. South, radically undermining the rigid black-and-white racial binary established during slavery and reinforced throughout the Jim Crow era. Yet the experience of these immigrants in a globalized, neoliberal South often includes forms of labor and poverty that exhibit uncanny echoes of earlier forms of exploitation in the region. Here we encounter the kinds of historical (and geographical) continuities between old, new, and globalized Souths that have been imaginatively traced by some of the authors discussed in subsequent chapters.

The third section of the introduction considers the transnational turn in relation to and within the new southern studies as well as relevant southern historiography. I consider the "hemispheric phase" of early new southern studies along with attempts to recast it in "global contexts." I also delineate some of the debates about globalization, and resulting disciplinary discontents, that have emerged between historians and the cohort of literary and cultural studies scholars associated with the new southern studies. I then adumbrate the emergence of a more materialist new southern studies that attends to ways in which the contemporary exploitation of immigrant workers in the globalized U.S. South recalls the fraught regional history of racialized labor. In the fourth and final section, I assess how such debates about economic globalization, immigration, and transnationalism have played out within the subfield of southern literary studies, where narratives by and about immigrants remain marginalized. I ponder the relative merits of "regional," "national," or "transnational" as scales for analyzing "the South" and call for attention to the dialectical relationship between these scales—not least as they register in the literature discussed in the chapters that follow.

Chapter 1 considers Zora Neale Hurston's representation of both intraregional and transnational migrant labor across the course of her richly idiosyncratic career. I trace how Hurston made the movements of black southern workers *around* and Caribbean laborers *into* the U.S. South integral to the narrative cartographies of *Jonah's Gourd Vine* (1934) and *Their Eyes Were Watching God* (1937). In both novels, key black southern characters migrate not northward but southward. However, rather than discursively displacing the Great Migration by focusing on the rural southern "folk" (as Hazel Carby has influentially charged), Hurston hereby engages with the lesser known history of black migrant workers *within* the South; moreover, the narrative shift south to the "muck" of the Everglades in *Their Eyes* emphasizes the encounter between black southern and Bahamian migrant workers. I also explore the main, largely overlooked historical source for the hurricane and flood that devastate the muck's diasporic black community: the huge storm that hit the Everglades in September 1928, killing thousands of black migrant workers. The chapter begins and concludes by considering the manuscript drafts of Hurston's unpublished 1958 essay on migrant workers in Florida. I argue that this essay can be considered as part of a continuum with the four books that Hurston published between 1934 and 1938. Across two decades, Hurston revealed the ongoing role of the U.S. South—especially south Florida—within an extended Caribbean characterized by the kind of migrant labor patterns more recently traced by historians.

Chapter 2 turns to another African American woman writer who, like Hurston, has been rescued from obscurity and recuperated as a major novelist of the Harlem Renaissance but whose representation of rural black southern culture is rather less adaptable to a revisionist reading of the Southern Renaissance. I discuss Nella Larsen's debut novel, *Quicksand* (1928), as a Danish-African-American author's remapping of the U.S. South at national and transatlantic scales. This remapping is mediated through the multiple migrations of semiautobiographical protagonist Helga Crane across the Mason-Dixon Line and the (black) Atlantic. Through Helga's frequent transregional and transnational relocations to and between various urban sites—Chicago, New York, Copenhagen—bookended by her two periods living in the rural U.S. South, *Quicksand* develops a comparative representation of two ostensibly contrasting "folk" cultures: black U.S. southerners (including rural migrants to Chicago and Harlem) and working-class Danes (including rural migrants to Copenhagen). The chapter concludes with a discussion of the controversial short story "Sanctuary" (1930), which generated accusations that Larsen had plagiarized Sheila Kaye-Smith's "Mrs. Adis" (1922). I read "Sanctuary"—Larsen's only work of fiction set entirely in the U.S. South—as extending *Quicksand*'s transnational, intertextual recasting of racial and regional folk identities: the story revises Kaye-Smith's account of rural English class and labor conflict as a more familiar (and folklike) fable of racial strife under the U.S. southern sign of Jim Crow.

Chapter 3 attends to the work of John Oliver Killens, a black southern author whose prominence during the 1950s and 1960s as the leading light of the Harlem Writers Guild and a political activist affiliated with Malcolm X stands in stark contrast to his marginalization within southern literary studies. I argue that Killens's writing anticipated, and constitutes a kind of case study for, Baker's and Nelson's insistence on "the nuanced inseparability of North and South in any fruitful model of American cultural studies."[12] I begin with Killens's best-known book, *Youngblood* (1954), a precocious debut novel in which he was already keen to emphasize that the regional was inextricable from the national. *Youngblood* insists that supposedly "southern" problems of race and labor relations in the fictional Georgia city of Crossroads (based on Killens's hometown, Macon) cannot be detached from his characters' experiences of white racism and black activism in New York and Washington. The novel thus foreshadows the formulation that Killens would articulate more explicitly over the next few years in speeches, essays, and an unperformed play: that "Downsouth" is inseparable from "Upsouth." Yet Killens's writing did not remain confined to the regional-national framework of his own terminology. In the politically tumultuous years leading up to his third novel, *'Sippi* (1967), during which Killens negotiated an activist position between internationalist socialism and black nationalism, he also remapped Downsouth and Upsouth in relation to the Global South. Killens's second and most compelling novel, *And Then We Heard the Thunder* (1963), follows the experiences of black soldiers training and fighting in the U.S. Army during World War II. *Thunder*'s textual migrations—from Georgia via California to the Philippines and Australia—relocate the (black) U.S. South at national *and* transnational scales. But where Hurston's focus is circum-Caribbean/hemispheric and Larsen's transatlantic/black Atlantic, Killens's is transpacific and global southern.

Chapter 4 focuses on the fiction of one of the major American writers of the last forty years, Russell Banks. I consider Banks's narrative cartographies of the economic, demographic, and cultural connections across the "north–south axis" linking New England, the U.S. South, and the Caribbean. Banks's own youthful experiences in Florida and Chapel Hill shaped his conviction that the traumatic encounter of European- and African-descended peoples in the New World generated the dominant narrative of U.S. and hemispheric history. I explore the crucial role of two "Souths" in Banks's life and writing: the U.S. South (especially south Florida) and the Caribbean (as a kind of deeper south on that hemispheric "axis"). I read Banks's most autobiographical novel, *The Book of Jamaica* (1980), in intertextual relation to Hurston's *Tell My Horse* (1938). In Hurston's book of Jamaica and Haiti, her pioneering status as a black southern female participant-observer in and of the extended Caribbean is compromised by a possessive, neo-imperial American "vision" of Jamaica, especially the Maroon colony at Accompong. In *The Book of Jamaica*, the narrator's increasing awareness of his situation as a privileged white American male, not least vis-à-vis the Maroons, engenders a sustained examination of U.S. hemispheric power. The core of this chapter, though, is a reading of Banks's breakthrough novel *Continental Drift* (1985): its representation of south Florida on a north–south axis that extends from New Hampshire to Haiti, particularly via transregional and transnational patterns of migration to Miami. The genesis of *Continental Drift* was Banks's interest in news stories of smuggled Haitians drowning at sea off the Florida coast: a grim microcosm of sociopolitical circumstances shaped by U.S. foreign policy in the Caribbean. In the novel, the northward migration of Vanise and Claude Dorsinville from Haiti intersects with the southward migration of white working-class Bob Dubois from New Hampshire. Through the tragic trajectories of these characters, Banks teases out different meanings of possession: Vanise finds sanctuary from racial and sexual exploitation in being possessed by *voudon* loas, whereas Claude gives himself over to the immigrant faith in American capitalism. Yet ultimately it is Bob who is most perniciously "possessed," becoming involved in the illegal smuggling and drowning of Haitian refugees. Like Hurston before him, Banks challenges stereotypical notions of voodoo/*voudon* possession, in this case by formulating an alternative definition of Reagan-era "voodoo economics": to be so possessed by the corrupting "spirit" of capitalism that one becomes, like Bob, *dis*possessed of one's identity and humanity.

Chapter 5 considers the writing of Jamaican sociologist and novelist Erna Brodber, especially *Louisiana* (1994), another work of fiction that can be read with intertextual reference to Hurston's insistent focus on the connections between the U.S. South and the Caribbean. I begin by exploring *Louisiana*'s innovative mapping of black (female) migration during the late nineteenth and early twentieth centuries: the Great Migration of black southerners to northern metropolises as well as movements between Jamaica and the United States. Much as Larsen in *Quicksand* mediates wider migrations through the individual movements of her protagonist, Helga Crane, so in *Louisiana* the transnational and transregional travels of Ella Townsend—northward from Jamaica to New York and then southward to New Orleans—are metonymic of larger migratory patterns. In New Orleans, Ella transforms herself from an academic anthropologist into a "horse" for spirit possession; here Brodber references both Hurston's anthropological writing and New Orleans' own storied history of voodoo. However, *Louisiana* also focuses on the historical and material conditions of black southerners, including strategies of resistance to the racist and capitalist exploitation of their labor. Unpacking the narrative's suitably oblique representations of these workers' resistance is crucial to a fuller understanding of the novel's own cultural work: as Ella's manuscript proceeds, spiritual and psychic forms of knowledge reveal a historical and political unconscious of black U.S. southern and Caribbean struggle in the canefields of late nineteenth-century rural Louisiana and on the waterfront of early twentieth-century New Orleans. Like *Continental Drift* and Brodber's own previous novel *Myal* (1988), *Louisiana* also reconfigures the more deleterious effects of spirit possession as analogous to capitalist exploitation or "possession" of black labor. Perhaps most striking, however, is Ella's gradual revelation of the hidden history of Garveyite activism among blacks in the rural South. Finally, *Louisiana* extends its material history of migrant labor to Jamaican guest workers in New Orleans during and after World War II, and recalls the kind of connections between the Civil Rights movement in the U.S. South and postcolonial revolution in the Global South that so captured Killens's imagination.

Chapter 6 focuses on Cynthia Shearer's *The Celestial Jukebox* (2005), which takes place in rural Mississippi during 2001 and features immigrants from Honduras, Mauritania, and China. Yet Shearer's novel refuses to represent such economic and demographic transformations as simply a "turning point" in southern history, much less as a complete global-southern break with a regional-southern past. Rather, like some of the newer new southern studies scholarship discussed in my introduction, *The Celestial Jukebox* emphasizes the eerie historical continuities between the exploitation of immigrant workers in the contemporary U.S. (and global) South and the socioeconomic structures and labor practices that characterized the region in earlier periods. I consider too the novel's depiction of continuities in rural land use, from antebellum plantation slavery to contemporary "casino capitalism." The chapter concludes by considering how one strand of the narrative—following Mauritanian immigrant Boubacar Traore from the Mississippi hamlet of Madagascar via Clarksdale and Memphis to New York—foregrounds more hopeful transhistorical *and* transnational continuities, sustained through the expressive form of music. Like New Orleans jazz in *Louisiana*, so in *The Celestial Jukebox* both jazz and Delta-derived blues circulate across and through the black Atlantic: as adapted and performed by Boubacar, this music amplifies cultural connections across the African diaspora.

Chapter 7 looks away from the hemispheric and transatlantic scales of analysis that predominate in most of the prior chapters and seeks to extend American studies' transpacific turn into the new southern studies. It does so by attending to three novels about Asian immigration to the U.S. South since the 1965 Hart-Celler Immigration and Nationality Act and the 1975 withdrawal of U.S. military forces from Vietnam. On one hand, by focusing on Vietnamese refugees and Chinese voluntary migrants, these novels may help move us beyond the nativism and black-white racial binary that remain stubbornly persistent even in contemporary southernist scholarship. On the other hand, Lan Cao's *Monkey Bridge* (1997) and Ha Jin's *A Free Life* (2008) might pose the most radical challenge yet to even revisionist approaches to the region by doing away with the concept and scale of "the South" altogether. Though it is tempting to read *Monkey Bridge* and *A Free Life* alongside Monique Truong's *Bitter in the Mouth* (2010) as narratives about "Asians in the South" or as contributions to a more multiethnic "southern literature," the immigrant protagonists of these novels do not necessarily see themselves as being either "Asian" or in "the South"—let alone as "southern." I conclude the chapter with a brief discussion of Brittani Sonnenberg's debut novel, *Home Leave* (2014), which depicts immigration in the opposite direction. The Kriegstein family moves through the transnational circuits of corporate globalization: from and between the urban and rural U.S. South (Atlanta, small-town Mississippi, mountainous North Carolina), major European cities (Hamburg, London, Berlin), and Asian capitals of global capital (Shanghai, Singapore). In the process, *Home Leave* traces the reconstitution, in a putatively postcolonial and post-American world, of uncannily familiar forms of white privilege as an enduring cultural logic of global capitalism.

The epilogue ponders further the implications, for both the new southern studies and transnational American studies, of re-scaling "the South" globally. It does so by considering how major books by four leading figures in contemporary American literature make a compelling case for the importance of a transnational American studies with "the South." In Toni Morrison's *Tar Baby* (1981, about the black diaspora from the Caribbean via Florida and New York to Paris), Peter Matthiessen's *Shadow Country* (2008, an epic account of Everglades entrepreneur Edgar J. Watson as an allegory of U.S. imperialism), Dave Eggers's *Zeitoun* (2009, mapping post-Katrina New Orleans through the traumatic experiences of a Syrian immigrant), and Laila Lalami's *The Moor's Account* (2014, a neoslave narrative told from the perspective of the first black African to encounter Florida), "the South" is not the most relevant scalar unit. Hence, reading *Tar Baby*, *Shadow Country*, *Zeitoun*, and *The Moor's Account* requires a "southern studies without 'the South'" (Leigh Anne Duck's term) stuck in amber as a homogenous and distinctive "region," yet still able to register that such texts—like many of the novels discussed in this book—collectively depict disturbing historical-geographical continuities between slavery, convict labor, and the abuse of immigrant workers today. But these books also beg a transnational American studies *with* "the South": a critical praxis which recognizes that although such exploitative labor relations are usually seen as distinctly "southern," they are also identifiably American. Ultimately, (new) southern studies and (transnational) American studies would benefit from a mutual understanding of how such literary narratives represent both region *and* nation as inextricable from the capitalist world-system that, circa 1981 or so, came to be called "globalization."

A word or two, too, about the title, which derives from the closing scene of

Killens's *And Then We Heard the Thunder*, in which a weary handful of African American and white southern soldiers meet in the aftermath of an armed battle in the streets of an Australian city. When the southern-born black protagonist declares, "This is the place where the New World is," it could be a dystopian vision of U.S. racism and capitalism's expansion into the Global South or a stubbornly utopian faith in the possibility of postcolonial solidarity between African Americans, Africans, Asians, and even working-class white southerners. Throughout my book, however, the phrase "where the New World is" contains other meanings. In the chapters on Hurston, Banks, and Brodber, it references the simultaneously regional and hemispheric history of New World slavery and colonialism.[13] In my last two chapters' focus on more contemporary immigrant trajectories from other continents—Shearer's depiction of Mauritanian Muslims in Mississippi; Truong, Cao, and Jin's representations of Vietnamese and Chinese characters settling in North Carolina, Virginia, and Georgia—"where the new world is" signifies that "the South" has become a key scale for mapping transnational migration in the era of neoliberal globalization, though the immigrant protagonists may not conceive of it as such.

The production of *Where the New World Is* has taken a few transnational turns of its own. My subject position as a white English male is not obviously comparable to that of Helga Crane in Larsen's *Quicksand*. Nevertheless, during the last few years of writing and revising, I have felt an affinity with Helga's sense of "the division of her life into two parts in two lands"—Denmark and the United States—while "moving shuttle-like from continent to continent." I began work on this book at the University of Copenhagen in 2005 during a teaching leave that allowed me to hash out rough drafts of the Hurston and Larsen chapters. Over the following five years in Copenhagen, I drafted sections of the chapters on Banks, Brodber, and Shearer. For providing intellectual and social sustenance during that longest of my five spells living in Copenhagen, I am grateful to Anne Dvinge, Justin D. Edwards, Trevor Elkington, Rune Graulund, Carl Pedersen, and Stuart Ward.

After taking up an associate professorship at the University of Mississippi in January 2011, I began the Killens chapter and wrote the essay on narratives of Asian immigration to the U.S. South that generated this book's final chapter. Special thanks are due to those colleagues who welcomed me to Oxford in complicated personal circumstances. For their support through a trying transition period, I am particularly grateful to Ivo Kamps, head of the English Department, and Karen Raber, who chaired the search committee that hired me. The English Department and the university's celebrated Center for the Study of Southern Culture provided the kind of environment in which to "do" southern (and American) studies that one can only dream about at most other

U.S. universities, let alone across the Atlantic. I am fortunate to have experienced a period in my career in which I could count among my colleagues the following fine southernists (fellow members of what, in early 2011, a professor from a rival university dubbed the "Mississippi Mafia"): Deborah Barker, Leigh Anne Duck—also, through even greater fortune, my colleague at the University of Copenhagen during 2009–10—Adam Gussow, Jaime Harker, Kathryn McKee, Annette Trefzer, and Jay Watson. For their collegiality and friendship, thanks as well to Adetayo Alabi, Cristie Ellis, Beth Ann Fennelly, Ann Fisher-Wirth, Richard Ford, Tom Franklin, Colby Kullman, Chris Offutt, Peter Reed, Jason Solinger, Daniel Stout, and Ethel Young-Minor. Though personal circumstances required me to return to Copenhagen in summer 2012, I was fortunate to get the chance to return to the University of Mississippi a mere eighteen months later. While a visiting professor during the spring 2014 semester, I finished the Killens chapter, extended the Banks chapter, and enjoyed the privilege of teaching the graduate course devoted to hometown hero William Faulkner (including a class on Graham Swift's *Last Orders* conducted around the kitchen table at Rowan Oak). Thanks to Annette for allowing me to gatecrash her office while she was on leave. For making both of my spells in Oxford so memorable, extra thanks to Mike Lesage and, especially, Elizabeth Rodriguez Fielder.

I began writing the introduction on my most recent return to Copenhagen in summer 2014 but finished the first draft at a café in summery Sydney, Australia, in January 2015. Thanks to my brother, Daniel, and his partner, Signe, for hosting me for those very welcome three weeks Down Under: I was especially happy to be in Sydney for the birth of my nephew Xander on New Year's Eve 2014 and to spend some precious time too with his older brother, Joshua. Portions of the manuscript developed in other locations. Thanks to everyone in New York who hosted me on various occasions between 2011 and 2013. The University of Copenhagen funded a summer 2013 stay in Cambridge, Massachusetts, where my participation in Harvard University's Institute for World Literature—especially Nirvana Tanoukhi's weeklong seminar "The Scale of World Literature"—helped sharpen parts of this book. Thanks to my parents, Janet and Raymond, for providing a sanctuary on those all-too-rare returns to my birthplace: Truro, Cornwall. In the last sixteen months of working on the manuscript, I have been very fortunate to spend downtime in Denmark and Sweden with Linnéa Havsfjord Lindgren and to use Linnéa's apartment across the border in Malmö as a writing retreat.

Research for the book also took me on shorter trips to various locations in the United States. Special thanks are due to the Center for the Study of the Global South at Tulane University for awarding me a generous grant to conduct research for three weeks during January 2009 in Austin and Gainesville. For assisting my research in the Russell Banks Papers at the University of Texas's Harry Ransom Center, I am grateful to archivist Gabriela Redwine. For similar assistance with the Zora Neale Hurston Papers in the George A. Smathers Libraries at the University of Florida, thanks to archivist Florence M. Turcotte and her colleagues in the special collections research room. In May 2014 I spent a week working through the John Oliver Killens Papers in the Stuart A. Rose Manuscript, Archives, and Rare Book Library (MARBL) at Emory University: thanks to associate archivist Kathy Shoemaker for her practical help and to Randall Burkett, curator of MARBL's African American collections, for his interest in the project. I am also grateful to Barbara Killens-Rivera for granting permission to quote from the Killens Papers and supporting my interest in her father's writing. Cheers as well to Det Kongelige Bibliotek in Copenhagen, the J. D. Williams Library at the University of Mississippi, and the New York Public Library for help in securing secondary sources.

I have been fortunate to road-test sections of this manuscript in various forums. Parts of the introduction were developed during invited talks at the University of Manchester (the Northwest Britain American studies postgraduate and postdoctoral conference, May 2013); the University of Graz (November 2013, thanks to an invitation from Silvia Schultermandl); the University of Mississippi (the "New South Identities" symposium, February 2014, organized by Michelle Coffey and Jodi Skipper); and the University of Sydney (a talk at the United States Studies Center in August 2015, organized by Sarah Gleeson-White and Thomas Adams). Parts of chapter 1 were first presented at the Southern Association for American Studies conference, Louisiana State University (February 2005); the Society for the Study of Southern Literature (SSSL) conference in Birmingham, Alabama (March 2006); and the Multi-ethnic Literatures of the United States conference at the University of Georgia in Athens (April 2015). Parts of chapter 2 were first presented at the Nordic Association for American Studies conference in Växjö, Sweden (May 2005); the "Denmark and the Black Atlantic" conference, University of Copenhagen (May 2006); the annual "Faulkner and Yoknapatawpha" conference, University of Mississippi (July 2008); and the "American Objects: Transnationalism of Southern Cultures" symposium, University of Northumbria (March 2014, organized by Michael Bibler). Parts of chapter 3 were first presented at the American Literature Association conference in San Francisco (May 2012); the British Association for American Studies conference, University of Exeter (April 2013); and the University of Mississippi Department of English research seminar series (February 2014). Parts of chapter 4 were first presented at the SSSL conference, College of William & Mary (April 2008), and at the first of the four "Understanding the South, Understanding Modern America" conferences, hosted by the University of Manchester (May 2008). Parts of chapter 5 were first presented at the (much missed) Southern Women Writers conference, Berry College (April 2008; thanks to Jim Watkins for welcoming me into his family's home), and the "Incarceration Cultures" one-day seminar, University of Leeds (March 2010, organized by Kate Dossett). Parts of chapter 6 were first presented in an English Department research seminar at the University of Texas, Austin (January 2009; props to Coleman Hutchison for the invitation and hospitality); the SSSL conference in New Orleans (April 2010); and in my keynote at the annual "Southern Writers / Southern Writing" graduate conference at the University of Mississippi (July 2011; thanks to Kyle Schlett for the invitation). Lastly, I was lucky enough to test parts of the epilogue in an American studies research seminar during my spring 2016 visiting fellowship at the University of Manchester and at the South Atlantic Modern Language Association (SAMLA) conference in Jacksonville (November 2016).

Some of the material in this book has appeared in different form elsewhere. Brief passages from the introduction and parts of chapter 7 derive from my chapter "You Don't Have to Be Born There: Immigration and Contemporary Fiction of the U.S. South" in *The Oxford Handbook to the Literature of the American South* (2016), edited by Fred Hobson and Barbara Ladd. Thanks to Oxford University Press for permission to reprint that material here. An earlier version of some of chapter 1 appeared as "The (Extended) South of Black Folk: Intraregional and Transnational Migrant Labor in *Jonah's Gourd Vine* and *Their Eyes Were Watching God*," *American Literature* 79, no. 4 (December 2007): 753–80. Thanks to Duke University Press for permission to reprint that material here. An early version of some passages from chapter 6 was included in my short essay "Narratives of African Immigration to the U.S. South: Dave Eggers' *What Is the What* and Cynthia Shearer's *The Celestial Jukebox*," *CR: New Centennial Review* 10, no. 1 (2010): 65–76. Thanks to Coleman Hutchison for soliciting that essay for inclusion in the "Souths" subsection that he edited and to Michigan State University Press for permission to reprint here. For permission to include the two images in chapter 1, from the Hurston Papers at the University of Florida, thanks again to the archivists at the George A. Smathers Libraries. The two postcard images of Copenhagen in chapter 2 are out of copyright and can be found at the website Indenforvoldene.dk; thanks to T. M. Sandau for corresponding with me about the postcards and for sending me high-resolution electronic copies. I am grateful to the *Chicago Defender* for their assistance in sourcing the *Defender* cartoon that is included in chapter 3. Thanks to Peter Lindeman at Fairfax Media for confirming I could use the George Aria cartoon from the *Sydney Sun* that also appears in chapter 3, and to the Australian War Memorial for providing a high-resolution copy.

At the University of Georgia Press, I am very grateful to acquisitions editor Nancy Grayson (now retired) for her proactive interest in this project from an early stage, which persuaded me that the press, and especially the New Southern Studies series, was the right match. I was fortunate to work with Walter Biggins a decade or so ago on the edited volume *Perspectives on Barry Han-*

nah; since succeeding Nancy at Georgia, Walter has been unwaveringly encouraging, both in person and over email. As ever, cheers to series coeditor Jon Smith, who has championed and challenged my work since I was a newly minted PhD. I am very grateful to the two anonymous peer reviewers for their unusually extensive and constructive feedback on what was (aggravatingly, no doubt) an unfinished version of the manuscript. Since submitting the final manuscript, I have had the pleasure of working with staff editor Jon Davies, assistant acquisitions editor Bethany Snead, and marketing content and exhibits manager Christina Cotter. Many thanks as well to Daniel Simon for his sterling work copyediting the manuscript.

Finally, I want to express the greatest gratitude to my three children: Samuel, Rosa, and Isaac. They have been remarkably tolerant of my "moving shuttle-like from continent to continent" over the last few years, while providing a core grounding during the decade-plus that the manuscript has been in progress. This book is dedicated to them.

Where the New World Is

INTRODUCTION

The Transnational Turn in the South

On June 23, 2011, CNN's Freedom Project against "Modern-Day Slavery" ran a report about a group of Thai farmers who had paid $9,300 each to recruiters for the multinational corporation Global Horizons, which supplies agricultural workers to U.S. farms under the Department of Labor's H-2A Temporary Agricultural Employment of Foreign Workers program. The Thai nationals were flown from Bangkok via Los Angeles to Hawaii, where their passports were confiscated and they were forced to work for eight hours a day without pay; after that, they were sent to farms in Maryland, Georgia, and Mississippi. Forced to labor for seven months, during which time they received only $4,000 total in salary, the farmers were told they had to keep working until they had paid off their original recruitment debts. A week and a half later, the *New York Times* published an editorial observing that draconian new laws restricting immigration "in Georgia, Alabama and South Carolina are following—and in some ways outdoing—Arizona's attempt to engineer the mass expulsion of the undocumented, no matter the damage to the Constitution, public safety, local economies and immigrant families." Noting the impact on local economies as undocumented foreign workers fled from the threat of deportation, the editorial pointed out that when "the purge takes hold in agriculture, there will be no one left to pick onions, peaches and cotton. The immigrant labor shortage is already being felt in Georgia, where crops are rotting and the governor has called for using jobless ex-convicts in the fields."[1]

As these two mainstream media reports suggest, globalization and immigration are paramount realities in the twenty-first-century U.S. South. These economic and demographic phenomena have compelled scholars across various disciplines to reconsider and recast familiar understandings of "the South." As historians James Cobb and William Stueck observe in their introduction to *Globalization and the American South* (2005), "A growing conviction [has emerged] that there is more value in studying the South as part of the world than as a world apart." In the introduction to *The American South in a Global World* (also from 2005), anthropologist James Peacock, historian

Harry L. Watson, and comparative literature scholar Carrie Matthews posit that contemporary "globalization is ... a turning point in southern history."[2] In similar fashion, traditional models of southern literature and culture, and southern literary and cultural studies, have come under reexamination. In 2004 Jon Smith and Deborah Cohn identified an imperative to "look away from the North in constructing narratives of southern identity" to resituate the U.S. South in hemispheric and "global-southern" terms. In 2006 Kathryn McKee and Annette Trefzer's introduction to their special issue of *American Literature*, "Global Contexts, Local Literatures," ventured that the present "new global phase is a crucial turning point in the South, and transnational and postcolonial perspectives yield a field of study fundamentally different from previous approaches."[3] That these four examples of U.S. southern studies scholarship appeared within a three-year period suggests a collective sense of not only social, economic, and demographic but also disciplinary transformation.

As we will see, cross-disciplinary consensus about the emergence and significance of a globalized "turning point" in the South has been rather less complete than such selective examples suggest. Still, this pervasive feeling that social, economic, and demographic changes in the contemporary era of globalization have generated a paradigm shift in scholarship is understandable if we consider that for something like a century and a half the South was characterized by rigidly racialized labor structures and, relatedly, a low level of migration to the region. The seismic growth in immigration to the U.S. South since 1965 is one major reason the present era of "globalization" (dated to 1981 or thereabouts) seems like such a "turning point" for the South and southern studies. However, I want to stress that any transnational turn in the South—be it socioeconomic, demographic, and/or disciplinary—should not be seen simply as a radical (much less liberating) *break* from regional tradition but rather as revealing discomforting historical-geographical continuities with what went before. After all, "globalization" is hardly a new phenomenon in the region—in profound ways it predates the ideological invention of "the South"— and there are striking similarities between the exploitation of immigrant workers in recent decades and the oppressive and often racialized labor practices that characterized the region in earlier periods. I want to begin, then, by adumbrating earlier examples of (and recent scholarly debates about) globalization, migration, and labor relations in the place we are so accustomed to call "the South."

Periodizing Transnational Turns in the South:
Before 1830, after 1965

In their introduction to *Imagining Our Americas: Toward a Transnational Frame* (2007), historian Heidi Tinsman and anthropologist Sandha Shukla identify the "[t]winned imperatives," when considering the "geographical and imaginative possibilities of *region*," of trying to "contend with contemporary globalization's intensity and to understand globality's historical depth." The region to which Tinsman and Shukla refer is hemispheric: after José Martí, "Our Americas."[4] However, a historical consciousness of how "globality" has shaped a region *within* a nation, such as the U.S. South, is similarly vital—perhaps especially so when that region has more usually been defined according to its alleged "distinctiveness" from the North or nation, in apparent isolation from wider global forces. If, as Leigh Anne Duck observes, "the contemporary intensification of globalization" has significantly "influenced" recent efforts to resituate the U.S. South in global contexts, then it can also make us more cognizant of "the old truth of transnational interactions and exploitations" that are too often obscured by narrowly "regionalist" visions of the U.S. South as distinctive or exceptional.[5]

Since the mid-2000s, a number of scholars across various disciplines have echoed economic historian Alfred E. Eckes's pointed observation that "the South has always been globalized." As Watson reminds us, an "earlier transnational economy virtually created the historical South." That history was defined by the forced migration of Africans via the transatlantic Middle Passage into New World slavery; it was part of what imperial historian A. G. Hopkins has identified as the era of "proto-globalization" between 1600 and 1800. Anthropologist Donald M. Nonini avers that, largely if not entirely due to the transatlantic slave trade, "the American South has been multicultural since at least the sixteenth century": "there have been few periods during which it [the South] has not experienced influxes of migrants from Europe, Latin America, the Caribbean, Asia, and elsewhere."[6] If slaves retained and adapted African cultural forms, their masters were major players in and beyond proto-globalization: literary scholar Patricia Chu has stressed that the world these slavemasters made encompassed multiple transnational routes as the Middle Passage intersected with the global spread of capitalism: "Plantation capitalists stood at the forefront of industrial technology and modern business practice. They were the first to establish and develop global networks to circulate labor (African slaves), raw materials, capital and credit, and commodities."[7] Indeed, white southern planters' global influence and ambition went beyond the Atlantic world's triangular trade in slaves and crops such as cotton. In *American Mediterranean: Southern Slaveholders in the Age of Emancipation* (2008), Matthew Pratt Guterl seeks to bring "to the surface a narrative of Southern history that exists outside of the nation-state" and "recast the nineteenth-century U.S. South as a messy, complicated borderland of sorts between North America and the Caribbean." Guterl does so by (like Chu) challenging the conventional notion of an "increasingly parochial Southern planter class," demonstrating that the planters themselves advocated the "supposedly predestined advance of the United States into the global South"—for example, via the annexation of Cuba as a "Southern version of manifest destiny"—and understood the "labor problem" both during and after slavery as paramount among "pan-American concerns" shared throughout other plantation societies like Cuba, Jamaica, Haiti, and Brazil.[8]

The simultaneously hemispheric and transatlantic worldview of "these cosmopolitan Southern slaveholders" can be understood as a manifestation of what Ifeoma Nwankwo calls "hegemonic cosmopolitanism, exemplified by the material and psychological violence of imperialism and slavery." It contrasts with but is inextricable from the "cosmopolitanism from below" of African-descended slaves in the U.S. South who, notwithstanding that they were the victims of such violence, envisioned themselves as subjects rather than objects. They did so by imagining the hemispheric "common experiences of slavery and discrimination and African heritage" and were especially encouraged by the rumors of revolution in Haiti (1791–1804) that so terrified white southern slavemasters.[9] This fraught New World master-slave dialectic was evident in the "racial panic discourse" that arose among whites in response to Denmark Vesey's thwarted 1822 slave rebellion in South Carolina (Vesey was born in the Danish West Indies and inspired by both the Haitian and American revolutions) and the 1831 Nat Turner insurrection in Virginia.[10] Importantly, this hemispheric and global southern history also reveals "patterns reminiscent of our own age of globalization and labor and capital movement": postbellum arguments about the importation of Chinese and European labor "anticipat[ed] current debates over immigration from Mexico and Latin America."[11] As we will see, Guterl is not the only scholar to compare today's globalized South with earlier periods in the region's hemispheric and Atlantic world history.

In other ways, however, slavery isolated the U.S. South from the wider world. Peter Coclanis—the historian who perhaps has done most to stress that globalization in the South is of a rather longer *durée* than the last few decades—has noted that voluntary (im)migration to the U.S. South was already declining during the early republican and antebellum eras "as slavery limited opportunities for free migrants."[12] The centrality of slave labor to both the South's earlier "globality" *and* the development of its own more local economy and identity can hardly be understated. Peacock has argued that following two centuries in which "the South was a node in a network stretching from Europe through the Caribbean . . . around 1830, the South as a region was invented, as people migrated inland and formed a regional identity that turned inward, in opposition to the new nation."[13] Though never total—there were significant local variations; foreign capital continued to flow in; members of the planter class continued to situate the South transnationally—this inward turn to defending the "peculiar institution" prevented significant further migration into the region. Between 1830 and 1861, the process of southern identity formation around a slave economy—and, as Paul Giles has recently remarked, Native removal, a forced migration *out* of the region—morphed into what Drew Gilpin Faust has called "the creation of Confederate nationalism."[14] Guterl notes that "[t]he establishment of Confederate nationalism" constrained "the South's peculiar borderland culture and Caribbean complexion": plans for imperial expansion were hardly practical in the midst of a draining military conflict, while on the ideological front "the Confederacy had to 'stave off the charge that it was becoming 'Latin'" by stressing its origins in the American Revolution.[15] Though much of the South was only recently settled, and many of the planters (and hence also their human property) were transient, its solidifying identity as a slave-based region *cum* nation hardly encouraged immigrant free laborers. Circa 1860, when approximately 14 percent of the nonsouthern population of the United States was comprised of immigrants, "in the South the figure was only 5 percent."[16]

In the longer term, the regional and neonational invention of "the South" not only "resulted in secession [and] the myth of the lost cause" but also "diminished global connection and migration during the nineteenth and twentieth centuries."[17] For at least a few decades following the end of slavery and the Confederacy, the tart assessment of a character in Nell Zink's zany novel *Mislaid* (2015) remained broadly true: "The South was built on the cheap labor of neighbors. No immigration, no out-migration, no upward mobility, no downward mobility."[18] To be sure, the postbellum South *tried* to attract immigrants: as masters without slaves, the planter class sought to solve the looming "postwar labor problem" by plugging into "an international network of migrating labor, who might relieve the South of its insufferable dependence on freedmen." Guterl dissects the "fantasies of immigrant labor" that enraptured former slaveowners: most notably, an archetype of the Asian "model minority" myth in which Chinese "coolie" workers were imagined as (in the words of one official report on Chinese immigration circa 1870) "industrious, frugal, obedient and attentive" and thus able "to perform with facility every kind of farm labor." Southern propagandists for coolie labor figured "John Chinaman" as "willing to work where white folks cannot and black folks will not," but in reality Chinese workers proved rather less docile and dependent, asserting their rights, demanding proper recompense, and leaving plantation labor behind. Official immigration bureaus in numerous southern states also campaigned to attract white working-class laborers from politically troubled areas of Europe, especially Ireland and Germany. But even more than the fantasy of John Chinaman, "[w]hite immigration was the fool's gold of the postwar South": European immigrants were aware of the South's reputation, forged by and during slavery, as the "hellish opposite" of the United States' image as "a sort of Shangri-La" for the diligent working-class immigrant. Hence immigrants remained oriented toward other areas of the reunited States, and circa 1870, "the South actually had fewer foreign-born residents than it did in 1860."[19]

With the end of Reconstruction in 1877, white southern authorities looked away from Europe and China and inward once again to the region's native black population. Although a significant number of former slaves took the rollback of Reconstruction as their cue to migrate northward (as in the famous "Kansas Fever" of 1879), the imposition of Jim Crow and the neoslavery of sharecropping—along with the use of convict labor, described by historian Alex Lichtenstein as "New South slavery"[20]—put black labor back in its "place." This again left few employment opportunities for prospective voluntary migrants. As historian David Reimers notes, "Plantation work was [still] identified with blacks," and "aside from agriculture there were few jobs to attract the foreign born," not least because "wages in the southern United States were lower than elsewhere."[21]

Toward the end of the nineteenth century, regional recalcitrance only intensified. Anthropologist Helen A. Regis remarks that "the post-1890 period" was one of "racial polarization, reinforcement of existing social hierarchies, and resistance to federalism," with the result that "[t]he profound transnational connections that shaped the southern United States were silenced."[22] By the early twentieth century, this ossification of the solid (white) South prompted a massive exodus out of the region: the "Great Migration" was underway as black southerners sought an escape from systematic racism and economic exploitation of their labor. Moreover, as historian James N. Gregory has detailed, poor whites joined blacks in a "southern diaspora" seeking better opportunities across the country.[23] Eckes observes, "Out-migration was a problem until the mid-twentieth century. Between 1910 and 1950, an estimated ten million people left the South."[24] It is worth qualifying that black and white southern migration was *intra*regional as well as *inter*regional. As historian Louis M. Kyriakoudes remarks, "The migration that swept black southerners to the cities of the North and West was just one portion of a broader black and white exodus from southern agriculture.... Highly mobile rural southerners moved across the rural South, seeking greater opportunities in the region's tenancy-dominated agriculture."[25] As we will see in chapter 1, Florida became a favored destination for black and white southern migrant workers, along with their counterparts from the Caribbean.

As black and white southerners began moving en masse across the nation, they encountered those arriving from abroad: by 1910, the influx of immigrants into the United States was such that fully 15 percent of the population was foreign-born, while the South's equivalent figure sank to only 2 percent.[26] "During the great wave of immigration to the United States between 1890 and 1920," Mary Odem writes, "small groups of immigrant workers from Europe and China settled in the [South]," but "the vast majority headed to urban areas in the Northwest, Midwest, and West to become part of the industrial workforce." The South was characterized by a "slower pace of industrial development and the presence of a large number of poor blacks and whites who provided a steady pool of low-wage labor" that continued to negate any need for immigrant workers.[27] Moreover, as David Goldfield has observed, the few southern and eastern Europeans who arrived in the South during the early twentieth century suppressed their "ethnic identity in favor of racial solidarity" with native whites, thereby adhering to and reaffirming the region's rigid biracial hierarchy.[28] When in 1916 Randolph Bourne posited his vision of the United States as "not a nationality, but a trans-nationality, a weaving back and forth, with the other lands, of many threads"—especially immigrants and the expressive cultures they brought with them—he identified the South as a conspicuous exception to that "cosmopolitan" vision. Bourne archly observed that the South was the "most distinctively 'American'" region of the nation, but only if one conformed to a retrograde model of national identity based exclusively on a conservative "Anglo-Saxon tradition" that smugly assumed "the inferiority of the non-Anglo-Saxon immigrant." For Bourne, the South was the antithesis to his "trans-national America": the *absence* of "foreign hordes" entering the region left it still "an English colony, stagnant and complacent" as well as "culturally sterile." (Here Bourne also anticipated by a year H. L. Mencken's infamous skewering of the South as "almost as sterile, artistically, intellectually, culturally, as the Sahara Desert.")[29] Though Bourne focused his ire on the national myth of melting-pot assimilation (and would, decades later, inspire American studies' "transnational turn"), he shared the increasingly normative view that the South's continued inclination to look away from the nation and world, while clinging stubbornly to an antiquated system of agricultural labor that discouraged immigration, went against the American grain. Even as Bourne redeemed American exceptionalism by celebrating "the uniqueness of this trans-nationalism of ours," he—like so many others since—reaffirmed an image of the South as what Barbara Smith and Jamie Winders call "a space of exception" to such exceptionalism, "a place where national trends of immigrant settlement and labor have been presumed not to apply."[30]

Of course, there were always local exceptions to the South's apparent exceptionalism from national patterns of immigration. Between the Civil War and World War I, "Greeks, Cubans and Italians went to Florida," with Italians also settling in New Orleans and the Mississippi Delta or working on Arkansas plantations.[31] While "[t]he popular stereotype of Mississippi" remains one "of a conservative agrarian society, with only limited openness to outside influence" and "limited migration," several of the essays collected in *Ethnic Heritage in Mississippi* (2012) suggest otherwise. That varying permutations of not only European and African but also Syrian and Chinese peoples entered Mississippi between the 1840s and 1890s prompts volume editor Shana Walton to propose, a tad hyperbolically, that today's seemingly unprecedented wave of "globalized" immigration really means that "Mississippi is returning to its early diversity."[32] Chinese immigrants began arriving in the Magnolia State during the late 1860s after being "hired by planters as an implicit and sometimes explicit threat to their own [newly emancipated] black labor."[33] But in a postslavery society overwhelmingly defined by the black-white racial binary, the niche available to such immigrant groups was narrow indeed. Though the "Mississippi Chinese" cannily exploited that binary by moving out of the cotton fields to establish grocery stores in black neighborhoods that white businessmen deemed beneath them, for decades they struggled to negotiate their own identity within a strictly segregated Jim Crow South. As Leslie Bow has observed—and as will be discussed in chapter 6 of this book—this tenuous and anomalous "racial interstitiality" in an otherwise rigidly demarcated black-and-white South meant that powerful whites were more likely to define the Mississippi Chinese as "partly colored" than "honorary whites."[34]

Given the South's neoslavery labor practices, its rigidly binary racial structures, and its exceptionalism vis-à-vis national (im)migration patterns—even after federal anti-immigration laws were implemented during the 1920s—it is not surprising that when foreigners and immigrants appeared in literature by major writers of the Southern Renaissance, they were usually figured as individual interlopers in otherwise fixed, isolated rural or small-town locales. One might point here to Joe Christmas's "Mexican" migrant father in William Faulkner's *Light in August* (1932), or the Argentine captain Gualdres in the title story from *Knight's Gambit* (1949); the Greek mute Antonapoulos in Carson McCullers's *The Heart Is a Lonely Hunter* (1940); the postwar Polish refugee Guizac and his kin in Flannery O'Connor's "The Displaced Person" (1955); Lady Torrance in Tennessee Williams's *Orpheus Descending* (first performed in 1957), the daughter of an Italian immigrant to the Mississippi Delta murdered by local whites; or Cuban migrant worker and guitar whiz Tico Feo in Truman Capote's "A Diamond Guitar" (1958), a "foreigner" who—along with "one Chinese"—constitutes the exception to the black-white binary of "one hundred and nine white men [and] ninety-seven Negroes" incarcerated at the story's Parchman-like "prison farm." (Tellingly, the anomalous Chinese inmate bunks with the black inmates, in accordance with his "partly colored" status, while Tico shacks up with the white prisoners: the Cuban's "yellow hair" is enough to mark him as "white" within the prison's microcosm of Jim Crow racial and spatial structures.)[35] To be sure, such starkly individual cases were not the only way of representing immigration during the renaissance era. I will discuss in chapter 1 how Zora Neale Hurston depicted Caribbean migrant workers in Florida. Still, it is telling that Hurston's work barely registered with southern literary scholars between the 1950s and the early 1980s: only more recently has her engagement with the black diasporic demographic and cultural connections between the U.S. South and the Caribbean dovetailed with critical debates in the new southern studies. It is surely not coincidental that the neo-Agrarian "image" of the South and southern literature as characterized by a "strong identification with a place" and "intense involvement in a fixed, defined society" was invented and institutionalized in academia during the 1950s and 1960s.[36] Though rarely addressed by southern literary scholars of the "Rubin generation," white "massive resistance" to the Civil Rights movement and its "outside agitators" ensured that Mississippi was not the only southern state that seemed more than ever a "closed society."[37]

Immigration to the Globalized U.S. South (and within the Global South): Turning Point and/or Historical Continuities?

Since 2005 or so, there has been widespread scholarly agreement that "the American South is once more subject to globalization."[38] Even Nonini, who stresses earlier globalizing processes in the South, acknowledges that "only during the last three decades have changes associated with globalization in the regional economies of the Americas called forth new flows of people and capital between the North American South and Mexico, Central America, the Caribbean, and Asia."[39] And, one might add, Africa. In *The Making of African America: The Four Great Migrations* (2010), historian Ira Berlin notes that while the conventional "slavery-to-freedom" metanarrative of black experience culminates with the 1965 Voting Rights Act, another piece of legislation passed later that year—the Hart-Celler Immigration Act—was arguably even more significant. Hart-Celler allowed the United States to reaffirm "the nation's heritage as a global sanctuary," at a time when the percentage of foreign-born peoples was at a historical low, and "initiated a transformation of black America" as an influx of voluntary African and Caribbean immigrants surpassed the numbers brought across the Atlantic during the slave trade. As Berlin, Nwankwo, and others have noted, this new influx has scrambled conventional definitions of "African American" identity.[40] But the fact that many of these African and Caribbean immigrants arrived and settled in former Confederate states—especially cities like Atlanta, Houston, and Miami—has also disrupted familiar notions of southern identity. Encounters as well as antagonisms between African immigrants and African Americans / black southerners are dramatized in important contemporary novels including Cynthia Shearer's *The Celestial Jukebox* (2005), Dave Eggers's *What Is the What* (2006), and Yaa Gyasi's fine debut, *Homegoing* (2016).[41]

Circa 1950, only 1.6 percent of the South's population had been born in other countries; by contrast, the 2000 census showed that "[f]oreign-born people" now "comprised 7.9 percent of population in the South."[42] In the 1990s, mass Latino/a immigration moved beyond the familiar destinations (Texas and Florida) so that "in virtually every other southern state the Hispanic growth rate surpassed the national growth rate in Hispanic population by three, four, five, or six times." In North Carolina, the census count revealed that the Hispanic presence had grown by 394 percent during the decade. This dramatic growth has led scholars to speak of the "Latinization" of a "region where change has always been slow and received with skepticism" and the emergence of a "*nuevo* New South."[43] Such terminology is problematic: the semantic reiteration of novelty threatens to elide the deep history of Latinos/as in older (and older new) Souths, dating back to early Spanish colonialism more than five centuries ago. We would do well to heed María DeGuzmán's warning that it would be "a mistake that perpetuates an ideology of Anglocentric white supremacist hegemony" to "conceive of Spanish, Mexican, and Mexican American cultural presence in ... the South as a mere alien presence making its appearance in the 1980s or early 1990s."[44] Having said that, contemporary "Latinization" is conspicuous partly because Mexican, Guatemalan, Salvadoran, Honduran, Puerto Rican, Dominican, Colombian, and Venezuelan newcomers "are not following the previous path of suppressed ethnic identity" taken by southern and eastern European immigrants during the early twentieth century.[45]

Nonini's reference to the "flows of people and capital" gestures to the inextricability of economic globalization and immigration, especially in the form of immigrant labor. Barbara Ellen Smith stresses that "globalization arrives in the U.S. South not only through the practices of transnational corporations but also in human form—specifically, new immigrants."[46] For some southern partisans, globalization—not least this influx of immigrants—has superseded "Americanization" as the latest external leviathan threatening "southern distinctiveness."[47] The flip side to such eschatological fears concerning the "Globalization of Dixie" is a tendency to figure free-market capitalism as a liberating force that has opened up the "closed society" and supplanted Jim Crow's biracial hierarchy with a multiethnic, multicultural populace. The reality is more nuanced: while these economic and demographic processes are clearly transforming the South, they also expose and even exacerbate the region's preexisting and distinctive—if not exceptional—social, racial, and spatial inequities.

Here it is worth noting that not only the ethnic variety but also the *class* of many (im)migrant workers entering the region has changed quite significantly from the indentured white European or enslaved black African of earlier southern history. The post-1965 acceleration of immigration has also generated "the formation of new transnational circuits made up of labor migrants, businesspeople, professionals, political refugees, students, and tourists."[48] Sawa Kurotani and Sayuri Guthrie-Shimizu have explored what happens when "the South meets the East" as white-collar Japanese corporate professionals are transferred from their home country to positions in North Carolina's Research Triangle. On one hand, they become an "urban, internationalized, middle-class part of today's American South"; on the other, they are largely "unaware of and unconcerned with the regional economic disparity" around them, including deep-rooted rural poverty and "rundown wooden shacks that stand precariously outside the glitter of globalization."[49] Ajantha Subramanian has critiqued the "corporate multiculturalism" promoted in political invocations of "a new South–South solidarity" between North Carolina and south Asia. Subramanian notes that while this vision—a version of what Joel Pfister has called "diversity capitalism"—facilitates the entry of affluent Indian professionals into "previously white-dominated social spaces" like universities, research institutions, and corporations, it also ensures their class-based segregation from less privileged whites, blacks, and Latino/as.[50] As Nonini notes, the "presence of cosmopolitan professionals" alongside poor local populations "distinguishes the globalized southern economy with a new and extreme form of economic and social inequality." But as sociologist Wanda Rushing sees it, economic globalization in a city like Memphis also "tends to reproduce old patterns of inequality, generating wealth and power for a few and maintaining the structure of poverty and inequality for many."[51] The intersection of the regional and global both erases *and* expands familiar "southern" forms of historical-geographical uneven development.

Hence, as historian Brian Ward warns, "despite a tendency to hail the liberating and progressive potential of globalization, there is little to suggest that transnational manifestations of private, though often state-supported, economic and cultural power are inherently liberating and progressive."[52] Literary scholar Hosam Aboul-Ela has scored the contributors (primarily historians) to *Globalization and the American South* for too easily accepting "the U.S.-centric, neoliberal narrative" that views economic globalization as a largely positive force, and for only secondarily considering immigration and its discontents.[53] Such critiques within and of southern studies recall Rob Wilson and Wimal Dissanayake's warning in *Global/Local: Cultural Production and the Transnational Imaginary* (1996) that "[t]oo much of cultural studies, in this era of uneven globalization ... can sound like a way of making the world safe and user-friendly for global capital."[54] Like Wilson and Dissanayake, Ward and Aboul-Ela identify the pitfalls of a "vulgar transnationalism" that (like corporate multiculturalism) uncritically accepts and recapitulates the cultural logic of global, neoliberal capitalism.[55] The CNN and *New York Times* reports referenced in the opening paragraph serve as a salutary reminder that despite the increasing numbers of well-educated white-collar corporate employees arriving from around the world, the globalization of labor in the U.S. South remains overwhelmingly characterized by manual, unskilled work performed by poorly paid, temporary, and undocumented nonwhite immigrants.

Indeed, under neoliberal capitalism, U.S. and especially southern agricultural employers hire immigrant workers because they lack even rudimentary rights or other forms of protection from the state; supposedly pliant Latino/a workers (like Chinese "coolies" after slavery) alleviate employers' "historic dependence on black labor."[56] There are historical continuities here too: as labor historian Cindy Hahamovitch demonstrates, this deregulation and denial of rights can be traced back to the Emergency Labor Importation Program instituted during World War II. Though the program was supposed to end with the war itself, Mexican and Caribbean "guest workers" continued to arrive in even larger numbers—not due to any lack of local labor but because large-scale employers like U.S. Sugar in Florida wanted flexible, low-wage employees. Facilitating this "agricultural exceptionalism," the U.S. government abdicated its wartime role of regulating employers. Unprotected by the state, Caribbean farmworkers in Florida during and after the war experienced conditions with obvious "parallels to slavery," but with the extra twist that "[i]n this new era of transnational labor, the threat of deportation became the new whip."[57]

Given such transhistorical parallels, one might well ask how "*nuevo*" the latest "New South" really is. Into the twenty-first century, many Latino/a immigrants have faced oppressive working conditions that recall the region's long history of racialized labor exploitation "from the days of slavery to post–Civil War freedmen to the Mexican braceros."[58] In 2004 the Southern Poverty Law Center founded the Immigrant Justice Project and published a report entitled *Close to Slavery*, which recorded extreme abuse of immigrant labor across H-2 guest worker programs. In *Nobodies: Modern American Slave Labor and the Dark Side of the New Global Economy* (2007), journalist John Bowe investigated the grim situation of Latin American and Caribbean fruit and vegetable pickers in rural Florida. Hired by contractors employed by agribusiness corporations and supermarkets (subcontracting absolves those big businesses of direct responsibility for labor abuses), foreign-born farmworkers often become mired in the kind of coercive working conditions that prompted one Justice Department official to term south Florida "ground zero for modern slavery." This echoes an earlier judgment by the U.S. Department of Labor that the *bracero* program, ended in 1964, amounted to little more than "legalized slavery."[59]

In *Fields of Resistance: The Struggle of Florida's Farmworkers for Justice* (2011), Italian activist and author Silvia Giagnoni explicitly links the exploitation of immigrant farmworkers in and around Immokalee, Florida, to a historical continuum of labor exploitation from chattel slavery via the convict lease system (finally abolished by Florida and Alabama in 1923) to the Emergency Farm Labor Program. As we will see in subsequent chapters, writers from Hurston to Cynthia Shearer and Peter Matthiessen have traced the long and disturbingly continuous history of agricultural labor exploitation in south Florida. However, Giagnoni also locates Immokalee in "the Global South" that extends across

Brazil, India, Pakistan, Bangladesh, Nepal, Thailand, Burma, Laos, Cambodia, and Mauritania. This is a very different form of global southern "solidarity" to that promoted via the Research Triangle's corporate multiculturalism. But there is an important distinction to be made here between "the Global South" and the "global South" or "globalized South" of which southern studies scholars more usually speak, referring more narrowly to the impact of economic globalization *within* the established boundaries of the U.S. South. Resituating the U.S. South in relation to or even as part of the Global South is a more far-reaching and complicated affair. Giagnoni wryly remarks that "Immokalee, Florida, in the United States is also one of these places" in the Global South: "hard to pronounce, hard to make sense of, metaphorically and physically, and hard to locate on the cognitive map of most Americans."[60] Her more serious point is that the exploitative labor relations practiced in south Florida are profoundly reminiscent of those forms of labor abuse and outright slavery found throughout the Global South countries she mentions and involve migrant workers *from* the Global South.

One of the difficulties involved in cognitively mapping the U.S. South vis-à-vis this Global South is that it is also part of the United States (still, for all its internal inequities and economic crises, the world's wealthiest nation) and the Global North. In *Southern Insurgency* (2016)—a title that in a more traditional southern studies context one might expect to refer to Confederate secessionism or "massive resistance" to desegregation—political scientist Immanuel Ness argues that during the era of "neoliberal globalization that began in the 1980s," capitalism's latest spatial fix involved the transfer of industrial labor from high-wage developed nations to the Global South. The result is that "globally Northern capital is completely dependent on the super-exploitation of low-wage [globally] Southern labor." On one hand, then, the inequality and exploitation experienced by both native-born and immigrant denizens of the contemporary U.S. South both recalls a *regional* history of labor abuse *and* compares with socioeconomic formations in countries across the contemporary Global South. (Ness notes that the neoliberal "development of capitalism in the modern world is compatible with the forms of unfree and bonded labor that are entrenched" already through earlier racialized or caste-based structures of exploitation.) On the other hand, the U.S. South is part of the privileged Global North—as well as "the hegemonic power in the world," the United States—that superexploits the Global South.[61] Because its regional history of racialized labor exploitation converges with its current identity as a preferred destination for migrant workers who are themselves exploited, the U.S. South has become an uncanny (if not "unique") kind of contact zone between Global North and South.[62]

Ness stresses that most contemporary labor migration on a global scale takes place within or between Global South nations: the "southern insurgency" to which he refers is the radicalization of a geographically reconstituted "New Industrial Proletariat" within the Global South itself. Nevertheless, an increasing number of Global South migrant workers have sought out the U.S. South: after all, as Ness acknowledges, "wages and material conditions in the imperialist core in Europe and North America remain far better in the era of neoliberal capitalism than those of almost all unionized workers in the [Global] South."[63] In a similar vein, James Cobb observes that "in the broader global context the [U.S.] South has become a high-wage region."[64] Immigrant workers earning wages in the U.S. South have become a crucial transnational source of income for not only their families back home but also the home nations themselves: sociologist Saskia Sassen emphasizes that in many Global South countries, immigrant remittances are an absolutely vital form of revenue. Here we see the contradictions of neoliberal capitalist globalization in effect: when "the growing immiseration of governments and economies in the global South launches a new phase of global migration and people trafficking," the U.S. South is simultaneously a favored destination for global southern peoples who have the agency and resources to migrate themselves (albeit often illegally) *and* a prime site for trafficking and neoslavery of the kinds critiqued by Hahamovitch, Bowe, Giagnoni, and even the Justice Department.[65]

Such historical continuities with earlier forms of labor exploitation in the U.S. South, and contemporary parallels with abusive labor relations across the Global South, are hardly confined to agriculture: immigrant workers are also heavily represented in construction, factories, landscaping, and the hotel industry. Large numbers of Latin American laborers arrived in New Orleans after Hurricane Katrina devastated the city in August 2005. They were recruited by contractors as part of what Allison Graham calls a "global search for cheap labor" that saw temporary workers arrive from as far away as India.[66] The local political response to the arrival of this impermanent and often illegal Latino/a population was at best ambivalent. Mayor Ray Nagin wondered out loud: "How do I ensure that New Orleans is not overrun by Mexican workers?" Journalist Jordan Flaherty has noted that such "inflammatory rhetoric" was being "delivered while blatant violations of workers' rights were ignored" by city and federal officials. Local civil rights veterans observed that such labor abuses echoed the exploitation of slaves in antebellum New Orleans; some of those veterans allied with "Latino immigrants in a fight against what some now call 'Juan Crow.'"[67] Within six years of Katrina and in the wake of the 2008 economic crisis, such harsh rhetoric and restrictions against immigrants had become widespread. Georgia and South Carolina passed laws against undocumented workers, but harshest of all was Alabama's draconian HB56 law, which allowed police to question anyone on "reasonable suspicion" that they were in the state illegally, while schools and other public services were empowered to request proof of citizenship. In Alabama as in New Orleans, critics compared the contemporary treatment of Latino/a workers to the history of slave labor in the Old South.[68]

Yet for all that this regional tradition of labor exploitation now encompasses recent immigrants, demographic flows across national borders—between the U.S. South and the (larger) Global South—reinvent the region in radical and hopeful ways. Labor historian Leon Fink has detailed how Mayan poultry workers in Morganton, North Carolina, hired in familiar "southern" fashion as cheap labor, nevertheless reconfigured "community" in transnational terms. Negotiating "the increasing fluidity" of both capital flows and labor markets, the workers maintained ties to their familial and village networks in Guatemala even while forging new political alliances in Morganton. As "transnational villagers" (Peggy Lewitt's term), they participate in what Sassen calls "counter-geographies of survival . . . on a global scale"; they practice what another sociologist, Ulrich Beck, termed (anticipating Nwankwo's use of the same phrase) "cosmopolitanism from below," made up from the "multiple alliances and affiliations" of the ordinary rather than elite "transnational migrant subject."[69] In another case study, anthropologist Steve Striffler reveals how in "less than two decades, the poultry industry has become a key site for 'workers of the world' to come together in a region of the United States—the South—that has received relatively few foreign immigrants during the twentieth century." For Striffler, solidarity between Latin American and southeast Asian laborers at a Tyson Foods poultry processing plant in northeast Arkansas provides a microscale example of how "globalization can lead not only to the internationalization of capital but to the internationalization of workers." Striffler concludes "that if we are going to understand transnationalism in a more profound way"—if we are to move beyond vulgar transnationalism—"then we need to see culture not just in terms of cultural difference . . . but also in terms of class formation."[70]

In 1945 erstwhile Agrarian Allen Tate opined that industrial capitalism had "destroyed the regional economies" and replaced them with a "world provincialism" in which it was "very difficult for 'backwards peoples' . . . to make their living independently of somebody else nine thousand miles away" (not unrelatedly, Tate declared that the regional distinctiveness of "the Southern literary renascence" was "over" too).[71] Yet as Fink and Striffler stress, the transformation of the South into a global capitalist "space of flows" (Manuel Castells's term) has also generated, however inadvertently and contingently, opportunities for the construction of a transnational sense of community or solidarity between previously disparate peoples.[72] A third and final example of this grassroots "internationalization of workers" can be found in the Coalition of Immokalee Workers (CIW), formed in 1993 and made up mostly of Mexicans, Guatemalans, and Haitians. In 2005 and 2007 the CIW organized for and achieved small but significant wage improvements from Taco Bell and Mc-

Donald's: both corporations agreed to pay pickers one cent more per pound of tomatoes, an ostensibly trivial increase that effectively doubled pickers' wages. In the same period, the CIW also won an Antislavery Award for their exposure of "six operations in which hundreds of farmworkers were being kept captive somewhere in the endless fields of Florida."[73] As I will demonstrate in chapter 6, the CIW provides a touchstone for the ways in which Shearer's novel *The Celestial Jukebox* imaginatively maps the relationship in today's "globalized" South between the history and legacies of slavery and the contemporary exploitation of immigrant workers from the Global South.

The Transnational Turn and the New Southern Studies

If globalization has generated a "turning point" in southern historiography, in southern literary and cultural studies it has dovetailed with the rise of the new southern studies. Jon Smith has identified new southern studies' genesis in the "banner year" of 1999, which witnessed the publication of pioneering work by Scott Romine, Deborah Cohn, and Jennifer Greeson.[74] But the "new southern studies" was not so named until 2001, by two major figures in American studies: Houston Baker and Dana Nelson, in their role as editors of *American Literature*'s special issue "Violence, the Body and 'the South.'" Given the long-standing marginalization of southern studies within American studies, and American studies' then-recent "transnational turn," such prominent Americanist attention to the South seemed auspicious. In the years since, some scholars have suggested that the new southern studies always "critiqued the field of southern studies from a theoretically-informed, transnational perspective."[75] Yet Baker and Nelson conceptualized "new southern studies" mostly within a regional-national framework: for them, it involved analyzing how "'The South' is the U.S. social, political, racial, economic, ethical, and everyday-life imaginary written as 'regionalism.'" Baker and Nelson usefully highlighted the tendency to displace U.S. racism and oppression onto the South as an abject regional other, thereby foreshadowing Duck's *The Nation's Region: Southern Modernism, Segregation, and U.S. Nationalism* (2006) and Greeson's *Our South: Geographic Fantasy and the Rise of National Literature* (2010). However, their special issue's introduction did not explore the implications of American studies' transnational turn for their "new southern studies," or the possibility that a transnational turn in or to the South might advance American studies. The closest they came was their hemispheric gesture to "yet another 'South'—the south-of-the-border space where Latino cultures construct, challenge, inform, and expand the economic, political, and violent social histories of 'our America.'"[76] Baker's book *Turning South Again*—also from 2001, and which both argues for and positions itself as part of "a new southern studies [that] is long past due"—exhibits an overt antipathy toward one transnational critical model in particular. *Turning South Again*'s incisive exposé of the suppressed homologies between southern regional and U.S. national imaginaries emphasized this approach over and against Paul Gilroy's black Atlantic, which Baker dismisses as the abstractly global yet also "Britishly 'provincial'" approach from which he "turn[s] away" to focus on "*the privileged, locative site of my entire discussion—namely, the 'South.'*"[77] Two years later, Riché Richardson rightly observed that "we have witnessed 'turns' towards the South in a number of areas," from V. S. Naipaul's travelogue *A Turn in the South* (1988) to Dirty South hip-hop; while *Turning South Again* was part of that rich body of creative and scholarly work, Baker's "*privileged, locative*" positioning diverged from Richardson's own "imperative that any 'turns' toward the South move beyond the nation-centered models that have been dominant within Southern studies" and that they facilitate "the development of an epistemology on global and transnational dispersals of the American South."[78]

As the new southern studies was originally formulated, then, there was little common ground with American studies' transnational turn. Over the next few years, however, Baker and Nelson's coinage was adapted to various agendas that moved beyond the shopworn regional-national model. For Jon Smith, it could be usefully yoked to his important hemispheric project with Cohn, the essay collection *Look Away! The U.S. South and New World Studies* (2004), which sought to "redirect the critical gaze of southern studies outward, away from the nativist navel-gazing that has kept mainstream southern studies methodologically so far behind American studies." Like Cohn's *History and Memory in the Two Souths* (1999), *Look Away!* did this by turning south of the U.S. South, relocating the region in the context of "New World plantation colonialism."[79] McKee and Trefzer's special issue of *American Literature*—a sequel of sorts to "Violence, the Body, and 'the South'"—explicitly redefined "The New Southern Studies" by emphasizing the "Global Contexts" of ostensibly "Local Literatures." Pointedly noting that "Baker and Nelson's volume remain[s] largely nation-bound and locked into the familiar racial binaries of black and white," McKee and Trefzer declared their intention "to showcase a new Southern studies based on the notion of an intellectual and practical Global South, a term that embeds the U.S. South in a larger transnational framework."[80]

By this time, despite the seemingly shared turn to studying the globalized U.S. South (and, less consistently, the Global South), there were clear signs of conceptual and methodological tensions between southern historians and the literary/cultural studies scholars associated with the new southern studies. In 2005 Barbara Ladd noted in *PMLA* that the emergence of the new southern studies seemed to have disrupted "the traditionally close but always testy relationship between southern historians ... and literary and cultural critics" (Jon Smith's feisty response to Ladd's "state of the field" essay amplified some disagreements among literary and cultural critics too).[81] Ladd's point was borne out over the next year or so. In *The American South in a Global World*, only Peacock's epilogue even acknowledges that there was "a growing body of literary studies positioning the South globally and comparatively."[82] In 2006 the *Journal of Southern History* review of *Look Away!* bemoaned its disciplinary bias, grumbling that most of the essays "deal with literary topics" and bridling at Smith and Cohn's "somewhat patronizing contention that southern historians continue to ignore all interdisciplinary perspectives and even comparative history."[83] But in *American Literary History*, Aboul-Ela noted the "irony" that, compared to *Globalization and the American South*, the largely literary-critical makeup of Smith and Cohn's collection revealed a "greater investment in historical precedent as compared to the historian who comments on globalization"; *Look Away!* thereby "lends itself less easily to a celebratory tone" regarding economic globalization.[84]

Some testiness between southern historians and literary/cultural studies scholars was also evident during the four conferences from 2008 to 2010 that formed the core of the "Understanding the South" research network at the universities of Manchester, Cambridge, Florida, and Copenhagen. As main organizer Brian Ward observed: "One of the goals of the Understanding the South, Understanding America Research Network is to promote dialogue between historians of the South and those scholars, principally from literary and cultural studies backgrounds, who are associated with 'The New Southern Studies.'" The four conferences and resulting trilogy of books went some way toward meeting this rationale and placed considerable emphasis on resituating the region in transnational frameworks. (Disclaimer: I was a co-organizer of the network and coeditor of the books.) However, historian Karen Cox complained "that literary/cultural studies scholars are just applying their methods to the New South and calling it NSS" (new southern studies); Cox called such work "maddening... filled as it is with jargon" and accused it of lacking "historical context."[85] A more measured and sustained historian's critique of the new southern studies emerged from Michael O'Brien's keynote during the second "Understanding the South" conference at the University of Florida in January 2009. In "Place as Everywhere: On Globalizing the American South"—reworked as the epilogue to *Creating Citizenship in the Nineteenth-Century South* (2013)—O'Brien began by noting certain similarities between the globalization of southern history and the globalizing imperative of the new southern studies. However, O'Brien proceeded to suggest that the "postmodern literary scholars" who practice the new southern studies are "less committed to the constraints of the historical imagination than was common among southern literary critics in, say, 1960." This was a criticism not likely to be well received by literary scholars who saw the neo-Agrarian mantras of the Rubin generation as less interested in historicizing the South than mythologizing a certain "image" of it.[86] But O'Brien went further, suggesting that the new southern studies constitutes a kind of academic analog to the neoliberal vision of globalization as a positive good. Having noted that "scholars of globalization" tend to be divided between those who believe in a neoliberal vision of "final freedom for economic man" and those who "see little but danger in unregulated freedom," O'Brien claimed that new southern studies "scholars seem curiously, if only implicitly, closer to the neoliberal position than they might prefer." According to O'Brien, "most of the New Southern scholars seem to assume that globalization, though its economics might often be pernicious, may have social consequences that may, if we are lucky, tend to increase human freedom."[87]

An astute reader will notice that O'Brien's accusation echoes Aboul-Ela's charge that the contributors—primarily historians—to *Globalization and the American South* too easily assumed a "neoliberal slant" that saw economic globalization in favorable terms; the difference is that the disciplines are reversed, and the historian is scoring the scholars in the new southern studies. Certainly, one can find examples of putatively new southern studies scholarship that seem sanguine, even blasé about the more pernicious dimensions of globalization, not least the exploitation of immigrant labor. O'Brien himself cites Peacock's *Grounded Globalism: How the U.S. South Embraces the World* (2007), wryly remarking that "the happy migrants inhabiting [Peacock's] pages seem to flow over borders with as much ease as though wandering over so many suburban lawns to reach a church picnic." I share O'Brien's skepticism regarding Peacock's sunny vision of the South's "grounded globalism." But though Peacock's book was the second volume in the New Southern Studies book series, its "commonsensical" (O'Brien's word) approach is notably removed from most new southern studies scholarship.[88]

If O'Brien's allegations that "postmodern literary scholars" were insufficiently critical of neoliberal globalization may have had some limited purchase in the early new southern studies era, it seems rather less persuasive now. Nor does Richard H. King's assessment of the new southern studies circa 2010 as "primarily an exploration of the way the South has been thought about" really hold a few years further down the line.[89] Even as the works of Duck and Greeson have inspired renewed attention to the relationship between region and nation, there has been a growing tendency elsewhere to focus on the material realities and inequities of economic globalization. Moreover, like many of the historians, sociologists, anthropologists, and journalists cited above (Guterl, Barbara Ellen Smith, Hahamovitch, Fink, Giagnoni, Flaherty, Bowe), these scholars seek to contextualize the contemporary exploitation of immigrant workers in the globalized U.S. South (and Global South) vis-à-vis the fraught regional history of racialized labor: slavery, sharecropping, convict labor, and anti-unionism. In 2006 Richardson called for attention to "the U.S. South within labor studies and to make labor a topic more organic to dialogues in contemporary Southern studies"; that same year and in the same venue, Tara McPherson cited Walmart as a case study of "the South as a key part of a global franchise economy, with intricate links to past histories of labor exploitation" from the slave trade to the *bracero* program.[90] In *I Don't Hate the South* (2007), Baker wrote: "In the U.S. South, squalid subsistence-living conditions are frequently the norm for Mexican and Central American farm workers; their labor and lives mirror in dark ways chattel slavery's worst deprivations of body and spirit."[91] In *Wounds of Returning*, also from 2007, Jessica Adams notes that in the contemporary South "[t]he image of the plantation as an uncomplicated site of white achievement" is challenged by "landscapes irrevocably shaped by industrialism and globalization" and increasingly staffed with immigrant workers.[92] In 2010 Duck remarked that a key concern for contemporary scholars is how "previous phases of globalization—including imperialism and the transatlantic slave trade—influence present-day forms of immiseration" in the U.S. South and beyond.[93] In the afterword to *Creating and Consuming the American South* (2015), McPherson insisted that "our readings of southern culture need to be more materialist and less southern, pushing beyond representation and narrative to conditions of production and the flow of capital." In the same volume, in an essay that directly responded to O'Brien's claims that the new southern studies is too invested in postmodernism and too dazzled by neoliberalism to discern its discontents, Jon Smith asserted that "very few of us in the New Southern Studies see globalization merely as an escape from more local oppressions." Smith posited a "post-postpolitical southern studies" that would move beyond what he (on this point, not unlike O'Brien) sees as the neutered postmodern focus on virtual or symbolic Souths to rediscover a kind of "real": the ways in which "real bodies" in the region continue to be subjected to the inequities of global capitalism, the rollback of the Civil Rights movement, and environmental degradation.[94] Whether or not this newest, notably materialist turn is entirely original, it suggests that O'Brien's 2009 characterization of the new southern studies was, at the very least, outdated. A more historicized and materialist attention to migration and labor—in regional *and* global Souths, both present *and* past—is animating an increasing amount of scholarship. This book is (among other things) a historical-geographical materialist contribution to and extension of this body of work.

Beyond Quentissentialism:
Migration and "Southern Literature"

How have these debates about transnationalism, economic globalization, and immigration impacted southern literature and southern literary studies? In 2004 Nahem Yousaf and Sharon Monteith wrote: "When new populations that enter the South are acknowledged in fiction, the tension between exclusionary definitions of Southern-ness and the exclusion suffered by 'minorities' produces a sea change within the Southern literary tradition."[95] Whether this change has happened is debatable; so too is the question of whether it could be contained "within" conventional notions of "southern literature." To be sure, fiction by contemporary, native-born southern writers has increasingly registered the presence of immigrants. As I noted in my first book, Barbara Kingsolver's *Prodigal Summer* (2003) features Mexican agricultural workers in rural Kentucky as well as a "Polish-Arab-American" protagonist, while Tom Wolfe's blockbuster *A Man in Full* (1998) interrogates the ways in which Atlanta's boosters have defined it as an "international city," a global capital of capital, by drawing attention instead to global flows of people, especially from southeast Asia.[96] However, in these and other novels, immigrant characters have relatively minor roles; indeed, as Monteith notes, "most fictions about migrants and exiles have focused on individual protagonists in stories of solitary foreigners who arrive in the post-war South."[97] In this regard, contemporary southern fiction's representation of immigrants has not diverged significantly from the Renaissance-era writing (by Faulkner, McCullers, Capote, et al.) mentioned earlier: it reconfirms Peacock's sense that in southern literature "the less diverse southern setting accentuates the foreigner as standing out."[98]

However, the incommensurability of immigrant narratives and stories with the "southern literary tradition" also has something to do with residual biases and boundaries in southern (literary) studies itself. Winders and Smith note that because much work in southern studies still "operates through a powerful discursive formation: a South contoured by a black-white binary," the field, "as currently configured, cannot account for [the] degree of variation and change" that has resulted from immigration. In a similar vein, Melanie Benson Taylor has observed that "one of the trends slowest to develop" in the new southern studies has been "a functional awareness of ... multiethnic disruptions to the region's black-white binary." Benson Taylor notes that even Patricia Yaeger's "otherwise visionary" *Dirt and Desire: Reconstructing Southern Women's Writing, 1930–1990* (2000)—a volume often identified with the inchoate (if then unnamed) new southern studies, and which vigorously broadcast its own desire to "dynamite the rails" of traditional southern literary studies—"fails to transcend its reductive racial contours" because of Yaeger's insistence that "southern literature, at its best, is ... about the intersection of black and white cultures as they influence one another and collide."[99] A similar criticism can be leveled at McPherson's *Reconstructing Dixie: Gender, Race, and Nostalgia in the Imagined South* (2003). Through the organizing idea of the South's "lenticular logic," McPherson reveals "the visibility of race" by emphasizing "blackness, even as the South as a whole becomes less black and white, because the black/white axis in southern culture remains so prominent." Yet McPherson's own logic risks inadvertently perpetuating the marginalization of those immigrants who have rendered the South "less black and white" or, in the case of those with African or Caribbean origins, complicated uniquely U.S. (southern) ideas of "blackness."[100] To maintain a focus on the black-white binary compounds (to take Smith and Winders's example) "the illegibility of a Latino presence within southern stories": "Latinos cannot be rendered 'southern'" in the usual "southern histories organized through defining racial difference between black and white."[101] Yet the flip side may be equally problematic: that we too easily integrate immigrant experiences and narratives into a more expansive "southern literary tradition," thereby implying that we have overcome the old racial binary—and the old racism. Leslie Bow astutely cautions that Asian Americans may be "all too readily incorporated into newer versions of the imagined South ... as a symbol of inclusiveness heralding the felicitous erosion of the historically sedimented black-white binary" and that their stories may become a kind of cultural capital through which "to rebrand southern studies." Bow's point that accounting for "Asians in the South" may be merely a "pluralist add-on to business as usual" within the field recalls McPherson's critique of that "additive strategy" whereby southernist scholars superficially qualified their primary focus on "recounting white experience" by "tacking on the experience of African Americans"—a move that "obeys the structural logic of the lenticular."[102]

Another persistent assumption is that only native-born writers produce "southern literature": a disciplinary version of what I have termed "the Quentissential fallacy." In Faulkner's *Absalom, Absalom!* (1936), Quentin Compson's declaration to his Canadian roommate Shreve McCannon that "[y]ou cant understand it. You would have to be born there" eerily anticipates the kind of southern literary-critical nativism that precludes dialectical national perspectives from beyond the U.S. South—or within "it," by immigrant authors and protagonists.[103] Monteith and Yousaf remark that native-born southernists "remain surprised that non-Southerners and non-native Southerners are vocal in critical debates around regionalism and identity." In 2007 Monteith noted: "Even very recent and exciting books in Southern Studies include expressions of surprise that the mapping of Southern studies is already—and has always been to some extent—a global process." In 2013 Yousaf reiterated that despite "new directions forged by scholars in New Southern Studies, immigrants usually remained quietly outside of Southern literary criticism."[104] As such, Suzanne Jones's pointed remarks a few years earlier remain relevant: "Instead of worrying about who qualifies as a Southern writer or rigidly delimiting southern literature, we might more fruitfully ask questions about who is writing about the U.S. South (no matter their birthplace or residence), and what stories they are telling." *Where the New World Is* seeks to move beyond Quentissentialism by assessing in detail how "international writers and writers who are new immigrants to the South"—as well as select southern- and U.S.-born authors—"can help us to think globally and comparatively about the region."[105]

Regionalism, Transnationalism, and the Scale of "The South"

One of the most prominent proponents of American studies' transnational turn, Paul Giles, argues that "since about 1981, the multidimensional effects of globalization have reconfigured the premises of U.S. national identity" in a "transnational era" that is "centered around the necessarily reciprocal position of the U.S. within global networks of exchange." For Giles, it follows that "in relation to the study of American literature and culture ... the rules of engagement have changed so significantly that old area-studies nostrums about exceptionalist forms of national politics and culture ... have become almost irrelevant."[106] From a new southern studies perspective, one might echo Giles by positing that the effects of globalization have rendered redundant the hackneyed nostrums informing *southern* studies' hoary emphasis on *regional* distinctiveness. By extension, they might yet undermine American studies' own enduring and "convenient southern exceptionalism," in which—notwithstanding the transnational turn—the region remains "the staid, backward Other" that allows a self-consciously "sexy" American studies to keep rebranding itself as "energetic, future-oriented, young, and passionate."[107]

What, though, might "the South," "southern literature," or "southern studies" then *mean*? Here it is worth pondering Matthew Lassiter and Joseph Crespino's observation in *The Myth of Southern Exceptionalism* (2010) that, even with widespread "[e]vidence of the globalization of the American South" and the related turn to "national and transnational themes" in southern historiography, "region" remains simultaneously "the most popular but also the most imprecise scale of analysis."[108] One of the difficulties in writing this introduction has been stressing that slavery and its labor legacies imposed restrictions on voluntary immigration to the region, while qualifying that there were always local exceptions to this demographically demonstrable form of southern distinctiveness. Another tricky balancing act has involved affirming how the present era of capitalist globalization and mass immigration constitutes a transnational "turning point" for (the study of) the South, while also insisting that such economic and demographic phenomena must be considered as continuous with regional histories of exploitation. In both cases, it might seem to some readers—especially those incredulous toward all forms of southern exceptionalism—that I am redeeming "the South" as a "scale of analysis" just when it seems more "imprecise" than ever before. Indeed, scholars within the new southern studies have gone further than Lassiter and Crespino by raising the question of whether "region" or "the South" is any longer a useful scale. In 2006 Barbara Ellen Smith pondered the dialectic between capitalist globalization and "place-based forms of social activism and resistance struggles" and posited: "The place that is both defended and created is rarely the region, for what is at stake is far more specific, concrete, and personal: the ten blocks of a neighborhood, a small watershed or hollow, a rural community. *The South* is too large and ambiguous to be mobilized as a meaningful place in these contexts." Yet Smith qualified that such microcosmic "struggles are in the South and of the South—shaped by the framework of Southern history and politics.... Indeed, these struggles *are* the South."[109] In 2007 Jon Smith, drawing on Michael Hardt and Antonio Negri's *Empire* (2000) as well as Immanuel Wallerstein's world-system theory, observed that "the U.S. South today offers a complicated mix of microregions" in which "Mississippi and much of Alabama qualify as semiperipheral," whereas "Atlanta and Charlotte now function as part of the core" of global-northern neoliberal capitalism. To the degree "the South" still exists here, it is as a kind of residual conceptual container of dizzyingly different "microregions" revealing socioeconomic realities (and inequalities) not at regional but rather local and global scales. More recently, Smith has suggested that "'the South' increasingly appears to be an unhelpful scalar unit: far better to work at a larger scale (the nation, conservatism, plantation America) or a smaller one (consumer culture in Mississippi, desegregation in Atlanta or Milwaukee)." The culmination of such "re-scaling" at more local *and* global levels is Duck's call for "Southern studies without 'The South.'"[110]

Such observations within historiography, sociology, and the new southern studies dovetail with current discussions about scale across a range of other disciplines, from human geography to comparative literature. Among geographers influenced by historical materialism, "it was CAPITALISM that was early on identified as the driver behind the production of scale."[111] Neil Smith, the leading theorist of geographical uneven development under capitalism, has adumbrated "a sequence of specific scales: body, home, community, urban, region, nation, global." For Smith, while region as a "site of economic production" is "closely bound up with the larger rhythms of the national and global economy," it remains distinctive because "[t]he social division of labor is most sharply expressed in spatial terms at the regional scale." Smith also identifies a conceptual and disciplinary division between "the metaphorical uses of space that have become so fashionable in literary and cultural discourse" and "the more material conceptions of space that have dominated the 'new' geographies." Yet literature (and literary studies) has a vital role to play in the conceptualization of scale under capitalist globalization precisely because, as Smith also notes, "the use of spatial metaphors, far from providing an innocent if evocative imagery, actually taps directly into questions of social power." Besides its alertness to the power of metaphors and metaphors of power, literature's imaginative capacity to (as Neil Smith puts it) "jump scales"—from the corporeal to the communal or from the regional to the global—enables it to both critique existing socioeconomic relations and create alternative ways of being in the world across a wide range of scales.[112]

Wai Chee Dimock wonders: "What is the appropriate scale for the study of culture and, in particular, the study of literature?" With reference to Wallerstein's world-system, Dimock concludes "that literary studies requires the largest possible scale," which she terms "planetary." If Dimock's claims for "[t]his immensity of time and space in the scale appropriate to literary studies" raises concerns about the loss of what Georg Lukács termed "particularity," this kind of scaling up and out to the global or planetary poses similar questions for a field like southern literary studies, with its traditional privileging not only of "region" but also "place," "community," and "roots" (all conventionally associated with rurality or small towns).[113] The field faces too its own version of what Nirvana Tanoukhi (channeling Wallerstein) describes as the challenge of formulating "a scale-sensitive procedure" that "would help us grasp the actually existing landscapes of literature" and in ways which move beyond familiar "metaphorical deployments of 'space' toward concrete discussions about the materiality of literary *landscapes*."[114] In the U.S. southern context, familiar spatial metaphors—"Dixie," "the former Confederacy," "the Bible Belt," "the closed society," or even "the South"—may be a hindrance rather than help to scholars within and beyond literary studies working on the significance of immigration to more local and/or global landscapes: for example, south Florida, as part of the contemporary "extended Caribbean"; New Orleans, as a post-Katrina case study of the "global search for cheap labor"; or Atlanta, as an "international city" connected to other global capitals of capital. In *The American South and the Atlantic World* (2013), Brian Ward employs another literary metaphor—poet William Blake's claim to "see a world in a grain of sand"—to suggest that "those studying the American South can also profit from a granular approach" in which larger scales like the Atlantic world "are revealed by close attention to a particular southern locale."[115] Yet it does not necessarily follow that a microregion or a metropolis, any more than "the Global South" or "the Atlantic world," is a more "scale-sensitive" unit of analysis than "the U.S. South." Depending on the object of (literary) study, the appropriate scalar unit might be more or less local, regional, or (trans)national; it might require too a dialectical "jumping" between scales.

As we reassess literature about the U.S. South "in the context of geographical materialism" and "through the variegated forms of its imaginary relations to the real dimensions of physical space," raising the possibility that the "old area-studies nostrums" (in southern as well as American studies) may no longer hold does not mean that, ergo, we should simply ignore "region."[116] "The South" may be a frustratingly imprecise, flawed, and contradictory scale of analysis—one ever more intertwined with rather than distinct from local, national, and global scales—but we must remain alert to the ways in which a broadly "southern" history of labor relations, involving both involuntary and voluntary immigrants, continues to resonate today. Indeed, many of the literary landscapes depicted in the stories and novels discussed across the following seven chapters and epilogue imaginatively excavate various local and transnational forms of migration and labor that challenge conventional ideas of a demographically solid or black-white South, even as they also dramatize the historical-geographical continuities of (racialized) labor exploitation throughout the region. Therefore, attending to the local in "the materiality of literary landscapes" is not necessarily nostalgic or conservative, even if that was often the case with neo-Agrarian "images" of autochthonous, organic communities and fixed, defined societies. As Wilson and Dissanayake note, "the local need not embody a regressive politics of global delinkage, bounded particularity, and claims of ontological pastness, where locality becomes some backward-gazing fetish of purity to disguise how global, hybrid, compromised, and unprotected everyday identity already is." The global has not simply erased the local; transnational routes have not completely displaced regional roots; the abstract "space of flows" of global finance capitalism has not entirely effaced an experiential "sense of place." Rather, the practice of everyday life throughout the transnational U.S. South involves a more "tricky version of the 'local' which operates within, and has been thoroughly reshaped by 'the global.'"[117] In *Reconstructing the World* (2008), Harilaos Stecopoulos—the literary scholar most attentive to theories of geographical scale while bridging the gap between American and (new) southern studies—decries the tendency of transnational Americanists to regard "the region and the regional" as "passé." Stecopoulos insists that such scholars "will be repaid richly by attending more carefully to the import of regionalism," especially "a transnational notion of region."[118] Or as Giles puts it: "Transnationalism... is not the antithesis to regionalism but crucial to its constitution: it is precisely the ways in which any given region configures itself in relation to the world around it that determines its internal sense of its own identity."[119]

In the seven chapters and epilogue that follow, I assess how fourteen writers—only two of them native-born southerners—over the course of nearly ninety years have challenged received readings and understandings of the U.S. South as a fixed, rooted, regional place largely untouched by the wider world. All these writers emphasize the role of migration and labor in reconfiguring the region's relation to the nation and a range of global scales: hemispheric (Haiti, Honduras, Jamaica), transatlantic/black Atlantic (Denmark, England, Mauritania), and transpacific/global southern (Australia, China, Vietnam). A few of the newer novels discussed focus on the post-1965 period most obviously characterized by contemporary processes of economic globalization and immigration, which has been the focus of recent scholarship. However, the first three chapters explore how between the 1920s and the 1960s African American authors who were only very rarely included in the neo-Agrarian canon of "southern literature" were already remapping the South on various intraregional, national, and transnational scales. Moreover, while none of the novels and stories discussed here were published before 1928—a periodization that may appear to vindicate those recent criticisms that the new southern studies has favored the twentieth and twenty-first centuries—the temporal scope of the fiction under discussion ranges from Reconstruction to the present era of globalization. Many of these novels and stories stress the historical continuities of labor exploitation that, as this introduction has stressed, run like a red thread from the Old South to today's globalized South. Let us begin, then, with Hurston's career-long engagement with intraregional *and* transnational migrant labor in Florida's "extended South."

CHAPTER 1

The Extended South of Black Folk
Intraregional and Transnational Migrant Labor in the Writing of Zora Neale Hurston

In summer 1958, at the instigation of a white friend in Fort Pierce, journalist Margaret Silver, Zora Neale Hurston began writing the first installment in a proposed series of articles for the *Miami Herald*. Entitled either "The Migrant Worker in Florida" or "Florida's Migrant Farm Worker," the typescript drafts demonstrate Hurston's keen awareness that the long-established role of migrant labor in Florida agriculture was being modernized in accordance with its vital importance to both the state's economic growth and the nation's food consumption: "From agriculture derives Florida's Number One income, and the migrant farm laborer is absolutely necessary to it now. The state is the hothouse of the nation, providing fruit and fresh vegetables during the long, cold months when such products could not be brought off elsewhere. As the nation depends upon Florida products, so does the farm industry depend upon the availability of the migrant worker apparatus." Hurston went on to delineate the changing demographics of this "apparatus" as "Texas-Mexican and Peurtorican [sic] elements" joined black southern and Caribbean laborers in Florida's fields and groves, address directly the *Herald*'s more privileged (and predominantly white) readership about their ignorance of this "subterranean force" of migrant workers, and detail via interviews the experiences and viewpoints of the workers themselves.[1] She thus deftly adumbrated how—as in geographer Neil Smith's analysis of scale—the region as a "site of economic production" is "closely bound up with the larger rhythms of the national and global economy" that extends northward across the United States and southward into the labor force of the Caribbean and Latin America.[2] But not for the first time in Hurston's career, her refusal to figure blacks as mere helpless victims of racist oppression and economic exploitation, and her insistent focus instead on what Alice Walker would later term "racial health—a sense of black people as complete, complex, *undiminished* human beings," was met with incomprehension.[3] In a letter dated July 9, 1958, George Beebe of the *Miami Herald* wrote to Doug Silver (Margaret's husband) that

> Zora Neale Hurston's approach to the migrant labor camp situation, doesn't quite jell.
>
> I had several editors read the first installment, and they couldn't quite figure what the purpose of the story was.
>
> The conversations and activities of the people [the migrant workers interviewed by Hurston] are probably unlike those of any Negro community and the question arises as to whether she is trying to prove that conditions are bad in these camps, or whether they are better than many believe.[4]

The *Herald* canceled the proposed series of essays, and Hurston seems never to have completed further planned installments.

This account of Hurston's failed report on Florida's migrant workers appears to confirm the conventional narrative of her declining career in the years following publication of the well-received autobiography *Dust Tracks on a Road* (1942). That narrative takes in the muted response to Hurston's fourth and final novel, *Seraph on the Suwanee* (1948); her failure to generate publisher interest in a long-planned book about King Herod; her piecemeal work as a maid and teacher during the 1950s; and her death and burial in an unmarked grave in Fort Pierce, Florida, in January 1960. There is a bleak pathos to the burn marks and missing words that mar the typed drafts of "Florida's Migrant Farm Worker": they were among the cache of Hurston's papers ordered to be burned after her death, only to be rescued from the fire by a passing neighbor.[5] Yet the unfinished essay can be read in a more affirmative fashion: as an important contribution to and reconfirmation of Hurston's decades-long interest in the role of black migrant labor in Florida, which began in the late 1920s and permeated her now-canonical published books of the late 1930s.

From this angle, "Florida's Migrant Farm Worker" might even recalibrate the extraordinary hypercanonization of Hurston's writing that followed her rediscovery by Walker and others in the 1970s. Since then, Hurston's eclectic body of work has registered deeply across various disciplines including African American studies, American studies, women's studies, and southern studies. However, critics have generally concentrated on the run of books that Hurston published in a remarkably prolific period between the mid- and late 1930s: most obviously her second novel, *Their Eyes Were Watching God* (1937), but also her anthropological volumes *Mules and Men* (1935) and *Tell My Horse: Voodoo and Life in Haiti and Jamaica* (1938). In 2011 Paul Giles ventured that Hurston's "critical reputation has been distorted by a privileging of her early work (*Their Eyes Were Watching God* in particular)."[6] Attending to a late unpublished essay like "Florida's Migrant Worker" may then revise our understanding of Hurston once again: not because the essay is a vital piece on its own terms or effects a conspicuous break from her canonical period, but rather for the way it reaffirms and amplifies the depth of Hurston's engagement with black migrant labor in and beyond the U.S South.

Hurston's representation of and relationship to the U.S. South has been a subject of debate across various disciplines. Despite Hurston's profound engagement with the region, southern studies was slower than other fields to recognize her significance. In the monumental 626-page *History of Southern Literature* (1985), Hurston's life and work merited merely two pages of an essay by Thadious M. Davis assessing "southern standard-bearers of the New Negro Renaissance" separately from white writers of the Southern Renaissance.[7] In the 1990s, Hurston finally emerged as a significant figure in southern literary studies as its practitioners made a concerted attempt to revise conventional definitions of "the South" and "southern literature." However, some of this scholarship relied heavily on residual neo-Agrarian notions of the South as exceptionally rooted, rural, and regional: "intimately attached to 'the soil'" and "not linked in any significant way to national or global forces that exist outside." Keen to demonstrate that Hurston "was always a southerner too," such criticism failed to fully engage with the complexities that characterize Hurston's representations of black life, labor, and migration in and "outside" the rural South.[8] Patricia Yaeger's *Dirt and Desire: Reconstructing Southern Women's Writing, 1930–1990* (2000) was more daring in utilizing brief, sometimes brilliant readings of Hurston texts to "dynamite the rails" of traditional southern literary studies. Yet Yaeger's more sustained (chapter-long) analysis of "the dirt-based economy" on the Everglades muck in *Their Eyes Were Watching God* was oddly incongruent with her rallying cry for "the relevance of southern studies within a world of globalized localities."[9] Only with the emergence of the new southern studies in its early hemispheric phase did scholars such as Annette Trefzer, Katherine Henninger, Leigh Anne Duck, and John Lowe begin to more fully explicate Hurston's depictions of the South (especially black southern culture) vis-à-vis the wider world (especially the Caribbean).[10] More recently, Hurston has taken a leading role in Keith Cartwright's study of the intersection of "deep southern time, circum-Caribbean space," and "Afro-creole authority." For Cartwright, Hurston's representations of Florida and the wider Gulf South counter "Anglo-nationalist readings of America (or African America)" because "[s]he knew that Cuban, Bahamian, Haitian, West Indian, and Seminole bodies of knowledge had been circulating in Florida in ever-creolizing ways."[11]

Critics working in African American studies were quicker to assess Hurston's relationship to and representation of the South, at both national and transnational scales. In this context, Hazel Carby's argument (developed in a series of essays between 1988 and 1991) that Hurston creates a "discourse of nostalgia" for black southern folk culture was both bracingly provocative and highly influential.[12] Carby herself was building on Susan Willis's claim in *Specifying: Black Women Writing the American Experience* (1987) that *Their Eyes* enacted "a utopian betrayal of history's dialectic" because Hurston "chooses not to depict the Northern migration of black people," instead sending her central characters to the Everglades, "a primal never-never land, more south than the rural South"—though Willis allowed that the "muck" possibly "articulates the recovery of Caribbean culture."[13] Carby too insists that Hurston conveniently ignored the Great Migration from the rural South to the urban North, in favor of "a continuity of [rural black southern] cultural beliefs and practices with beliefs and practices in the Caribbean." From *Mules and Men* via the "highly romanticized" *Their Eyes* to *Tell My Horse*, Hurston rewrote "the geographical boundaries of representation by situating the southern, rural folk and patterns of migration in relation to the Caribbean rather than the northern states."[14] Carby also contrasts Hurston's "romantic imagination" unfavorably with Richard Wright's Marxist-realist representation of modern black life in northern cities and complains that whereas "Wright has recently been excluded from contemporary formations of the African American canon," scholars like Houston Baker and Henry Louis Gates had elevated Hurston to advance a "mythology of the rural South" and bolster "ideas of an African American literary tradition [that] are dominated by an ideology of the 'folk.'"[15] This "academic reclamation of Zora Neale Hurston's southern folk aesthetics," as Madhu Dubey dubs it, is evident in Baker's *Workings of the Spirit: The Poetics of Afro-American Women's Writing* (1991), which valorizes Hurston for capturing "a full-muscled heroically womaned, fiercely articulate vernacular community" in the folktales of *Mules and Men*. Like Carby, Dubey suggests that such an ideological aesthetics of the black southern folk is "politically conservative" because it fetishizes a "premodern, rural South" and retreats from the modern, urban realities of African American life (in both Hurston's own time and the critics' present).[16]

For all the vibrancy of these debates, Hurston's career is not quite so easily reducible to the binary oppositions through which they have often proceeded: southern versus northern; rural versus urban; premodern versus modern; conservative versus progressive; the Great Migration versus the circum-Caribbean; folk aesthetics versus social realism; and Hurston versus Wright (or, as we will see in chapter 2, Hurston versus Nella Larsen). If the vernacular-critical focus on Hurston's southern folk aesthetics was not the full story, neither did Carby's theory of "discursive displacement" allow for Hurston's deep engagement with the historical-geographical realities of *intraregional* and *transnational* patterns of black migration: demographic movements *within* the South and from the Caribbean *into* the South. These movements may be less familiar than the mass relocation of rural southern blacks to northern cities, but they were substantial, and Hurston made them central to the narrative cartographies of her first two novels: *Jonah's Gourd Vine* (1934) and *Their Eyes Were Watching God*. Particularly important here is Hurston's representation of migrant workers on "the muck" of the Florida Everglades in

Their Eyes. The novel imaginatively recasts the devastating storm that hit the Everglades on September 16, 1928, killing thousands of black migrant workers, including a significant number of Bahamians. Through these first two novels and her nonfiction from the late 1920s to the late 1950s, Hurston depicts the U.S. South (especially south Florida) less as a romantic site of rooted rural "community" than as a simultaneously oppressive and liminal locus traversed by intraregional *and* transnational flows of migrant labor. In doing so, Hurston stressed that the rural South was not merely the premodern, folk-cultural departure point of a modern Great Migration to the metropolitan North; it was a key site and geographic scale within that more complex network of regional, national, and hemispheric migrations occurring throughout the New World black diaspora, under the aegis of a capitalist agribusiness that itself extended beyond U.S. (southern) borders.

This first chapter, then, seeks to extend critical debates in both (new) southern studies and African American studies about the links between the U.S. South and the Caribbean that recur throughout Hurston's writing. Whereas Cartwright prioritizes Hurston's "limbo imagination" of a "Gulf sublime" and reads circum-Caribbean hurricanes through her channeling of spiritual "repertoires of the orisha Oya," I place a more materialist emphasis on Hurston's representation of black southern and Caribbean migrant workers.[17] This is not to insist that readers should uncritically accept either *Jonah's Gourd Vine* or *Their Eyes* as (to borrow a phrase from Leigh Anne Duck) "a realistic representation of southern African American life"—or, for that matter, *Their Eyes* as an authentic documentary of the Bahamian migrant worker experience.[18] After all, Richard Wright's notoriously withering review of *Their Eyes* proceeded precisely from his worry that white readers would (mis)read Hurston's novel as a realistic representation of "the Negro" and "Negro life."[19] Rosemary Hathaway has anatomized how *Their Eyes* remains subject to the perils of "touristic reading," "whereby a [white] reader assumes ... that the text is necessarily an accurate, authentic, and authorized representation of that 'Other' cultural group." Hurston's "use of folkloric material" in fictional form may facilitate touristic reading by appearing to offer "some sort of unmediated grounding in cultural authenticity": indeed, this was the basis for "Wright's objections to the folkloric aspects of Hurston's writing."[20] Wright's infamous charge that Hurston's focus on "the Negro folk-mind" is "quaint" and "carries no theme, no message, no thought" continues to resonate through Carby's assessment (adopted and adapted by other critics) that Hurston's "discourse of nostalgia" for the black southern folk displaced modernity and the Great Migration. Hence, as Cartwright notes, Hurston continues to be "accused of not being national enough, urban-contemporary enough, *real* enough."[21] At the same time, the vernacular-critical valorization of Hurston's "southern folk aesthetics" also fails to fully account for her hardheaded focus on the socioeconomic realities faced by black migrant workers moving *within* and *into* the South: not least, in *Their Eyes*, the dystopian experience of living and dying Jim Crow during and after the hurricane. So, while I would not dispute that Hurston's fiction and nonfiction alike formally and thematically foreground the "folk," her depictions of black southern and Caribbean migrant labor should not be dismissed as "quaint," "nostalgic," or "utopian" and may be rather more "realistic" than such readings usually allow. My hope is that a more historical-geographical materialist approach to Hurston's representations of intraregional and transnational migrant labor may help negotiate a conceptual third space between the critical history of attacks on Hurston's alleged antirealism and the more recent fetishization of her southern folk aesthetics.

"Ahm goin' tuh Zar, and dat's on de other side of far": Black Southern Migrant Labor in *Jonah's Gourd Vine*

In *Dirt and Desire*, Yaeger argues that Hurston interrogates the sociohistorical realities of racial segregation and labor exploitation, even while celebrating the relative autonomy and agency of rural black southern life. Yaeger sees John Pearson's first encounter with a train in *Jonah's Gourd Vine* not as a naïve "depiction of the black southerner as primitive"—one of the grounds on which Alain Locke, as well as Wright, criticized Hurston's work in the 1930s[22]—but as an indication of "the myriad ways the southern world was changing for African Americans born just after emancipation who were still harnessed by the scarcity and immobility of the sharecropping system." This suitably lococentric take on *Jonah's Gourd Vine* constitutes one of *Dirt and Desire*'s most successful attempts to "dynamite the rails" of southern literary studies and affirms the potential of drawing out Hurston's emphasis on the socioeconomic realities, rather than "folk" residues, of sharecropping. Criticizing southern literary critics' tendency to talk about "the South's 'monumental historical consciousness,'" Yaeger proceeds to ask: "In *Jonah's Gourd Vine*, when a black sharecropper [John Pearson] moves off the plantation to go farther south—all the way to the Florida frontier—why can't Zora Neale Hurston's account of his first train ride count as 'monumental'? What about this man's labor in constructing southern railroad lines?"[23] While these are important questions, the reference to Pearson "go[ing] farther south" inadvertently echoes Carby's argument that the movement "from the southern states further south" in Hurston's work discursively displaces the Great Migration.[24] In particular, John Pearson's initial train journey from rural Alabama to Florida may seem to anticipate Janie, in the company of Joe Starks, "turn[ing] south" from her birthplace in west Florida to Eatonville.[25] When John's adulterous ways force him off the

Pearson plantation in Notasulga, Alabama, he takes a train south—or, more precisely, southeast—to Sanford, Florida:

> John's destination was purely accidental. When he came out upon the big road to Chehaw, he overtook another Negro. They hailed each other gladly in the early dawn.
> "Where you bound fuh?" John asked.
> "Tuh ketch me uh high henry."
> "Whuss dat?"
> "Uh railroad train, man, where you been all yo' days you don't know de name of uh train?"
> "Oh, 'bout in spots and places. Where you bound fuh when you git on de train?"
> "Tuh Florida, man. Dat's de new country openin' up. Now git me straight, Ah don't mean West Florida, Ah means de real place. Good times, good money, and no mules and cotton."
> "B'lieve Ah'll go 'long wid yuh."[26]

The narrator's remark that John's peregrinations are "purely accidental" may seem to bolster the argument that throughout the mid-1930s Hurston repeatedly and disingenuously rewrote "the geographical boundaries of representation" to displace the Great Migration. However, the full complexity and meaning of Pearson's personal movements only emerge if one attends more closely to the first half of *Jonah's Gourd Vine* and to the history and demography of migrant labor in the South during the 1920s and 1930s. Through John's frequent and numerous changes of location and employment, Hurston constructs a detailed narrative cartography of migrant labor patterns around the rural South—patterns more localized but no less "monumental" than those involving the more familiar Great Migration to the urban North. As historian R. Douglas Hurt reminds us, "between 1910 and 1930, more than 1.5 million African Americans, mostly farmers, left the South, pushed by the boll weevil, poverty, and want and pulled by industrial jobs outside the region . . . an additional 2 million departed from the region between 1930 and 1950." However, Hurt also notes: "Despite the Great Migration of African American farmers from the countryside during the first third of the twentieth century, by 1940, 77 percent of the U.S. black population still lived in the South, and 64 percent lived in rural areas."[27] Another historian, Louis M. Kyriakoudes, argues that the oral accounts of black southern migrants collected during the 1930s by the Federal Writers' Project (FWP) "complicate our view of the early-twentieth-century southern rural exodus we call the Great Migration. . . . [T]he frequent moves of black and white southerners created migration patterns of great complexity. Highly mobile rural southerners moved across the rural South, seeking greater opportunities in the region's tenancy-dominated agriculture."[28] Hurt and Kyriakoudes's work usefully contextualizes Hurston's writing in historical-geographical materialist terms by clarifying her emphasis on rural migration *within* and *between* the southern states. It helps us to see how John Pearson's "highly mobile" search for "greater opportunities" encompasses not only the interstate train journey from plantation life in Alabama to "de new country" of Florida but also his intrastate movements even before leaving Alabama.

From almost the very start of *Jonah's Gourd Vine*, John Pearson is an economic migrant. He arrives on the Pearson plantation in Notasulga after leaving his family back "over de Creek" to escape his stepfather Ned's neoslaver attitude to African American labor. Ned insists that "[n]iggers wuz made tuh work and all of 'em [John and his siblings] gwine work right long wid me" (5), to which John responds, "[d]is ain't slavery time and Ah got two good footses hung onto me" (8). John's initial journey on foot over Songahatchee Creek to Notasulga—with its accompanying shift from cotton sharecropping to plantation labor—is almost as significant as his subsequent migration by train to Florida. Moreover, John's first encounter with a locomotive coincides with his arrival in Notasulga.[29] Overcoming his shock at the "fiery-lunged monster" before him, John begins to freight the train with symbolic meaning, albeit without yet understanding its significance: "It say something but Ah ain't heered it 'nough tuh tell whut it say yit.... Ahm comin' heah [the station] plenty mo' times and den Ah tell yuh whut it say" (16). When John is confronted the following spring by the grim prospect of returning back "over dat Creek" (40) to sharecropping, he more clearly comprehends and articulates the sense of freedom that he has projected onto the train since his arrival: "No, he couldn't leave Notasulga where the train came puffing into the depot twice a day. No, no! He dropped everything and tore out across the fields and came out at last at the railroad cut just below the station. He sat down upon the embankment and waited." On one level, then, the train represents John's initial, relatively liberating migration to Notasulga and away from sharecropping. But on another level, he is beginning to read into the train's "words" the possibility of a "great[er] away," a "distance" that extends beyond Notasulga. John hears the refrain "Opelika-black-and-dirty, Opelika-black-and-dirty!" (41) in the "chanting" of the engine and "the powerful whisper of steam." Here John anticipates his first (temporary) break with the Pearson plantation when he goes to work in the tie-camp near Opelika (57), itself a move that foreshadows John's interstate migration by train to Sanford, where he is recruited to another railroad camp in Wildwood, west of Sanford (105).

The second half of *Jonah's Gourd Vine*, focusing on John's comparatively settled (albeit scandal-ridden) later life as a carpenter and preacher in Sanford, also maps the impact of black southern migration to the urban North before and after World War I—the mass migration that, according to Carby and other critics, Hurston's major work "ignores."[30] Chapter 19 depicts northern industrial capitalism's active recruitment of black labor from "[t]he South—land of muscled hands" and how the "call of the North" (149) subverts the authority of the white southern state apparatus and its surveillance of rural African Americans:

> Do what they could, the State, County and City all over the South could do little to halt the stampede. The cry of "Goin' Nawth" hung over the land like the wail over Egypt at the death of the first-born. The railroad stations might be watched, but there could be no effective censorship over the mails. No one could keep track of the movements of cars and wagons and mules and men walking. Railroads, hardroads, dirt roads, side roads, roads were in the minds of the black South and all roads led North.

This passage provides compelling support for Yaeger's argument that Hurston "is rewriting black public history—capturing the train's [and, one might add, the road's] historic meaning for southern black men and women"; more generally, it makes "[t]he southern literary landscapes of the 1930s look much less regionally insular" than traditional southern literary studies has allowed.[31] Yet when John himself makes one final migration, he does not go "[o]n to the North! The land of promise" (151). John's authority over his congregation and his standing within the wider Sanford community has been seriously imperiled by his philandering and sensational divorce from second wife Hattie. Because many of his most loyal supporters have already gone north (149, 154), John recognizes that "[m]aybe it's meant for me tuh leave Sanford" (185). But rather than reconnecting with his former congregation in a northern metropolis, John heads further south—or southwest—to Plant City (186), where he struggles to find work as a carpenter before marrying the wealthy widow Sally Lovelace.[32]

This latest "haphazard" (186) southward migration, continuing John's trajectory from Notasulga southeast to Sanford and Eatonville and finally southwest to Plant City, foreshadows Janie's general movement further and "further south" in *Their Eyes*. However, Hurston is mapping across both novels the kind of rural, intraregional migrant labor patterns too easily overlooked in overly simplistic models of the Great Migration from the rural South to the urban North. There is compelling historical evidence to bolster Hurston's point, first dramatized in *Jonah's Gourd Vine* and subsequently reiterated throughout her career, that Florida was a major destination for black southern migrant workers. Even as much of the agricultural South was going into decline in the early twentieth century—a process that would intensify during the Great Depression—Florida was experiencing a widely hyped land boom. The construction of massive new urban developments for both residents and tourists was accompanied by an expansion of agricultural production around Lake Okeechobee; most of the required farm labor was provided by migrant workers. As Kyriakoudes observes, "[T]he advent of the 1920s farm depression sent southern blacks on the road as migrant laborers, working the fruit and vegetable crops in the burgeoning truck farms of Florida and New Jersey."[33] Such localized variations within the South's agricultural economy were not the only factor that fueled black migration to Florida before the Great Depression. Sociologists Stewart Tolnay and E. M. Beck have demonstrated that between 1910 and 1930 racial violence in the Deep South, especially Mississippi and Georgia, generated a significantly larger exodus of African Americans from those states than from others in the region: "Not all black migrants during the era of the 'Great Migration' were headed northward, however. There was a great deal of circulation *within* southern states." For example, "[B]etween 1920 and 1930 ... Georgia lost 260,000 blacks and Florida gained over 54,000 via net migration."[34]

In her introduction to *Mules and Men*, Hurston recounts a conversation with her mentor, Columbia anthropology professor Franz Boas, in which she justified her decision to begin fieldwork on "Negro folklore" in the far southeast: "'Florida is a place that draws ... Negroes from every Southern state surely and some from the North and West.' So I knew it was possible for me to get a cross section of the Negro South in the one state."[35] Carby quotes this passage to bolster her argument that with *Mules and Men* Hurston began deliberately displacing the demographics of northward urban migration.[36] Yet one might reasonably cite this quote to amplify the point that Hurston makes in both *Jonah's Gourd Vine* and *Mules and Men*: mass movement to northern cities was hardly the whole story of rural black southern migration during the 1920s and 1930s. Labor historian Cindy Hahamovitch stresses that "forty- to sixty thousand destitute people hurried to Florida every winter during the Great Depression": these "[p]oor people—black and white—came to Florida ... because the draining of the Everglades had recently exposed rich farmland that could produce hundreds of thousands of acres of vegetables in the winter when there was little work elsewhere."[37] As David G. Nicholls notes, Polk County's truck farm and logging camps employed "migrant workers from throughout the South"; Nicholls quotes a 1931 study reporting how "as the forests have been cut out the movement of Negro workers from one southern state to another in search of work in the lumber camps has increased." The intraregional mobility of these migrant workers allowed Hurston to collect "together stories from disparate geographical origins" that often dramatized conflict with and resistance to exploitative employers.[38] *Mules and Men* thus foregrounds both the workers' mobility *and* their experience of exploitation throughout the Jim Crow South. Arriving at the Everglades Lumber Cypress Company camp in Loughman, Hurston was quick to realize "that this group of several hundred Negroes from all over the South was a rich field for folklore."[39] The discovery vindicated her claim to Boas that Florida held unique drawing power for rural southern blacks; more than that, though, it demonstrated that focusing on the "folk" (and, formally, on "folklore") did not preclude engaging with major contemporary patterns of migration. As Duck remarks in *The Nation's Region* (2006), in *Mules and Men* "Hurston's folk appear to be surprisingly modern," and her "folklore comes mainly from wage laborers in a lumber mill" who creatively adapt "old-time tales" (8) and songs to their own lives; moreover, these mobile black southern "folk are linked to the national economy through both production...and consumption."[40]

Much like *Mules and Men*, *Jonah's Gourd Vine* foregrounds the black southern folk and their lore. But here too, what Eric J. Sundquist terms "the intersection of [the novel's] folk and narrative registers" elucidates rather than elides the material realities of black southern lives transformed by modernity and migrant labor. This is evident in the echoes between the African retentions of "[t]he drum with the man skin" (29) on the Pearson plantation and what Sundquist terms "the onomatopoeic 'chanting' of the train," sounding (as we have already seen) "its rich association with movement and migration in modern black history"; it is also apparent in the resonances between the biblical, metaphorical "hammers of creation" and "anvils of Time" (175) in John's sermons, and the material, literal hammers and axes that he wields while working in the tie- and lumber camps. *Jonah's Gourd Vine* has often been overlooked by critics (including Carby) who concentrate on Hurston's next three published books, even though *Mules and Men* was written before her debut novel. Yet if we read *Jonah's Gourd Vine* with attention to how its seemingly uneven—or in Sundquist's term, "jagged"—fictional fusion of folklore and migrant labor serves to register (rather than repress) a dramatic sense of social and demographic change, we can see more clearly how Hurston was concerned, at this key point in her career, with representing those blacks who, despite the Great Migration and Great Depression, stayed in and moved around the rural South.[41] As Riché Richardson has observed, "[W]hile Carby valuably instructs us about the costs of a hegemonic black rural folk ideology for blacks in urban contexts," her theory of discursive displacement itself "renders invisible and insignificant blacks who *do* continue to live in the rural South."[42]

Bahamian Migrant Labor
in *Their Eyes Were Watching God*

Still, it is not *Jonah's Gourd Vine* but *Their Eyes* that Carby reads for evidence of Hurston's discursive displacement of the northward Great Migration. It is also *Their Eyes* that takes the more prominent role in Yaeger's project, as the Everglades "muck" becomes a privileged locus within *Dirt and Desire*'s reconstructed southern literary landscape. Discussing the ways in which southern women writers map "a southern social geography that should make the quiddity of 'southern' places more interesting," Yaeger applauds Hurston for generating "an incredible instability of place; she sends her African American characters southward" from Eatonville to the Everglades. Yaeger thus echoes both her own observations about John traveling "farther south" in *Jonah's Gourd Vine* and Carby's considerably more skeptical view that migration "from the southern states further south" in *Their Eyes* obscures northward urban migration.[43] Duck too remarks that "unlike protagonists of Great Migration narratives, Janie, in pursuing the horizon, generally goes south"; this tallies with *Their Eyes'* "chronotope of the folk," which "often appears allotemporal, existing outside that of the nation and its economy."[44] Yet the narrative trajectory and literary geography of Hurston's second novel look rather different if one considers another migratory movement that Carby fails to take seriously and that Yaeger overlooks in her brief analysis of "the indigent situation of migrant workers" on the muck.[45] The Bahamian presence in *Their Eyes* further destabilizes both neo-Agrarian *and* revisionist notions of "'southern' places" by extending Hurston's representation of migrant labor in the rural South from the intraregional to the transnational.

In Jan Cooper's assessment, Janie regains "[b]riefly with Tea Cake and the other workers in 'the muck' ... something as close to the agrarian ideal as a modern Southern writer could imagine, a community in which all members have a well-defined role and are fundamentally at harmony with the luxuriant natural world surrounding them."[46] Cooper acknowledges the gendered limits of this black (folk) community but does not recognize how the events engendering Janie's killing of Tea Cake and the resulting split within this black "community" (so starkly evident during Janie's trial) are inextricable from the more pervasive power of white southern racism both on and beyond the muck. The claim that Janie, Tea Cake, and their fellow workers live in "harmony" with nature also sidesteps what happens when they are displaced from the muck by a devastating hurricane—an oversight repeated by Mary Weaks-Baxter.[47] Like *Jonah's Gourd Vine* and *Mules and Men*, *Their Eyes* maps south Florida as a mecca for black migrant workers fleeing racial oppression and economic depression elsewhere in the South. After the hurricane, however, Hurston stresses the sociospatial practice of white southern power, the grimly familiar experience of living and dying Jim Crow, and how these regional realities ensnare other members of the New World black diaspora.

As the storm gathers, the narrative registers the black migrant laborers' jarring loss of "harmony" with the "natural world surrounding them" by shifting from the image of a worker (Janie and Tea Cake's friend Stew Beef) to a biblical figure sounding the storm's awesome dimensions: "Sometime that night the winds came back. Everything in the world had a strong rattle, sharp and short like Stew Beef vibrating the drum head near the edge with his fingers. By morning Gabriel was playing the deep tones in the center of the drum"

(158). As Janie, Tea Cake, and their Bahamian friend Motor Boat sense the loss of their affective link to—or laboring power over—the "natural world," so too they identify a shift in ultimate authority over nature (the whipping winds, the swelling lake) from white landowners to a different kind of "bossman" (158):

> "[...] Ole Massa is doin' *His* work now. Us oughta keep quiet."
>
> They huddled closer and stared at the door.... The time was past for asking the white folks what to look for through that door. Six eyes were questioning *God*. (159)

This invocation of a supreme *super*natural or *non*worldly authority (elevated further by the novel's title) may appear at first glance a "folkloric" distraction from, or religious mystification of, southern social and racial relations. But as Lake Okeechobee floods the surrounding landscape and the field workers are unceremoniously displaced from the muck, the narrative deftly depicts local white authorities attempting to reassert their social power over black workers, even amid the chaos and destruction caused by the storm. Tea Cake is commandeered by two white men in the hurricane's aftermath and, despite protesting that he is "uh workin' man wid money in mah pocket," forced to help bury the storm's victims in segregated mass graves:

> "Hey, dere, y'all! Don't dump dem bodies in de hole lak dat! Examine every last one of 'em and find out if they's white or black."
>
> "Us got tuh handle 'em slow lak dat? God have mussy! In de condition they's in got tuh examine 'em? Whut difference do it make 'bout de color? Dey all needs buryin' in uh hurry."
>
> "Got orders from headquarters. They makin' coffins fuh all de white folks. 'Tain't nothin' but cheap pine, but dat's better'n nothin'. Don't dump no white folks in de hole jus' so."
>
> "Whut tuh do 'bout de colored folks? Got boxes fuh dem too?"
>
> "Nope. They cain't find enough of 'em tuh go 'round. Jus' sprinkle plenty quicklime over 'em and cover 'em up."
>
> "Shucks! Nobody can't tell nothin' 'bout some of uh dese bodies, de shape dey's in. Can't tell whether dey's white or black."
>
> The guards had a long conference over that. After a while they came back and told the men, "Look at they hair, when you cain't tell no other way. And don't lemme ketch none uh y'all dumpin' white folks, and don't be wastin' no boxes on colored. They's too hard tuh git holt of right now."

Though Tea Cake remarks ruefully, "Look lak dey think God don't know nothin' 'bout de Jim Crow law" (171), the situation makes clear that local, material-worldly authority has reverted back from God to the white "bossmen."

Noting that "the pleasures of life on the muck" are turned upside-down by the storm, Yaeger identifies these Jim Crow burials as a case study in "reverse autochthony," her term for a relatively uncharted dimension of southern writing in which "both grownups and children are hurled into water or earth without proper rituals, without bearing witness to grief, without proper mourning."[48] Despite Wright's scorn for *Their Eyes*' supposed focus on a simplified "Negro folk-mind" and its lack of political "message," Hurston's representation of the storm and its aftermath as a parable of racism in the Jim Crow South connects it to Wright's story "Down by the Riverside," from *Uncle Tom's Children* (1938)—the collection that Hurston reviewed almost as harshly as Wright had *Their Eyes*. Also set during a flood, the story features a black male protagonist, Mann, who fears being press-ganged in a fashion and context similar to Tea Cake's: "He had heard that the white folks were threatening to conscript all Negroes they could lay their hands on to pile sand- and cement-bags on the levee.... Shucks, in times like these theyll shoota nigger down jus lika dog n think nothin of it." "Down by the Riverside" ends with the death of Mann, shot by white troops and "hurled into water . . . without proper mourning": "One of the soldiers stooped and pushed the butt of his rifle under the body and lifted it over. It rolled heavily down the wet slope and stopped about a foot from the water's edge; one black palm sprawled limply outward and upward, trailing in the brown current."[49] Yaeger connects reverse autochthony to more recent southern history—the brutal 1998 murder of James Byrd in Jasper, Texas—but does not reference Hurston's more immediate historical source.[50] Much as Wright based "Down by the Riverside" on the Mississippi flood of 1927, the storm in *Their Eyes Were Watching God* draws upon the Lake Okeechobee hurricane of 1928.

On September 16, 1928, a hurricane with winds of 140 miles per hour struck south Florida, having already killed hundreds of people in Puerto Rico and the Bahamas. The winds demolished the feeble four-foot dikes holding back the seven hundred square miles of Lake Okeechobee, sending eight-foot tidal waves sweeping through the surrounding landscape. The official death toll was 1,838, but this figure has been disputed by scholars who believe up to 6,000 people died, and that "four-fifths of them [were] poor blacks working the fertile sugar cane and bean fields near Lake Okeechobee."[51] In a "natural" example of reverse autochthony, some bodies were "swallowed whole by the Everglades muck" and thus never recorded in the official death toll.[52] As the recovered corpses accumulated, the grotesque reality of southern racial segregation was starkly illustrated. While 69 whites were being buried in pine boxes in Palm Beach's Woodland Cemetery, 674 black bodies were separated out and buried in a vacant lot in West Palm Beach that, as Robert Mykle recounts, "served as a clandestine burial ground" for poor blacks. Moreover, "The black survivors were treated little better. Many were rounded up for the worst of the cemetery detail work, loading and unloading the stinking, rotting bodies. White National Guardsmen watched over them as they worked. Many were single men with few ties to the area and little incentive to help."[53] Like Tea Cake in Palm Beach, these coerced black migrant workers were ordered to "rely on facial features or hair texture if necessary" to ensure that no white bodies were thrown into the mass graves.[54]

Here we see how the links between black migrant labor on the muck and the hurricane of 1928 historicize a novel that has been read by critics ranging from Wright via Carby to Duck as a "quaint," "nostalgic," and "allotemporal" depiction of black southern folk culture. Furthermore, the history of the Lake Okeechobee hurricane helps contextualize another rarely considered aspect of Hurston's representation of black life and labor in the Everglades: the presence of Caribbean migrant workers. Mykle remarks that among the "four thousand strong" cohort of black migrant workers on the muck, "many were from the Bahamas, joined by a few Jamaican and other Caribbean islanders."[55] Journalist and historian Eliot Kleinberg remarks that "as many as 5,000 migrant workers [were] believed to come from the impoverished islands of the Caribbean." Local white landlords' reliance on "black migrants from the Deep South or the Caribbean" had increased as the mode of agricultural production in the Everglades shifted from small farms to "a collection of larger farms owned by big business."[56] As Howard Johnson observes in his study of late nineteenth- and early twentieth-century migration from the Bahamas to Florida, "the Bahamas provided the mainly black labor force" that "was responsible for the expansion of agrarian capitalism in South Florida."[57] Hahamovitch too points out that "the histories of Florida and the Bahamas had long been intertwined" through migrant labor: she quotes an early historian of south Florida who acknowledged that "All our heavy laborers were Bahamian negroes." Although the United States enacted strict anti-immigration legislation in 1917 and 1924, Bahamian workers kept coming, legally or not. During World War I, the Department of Labor's Immigration Service had established the country's first foreign guest-worker program, importing temporary agricultural labor from the Bahamas, Mexico, and other neighboring countries. Temporary labor contracts for foreign agricultural workers continued via a loophole in the otherwise punitive 1917 Immigration Act. There were other ways around the legal restrictions: in August 1921 the Immigration Service began investigating "the smuggling of Negroes from the Bahama Islands."[58] Overall, however, the postwar anti-immigration acts rendered the status of Bahamian workers in the Everglades even more marginal: by 1928 they were generally "unseen, uncounted, unwanted, except at planting and harvest time. No one thought very much about them, though it was their labor that brought most of the prosperity."[59]

These Caribbean laborers, along with their African American counterparts, suffered most when the storm hit Lake Okeechobee: "Living in flimsy shanties, many built of tarpaper and scrap wood in the least desirable areas ... migrant farmhands had no place to retreat to.... There was no one to miss them, no one to look for them, and no one who cared whether they were found or not."[60] In the disaster's immediate aftermath, the newsletter of the Florida State Board of Health reported: "Most of the deaths were among the negro laborers who entered the Everglades for the planting season which had opened a short time previously. Since a large percentage of these negroes were from Nassau, which is outside of the state, it was not possible in a great many instances to identify the bodies."[61] Despite the efforts of journalists, historians, and community activists, it has remained all but impossible to trace the lives and deaths of the storm's Caribbean victims because of their tenuous social and legal status as foreign black migrant workers.[62]

The Caribbean migrant workers' absence from the official history and death toll of the 1928 hurricane is eerily echoed by the lack of literary-critical attention to the Bahamian presence in *Their Eyes*, even among scholars drawing on the new southern studies and arguing for "Hurston's privileging of mobility and migrancy" as "a turn to the global."[63] Despite the critical efforts since 2000 or so to resituate both Hurston's work and (new) southern studies in relation to the Caribbean, Carby remains one of the few critics to have volunteered more than a passing remark on the Caribbean workers' role in the novel. However, Carby sees the introduction of these foreign workers as part of the dubious narrative strategy resulting from Hurston's "decision to rewrite the geographical boundaries of representation by situating the southern, rural folk and patterns of migration in relation to the Caribbean rather than the northern states." So whereas Janie keeps turning south again, "Migration in a northerly direction is undertaken only by the Barbadians [sic] who join Janie and Tea Cake on the 'muck.'"[64] A closer reading of *Their Eyes* with reference to intraregional and transnational labor history exposes the limitations of this argument: even during the Great Migration, vast numbers of black migrant workers continued to move not only around the rural South (especially Florida) but also into the region from the Caribbean (especially the Bahamas).

Their Eyes pointedly renders the mass arrival of migrant workers on the muck from multiple directions: "They came in wagons from way up in Georgia and they came in truck loads from east, west, north and south" (131). By introducing the Bahamian workers, the novel reveals that many of these arrivals from south of the Everglades were coming from south of the U.S. South. Initially, the Bahamians seem to be merely minor characters; moreover, their representation is heavily mediated through Janie's point of view. Yet it is precisely the narrative's subtle exposure of Janie's initial shortsightedness that facilitates our understanding of how, rather than consolidating Hurston's alleged ideology of the black southern folk, the Bahamian presence exposes another gaping flaw in the agrarian "community" celebrated by critics like Cooper and Weaks-Baxter. The U.S.-born workers' limited empathy for and solidarity with their Caribbean counterparts manifests itself less as a neo-imperial American gaze—the kind of worldview which, as we will see in chapter 4, informs Hurston's ethnographic vision of Jamaica in *Tell My Horse*—than as a regional (black southern) and national (African American) blindness. At first the Bahamians are all but invisible to the U.S.-born migrant workers, including Janie. When she arrives with Tea Cake it seems "[t]o Janie's strange eyes, everything in the Everglades was big and new. Big Lake Okechobee, big beans, big cane, big weeds, big everything.... Wild cane on either side of the road hiding the rest of the world. People wild too" (129). The Bahamians first come into Janie's focus some months later when she begins "to look around and see people and things she hadn't noticed during the [picking] season." Janie belatedly begins to engage with the Bahamians and their culture: "[W]hen she heard the subtle but compelling rhythms of the Bahaman drummers, she'd walk over and watch the dances. She did not laugh the 'Saws' to scorn as she had heard the people doing in the season" (139). Only after "Tea Cake and Janie had friended with the Bahaman workers" do the other African Americans follow suit: "[T]hey, the 'Saws,' had been gradually drawn into the American crowd. They quit hiding out to hold their dances when they found that their American friends didn't laugh at them as they feared. Many of the Americans learned to jump and liked it as much as the 'Saws.' So they began to hold dances night after night in the quarters, usually behind Tea Cake's house" (154). Not until this point does what Edward Pavlić calls the muck's "transnational diasporic community" truly begin to coalesce.[65]

Daphne Lamothe rightly notes that this encounter between "the Bahamians and Black Americans" is "an easily overlooked passage in the novel" before positing that "[t]he relative ease with which these groups overcome their differences suggests that national and ethnic identification can be blurred with a greater awareness and cultivation of cultural similarities, and a greater tolerance of and interest in cultural difference."[66] Lamothe's claim is supported by a later scene, during the storm, in which we learn that Tea Cake has pledged to travel to the Bahamas to visit Motor Boat: "Goin' over tuh Nassau fuh dat visit widja when all dis is over," to which Motor Boat replies: "Definitely, Tea Cake. Mah mama's house is yours" (164). However, an earlier conversation between Tea Cake and Lias, another "of the Bahaman boys" (155), suggests that the development of a diasporic "awareness" and "tolerance" among the U.S.-born workers is not quite as simple as Lamothe suggests. Rather than heed Lias's uncle's warning about the imminent arrival of the hurricane that will devastate the muck and lead indirectly to his death, Tea Cake accedes to the supposed authority of white southern landowners. Indeed, the encounter reveals Tea Cake's dismissive attitude toward not only the Bahamian "boy" and his uncle but also the local Native Americans: another demographic on the muck rarely discussed by Hurston scholars. Although the Seminoles are the first group to recognize that a storm is approaching (154)—much as they are said to have anticipated the 1928 hurricane—Tea Cake is dismissive. When Lias warns that "De Indians gahn east, man. It's dangerous," Tea Cake responds disdainfully that

> "Dey don't always know. Indians don't know much uh nothin', tuh tell de truth. Else dey'd own dis country still. De white folks ain't gone nowhere. Dey oughta know if it's dangerous. You better stay heah, man. Big jumpin' dance tuhnight right heah, when it fair off."
>
> Lias hesitated and started to climb out, but his uncle wouldn't let him. "Dis time tuhmorrer you gointuh wish you follow crow," he snorted and drove off. Lias waved back to them gaily.
>
> "If Ah never see you no mo' on earth, Ah'll meet you in Africa."
>
> Others hurried east like the Indians and rabbits and snakes and coons. But the majority sat around laughing and waiting for the sun to get friendly again. (156)

Tea Cake's rejection of the Seminoles' storm warning on the premise that they surrendered to white colonial supremacy is laden with dramatic irony: when the storm hits, Tea Cake is finally forced to abandon his own faith in the white "bossmen" who literally "own dis country": "The time was past for asking the white folks what to look for" (159). Perhaps because Tea Cake himself is a transient worker and thus unfamiliar with Florida history, he overlooks the Jackson administration's genocidal terror during the Seminole wars of the 1830s—which led to the Seminoles migrating further south into the Everglades, where they also welcomed runaway slaves—and the Miccosukees' proud status as "the only known Native Americans to have never signed a treaty with the United States because they never surrendered."[67]

Interpreting Hurston's depiction of Caribbean "migration in a northward direction" only with reference to the Great Migration within the United States devalues the historical experience of those thousands of Bahamians who migrated north to the U.S. South—not least those who died during the storm of 1928 and went unremembered outside the pages of Hurston's novel. Having said that, critics more sympathetic to Hurston's attempts to connect black "southernness ... to cultural practices and beliefs of the Caribbean" also tend to privilege her life and career between 1935 and 1938—understandably so, given that this period included her extended stays in Jamaica and Haiti (where, famously, Hurston wrote *Their Eyes*). Trefzer argues persuasively that "Hurston's work on black Southern folk culture in *Mules and Men* (1935) and her travels in the Caribbean prompted her understanding of what might be termed black cultural globalism. By extending her research on folklore and voodoo from the Southern United States into the Caribbean Basin [in *Tell My Horse*], Hurston articulates a cultural continuum that stretches from West Africa through the Caribbean into the black American South." John Carlos Rowe suggests that *Mules and Men* and *Tell My Horse* "stage a drama in which the scientific and literary observer is reintroduced to her rural roots in the South, then initiated into her Afro-Caribbean heritage in New Orleans, Jamaica, and Haiti." Trefzer, Rowe, and Pavlić all concentrate on the continuities between the two anthropological-folkloric texts *Mules and Men* and *Tell My Horse*.[68] While this focus makes sense, it should be noted that Hurston's earlier research trips to the Bahamas during 1929 and 1930 had long since convinced her of the connections between blacks in the U.S. South and the Caribbean. Indeed, as Keith Cartwright has noted, Hurston's first scholarly publication—"Communication," an October 1927 essay in the *Journal of Negro History*—already "points to Florida's foundational colonial difference [as Spanish] and its strong ties to Cuba and the rest of the Caribbean."[69] By considering these early engagements with the connections between the U.S. South, the Bahamas, and the wider Caribbean, we can begin to understand the significance of the Caribbean presence not only in Hurston's work but also for a new southern studies that prioritizes long-standing "globalized localities" like south Florida.

In October 1929 Hurston traveled to Nassau because "I had heard some Bahaman music and seen a Jumping Dance out in Liberty City and I was entranced."[70] This prior contact with Bahamians in Miami also prompted Hurston to write to Langston Hughes that "There are so many of them in America that their folk lore definitely influences ours in South Fla."[71] After further research in the Bahamas during January and February 1930, Hurston published "Dance Songs and Tales from the Bahamas" in the July–September 1930 issue of the *Journal of American Folklore*. As if to drive home the connections between the Bahamas and south Florida, Hurston concluded the article with four folktales "recorded in Miami from Bahamian settlers." As in *Mules and Men*, Hurston stressed the mutability of "old-time tales" as they traveled with and were adapted by modern-day migrants. It is striking too that "Dance Songs and Tales" employs the term "great migration" to flag a hemispheric history of demographic and cultural exchange between the Caribbean and the U.S. South: Hurston remarks that the Bahamian jumping dance "resembles the Cuban *rumba* and the dances held in New Orleans after the great migration of Haitian and Santa Dominican Negroes after the success of [Toussaint] L'Ouverture."[72]

To be sure, Hurston's conception of Bahamian culture occasionally does appear invested in a romanticized *diasporic* ideology of the folk. In *Dust Tracks on a Road*, Hurston recalls how "I introduced Bahaman songs and dances to a New York audience at the John Golden Theater" in her off-Broadway production *The Great Day* (1932), which focused on life in a Florida railroad work camp. By retrospectively celebrating these songs and dances as "primitive" and "genuine Negro material"—in implicit contrast to the allegedly adulterated and commercialized African American songs that she dismissed in a 1934 essay as "neo-spirituals"—Hurston seems to be turning from U.S. southern to Bahamian folk culture in order to rescue what Carby calls "a representation of 'Negroness' as an unchanging, essential entity."[73] In "Other Negro Folklore Influences," an essay that Hurston wrote during her tenure circa 1938–39 with the Florida division of the FWP, she attributed the divergences between black U.S. southern and Bahamian culture to the contrasting historical experiences of black-white contact in the U.S. South and the Caribbean: "Bahamian music is more dynamic and compelling than that of the American Negro, and the dance movements are more arresting; perhaps because the Bahamian offerings are more savage. The Bahamian, and the West Indian Negro generally, has had much less contact with the white man than the American Negro. As a result, speech, music, dancing, and other modes of expression are infinitely nearer the African." Here Hurston seems less interested in turning south of the U.S. South to recover an essential, ahistorical "Negroness" than in explaining the stronger African retentions that she detects in Bahamian culture: "African-Bahamian folk arts," which are now dynamically "seep[ing] into the soil of America" by way of Florida.[74]

As I have tried to demonstrate, Hurston's major works between 1934 and 1937 generally posit a more flexible, fluid, and modernized model of black southern *and* Caribbean folk cultures, subject to and transformed by intraregional and transnational migration. Among all Hurston's voluminous writings throughout the 1930s, *Their Eyes Were Watching God* most vividly dramatizes the presence of Bahamian labor *and* culture in the U.S. South, such as how Bahamian expressive forms like jump dances were—as Hurston observed in 1939—"brought to Florida by immigrant Negro workers from the Bahama Islands."[75] Crucially, however, *Their Eyes* does not portray such folk cultural practices as static or "primitive." As she put it elsewhere, "Negro folklore is not a thing of the past. It is still in the making"; in *Their Eyes*, that process of "making" proceeds not despite but because of migration.[76] However, Hurston's depiction of the African American muck workers' initially aloof and condescending attitude toward "the Saws" and their dances suggests that she was hardly "utopian" about the prospects for circum-Caribbean cultural and political solidarity. Although Janie's pioneering personal embrace of the Bahamians and their culture eventually generates an inchoate "transnational diasporic community," Tea Cake's conversation with Lias signals Hurston's awareness that there remained significant national and ethnic barriers to the formation and endurance of any such community.

"The Subterranean Force":
Hurston and Florida's Migrant Farmworkers
after World War II

Hurston's research into intraregional and transnational migrant labor in Florida did not end when she left the state FWP in 1939. As we saw at the start of this chapter, almost two decades later Hurston returned to the subject of "Florida's Migrant Farm Worker" in an unfinished essay that exhibited her undimmed interest in the role of both southern- and foreign-born migrant workers in Florida's national "farm industry." Riffing on Cold War–era fears about Soviet infiltration of national borders, Hurston remarks that if "American Negroes make up the bulk of the Florida migrant farm laborers," then "the majority of these workers are 'Rushians', they rushed down here from Georgia." But Hurston emphasizes too the presence of "5,000 Bahaman workers contracted to the Florida Fruit and Vegetable Association" as well as two newer groups who, unregulated by government agencies, had carved a niche alongside their black U.S. southern and Bahamian counterparts: "The state found use for 45–60,000 migrant workers in the 1957–58 season just past, which was sub-normal because of the freezes. The reason that the figures cannot be pinned down too definitely is the Texas-Mexican and Peurtorican [sic] elements, who [word illegible due to burn damage] American nationals, can and do move about independently of the farm agencies at their own expense." These Tex-Mex and Puerto Rican "free-wheelers," Hurston notes, now "add up to many more thousands than the Bahamans."77

Hurston here registers the massive rise in the number of agricultural laborers arriving in Florida from the Caribbean and Latin America during and after World War II. Hahamovitch describes how this demographic spike directly resulted from the U.S. state's expansion and liberalization—in response to intensive lobbying led by south Florida planters—of the guest-worker program policies established during World War I. During the first half of 1943, Caribbean agricultural workers—first Bahamians, then Jamaicans—began to arrive on south Florida farms and plantations as "alien negro laborers" under the government's Emergency Wartime Labor Program. Already by 1944, Jamaican guest workers were harvesting 65 percent of Florida's sugarcane crop. Though the "emergency" program was supposed to conclude with the end of the war, a policy of "agricultural exceptionalism" in the immediate postwar period ensured an increase rather than reduction in the number of guest workers arriving from Caribbean countries and Mexico, through the *bracero* program. There was no labor shortage in south Florida—quite the opposite, with black southern agricultural workers returning from military duty. But corporate growers such as U.S. Sugar benefited from and lobbied for the retention of cheap, temporary foreign labor. Caribbean guest workers were also used to stymie black southern labor's demands for better wages and working conditions: already in 1943 white employers at an Okeechobee work camp began to play Bahamian and black southern workers against one another, generating significant hostility between the two groups.[78] Caribbean guest workers—"non-immigrant workers," as they were classified after the war—were themselves cowed by the threat of deportation. Hurston astutely observed that as "the imagination, enterprise and daring of the growers grew, the migrant worker device grew with it until now in 1958, it has...evolved into a production machine, a device, an apparatus, an invention, under the supervision of both state and government."[79]

Hurston also notes the connection and chasm between these migrant workers and the Sunshine State's wealthier denizens. She begins by addressing directly her privileged readership: "You, the favored inhabitants of the Sun God's Golden Land...how aware are you of the subterranean force which flows beneath your fabulous mansions?" Hurston stresses that "under the state's $475,863,000 agricultural take at farm level of [word/s missing due to burn damage] flows the plancton-rich [sic] stream of migrant labor," wryly adding that "[o]nly when the unusual occurs...is public attention called to this underground flow which nevertheless, affects powerfully the economics, and everybody who lives in this green-and-gold hot-house of the nation." Perhaps by "the unusual" Hurston meant the mass death of migrant workers during the 1928 hurricane as well as the "destructive freezes" of 1957–58 to which her article directly refers.[80]

However, the second half of "Florida's Migrant Worker" focuses not on the "subterranean" social and economic ligatures between wealthy Americans and migrant farmworkers but on the agency and voices of the migrants themselves. Presenting a kind of heteroglossia from the field, Hurston's approach allows workers to articulate their varying motives for traveling to Florida: even allowing for selective editing on Hurston's part, they often seem to have seen the move as an opportunity for relative autonomy from white authority rather than as another form of oppression. "One young man who swaggered as if he had some delightful surprises for the female folks" asserted that "Its [sic] better to change spots and places and get hold of some spending-change and be looked upon as folks," while a woman worker declared, "I sure was glad when I found out about this kind of work. I abomin[a]tes working in a house with some woman haggling me around. I make more money outside, and then again, I just likes to be out where a lot of folks is working. The work aint hard and [word illegible due to burn damage] boss aint mean." From these various voices explaining "why migrant farm workers come to be migrant," Hurston draws out "two basic reasons": "The work bettered their financial condition. No [word illegible due to burn damage] distinctions existed to make a person feel inferior."[81] Though Hurston seems here to downplay obvious and institu-

FIGURE 1. Hurston's accompanying text for this "[Miami] *Herald* photo by Ernie Tyner," apparently slated for inclusion in her 1958 essay "Florida's Migrant Farm Worker," emphasized the female tomato picker's agency in choosing field work over domestic labor. The picker is quoted saying, "I never want to go back to doing no maid's work. I love to feel free." Photographs Series E. Migrant Farm Workers, box 14, folder 5, Zora Neale Hurston Papers, Special and Area Studies Collections, George A. Smathers Libraries, University of Florida, Gainesville.

FIGURE 2. Hurston's caption for this photo, also by Ernie Tyner and intended for use in "Florida's Migrant Farm Worker," read: "Returning from the field by truck. Fewer and fewer trucks are used. The trend is towards busses which are even heated during winter." Photographs Series E. Migrant Farm Workers, box 14, folder 5, Zora Neale Hurston Papers, Special and Area Studies Collections, George A. Smathers Libraries, University of Florida, Gainesville.

tionalized southern social "distinctions" between blacks and whites, the financial benefits were equally appealing to black southern and Caribbean migrant workers. Hahamovitch notes that, despite the vicissitudes involved in cutting cane on south Florida's neoplantations, around "one in twenty Jamaican *agricultural workers* spent part of 1960 in the United States under contract, and fully half of all Jamaican farmworkers lined up for a chance to go." After all, "For rural Jamaicans, the farmworker program was their best hope of getting a little ahead, of earning wages three times higher than they could make at home doing similar work."[82]

In his letter to Doug Silver, *Herald* editor Beebe seems surprised that Hurston's "first installment" does not emphasize white growers' exploitation of the migrant workers (the "conditions... in these camps"). Yet it was characteristic of Hurston to focus on black life and labor as at least semiautonomous from white "bossmen," even at the risk of seeming to elide racial and economic oppression (that familiar charge against Hurston, dating back to Wright and Locke). The 1958 essay drafts are also consistent with Hurston's career-long tendency to emphasize the individual agency, rather than collective exploitation or potential solidarity, of black people in general and black migrant workers in particular: where once the spotlight was on John Pearson or Janie Woods, twenty-plus years later we have the swaggering young ladies' man. Duck has critiqued this individualist inclination, noting that *Their Eyes* ends with Janie's "folkloric practice" in the isolated space of her house in Eatonville, a form of "individual sustenance" that, however, is "not readily conducive to thinking about social or political solutions for the community." For Duck, Janie's final "voluntary segregation of the self... preserves African American folkloric culture" but formally "displaces the enforced racial segregation of the South."[83] It is possible to perceive continuities here with Hurston's thinking almost two decades later, by which point she was best known for controversial essays and letters like "Court Order Can't Make Races Mix." Published in the *Orlando Sentinel* in August 1955, "Court Order" bemoaned the impact of federally enforced integration on both "the self-respect of my people" and Hurston's own sense of self—"How much satisfaction can I get from a court order [*Brown v. Board of Education*] for somebody to associate with me who does not wish me near them?"—while ignoring overwhelming evidence that segregated black schools throughout the South were severely underfunded.[84] But whereas "white southern newspapers eagerly circulated her attack on desegregation," the *Herald* canceled the proposed essay series on Florida's "migrant worker apparatus," including a planned installment on "the coming of the Bahamian workers."[85] Hurston's views on desegregation and the burgeoning Civil Rights movement may have been conservative, but migrant labor in Florida was a subject she was perhaps uniquely placed to elucidate.

Even after the publication of rediscovered manuscripts dating from Hurston's collection of "Negro folk-tales from the Gulf States" in the late 1920s (*Every Tongue Got to Confess* [2001]) and her work with the Federal Writers' Project in the late 1930s (*Go Gator and Muddy the Water* [1999]), Hurston's late 1950s manuscripts about Florida's migrant labor remain unpublished. In this chapter, I have tried to show that they can be read as part of a career-spanning continuum with Hurston's (now) canonical books between 1935 and 1937 as well as her anthropological scholarship and debut novel earlier in that decade; in the process, Hurston tracked the U.S. South's historic and ongoing role within what Immanuel Wallerstein was the first to call the "extended Caribbean."[86] Taken together, this extraordinary body of writing vividly details how south Florida's powerful economic position within an extended Caribbean—or an extended South—was driven by intraregional and transnational migrant labor. That Hurston returned to the situation of Bahamian and other immigrant workers in 1958, only eighteen months before her death, suggests her ongoing sense of the significance of nonnative labor to Florida's status as "the hot-house of the nation."

Though unpublished, Hurston's *Miami Herald* piece anticipated the landmark CBS documentary *Harvest of Shame*, aired on November 26, 1960, which focused on Belle Glade and finally drew national attention to the ways in which Florida agribusiness mistreated migrant workers. Abuse of "the migrant worker device" continued over the next few decades: Hahamovitch demonstrates in often harrowing detail how, from the 1950s until the 1990s, Florida's sugar industry was the nation's largest employer (and exploiter) of H-2 labor: in that period, between five and twenty thousand guest workers cut sugarcane for five to six months of each year.[87] As Haitian American writer Edwidge Danticat has noted in her foreword to the 2006 edition of *Their Eyes*, "migrant labor and hurricanes remain very concrete elements of life in Florida."[88] Hurston's novel remains eerily resonant in today's globalized South, where wealthy sugar producers have "bought land in the vicinity of Lake Okeechobee ... and imported platoons of poorly paid Caribbean migrant workers," and where Hurricane Katrina—officially the deadliest hurricane to hit the United States since the Lake Okeechobee hurricane seventy-seven years earlier—displaced an estimated three hundred thousand Central American and Caribbean immigrants from in and around New Orleans.[89] By failing to consider either the intraregional movements of rural black southerners or the transnational border crossings of Caribbean guest workers, Carby's influential critical model itself discursively displaces the (extended) South of black folk. As Hurston wrote in the late 1930s: "If Florida lore is richer it is because the lore and lushness of other states and countries have been heaped upon Florida by her great attraction for workers."[90]

CHAPTER 2

Transnational/Intertextual Migrations and U.S. Southern, Danish, and English "Folk" Identities in Nella Larsen's Fiction

In chapter 1, I argued that critics in (new) southern studies and African American studies have not fully registered the intraregional as well as transnational scales of Zora Neale Hurston's writing about black labor and migration in the U.S. South. But what if we turn now to another black woman writer from the same era who, like Hurston, was lost to literary history and then recovered as a major figure of the Harlem (rather than Southern) Renaissance? What too if that writer's representation of the rural South is less amenable than Hurston's to either revisionist models of "southern literature" or black "southern folk aesthetics"? In *Dirt and Desire* (2000), Patricia Yaeger makes the parenthetical observation that "Nella Larsen's reflections on the South in *Quicksand* (1928) and *Passing* (1929) offer still wider reference points for gendered remappings of the New South's racial coordinates."[1] Yaeger's tantalizing but unpursued observation offers a starting point for this second chapter's exploration of the ways in which Larsen's fiction uses (mostly individual) migrations to remap the South's racial and spatial coordinates at various regional, national, and transnational scales.

I have no interest in claiming that Larsen "was always a southerner too" or that we should see Larsen as a "southern writer." However, the vexed issue of Larsen's relationship to black southern culture has had a significant bearing upon how her life and work have been understood. During the 1990s, influential scholars criticized Larsen for her alleged lack of identification with the black southern "folk." Seeking "to conceptualize a southern, vernacular ancestry" for black women's writing in *Workings of the Spirit* (1991)—a valuable project at a time when such conceptualizations remained rare—Houston Baker charged that "[b]lack southern vernacular energies remain an absence" in Larsen's novels: the "mulatto aesthetics" of *Quicksand* and *Passing* lack "a fleshing out of . . . the southern, vernacular, communal expressivity of black mothers and grandmothers." By contrast, Baker praised Hurston's work for featuring "a full-muscled heroically womaned, fiercely articulate vernacular community represented by the Everglades camp" in *Mules and Men* (1935) and "a poetics of Afro-American woman's everyday life" in *Their Eyes Were Watching God* (1937).[2] In her important study of the twentieth-century African American migration narrative, *"Who Set You Flowin'?"* (1995), Farah Jasmine Griffin claimed that both Larsen and *Quicksand*'s protagonist, Helga Crane, exhibit "disdain and contempt ... for the black 'folk'"; that "[t]here are no wisdom-bearing sages in Larsen's South—only ignorant, superstitious black folk"; that there was "no mention of a folk culture"; and that "[t]here are no ancestors in *Quicksand*."[3] J. Martin Favor's insightful chapter in *Authentic Blackness: The Folk in the New Negro Renaissance* (1999), which recognized that "Larsen asks her readers to complicate their notions of black identity" because "Helga can accept the cultural life of neither bourgeoisie nor folk," nevertheless concurred that Helga "despises members of the folk."[4]

There are reasons why Larsen's life and work fare poorly in a critical model that foregrounds what Madhu Dubey identifies as a matrilineal "southern folk aesthetics."[5] Helga Crane's mother is neither black nor southern: she is white and Danish, much like Larsen's own immigrant mother, Mary Hansen. Larsen was born in Chicago in April 1891 to Mary and a black father, Peter Walker, who was not (African) American: in a 1926 Alfred Knopf publicity statement, Larsen described herself as "a mulatto, the daughter of a Danish lady and a Negro from the Virgin Islands, formerly the Danish West Indies." Larsen added: "When she was sixteen she went alone to Denmark to visit relatives of her mother in Copenhagen where she remained for three years."[6] This extended stay in Demark tallies with a conspicuous four-year gap in the record of Larsen's life between June 1908, when seventeen-year-old Nella was expelled from Fisk Normal School in Nashville, and May 1912, when she began her studies at a nursing school in New York. However, Larsen's first two biographers cast doubt on their subject's claim upon a mixed Afro-Danish heritage. In *Invisible Darkness* (1993), Charles Larson concluded that "her Denmark years are a total fabrication, a fancy embroidery upon the tragedy of her early life" as the abandoned daughter of a white Danish mother.[7] In *Nella Larsen, Novelist of the Harlem Renaissance* (1994), Thadious M. Davis declared that "throughout her public life [Larsen] displayed little intimate or firsthand knowledge of that country [Denmark], even though she could speak and read Danish," and that Larsen exhibited a lifelong tendency to formulate "public fictions of her past" as "not merely a 'mulatto,' but one who had grown up in a white, foreign country"—a background that allegedly enabled Larsen to elevate herself above the African American masses.[8]

Almost simultaneously with these critiques of Larsen's relationship to and representation of both the U.S. South *and* Denmark, Paul Gilroy published his groundbreaking book *The Black Atlantic* (1993). In the introduction, Gilroy wondered out loud: "What of Nella Larsen's relationship to Denmark?"[9] An answer was forthcoming four years later, when George B. Hutchinson proved that Larsen visited Denmark at least twice in her youth and remarked: "The effect of discounting Larsen's Danish experience and Danish background and her connection to her mother is to subordinate her mature story of her life to a story that cannot accommodate the possibility of someone being both African American and Danish American."[10] In the wake of Hutchinson's essay and mammoth 2006 biography, not only southern folk aesthetics seemed inadequate as an approach to Larsen's life and work. Hazel Carby's final chapter in *Reconstructing Womanhood* (1987) drove home her argument that Hurston "avoided the class confrontation of the Northern cities" through a "reconstruction of 'the folk'" by lauding Larsen for writing "more directly out of this urban confrontation" between northern metropolises and the migrating black southern masses. However, Carby's view that Helga's movement "from South to North" and back again "reproduces the tensions of migration into a structure of oppositions between country and city" elided black life in southern cities such as Nashville (where Helga once studied at "Devon," an allusion to Larsen's teenage years at Fisk Normal School) and Atlanta (the hometown of bourgeois black southern teachers featured in the first section of *Quicksand*). This rural-urban, south–north framework also sidelined Helga's transnational travels and familial connections to Denmark: briefly considering "[t]he section of the novel set in Copenhagen," Carby claimed that "Larsen displaced to Europe an issue of central concern to the intellectuals of the Harlem renaissance: white fascination with the 'exotic' and the 'primitive.'" But rather than refracting the Copenhagen chapters through the lens of 1920s Harlem, we might consider on their own terms the historical-geographical contours of Larsen's links to and depiction of Denmark's capital city in the early twentieth century.[11]

In this chapter, then, I read *Quicksand* as a Danish-African-American author's remapping of the U.S. South at national and transnational scales experienced through migration: Helga Crane's multiple movements back and forth across both the Mason-Dixon Line and the (black) Atlantic. Helga's frequent relocations during her early twenties between various urban sites—Chicago, New York, and Copenhagen—are bookended by two periods living in the U.S. South: as a teacher at the black school Naxos, and as the wife of a black minister in rural Alabama. Tracing Helga's individual travels across regional and national borders, I draw out the novel's representations of various "folk" cultures: the rooted black folk culture of the rural South, the rerouted folk culture of black southern migrants in the urban North, and residues of rural Danish folk culture in modern Copenhagen. Against the critical view that Helga Crane despises "the folk," I argue that Helga (a notoriously contradictory character) at times tends to *romanticize* the folk—not least rural southern black folk. However, *Quicksand* also flirts with a romance of the rural *Danish* folk, even as the narrative of Helga's life in Copenhagen vividly reveals the realities of racism and rural-urban migration in early twentieth-century Denmark. I conclude with a brief discussion of Larsen's final publication, the short story "Sanctuary" (1930), which extended *Quicksand*'s cross-racial, transatlantic exploration of folk identities via a controversial recasting of Sheila Kaye-Smith's "Mrs. Adis" (1922), a story about rural class conflict in southeast England, as a folklike tale of racial strife in the U.S. South. All told, this chapter seeks to show how, much as Hurston's overt focus on black southern folk culture should not obscure her more materialist attention to the "subterranean force" of migrant workers moving within and beyond the region, the view that both the author and protagonist of *Quicksand* are detached from or disdainful of the black South can be productively complicated by considering Larsen's rendition of folk identities across borders and between texts.

Containing the Rural Southern Black Folk: Naxos

Quicksand opens with an often scathingly critical rendition of a southern black school that draws on Larsen's own negative experiences both as a student at Fisk Normal School in Nashville (1907–8) and as a nurse at Tuskegee Institute in Alabama (1915–16). In 1926 Larsen recalled that "her dislike of conditions there [Tuskegee] and the school authorities [sic] dislike of her appearance and manner were both so intense that after a year they parted with mutual disgust and relief."[12] Davis astutely observes that in making Helga "emblematic of her own youthful self escaping this particular southern and racial prison," Larsen was also "[a]nticipating and prefiguring Ralph Ellison and other midcentury respondents to the Tuskegee machine."[13] Intriguingly, *Quicksand*'s indictment of Tuskegee—"This great community, [Helga] thought, was no longer a school. It had grown into a machine"—anticipates another critic of Booker T. Washington and Tuskegee writing almost fifty years after Ellison's *Invisible Man* (1952).[14] Ten years after assessing Larsen negatively in *Workings of the Spirit* and nearly two decades after portraying Washington sympathetically in *Modernism and the Harlem Renaissance* (1983), Baker offered a stinging analysis of Tuskegee in *Turning South Again: Re-thinking Modernism / Re-reading Booker T* (2001) that strikingly dovetails with Helga's criticisms of Naxos in *Quicksand*. *Turning South Again* develops the tour de force argument that Washington's lifelong "black male public performance" was compromised by his profound shame regarding (his own origins in) "the 'country districts' of the South." Baker tracks Washington's career from his initial turn "away from the laboring classes, from restrictions of common black-South experience" to Tuskegee, the "announced project" of which was "to overcome the stigma of the black-South's mass body ... in order to create bountiful black craft workers."[15] The first four chapters of *Quicksand* similarly suggest that Tuskegee, fictionalized as Naxos, represses rather than uplifts the desires—political, economic, and sexual—of the rural black southern "country districts." *Quicksand* also anticipates *Turning South Again* by suggesting that the Tuskegee model of racial uplift was inextricable from white southern efforts to keep black folk in their place as skilled but cheap agricultural labor.

In *Quicksand*'s opening scene, the reader is privy to Helga's thoughts about the school and its modus operandi; within six paragraphs, an agitated Helga is considering her hatred of "'The South. Naxos. Negro education" (7). Griffin takes this quote as an epigram to her argument that Helga exhibits an "unflinching disdain for poor, illiterate, dark-skinned Southern blacks [that] leads her to conclude the black race is doomed to the role of history's despised burden."[16] Yet even in the novel's opening scene, a closer reading clarifies that Helga's "disdain" is directed not at her black southern students but rather Naxos's institutional complicity with the views expressed by a visiting white southern preacher "to the black folk sitting so respectfully before him" (6) earlier that day:

> This was, he had told them with obvious sectional pride, the finest school for Negroes anywhere in the country, north or south.... And he had dared any Northerner to come south and after looking upon this great institution to say that the Southerner mistreated the Negro. And he had said that if all Negroes would only take a leaf out of the book of Naxos and conduct themselves in the manner of the Naxos products, there would be no race problem, because Naxos Negroes knew what was expected of them.... They knew enough to stay in their places ... satisfied in the estate to which they had been called, hewers of wood and drawers of water. (6–7)

The white preacher's rhetorical reaffirmation of black southerners' social and spatial "place" foreshadows Baker's key point that the "containment" of black students at Tuskegee was bound up with broader southern labor relations. What Washington identified as "the black body's uninstructed appetites" can be interpreted instead as rural southern blacks' "urge to abandon manual labor" and "to desert agriculture"—a yearning to throw off the yoke of white southern authority over their laboring bodies. As Baker observes: "If instinctual, or even bestial, desires to escape manual labor and the soil were 'native' to the black masses of the 'country districts,' then Washington felt qualified to institutionalize at Tuskegee the sanitizing of such desires. He would purify black desires allied to the black libidinous body—a body screened, and held in mythic suspension, by the white mind of the South."[17] In *Quicksand*, this white southern mind-set is articulated by the preacher but interpolated by Helga's "hot anger and seething resentment" in her room that evening. The preacher's speech and its reception amid "considerable applause" has proven to Helga that Naxos's vision—a vision that once "she had ardently desired to share in" (7)—is subservient to southern racial and labor hierarchies.

However, Helga exempts the mostly poor rural southern blacks who constitute the student body from her assessment of Naxos: "No, it wasn't the fault of those minds back of the diverse colored faces. It was, rather, the fault of the method, the general idea behind the system" (8). Contemplating her two years as a teacher in this "system," Helga distinguishes the decline of her "zest" for "the Naxos policy of uplift" from her continued personal engagement with the students: "Yet she had continued to try not only to teach, but to befriend those happy singing children, whose charm and distinctiveness the school was so surely ready to destroy" (9). Helga hones her critique of the school's discipline and punishment of "the black-South's mass body" the next morning. Refusing to attend the ritual breakfast, Helga witnesses from her window a variation on what Baker terms Tuskegee's "marshaling of the black body to attention, discipline, regimentation": "the multitude of students . . . assembling into neat phalanxes preparatory to marching in military order to the sorry breakfast. . . . Here and there a male member of the faculty, important and resplendent in the regalia of an army officer, would pause in his prancing and strutting, to jerk a negligent or offending student into the proper attitude or place" (16).[18] Helga also witnesses the dormitory matron Miss MacGooden imploring the female students to "*please* at least try to act like ladies and not like savages from the backwoods"—even though most of the students "had actually come from the backwoods. Quite recently too" (15).

Much as Miss MacGooden "prided herself on being a 'lady' from one of the best families" (16), Helga's fiancé, James Vayle, has the appropriate black southern bourgeois heritage. By contrast, Helga is a "solitary girl with no family connections" (9)—that is, no connections acceptable to Vayle's family in "near-by Atlanta": "They had never liked the engagement, had never liked Helga Crane. Her own lack of family disconcerted them. No family. That was the crux of the whole matter. For Helga, it accounted for everything, her failure here in Naxos, her former loneliness in Nashville. . . . If you couldn't prove your ancestry and connections, you were tolerated, but you didn't 'belong'" (12). This focus at Naxos (and at Devon in Nashville) on racial and ancestral credentials is recapitulated by the principal, Robert Anderson. Attempting to head off Helga's threat to resign, the suave Anderson almost succeeds until he utters "that trite phrase, 'You're a lady.' You have dignity and breeding." This goads Helga to state explicitly her biracial, northern, urban, lower-class background: "If you're speaking of family, Dr. Anderson, why, I haven't any. I was born in a Chicago slum. . . . My father was a gambler who deserted my mother, a white immigrant. It is even uncertain that they were married. As I said at first, I don't belong here. I shall be leaving at once." This sequence drives home not only that Helga herself has no black southern roots but also her recognition that the black bourgeoisie's relentless emphasis on ancestry and "good stock" (24) perpetuates its superiority over the very "folk" it claims to be uplifting. In *Turning*

South Again, Baker remarks that the concept of a Talented Tenth formulated by Washington's great rival W. E. B. Du Bois "entails, without seeming equivocation, an 'untalented,' infertile, bereft nine-tenths—that is to say, the black majority."[19] In *Quicksand*, the black southern bourgeoisie's fetishization of "family" and "ancestry" entails a black folk majority that is *too* fertile and inferior to the point of being barely human at all: in MacGooden's term, they are "savages." When Helga reencounters Vayle at a Harlem party, he posits a frankly eugenicist view that the black elite must procreate because "if we—I mean people like us—don't have children, the others will still have.... The race is sterile at the top. Few, very few Negroes of the better class have children.... We're the ones who must have the children if the race is to get anywhere" (104). Despite her lower-class, mixed-race origins in a northern urban slum, Helga demonstrates notably more sympathy and solidarity with the black southern folk than does Vayle, MacGooden, or Anderson.

I have been arguing that Helga does not look down on the "black folk" who make up her students; she does, however, romanticize them. One of Helga's ostensibly more trivial gripes about the Naxos "system" is its insistence that, as the dean of women puts it, "Black, gray, brown, and navy blue are the most becoming colors for colored people." By contrast, Helga's "intuitive, unanalyzed driving spirit of loyalty to the inherent racial need for gorgeousness told her that bright colors *were* fitting and that dark-complexioned people *should* wear yellow, green, and red"; she recalls "[o]ne of the loveliest sights [she] had ever seen... a sooty black girl decked out in a flaming orange dress, which a horrified matron had next day consigned to the dyer." Helga's half-baked belief that rural black southern folk culture exemplifies an "inherent racial" aesthetic devolves into essentialism as she extols a "love of color, joy of rhythmic motion, naïve, spontaneous laughter" as the "essentials of spiritual beauty in the race" (20–21). This "unanalyzed" romance of the black southern folk is inseparable from Helga's related sense that the school subjugates the "natural" South. In the opening few pages, the adjective "southern" is repeatedly associated with nature: Helga's room is "flooded with Southern sun" (5); she is tired by the "sultry hot Southern spring" (6); and she is absorbed by the "sweet smell of early Southern flowers" (7). Helga sees Naxos as a kind of machine in the southern garden, each morning cranking into operation "[a]lmost naturally" as the militaristic marching of the student "automatons" "blot[s] out" the "bare earth, and grass" (16). Helga and James joke about his being "completely 'naturalized'" to "the unmistakable Naxos mold" (11), but she is attracted less to her fiancé than to the landscape of the school grounds: "Seductive, charming, and beckoning as cities were, they had not this easy unhuman loveliness. The trees, she thought, on city avenues and boulevards, in city parks and gardens, were tamed, held prisoners in a surrounding maze of human beings. Here they were free." This rhapsodic vision of a liberated *natural* landscape is useful to

Helga because it sharpens her awareness that the *social* landscape of Naxos is (as Davis puts it) a "southern and racial prison": the apparent freedom of the trees on campus contrasts with the stark social reality that here "[i]t was human beings who were prisoners." Hence Helga realizes that while "the scene spread out before her" is "incredibly lovely," it is also "facile" in the larger socioeconomic context of Naxos and the South more generally (19); she is alert to how, as Baker observes in *I Don't Hate the South* (2007), "Awe-inspiring natural beauty is but a metonym for the regional trap and southern incarceration of the abjected black body."[20] Later in the novel, however, Helga has recourse to a romance of the rural South and its black folk: viewing the region as a repository of authentic racial identity and as a sanctuary from the irresolvable complexities of her biracial, transnational life, Helga will turn south again—with fateful consequences.

Passing among the Northern Urban Black Folk: Chicago and New York

Arriving in Chicago following her abrupt departure from Naxos, Helga embraces the Windy City's foreboding climate as the antithesis of the school's dangerously "seductive" southernness: "She had forgotten how cold March could be under the pale skies of the North. But she liked it, this blustering wind. She would even have welcomed snow, for it would more clearly have marked the contrast between this freedom and the cage which Naxos had been to her" (30). If for Helga the journey from Naxos to Chicago represents a return to her birthplace, this striking image of contrast between northern freedom and southern imprisonment intones the promise of the Great Migration for rural southern blacks more generally. Baker argues that the reinforcement of "*domesticated immobility*" at Tuskegee denied rural black southerners the liberating possibilities of northern, urban modernity: glossing Baudelaire, Baker charts "the emergence of the 'big city' as a space of convergence for class and race" negotiated by the "*mobility of the black flâneur* . . . suited to opportunities of 'Progress' . . . in the northern sense of that term."[21] Yet for all Helga's anticipation of relative freedom "under the pale skies of the North," her own *flânerie* in Chicago reveals the racial and spatial realities of her status as an (over)educated yet impoverished "Negro" woman.

Helga calls upon her Danish immigrant uncle, Peter Nilssen, in search of financial support. Her mother's brother, Peter also funded Helga's six years of education at Devon in Nashville, thereby cementing her identity as "Negro" and establishing her educational (if not ancestral) connection to the U.S. South. Now, however, Peter's new wife denies Helga's claim upon her Danish family through some decidedly spurious logic: "'*Well*, he isn't exactly your uncle, is he? Your mother wasn't married, was she? I mean, to your father? . . . please remember that my husband is not your uncle. No indeed! Why, that, that would make me your aunt! He's not—'" (31). Refused access to her only surviving relative in the United States, Helga has further cause to worry about her economic insecurity given that, as Carby observes, in Chicago "[m]oney replaces kinship as the prime mediator of [Helga's] social relations."[22] Yet "while admitting [money's] necessity, and even its undeniable desirability, she dismissed its importance" (32); rather than finding a job, Helga spends "hours in aimless strolling about the hustling streets of the Loop district" (35). Initially Helga is "drawn by an uncontrollable desire" to both observe and "mingle with the crowd" on the "glimmering street"; the "myriad" and "moving multi-colored crowd" (32–33) seems to offer the modernist "convergence [of] class and race" that Baker describes. But when Helga secures an appointment at the employment office, her relatively privileged status as a "graduate of Devon" (36) and a former teacher at Naxos precludes her from the domestic work usually doled out to "Negro" women. When we next witness Helga "travers[ing] acres of streets," she is doing so with a growing sense of desperation that "in that whole energetic place [Chicago] nobody wanted her services" (37). Larsen's race-, class-, and gender-based critique of the (white, male, bourgeois) *flâneur*'s leisurely perambulations culminates when "the smallness of her commercial value" is calculated in the crudest sense by a "few men, both white and black, [who] offered her money" for sexual favors (37–38).

Helga is rescued by Jeanette Hayes-Rore, a prominent member of Chicago's black bourgeoisie who takes Helga to New York as a private secretary. Yet already on the train east, Hayes-Rore raises the same issue of "your people" (41) that plagued Helga among the black southern middle class at Naxos. Base economic need ("She couldn't afford anger" [38]) compels Helga to explain her origins again, but Hayes-Rore's muted response reveals the extent to which Helga's biracial background is regarded as beyond the pale in both the North *and* the South, among blacks *and* whites: "The woman felt that the story, dealing as it did with race intermingling and possibly adultery, was beyond definite discussion. For among black people, as among white people, it is tacitly understood that these things are not mentioned—and therefore they do not exist" (42). As sociologist F. James Davis remarks in *Who Is Black?* (1991), the "'one-drop rule,' meaning that a single drop of 'black blood' makes a person black," had "emerged from the American South" during slavery "to become the nation's definition, generally accepted by whites and blacks alike." By 1925 not only white southerners but also "mulattoes and blacks in general were convinced that no alternative definition was possible."[23] Hence Hayes-Rore's recommendation that upon arriving in Harlem, Helga repudiate her Danish family: "I wouldn't mention that my people are white, if I were you. Colored people won't understand it. . . . I'll just tell Anne [Grey, Helga's future landlady] that you're a friend of mine whose mother's dead. That'll place you well enough and it's all true" (44). This rhetorical displacement of Helga's matrilineal heritage demonstrates how, as Jessica Wegmann-Sánchez puts it, "Helga may not be African-American *and* Danish; she must be Black *or* White," with the result that "Helga is passing in Harlem, except that she passes as Black, not White."[24]

Initially, passing as black serves Helga well by facilitating "that magic sense of having come home" (46), even though she has no more personal or familial connection to Harlem than she does to the U.S. South. Identifying with Harlem's "black folk," she dismisses white New Yorkers as among those "[s]inister folk ... who had stolen her birthright" (48). However, Helga also exhibits a creeping inclination to idealize her relationship to Harlem's black masses by convincing herself that "[m]oney isn't everything. It isn't even the half of everything. And here we have so much else—and by ourselves. It's only outside of Harlem among those others that money really counts for everything" (49). Here Helga's willingness to situate herself as a member of the newly urbanized, northernized black masses involves glossing over the economic gap between Harlem's poor "black folk" and her own relatively privileged status among Harlem's bourgeoisie. Though Helga perceptively skewers the glaring class prejudice beneath Anne's "proclaiming loudly the undiluted good of all things Negro" (51), her own complacent claim to racial unity over and above clear class divisions enables her to believe that, by "com[ing] home" to Harlem, "she had, as she put it, 'found herself'" (46). By homogenizing Harlem's "black folk," Helga convinces herself that she has also "found" an essential blackness within her.

However, "it didn't last, this happiness of Helga Crane's": "Somewhere, within her, in a deep recess, crouched discontent." To the degree that this dissatisfaction represents a return of the biracial repressed—a recrudescent longing for the Danish family she has been required to disown—it is disturbingly expressed through Helga's emerging distaste for the urbanized "folk" she has previously embraced: "As the days became hotter and the streets more swarming, a kind of repulsion came upon her. She recoiled in aversion from the sight of the grinning faces and from the sound of the easy laughter of all these people who strolled, aimlessly now, it seemed, up and down the avenues" (50). According to Thadious Davis, Helga's aversion to the strolling street-level presence of the black masses resembles Larsen's own resentment while writing *Quicksand* "that she was trapped in an external environment populated by lower-class blacks and southern émigrés." In a 1927 letter to Dorothy Peterson, Larsen wrote: "Right now when I look out into the Harlem Streets I feel just like Helga Crane in my novel. Furious at being connected with all these niggers."[25] Given the massive influx of black southerners to Harlem during the Great Migration, this does seem suspiciously akin to what Griffin deems Helga's "unflinching disdain for poor, illiterate, dark-skinned Southern blacks." But it is important to recognize that Helga's disillusionment with life in Harlem derives primarily from her growing anger at being required to deny the full scope of her biracial, transnational, Afro-Danish identity. Indeed, while Helga is "annoy[ed]" by "the crowds of nameless folk on the street," she begins "actually to dislike her friends" among Harlem's black middle class (50): by requiring Helga to renounce her maternal heritage and by furiously denouncing any form of social or sexual interaction across the color line as "positively obscene" (63), the likes of Hayes-Rore and Grey have denied her "birthright."

After receiving a letter from Uncle Peter suggesting she visit her aunt in Denmark, along with a check for five thousand dollars, Helga decides to recover that maternal "birthright." Offered this opportunity to escape the United States' one-drop rule, Helga wonders, "Why... should she be yoked to these despised black folk?" Yet as she begins withdrawing from Harlem society, Helga does not lapse into mere disdain for the urban northern (or migrant southern) masses. Even when Helga makes a clumsy attempt to affirm her maternal heritage by claiming to sense "something in the racial character" of the "black folk" that is "alien" to her, she still identifies with Harlemites as "my own people, my own people" (57). Still, Helga prepares to remove herself from a nation that has imposed on her a (mono)racial identity at the expense of her own more complex family history: "She didn't, in spite of her racial markings, belong to these dark segregated people. She was different. She felt it. It wasn't merely a matter of color. It was something broader, deeper, that made folk kin" (58). Disconnected from not only "black folk" but also a nation where (in the urban North as well as rural South) racial segregation reigns supreme, Helga wants to reclaim her kinfolk: the catalyst for Helga's transnational turn to Copenhagen.

Connecting with the Danish Kinfolk: Copenhagen

Paul Gilroy defined the black Atlantic as a chronotope "crisscrossed by the movements of black people," especially black sailors, "engaged in various struggles toward emancipation, autonomy, and citizenship." In *Quicksand*, Helga envisions crossing the Atlantic in terms of her own "struggle toward emancipation, autonomy" and the achievement of a selfhood beyond the strictures of U.S. racial ideology: "Helga was a good sailor... even the two rough days found her on deck, reveling like a released bird in her returned feeling of happiness and freedom, that blessed sense of belonging to herself alone and not to a race" (66). However, Helga's vision of an autonomous subjectivity denuded of racial and national markers proves to be decidedly naïve. Gilroy observes that black Atlantic ships "were mobile elements that stood for the shifting spaces in between the fixed places that they connected."[26] While being a "good sailor" in the fluid space between New York and Copenhagen allows Helga to briefly entertain the conceit that she can escape racial and national categories and achieve a monadic sense of self, her identity remains contingent on "the fixed places" between which she oscillates: the United States and Denmark. That Helga achieves a degree of "freedom" during her transatlantic passage derives partly from the fact that social relations aboard the Scandinavian-American liner are more Scandinavian than American. On her first evening aboard, Helga is invited to dine with the ship's "purser, a man grown old in the service of the Scandinavian-American Line [who] remembered her as the little dark girl who had crossed with her mother years ago." The purser's insistence that Helga "must sit at his table" (65) contrasts starkly with the ways in which Helga's designated status as "Negro" often precludes such social mixing in the United States (for example, during her Jim Crow train journey from Naxos to Chicago).[27]

The purser's association of Helga with her Danish mother, the parent who at Naxos and in Harlem she was required to pretend "did not exist," seems to augur well for the reclamation of her matrilineal "birthright" on Danish soil. But while relocating to Denmark enables Helga to escape the U.S. color line, she experiences other forms of racism in Copenhagen. Helga's aunt and uncle, Katrina and Poul Dahl, dress her up in outlandish costumes and colors—a performance of exotic otherness with which Helga complies because the Dahls' bourgeois lifestyle provides "the things which money could give, leisure, attention, beautiful surroundings. Things. Things. Things" (69). Hence, for all that Helga finds a form of "kinship" in Copenhagen, money remains just as significant a "mediator in her social relations" as it was in Chicago and New York. Helga is aware that she too is being made into a thing: "her body is objectified, commodified, and placed on the marriage market," as Thadious Davis puts it.[28] However, she never confronts the full implications of her complicity in "the fascinating business of being seen, gaped at, desired"; by deliberately maintaining "the slow, faltering Danish" (76) and other devices designed to dramatize her difference, Helga compromises her claim to a "birthright" in Denmark.

The differences between U.S. and Danish racial ideologies—differences that Helga frequently encounters but never fully comprehends—can be related to the contrasting histories of slavery and colonialism in the United States and Denmark. In the list of countries with the dubious distinction of being the world's leading slave-trading nations, Denmark lies seventh, one place behind the United States.[29] But whereas the U.S. South introduced thousands of Africans to its own soil and developed slave plantations within its own borders, Denmark confined its own form of racial slavery to three small Caribbean islands collectively known as the Danish West Indies. Even after the emancipation of slaves in the Danish West Indies in 1846 and the abolition of slavery in 1848, few "black Danes" traveled to Denmark itself; when they did, such journeys were usually bound up with Copenhagen's continuing colonial power over the Caribbean islands. Arne Lunde and Anna Stenport have argued that this history of Danish slavery and colonialism constitutes "a structuring absence" in *Quicksand* that "haunt[s] the text in ways that have not been sufficiently interrogated."[30] How can Danish slavery and colonialism structure a novel that never directly mentions them? Here we might ponder Hutchinson's persuasive argument that "although the novel seems to be set in the 1920s, Larsen's physical descriptions of the city [Copenhagen] pertain to an earlier decade" when Larsen herself was in the city.[31] If *Quicksand*'s Copenhagen is temporally displaced back to the period between 1908 and 1912, Helga experiences the city before Denmark sold the Danish West Indies to the United States in 1917. Yet for all that Helga rails against the legacy of slavery in the United States, from the moment that she decides to return to Copenhagen on the premise that "there were no Negroes" and thus "no problems, no prejudice" there (58), Helga remains notably silent about Denmark's status as a former slave-trading nation and present-day colonial power. It is here that, in Pierre Macherey's terms, "we must investigate the silence, for it is the silence that is doing the speaking." For if "knowledge of the book must include a consideration of this absence," it is precisely the absence of and silence about other black Danes that accentuates Helga's own status as Copenhagen's supposedly singular black person: "*Den Sorte*" (the black), as she is "freely, audibly" designated when she appears on the streets of the city (75).[32] On one hand, Helga's racial exceptionalism as *the* black facilitates her acceptance into bourgeois society as an exotic curio. On the other hand, Helga's supposed uniqueness ensures that she will always remain *the* Other, allowing Copenhagen's society women to conclude that "she was attractive, unusual, in an exotic, almost savage way, but she wasn't one of them. She didn't at all count" (72).[33]

Besides race and nationality, class too mediates Helga's relationships with native Danes. It would be fallacious to claim that Helga demonstrates solidarity with the working class: she is too enamored of "things" and the Dahls' aspirational lifestyle for that; moreover, her privileged status in the Dahls' household at Marie Kirkeplads means that she is never associated with the "small, but nevertheless present, group of servant blacks of African or Afro-Caribbean descent" in early twentieth-century Copenhagen.[34] Having said that, Helga does demonstrate a willingness to confer with and defer to lower-class white Danes.[35] The most significant of Helga's encounters with a working-class Dane occurs during one of her walks through the center of the city:

> There was also the Gammelstrand, the congregating-place of the vendors of fish... where Helga's appearance always roused lively and audible, but friendly, interest.... Here it was that one day an old countrywoman asked her to what manner of mankind she belonged and at Helga's replying: "I'm a Negro," had become indignant, retorting angrily that, just because she was old and a country-

woman she could not be so easily fooled, for she knew as well as everyone else that Negroes were black and had woolly hair. (78)

It would be easy enough to read this encounter as merely a comic play on the fishwife's unworldly ignorance about the possibility that a "Negro" can be light skinned. Yet like the scene with the purser, this is "one of the many instances in which Larsen dramatizes the differences between Danish and American perceptions of racial identity.[36] The "old countrywoman" does not define Helga's physical characteristics in the pejorative sense with which Helga is familiar from U.S. racial discourse. The fishwife's rudimentary grasp of "race" also lays bare the crudity and absurdity that lurks beneath the supposedly more sophisticated attempts of the Copenhagen bourgeoisie to define Helga. Whereas Katrina figures Helga as a "foreigner, and different" rather than as a family member and fellow Dane (70), the fishwife folds Helga's unusual "appearance" into a more inclusive vision, beyond black and white, of "mankind." Even when the fishwife's mood shifts from friendliness to "indignant" fury, it says as much about the limits of Helga's racial thinking as the old woman's: by telling the fishwife "I'm a Negro," Helga again reveals her own inability to think beyond U.S. racial categories, claim her Danish maternal "birthright," and affirm her biracial, transnational subjectivity.

But why does *Quicksand* put this subtle critique of U.S. racial classifications in the mouth of an "old countrywoman" when the Danish section of the novel takes place exclusively in modern, urban Copenhagen? By relying on the figure of the fishwife to articulate a vision of "mankind" that appears to transcend both racial "folk" and "kinfolk," *Quicksand* flirts with an individualized romance of folklife and lore that, for a symbolically loaded moment, displaces the changing social reality of early twentieth-century Copenhagen. Industrialization, urbanization, and technological modernization were transforming the lives of Danes in and around the capital city at the turn of the century in ways that parallel the radical remaking of African American life via the Great Migration. As historian W. Glyn Jones observes, in the period between 1864 and 1901 "[t]he transition from old-fashioned industry to the beginnings of modern capitalism ... brought a change not only in the pattern of trade and industry, but also in the pattern of society." This social transformation was particularly apparent in the demographic shift "from the villages and the countryside" as rural Danes were pushed toward Copenhagen by the advent of mechanized farming and pulled by an expanding industrial labor market.[37] In her study of the fishwives' trade at Gammel Strand, ethnologist Birgit Vorre demonstrates that such social and demographic processes had a profound impact on fishing villages such as Skovshoved, the home of Gammel Strand's most famous fishwives, the *Skovserkoner*. Young people from Skovshoved and other fishing villages north of Copenhagen started taking factory work in the city rather than

FIGURE 3. A postcard portrait of Gammel Strand published in 1912—the year that Larsen likely returned to the United States after spending at least some of the preceding four years living in Copenhagen. The *fiskerkoner* (fishwives) can be seen selling their wares while wearing their distinctive white headscarves. Photograph courtesy of T. M. Sandau, www.indenforvoldene.dk.

FIGURE 4. In this portrait of Gammel Strand, issued as a postcard in 1910 by the Copenhagen photographer and publisher Fritz Benzen, the "folk" dress of a fishwife appears in striking contrast to the fashionable clothing of a Copenhagen customer. That such postcards were available for sale suggests that the fishwives themselves were not the only Danes aware that their "folk" image could be commodified. Photograph courtesy of T. M. Sandau, www.indenforvoldene.dk.

following their elders into the family trade. At Gammel Strand itself, the shift to modern capitalism took place between the 1870s and 1890s: during these decades, middlemen muscled in on the fish trade. But between 1880 and 1920, the fishwives managed to hold their own, partly because they made capital out of their image as representatives of a traditional "folk" way of life. As Vorre notes, the *Skovserkoner* continued to wear "old folk dress" even though they "had continual contact with the urban environment" and "[i]n most places [in Denmark] regional dress had already been replaced by more fashionable town dress." Though this choice of folk dress can be partly attributed to the fishwives' desire to demonstrate their solidarity during a time of economic and demographic upheaval, it was also a canny piece of branding: the *Skovserkoner* gained "commercial advantages" by promoting themselves as exponents of a traditional, rural way of life.[38]

Given that the fishwives' performance of a folk identity was informed by commercial nous, we might question *Quicksand*'s freighting of the fishwife with a form of folk wisdom explicitly dissociated from financial exchange: the "old countrywoman" passes up the opportunity to sell her piscine wares in order to express her "indignant" skepticism about Helga's self-declared "Negro" status. There is here a hint of the individualized experience of folk culture that (as we saw in chapter 1) Leigh Anne Duck perceives in Hurston's depiction of Janie as part of *Their Eyes Were Watching God*'s attempt to reconcile "folkloric practice" with a modern "bourgeois ideology" that privileges individual subjectivity: the fishwife represents what Duck calls a "folkloric selfhood."[39] Much as Helga's isolated status as *"Den Sorte"* obscures the structuring absence of other black Danes, so this single fishwife's symbolic significance as an individualized expression of the rural Danish folk threatens to overshadow the representation of the urbanizing working class. The rapid growth via rural-urban migration of this working-class population dramatically altered Copenhagen's built space between the 1880s and the early 1900s: "The move from the countryside to the towns, occasioned by industrialization, led to the building of potential slum areas."[40] These slum areas were concentrated in the new neighborhoods of Vesterbro and Nørrebro, and were largely comprised of buildings divided into cramped one- and two-room apartments. As Rich Willerslev notes in his study of workers' housing conditions in late nineteenth-century Copenhagen, already by 1885 there was "extreme overpopulation... without parallel in Vesterbro."[41] Yet despite the fairly detailed narrative cartography of Helga's *flânerie* between city landmarks like the department store Magasin du Nord and the high-cultural institutions at Kongens Nytorv, there is only one brief description of a working-class neighborhood. Strikingly, this description is incorporated into Helga's "impressed" sense of "the general air of well-being" throughout Copenhagen, in contrast to the urban United States—both North *and* South:

Even in the so-called poor sections there was none of that untidiness and squalor which she remembered as the accompaniment of poverty in Chicago, New York, and the Southern cities of America. Here the door-steps were always white from constant scrubbings, the women neat, and the children washed and provided with whole clothing. Here were no tatters and rags, no beggars. But, then, begging, she learned, was an offense punishable by law.... if misfortune and illness came upon one, everyone else, including the State, felt bound to give assistance, a lift on the road to the regaining of independence. (77)

There is some merit to Helga's transnational comparison of Copenhagen's "poor sections" with the equivalent areas of American cities. Since her birth in a Chicago slum, Helga has had considerable experience with racialized urban inequality throughout the nation (the "Southern cities" are presumably Nashville, where Helga studied, and Atlanta, where Vayle's relatives lived). From this perspective, the protection of working-class Danes by the welfare state, following reform and extension of earlier Poor Laws—a June 1890 piece of constitutional legislation reiterated that "Anyone who cannot support himself or his dependents, and is not himself the dependent of someone else, has a right to help from the public"—contrasts with the state's segregation and neglect of poor blacks in U.S. cities.[42] Hence Helga's perception of Copenhagen's less wealthy neighborhoods as a site of well-scrubbed whiteness might be understood as a sublimated expression of her anger at the racialization or "blackening" of urban poverty in the United States. However, Helga's idealized take on "the so-called poor sections" more immediately recalls her attempt to gloss over Harlem's *class* distinctions by incorporating herself into a generalized (northernized and urbanized) "black folk." By homing in on the "white" door-steps and "washed" children, Helga's own gaze whitewashes the poverty and crowdedness that distinguishes the slums from those more salubrious middle- and upper-class areas of Copenhagen in which she usually moves.

During its second year, Helga's life in Copenhagen cracks under the pressure of her status as the singular "*Sorte.*" Helga begins to romanticize Harlem once more: "she found her thoughts straying... to Harlem, its dirty streets, swollen now, in the warmer weather, with dark, gay humanity." This renewed yearning for black folk is fueled by a concert production of the *New World Symphony*. Antonín Dvořák's symphony was a transnational work that combined two folk music cultures. Written while the Czech composer directed the National Conservatory of Music in New York and significantly indebted to his African American student Harry T. Burleigh, the Ninth Symphony in E Minor, *From the New World* (1893), combined Dvořák's immersion in the folk musical traditions of his native Bohemia with his fervent belief that "Negro melodies" were the equivalent folk musical expression of the United States.[43] *Quicksand's* Copenhagen performance of the symphony adds another transnational turn to

Dvořák's production, but Helga focuses on the first movement's take on the spiritual "Swing Low, Sweet Chariot," figuring it as an expression of (her own) essential blackness and feeling "homesick, not for America, but for Negroes." This recourse to a "Negro" identity is such that "Helga Crane felt sympathy rather than contempt and hatred" for her black father, the only occasion in the narrative when Helga prioritizes her *paternal* heritage: Helga "sympathize[s] with his facile surrender to the irresistible ties of race, now that they dragged at her own heart" (94). This focus on—and, ominously, "facile surrender" to—a distinctly romantic idea of "race" as blackness displaces Helga's desire to claim her matrilineal "birthright" in Copenhagen and bolsters her decision to return "home" to Harlem.

Romancing the Black Southern Folk: Turning South Again

Helga's decision two years earlier to dissociate herself from a racial "folk" (black, American) and embrace the "broader, deeper" relationship to her "kin" folk (white, Danish) is now reversed, with "kinship" itself becoming less familial than (mono)racial:

> she had again found herself surrounded by hundreds, thousands, of dark-eyed brown folk.... *These* were her people. Nothing, she had come to understand now, could ever change that. Strange that she had never truly valued this kinship until distance had shown her its worth. How absurd she had been to think that another country, other people, could liberate her from the ties which bound her forever to these mysterious, these terrible, these fascinating, these lovable, dark hordes. Ties that were of the spirit. Ties not only superficially entangled with mere outline of features or color of skin. Deeper. Much deeper than either of these. (97)

Helga's subsequent seduction and shattering rejection by Robert Anderson ruptures these renewed "ties" to Harlem's "brown folk," but she does not abandon her vision of racial "kinship." On the contrary, she embraces it more fervently: when Helga meets Reverend Pleasant Green and his southern migrant congregation immediately after her rejection by Anderson, it provides Helga with the fateful opportunity to relocate her romance of black folk "spirit" back to the rural South. Thadious Davis notes that the Alabamian Reverend Green is "synonymous with ... southernness (as seen in the rural, unglorified black folk)," while Hutchinson identifies a direct link between Helga's "rather condescending as well as romantically idealized" view of the "loveable dark hordes" in both Harlem and "the rural South, the spiritual home of the 'dark hordes.'"[44] That Helga encounters Green and his congregation in a Harlem storefront church is a salutary reminder that the routes of the Great Migration sustained rather than sundered the familial and communal roots connecting black émigrés in the urban North back to the rural South. Green's visit to Harlem can be seen as a variation on John Pearson's dilemma in *Jonah's Gourd Vine*: "we preachers...don't know whether tuh g'wan Nawth wid de biggest part of our churches or stay home wid de rest."[45] The storefront church allows Green to preach to southern émigrés while he retains his religious base in rural Alabama. But Helga's Harlem encounter with the southern preacher and his congregation is also a narrative device through which Larsen emphasizes the dangers of romancing the South and its black folklife as a locus of racial and ancestral authenticity. Helga's "conversion" results in the redirection of her search for identity away from her modern, urban life in Chicago, New York, and Copenhagen into a spiritualized, ahistorical romance of the rural black southern folk. The final section of *Quicksand* plays out in excruciating detail the outcome of Helga's desperate embrace of the rural South as a sanctuary from the trials involved in trying to negotiate her biracial, transnational identity.

As we have seen, already at Naxos Helga held an "unanalyzed" belief that rural black southerners embodied the "essentials of spiritual beauty in the race." During the storefront church scene, Helga's essentialist vision of racial "spirit" and "spiritual beauty" takes on more explicitly religious dimensions; her conversion includes a vision of the South and the southern folk as not only separate from the urban North but outside of time, space, and history. As Duck has argued, much New Negro writing of the 1920s depicted the northward Great Migration in temporal as well as spatial terms "as a movement toward modernity" away from "the space of the South [which] is characterized by both a different developmental era and a different experience of time" that on occasion "exist[s] outside modernity" altogether. In a brief discussion of *Quicksand*, Duck observes that "the modern, cosmopolitan Helga Crane is paralyzed by an encounter with southern migrants' cultural practices" during their "folk religious service": "Observing these folk...she fears she may become entangled in, or infected by, their atavism."[46] Yet Helga overcomes such fears and embraces Green and his congregation because she convinces herself that they offer a conduit away from the transregional and transnational "complexities of the lives she had known" and "back into the mysterious grandeur and holiness of far-off simpler centuries" (115).

Helga turns south again for two reasons. First, having surrendered her matrilineal Danish "birthright" and despite having no black southern ancestry, Helga figures the region's rural folk as a surrogate racial family. Helga is helped in this direction when Green identifies her as "our errin' sistah" and a female member of the congregation comforts her by repeating, "Yes, chile, yes, chile" (113). Second, Helga comes to believe that the apparently atavistic religiosity of "a nameless people, observing rites of a remote obscure origin" (114) will provide an escape from the modern urban capitalist relations that, in both the U.S. North and in Denmark, have so defined her subjectivity. By giving "herself freely" (113) to Reverend Green—without money mediating their relationship—Helga believes she can negate not only her humiliating rejection by Anderson but also her prior commodification on Copenhagen's middle-class marriage market.

The profound flaws in Helga's conception of the rural South as a locus of premodern, precapitalist folklife become glaringly evident once she arrives in rural Alabama. According to Griffin, "During her immersion in black folk life, Helga comes to have an even greater disdain for black people."[47] The real problem is that Helga *romanticizes* rather than disdains the rural southern folk. Much as she ignored the transparent poverty of the black masses in Harlem and whitewashed her image of the working-class districts in Copenhagen, so now she willfully overlooks socioeconomic realities in order to sustain her romantic vision of folklife: "Eagerly she accepted everything, even that bleak air of poverty which, in some curious way, regards itself as virtuous, for no other reason than that it is poor" (119). Helga's vision of the rural southern folk as an essential source of "spiritual beauty" is a form of false consciousness: "And the people ... were to Helga miraculously beautiful. The smallest, dirtiest, brown child, barefooted in the fields or muddy roads, was to her an emblem of the wonder of life, of love, and of God's goodness." That the convert's faith in "this illumination" (122) of the black southern folk is a fallacy becomes apparent when, "the luster of religion [having] vanished" (130), Helga is left railing bitterly at "ten million black folk" worshiping "[t]he white man's God" (131). To be sure, *Quicksand* here exhibits little empathy with the role of black southern Christianity as a source of cultural endurance and resistance to Jim Crow. Thadious Davis notes that "Larsen's in-laws took it as an insult to the Imes family, which for two generations had been prominent in the black church and in the missionary field of Alabama."[48] But it is important to recognize that Helga's initial, highly idealized embrace of Reverend Green and his congregation is inextricable from her desperate need to see black southern folklife as a sanctuary from the capitalist modernity that so thoroughly mediated her experiences in Chicago, New York, and Copenhagen.

In rural Alabama, Helga tries to engage with the "miraculously beautiful" folk directly. However, the local women respond at best ambivalently to Helga's eagerness: they see her as "dat uppity, meddlin' No'the'nah" (120), and as the reverend's wife she remains elevated above them. Helga's social standing in relationship to her husband is fundamental, and fatal, to her life in Alabama. If on one hand the marriage hinders direct contact with local people, on the other Helga's "relative importance" as Green's spouse is "[o]nly relative" (119): Helga remains defined as a possession of her husband—"the preacher's Northern wife" (127)—and like the rest of "the female portion of the flock" she is expected to submit to and display "open adoration" for Green's patriarchal authority. At first, Helga believes that marriage to and sex with Green has enabled her to discover "the intangible thing for which, indefinitely, always she had craved. It had received embodiment" (121). However, this supposed materialization of that essential racial (and sexual) self, which Helga has long believed was "hidden away" inside her, results in repeated pregnancies. Whereas other contemporaneous novels of black southern life are conspicuously silent on the possibility that female sexual agency might lead to pregnancy (Hurston's *Their Eyes Were Watching God*) or fetishize black southern women as corporeal emblems of fertility (Jean Toomer's *Cane* [1923]), Helga's "embodied" sexuality traps her in a folk romance turned nightmare. Helga's pregnancies and related illnesses do elicit sympathy from the local women, and Helga is "humbled" by the "superhuman" mothering of Sary Jones (126). Ultimately, though, motherhood cements Helga's highly gendered "place" in a rural Alabama society rigidly defined by patriarchy as well as racial segregation.[49]

If Helga's inclination to romanticize the rural southern folk returns with a self-destructive vengeance, so too does her tendency to conflate southernness with the natural landscape. At Naxos, Helga resisted the "incredibly lovely" and "appealing" enticement of the landscape because she realized how "facile" it would be to detach nature's "unhuman loveliness" from the social structures of Jim Crow with which the school is complicit. But in rural Alabama, Helga imagines that nature merges with the folk: "Everything contributed to her gladness in living. And so for a time she loved everything and everyone. Or thought she did. Even the weather. And it was truly lovely" (121). The landscape is also equated with her embodied sexuality: "all that was living in her sprang like rank weeds at the tingling thought of night, with a vitality so strong that it devoured all shoots of reason" (123). The identifiably "southern" natural objects of the opening sequence at Naxos—sun, spring, flowers—have been replaced by "rank weeds"; as Helga's creativity is reduced to procreation, such fertile motifs for the physical landscape mutate into the perilous "quagmire" (134), "bog" (135), and "quicksand" of the novel's title. Helga experiences a version of Yaeger's "reverse autochthony," that "peculiar literary pattern" in southern women's writing which involves "a movement from relative freedom to disanimation" as female bodies and identities are depicted via vivid "figures of speech" as being absorbed "into the ground."[50] Helga herself realizes too late that this sinking into a suffocating southern landscape derives in no small measure from her own romance of the regional folk, "the quagmire in which she had engulfed herself" (134).

Helga turned south again despite having no black southern mother or grandmothers; at the end of the novel, she cannot escape because she has sons and daughters. We learn that Helga "meant to leave" Green—quite possibly an intertextual allusion to Nora Helmer's decision to abandon her husband, Torvald, and their children in the hugely controversial climax of Henrik Ibsen's play *A Doll's House*, which premiered in Copenhagen in 1879. However, Helga cannot bear to go because "through all the rest of her lifetime she would be hearing their cry of 'Mummy, Mummy, Mummy,' through sleepless nights. No. She couldn't desert them" (136). Helga's romance of the folk has condemned her own children to the strictest southern strain of U.S. racial ideology. Favor remarks that *Quicksand*'s use of the "birthright" metaphor recalls James Weldon Johnson's 1912 novel *The Autobiography of an Ex-Colored Man* (republished in 1927, the year before *Quicksand* appeared), which ends with Johnson's southern-born, northern-raised, Europe-traveling, biracial narrator bemoaning that, by passing as white in New York, "I have sold my birthright for a mess of pottage." Favor asks: "Is Larsen's ending an ironic rewriting of the African American's 'birthright' as a deserved, desired, and stable life among the folk?"[51] However, Helga's situation at the end of *Quicksand* is more tragic than ironic: she stays in Alabama because, though she is "used . . . up" by motherhood, the children are "still miraculously her own proud and cherished possession" (124). Helga may have renounced money and "things" as the prime mediators of her social relations, but by the end of *Quicksand* Helga has "paid" for her romance of the southern folk: "Enough. More than enough" (134).

The oft-criticized ending of *Quicksand* can thus be read as a deconstruction of the dangers involved in pursuing a southern folk aesthetic. If the ending seems "incredible" or unrealistic, it is because Helga's bad faith in an ahistorical, spiritual vision of the folk was itself neither credible nor realistic but rather a desperate reaction to the unresolved dilemmas of her nonsouthern, transnational, Afro-Danish-American heritage.[52] It does not follow, however, that Larsen (or Helga) disdains black southern life and culture; throughout *Quicksand* the representation of the South and black southern folk is considerably more sophisticated and sympathetic than some critics have allowed. In the first section of the novel, Helga Crane's frustration with the Naxos "system" derives partly from her own empathy and engagement with the black southern children who make up the student body. But the final section plays out the result of *romanticizing* black southern folk life: a tendency that Helga had exhibited fleetingly at Naxos, but in which she invests more fully and ill-fatedly in rural Alabama.

From Rural Sussex Folk to Rural Southern Folk in "Sanctuary"

Having published a second novel, *Passing* (1929), set in Chicago and Harlem, in 1930 Larsen published her first piece of fiction set entirely in the South and among black southerners: a short story entitled "Sanctuary." Almost immediately after "Sanctuary" appeared in *Forum*'s January issue, gossip began circulating that it bore a strong resemblance to a 1922 short story, "Mrs Adis," by the popular English author Sheila Kaye-Smith. Harold Jackman wrote to Countee Cullen: "Boy, that gal has used some of the identical words Miss Smith uses in her *Mrs. Adis*, and as for the dialogue, little Nell, I'll call her this time, has just changed it to make it colored.... All literary Harlem knows about it."[53] Larsen defended herself in *Forum*'s April 1930 issue by locating the genesis of the story in black folk culture. She claimed to have first heard a version of the story from an elderly black woman when she worked at Lincoln Hospital and Home in New York. Having initially "believed the story absolutely," Larsen had come to realize that it was a form of folktale: "lately, in talking it over with Negroes, I find that the tale is so old and so well known that it is almost folklore.... A Negro sociologist tells me that there are literally hundreds of these stories. Anyone could have written it up at any time."[54]

Larsen's defense was cunning but less than convincing. She was surely aware that Hurston was in this period "writing up" folktales from the rural South, and therefore may have hoped that her own use of "folklore" as source material would seem more plausible and acceptable. In *Pocahontas's Daughters* (1979), Mary Dearborn takes Larsen's defense at face value and poses a series of rhetorical questions implying that the use of a folk tradition complicates conventional definitions of plagiarism: "Does the woman who sets down a folk tale then own the tale? Are folk tales fit matter for fiction? ... If Larsen had set it all down as it happened—recounting her meeting with the black patient, then the story—would 'Sanctuary' be fiction?"[55] The problem is that Larsen's account, as Cheryl Wall has observed, "contains a signal flaw. No source for the story in the 'folk' tradition has ever been identified," despite Larsen's claims that the anonymous "Negro sociologist" had verified "hundreds of these stories."[56] "Mrs Adis" and "Sanctuary" contain too many thematic, structural, and linguistic resemblances for it to be coincidental. There is then little to be gained in lingering on Larsen's attempt to situate "Sanctuary" in relation to black folk tradition—a tradition to which she was sympathetic but hardly suffused in. It might be more productive to recognize that while the plagiarism charge is not easily dismissible, "Sanctuary" constitutes a complex case of creative revision: what Joshua L. Miller calls "an act of intertextual adaptation."[57] Indeed, "Sanctuary" extends what Anna Brickhouse has termed the "intertextual geography of *Quicksand*." Brickhouse shows that *Quicksand* enacts "a subtle intertextual conversation among a diverse array of works by both African American and white authors" that, developed via Helga's various migrations, constitutes "a kind of intertextual geography, a series of allusive literary landscapes." Elsewhere I have drawn on Brickhouse's approach to argue that *Quicksand* and William Faulkner's *Light in August* (1932) develop an almost simultaneous exploration of the ways in which U.S. racial classifications are interrogated via Helga and Joe Christmas's respective migrations between the rural South, urban North, and abroad: Denmark for Helga and Mexico for Joe.[58] Here I want to suggest that "Sanctuary" moves beyond *Quicksand*'s mapping of "the perilous territories of American literary history" by crossing the Atlantic and intertextually adapting an English story of class division—itself "almost folklore" in form and theme—to the race *and* class inequities that structured black life in the U.S. South.

Both "Mrs Adis" and "Sanctuary" revolve around a woman who helps protect a fleeing killer whose victim, it transpires, is her own son. In "Mrs Adis," the eponymous heroine is a forty-two-year-old mother "in the agricultural districts of Sussex" whose son Tom works on Ironlatch Farm. Mrs. Adis shelters Tom's childhood friend Peter Crouch at her modest home in "the old hammer-woods of the Sussex iron industry" after Crouch tells her that he shot a gamekeeper who caught him poaching in the woods on the grounds of Scotney Castle.[59] As Kelli A. Larson has demonstrated, these references to the area's now-defunct iron industry serve to suggest how "a once-thriving laboring class has been forced into the caste of the agricultural poor"; in such dire economic circumstances, Crouch's apparently petty poaching is perceived as a threat to "the sanctity of the class system." This class tension structures the plot of "Mrs Adis." Though the protagonist sees her son's friend as a ne'er-do-well, she is acutely aware of the social chasm between Crouch and the Adises, on one side, and the landed gentry and their gamekeepers on the other: indeed, the gamekeepers are "considered class traitors by Crouch and others of their station."[60] Mrs. Adis states her reasons for sheltering Crouch explicitly in terms of class solidarity: "shooting a keeper ain't the same as shooting an ordinary sort of man." Soon a group of men led by the castle gamekeeper Vidler visit Mrs. Adis's house seeking Crouch and bringing with them the body of Tom Adis, the actual—and accidental—victim of Crouch's gun. Despite Mrs. Adis's shock and grief at the death of her son, she does not surrender Crouch to the posse because she knows that he "shall swing" for his crime. The story ends with Mrs. Adis shut in a room with the body of her son while Crouch does "the only thing she wanted him to do, the only thing he could possibly do: he opened the door and silently went out."[61]

Larsen transposes Kaye-Smith's basic plot to "the Southern coast, between Merton and Shawboro," and among black southerners. In "Sanctuary," the fleeing killer is Jim Hammer, a black childhood friend of Annie Poole's son, Obadiah. Annie agrees to shelter Jim after asking him if the victim was "White man o' niggah?" and he replies: "Cain't say, Mis' Poole. White man, Ah reckons." Even though Annie, like Mrs. Adis, views her son's friend negatively ("Ah shuah don' see nuffin' in you but a heap o' dirt"), she knows that as a "po' niggah," Jim will be at the mercy of white southern men without her help.[62] As in Kaye-Smith's story, it turns out that the mother's son is the actual victim of the shooting, though in contrast to Peter Crouch's accidental killing of Tom Adis, it remains unclear whether Jim knew the man he shot was black rather than white. Once again the mother does not give up the murderer to the local authorities, represented by the white sheriff Lowndes and posse who visit the Poole home.[63] But whereas "Mrs Adis" concludes without the mother articulating her reasons for letting Crouch go, "Sanctuary" ends with Annie Poole explicitly stating to Hammer that *racial* solidarity is the reason she did not surrender him to the sheriff: "Git outer mah feather baid, Jim Hammer, an' outen mah house, an' don' nevah stop thankin' yo' Jesus he done gib you dat black face."[64]

If the "problem" of *Quicksand*'s ending in rural Alabama has hampered without ruining its reputation, turning south once again in "Sanctuary"—by way of an intertextual migration across the Atlantic to rural southern England—did irreparable damage to Larsen's public image. After the plagiarism scandal, she never published again. However, "Sanctuary" is more than a mere addendum to Larsen's dismayingly brief literary career. In this final published piece of fiction, Larsen expanded the transnational, comparative analysis of class, racial, and folk identities that permeated her debut novel. "Sanctuary" extends the intertextual geography of *Quicksand* by revising Kaye-Smith's story of rural English class and labor conflict as a folklike fable of racial strife under the U.S. southern sign of Jim Crow. Today the level of interest in Larsen's life and career, ranging across disciplines as disparate as African American studies and Scandinavian studies, is comparable to that of the Hurston revival. Yet years after Larsen's own biographers dismissed her claims upon an Afro-Danish identity, Larsen's transnationalism has remained difficult to square with disciplinary trends: in 2006 Patricia Chu warned that Larsen "is an example of an author whose work will suffer under an impetus toward nationalization of modernist studies." But region too remains a relevant scalar unit for assessing Larsen's fiction: throughout this chapter, I have tried to show that *Quicksand* and "Sanctuary" might benefit from a (new) southern studies approach that takes her representation of the U.S. South more seriously than earlier scholars have done. In Larsen's first novel and final story, the South is not a static, distinct, or separate region; it is fluidly, intertextually, and inextricably connected to various national *and* transnational geographies. Chu notes too that there remains "very little discussion of Nella Larsen in terms of... racialized global modernization."[65] This may be true, but *Quicksand* and "Sanctuary" render "global modernization" in racial *and* class terms: across the Atlantic, black U.S. southern, Danish, and British working classes alike must negotiate the shifting material realities of urbanization, industrialization, and technological modernization, not least through new forms of migration and labor relations. In ways we are only now beginning to fully fathom, Larsen's fiction offers (to paraphrase Yaeger) yet wider reference points for remappings of the South's social, economic, and racial coordinates: points beyond rural Alabama and "the Southern coast"; beyond Nashville and Atlanta; beyond even Chicago and New York, all the way to Copenhagen and rural Sussex.

CHAPTER 3

Downsouth, Upsouth, Global South

Migration and the "New World" in John Oliver Killens's Writing

In a foreword to the 1982 reissue of John Oliver Killens's debut novel, *Youngblood* (1954), Addison Gayle argued that "at a point in time when the Afro-American novelist explored, almost exclusively, the northern urban environment"—Ralph Ellison's *Invisible Man* (1952) and James Baldwin's *Go Tell It on the Mountain* (1953) being the most prominent examples—"*Youngblood* returns to the terrain explored so well by Richard Wright and becomes a novel that serves as a symbol of the civil rights movement, then in its infancy."[1] Gayle's figuration of Killens as a keeper of Wright's flame, focused on black life in the rural and small-town South, contrasts strikingly with Hazel Carby's charge a few years later (see chapter 1) that recent African American literary studies had fetishized black southern folklife and literature, privileging Zora Neale Hurston's writing over and above Wright's realist representations of black experience in northern cities following the Great Migration. Yet *Youngblood*, like so much of Killens's subsequent writing (and, as I have already argued, like the writing of Nella Larsen and Hurston herself), complicates these familiar binaries: rural versus urban, southern versus northern, folk versus modern, folk aesthetics versus social realism. Throughout his career, Killens developed a nuanced array of perspectives on black (southern) spatial experiences and practices at regional, national, and global scales.

By 1957, Killens was beginning to finesse his first novel's insistence on the ways that racism bound (rather than distinguished) region and nation by formulating the terms "down-South" and "up-South." During an address in Montgomery, Alabama, Killens observed that "[t]he Northern Negro seems to consider himself thousands of miles removed from the so-called problem" recently brought into focus by the bus boycott in Montgomery itself: "But some of us more realistically look upon Alabama, Georgia and Mississippi as *down*-South, and Harlem, New York, as *up*-South. They are not very far apart!"[2] Two years later, during a New York conversation with nightclub singer Maya Angelou, Killens repudiated her suggestion that "California blacks were thousands of miles, literally and figuratively, from these Southern plagues" of massive white resistance to the Civil Rights movement. Killens told Angelou: "Girl, don't you believe it. Georgia is Down South. California is Up South. If you're black in this country, you're on a plantation."³ Killens subsequently developed this terminology in an unproduced play, *Lower Than the Angels* (1960), and "Downsouth-Upsouth," included in his essay collection *Black Man's Burden* (1966). The essay opens by declaring: "We are a Southern country, fundamentally. At least for me, Macon, Georgia, where I was born is 'Down South,' and New York City, to which I escaped, is 'Up South,' and the difference is far less than the eight hundred miles that uneasily divide them."⁴ At the peak of the south-centered movement, Killens was warning against what historians Matthew Lassiter and Joseph Crespino have more recently termed the "myth of southern exceptionalism": the persistent figuration of the South as a racist and "intractable region" that in turn maintains the image (itself a myth) of the United States as "an otherwise liberal nation."⁵

Killens passed away in 1987, but fourteen years later his terminology resurfaced in Houston Baker and Dana Nelson's special issue of *American Literature* announcing the "new southern studies." Baker and Nelson cited Killens alongside Malcolm X to stress "the nuanced inseparability of North and South in any fruitful model of American cultural studies" (though as if in unwitting anticipation of the 2008 comedy folk song "There's No One as Irish as Barack O'Bama," by Hardy Drew and the Nancy Boys, Killens was misidentified as "John O'Killens").⁶ Yet since 2001, no scholars identified with the new southern studies have explored the significance of this black southern writer's substantial body of work: not only for its challenge to the ways in which "southern exceptionalism still structure[s] the popular mythology of American exceptionalism," but also for how it resituates the U.S. South at national *and* global scales.⁷ Here the new southern studies has perpetuated the almost total absence of critical attention to Killens within more traditional, "regionalist" southern literary studies. That absence surely had something to do with Killens's coruscating critiques of white southern racism and economic exploitation, and his insistence throughout the 1950s and 1960s that "[t]here is no such thing as art for art's sake. All art is propaganda, although there is much propaganda that is not art"—the kind of position that saw Wright dismissed as merely "sociological" by neo-Agrarians.⁸ Like Wright's writing, Killens's fiction remained staunchly social realist; however, as a first book, *Youngblood* both formally and thematically rendered black southern folk culture—especially spirituals—as a source of political and historical consciousness far more affirmatively than Wright did in *Uncle Tom's Children* (1938).⁹ Killens's belief in the combined aesthetic *and* political importance of black southern writing at both regional and national scales compelled him, shortly before his death, to charge that "the American literary establishment has relegated the black Southern writer to a state of invisibility and oblivion," and to affirm that "there is a black Southern literary tradition, a voice that is special, profound, and distinct from any other in the country." Typically, however, Killens qualified that "what we're really talking about are '*Black Down-Southern Voices*'": if black regional or down-southern writing was in some sense a distinctive tradition, it was inseparable from national or up-southern concerns.[10]

However, Killens's emphasis on regional-national relations through his downsouth-upsouth dialectic should not obscure the depth and significance of his internationalist outlook. Among the few scholars who have attended to Killens's career, a consensus has emerged that, during the early 1960s, Killens embraced black nationalism and that he did so because white southern massive resistance to the Civil Rights movement left him disillusioned with the (old) leftist ideal of cross-racial solidarity between the black and white working class. To be sure, there was good reason for Killens to recoil from the ugly reality of white southern racism, and, like many other African American writers and activists, he was energized by postcolonial revolutions in Africa and elsewhere; traveling through Africa in 1961 filled him with optimism about a "New World" of resistance to white supremacy. Yet Killens's interest in black nationalism was not new: it dated to the late 1940s and derived from his formative interest in black communist Harry Haywood's vision of the U.S. South as a separate black nation. What is more, Killens's alertness to the possibility of a coordinated global movement of "colored peoples" against white colonial power went back even further, to his service with the U.S. Army in the South Pacific during World War II. Hence Killens's hopes for cross-racial solidarity among southern workers and his black (inter)nationalist vision of a "New World" cannot easily be decoupled or conveniently assigned to discrete periods of his career. Even when Killens's engagement with postcolonial and pan-African cultural politics was at its peak, informing both his fiction and nonfiction between 1963 and 1967, he never completely abandoned those hopes that black and white working-class southerners could yet come together.

The first section of this chapter assesses the literary geography of *Youngblood* through the lens of Killens's later downsouth-upsouth terminology to reveal how already circa 1954 he was acutely aware that regional and national scales were inextricable: ostensibly "southern" problems of race and labor relations in small-town Georgia are linked to white racism and black activism in New York and Washington, D.C. However, I proceed to consider how and why Killens's collected writing cannot be confined to the regional-national framework that his own downsouth-upsouth discourse may appear to privilege, and which (as I noted in the introduction) Baker and Nelson's model of new southern studies recapitulates. If Hurston's focus on the black southern "folk" facilitates a materialist mapping of the extended Caribbean via migrant labor, and Larsen offers a comparative, intertextual take on the transatlantic "folk" cultures of the rural black southern, Danish, and English laboring classes, Killens's key texts also resituate the U.S. South but at a different global scale. Crucially important here is Killens's second and best novel, *And Then We Heard the Thunder* (1963), which emerged out of his own military experiences during World War II. The second section of the chapter analyzes *Thunder*'s textual migrations from the U.S. South via the U.S. West (California) across the Pacific into the Global South (the Philippines and Australia). In the process of charting this regional, national, and transnational narrative cartography, Killens explored how, as Harilaos Stecopoulos has put it, "the U.S. South and certain locations in what is now called the global South often manifested disturbing similarities" due to the omnipresence of white supremacy and racial segregation. But as a novel about black soldiers' experiences of a truly worldwide war, *Thunder* also foregrounds how "African Americans long have combated regional, national, and global manifestations of white power"—not least when such manifestations, from the U.S. South to the Global South, emanate from organs of the U.S. state apparatus like the military.[11]

Downsouth, Upsouth, and "The Crossroads of the U.S.A.": *Youngblood*

Midway through the first chapter of *Youngblood*, sixteen-year-old Joseph Youngblood of Glenville, Georgia, hears from a Detroit drummer "about the glories of the Promised Land, Up the Country, where freedom was natural fact, and a man was a man." Inspired by such seminal "narrative of ascent" imagery, at eighteen Joe boards a "[g]ood old, powerful going-north train" for Chicago.[12] But just after the train crosses the Tennessee-Georgia border, a group of white men board and force Joe and other black passengers to disembark and work on a plantation. Joe escapes and catches "a freight back to Georgia and settled in Crossroads" (22), where he meets and marries Laurie Lee Barksdale and where their two children, Robbie and Jenny Lee, are born. The novel's chronotopic focus hereby settles early on Crossroads, based on Macon, where Killens was born in January 1916 and remained until he enrolled for college in Jacksonville eighteen years later. As Killens's biographer Keith Gilyard notes, "Macon sat virtually at the geographical center both of Georgia and the Confederacy" and has been identified by historians as a key node within "the Lower South Industrial Complex."[13] Yet in *Youngblood* the legend at Crossroads' railway station states that "CROSSROADS, GEORGIA, IS THE CROSSROADS OF THE U.S.A." (27). This is quite literally the first sign that the narrative will dramatize the centrality of a seemingly provincial city to not only the Lower South but also the economic geography of the nation.

The Youngbloods live in Pleasant Grove, which correlates to the all-black Pleasant Hill neighborhood of Macon where Killens grew up, and which was established in the 1870s as one of the nation's first black townships.[14] Joe works at a turpentine mill owned by the town's most prominent white businessman, the paternalistic George Cross Jr.; gradually, however, Joe's drive and dignity are eroded by his white supervisor, the sadistic Mr. Pete. This degradation feeds Joe's enduring hope of ascending to the urban North and taking his family with him. But Joe also begins to hear how "some folks said it wasn't any different up-the-country" (35); his mill colleague Ray Morrison "said a cracker was a cracker wherever you went, and he ought to know. Ray had lived in all those big cities up there after he had got out of the army" following World War I (77). Joe's increasing concern that there is no guarantee of a better life in northern cities complements his firm belief that "Georgia was as much his home as it was the crackers'" (44). Laurie too vacillates between a sense that her own dreams of "leaving Georgia" (40) are succumbing to the drudgery of domestic labor and a fervent conviction that "I was born in the south. This is as much my home as it is any of these evil old crackers. Why should we be running away? Suppose we find the same old thing up there. What we going to do then? Just keep on running the rest of our lives?" After Joe's back is badly injured in an industrial accident at the mill, his remaining dreams of migrating to the North recede, and the Youngbloods become even more rooted in their adopted hometown. Joe ponders in both spatial and temporal terms his present sense of stasis in Crossroads versus the dynamic former possibility of northward migration: "He often wondered how it would have been if those crackers hadn't stopped that train that time he was headed for Chicago. Seemed like a hundred years ago" (77). Joe himself often "felt like a hundred years old" (83), and though sometimes "an old familiar glow seized hold of him and flowed like newly-gotten old-time religion all through his great body," increasingly he is unable to transcend the racialized reality of manual labor at the mill: "the moment passed and the tiredness and the awful awful pain in his back and terrible hopelessness grabbed him again" (84).

This sense that Joe has become trapped in both time and place is formally expressed in the shift of narrative focalization from Joe to his son, Robbie, who does manage to migrate to the North. But before turning to Robbie, I want to consider how and why the narrative first switches at the start of part 2 to another father and son, Charles and Richard Myles. Unlike Joe, Charles got out of the South, moving from his position as a teacher in "a little town outside of Birmingham, Alabama," to a new life in Brooklyn. Charles's son Richard is thus undertaking a kind of reverse migration when, after studying in Washington, D.C., and New York, he takes a teaching post at the black school in Crossroads attended by Robbie and Jenny Lee. Through these Myles family migration narratives, *Youngblood* begins to interrogate the belief (apparently shared by Joe) that there is a spatial *and* temporal chasm between the modern, urban North and the backward, small-town South. The first chapter of part

2 opens with Richard arriving in Crossroads and wondering, "What the hell am I doing in this jerkwater town?" (125); the chapter ends with the same refrain (149). Yet rather than developing through Richard a narrative of descent into Deep South dislocation and despair, the bulk of the chapter moves back in time to Richard's troubled upbringing in Brooklyn and truncated student life in Washington. Richard recalls how as a young boy he witnessed informal political forums hosted by his father at the Myles family home: "None of these men were native New Yorkers. They came from South Carolina and Georgia and Mississippi and Barbados and Trinidad and other points south" (126). The scene attributes black political radicalism in Brooklyn to a combination of southern migrants and immigrants from south of the U.S. South; here black southerners (and Caribbean blacks) are figured not as "backward" but as the vanguard of progressive politics in the urban North. The chapter also dramatizes Richard's revelation that his father was not a proud New York department store clerk but rather "a little black man in overalls" working in the storeroom under the bullying supervision of a "great big giant of a white man" who calls Charles "boy" (132). The distance between downsouth and upsouth is closer than it may at first appear: there are clear parallels here with Joe's treatment by Mr. Pete at the mill in Crossroads. Though Charles managed to escape the South, he later admits to his son, "I've been struggling... ever since I first came up-the-country a young man. It's just as far out of reach as it ever was" (147). Charles's encounters with racism in New York vindicate Morrison's view from Crossroads that "a cracker is a cracker all over the country, and a Negro is a Negro" (109).

Morrison also insists that "Washington, D.C. is specially bad, like Mississippi" (109). Richard Myles gains some sense of this when he leaves New York to study at a black university in D.C. apparently based on Howard. In April 1936 the nineteen-year-old Killens himself moved to Washington, where he became the first African American employee of the National Labor Relations Board (NLRB). In 1937 Killens took night classes at Howard with E. Franklin Frazier and became involved in local black political groups; the move to D.C. helped Killens synthesize "an ever-present and deeply felt racial consciousness with a class analysis that construed contemporary racism as one of the ravages of capitalism"—a worldview that informs his debut novel.[15] In *Youngblood*, Richard is exposed in D.C. to "all kinds of radical stuff, like the trade union movement and the working class and the Negro Problem" (135). Richard's radicalization accelerates when he becomes involved with restaurant employee and activist Henrietta Saunders, for whom the nexus of racial and economic exploitation in the nation's capital makes it "the ugliest dirtiest city in the whole damn world" (140). Henrietta is organizing a strike at the restaurant where she works because the white owner "thinks he's got slaves on a plantation" (144). This statement, uttered by a black female worker in the urban center of U.S.

state power, anticipates Killens's rejection of Angelou's southern exceptionalism circa 1959 ("If you're black in this country, you're on a plantation") as well as *And Then We Heard the Thunder*'s depiction of the U.S. Army as a nationalized and globalized military-agricultural complex.

Part 2 of *Youngblood* subsequently reverts to the narrative present and Richard Myles's encounter with downsouth, Depression-era racism in Crossroads. Richard's first meeting with the racist school superintendent leaves him feeling that "Washington, D.C. was such a long ways off and New York City seemed a million miles away" (152). For the first month, he lies in bed at night musing on his apparently altered state as "Richard Wendell Myles—way down south in Crossroads, Georgia—Away down south in Dixie.... It had been like getting aboard a train and taking a long trip across the border into another country" (161). Here Killens adopts but also adapts the familiar Harlem Renaissance tactic of figuring the rural and small-town South as both spatially and temporally different from the putatively modern urban North. As noted in chapter 2, Leigh Anne Duck argues in *The Nation's Region* (2006) that in *Quicksand* and other Harlem Renaissance texts, "the space of the South is characterized by both a different developmental era and a different experience of time": black southern "folk" time.[16] In 1925 Alain Locke posited that black migrants were moving not only from the rural South to the urban North but also from the primitive past to the civilized present: "A railroad ticket and a suitcase, like a Bagdad carpet, transported the Negro peasant from the cotton-field and farm to the heart of the most complex urban civilization. Here in the mass, he must and does survive a jump of two generations in social economy and of a century and more in civilization."[17] *Youngblood* appears to reiterate this sense of what Duck terms "temporal distance separating the North and the South" through Richard's perception that Brooklyn now seems "a million miles" away (161) and that Crossroads is so different that it seems to be not only "another country" but also another time: the "Away down South" of the Confederacy and his father's Alabama childhood.[18] But as Richard becomes an integral part of the local black community, so the chasm between the seemingly discrete chronotopes of Brooklyn and Crossroads dissipates, and connections between upsouth and downsouth become apparent. These transregional connections are both positive, in the form of communal and neo-familial relations that transcend the Mason-Dixon line, and negative, via a grim recognition that white racism and economic exploitation are pervasive in the North as well as South.

Alan Wald argues that Killens's depiction of the Youngbloods as "an exceedingly unpathological, un-'damaged' Black family" was a rejoinder to Ellison's representation of the Truebloods in *Invisible Man*, while Lawrence Jackson remarks that "Killens showcased the undying love and understanding within the Youngblood family" to counter Wright's bleak rendition of his own black southern family in *Black Boy* (1945).[19] Equally important, however, is this black southern working-class clan's bond with the educated but alienated northern outsider: Richard begins "carrying within him an unexplored feeling of being a part of the Youngblood family" (270). Indeed, the affinity between the New York teacher and the southern "folk" family—such a striking contrast with Chicago-born Helga Crane's sense of exclusion from the black southern bourgeois fetishization of "family" at Naxos—develops so deeply that Richard no longer sees the South as "another country." Instead, it is the particular social geography of Crossroads' white power structure that makes Richard feel like a foreigner: "Over in Pleasant Grove he always knew a secure kind of feeling of being at home and among his people. But the moment he came downtown to attend to any kind of business, he was back in that foreign country again" (258). Richard's neo-familial bond with the Youngbloods is also political: after Laurie Lee has been ordered by the Crossroads police to beat Robbie, Richard initially counsels that "it wasn't your fault.... It's the white folks. The crackers. It's the *southern way of life*." Immediately, though, Richard qualifies that "I'm beginning to believe it's the whole American way of life—north and south" (200). Mindful of his southern migrant father's travails in New York and his experiences with Henrietta in Washington, D.C., Richard repudiates the myth of southern exceptionalism and recognizes that racialized oppression and exploitation is a national rather than regional problem.

When Richard begins insisting that "we have to band together—got to organize ourselves," Joe is skeptical: "It was so easy for him to talk about fighting. New York City was a damn sight different from Crossroads, Georgia" (201). Yet Richard insists on a transregional, cross-racial solution to the ostensibly "southern" problem of black labor exploitation: "We have friends all over this country—colored and white.... We could use a branch of the National Association for the Advancement of Colored People... the labor unions—th—the white workers—and some of the more educated liberal-minded white people." Joe's bitter experience of black and white labor divided by the color line (a reality that Richard's stutter registers without fully recognizing) is such that he remains doubtful about the efficacy of such national, interracial organizing: "down here in Georgia the poor white peck is the black man's worstest enemy. Labor unions—These pecks down here won't let you get one foot in the door" (204). Nevertheless, Richard's vision reinvigorates Joe and he reemerges as a focal character in the narrative, confronting the mill foreman Mack for withholding part of his salary—a stand which in turn attracts the sympathy of white millworker and union member Oscar Jefferson.

Richard's teaching of black history and culture is also an inspiration to Robbie, who begins to believe that "[h]e would go anywhere. Maybe Atlanta or Savannah, or even New York where Richard Myles came from, a place where they wouldn't treat him like he was a dog or a slave just because he was colored" (188). After graduating high school Robbie migrates northward but spends only a single summer in New York before the Depression and the Youngblood family claim on the South as home ("Georgia was just as much his as it was the crackers'") brings him back to Crossroads. On one hand, "the City [New York] had given him a Great New Hope" exemplified by unionized labor action in which "the colored and white workers had stuck together and the Puerto Ricans too." On the other hand, Robbie "came back home because the City had given him a Great Disappointment": even united the workers "had lost the strike," and Robbie's experiences in Harlem forced an awareness that racism and segregation exists in New York too (328). On returning to Crossroads, Robbie initially (like Richard before him) perceives a spatial and temporal gap between metropolitan North and small-town South: "In three months time it [Crossroads] seemed to have contracted to one half its size.... He thought about the swiftness of New York City... speed speed speed, and he shook his head. Even Mama and Daddy were somehow different—Almost like country people" (330). An encounter with a racist white storeowner compounds this sense of regional difference as briefly "he forgot about what Harlem was really like, he forgot about jobs in New York that were not for Negroes, he forgot about the restaurants and hotels where Negroes weren't allowed, he only remembered that New York was North and New York was different from Crossroads, Georgia" (329). Ultimately, though, Robbie's experiences of racism and labor strife *as well as* unionization and cross-racial solidarity in Harlem inform his turn to labor activism in Crossroads. Robbie gets a job at the downtown Oglethorpe Hotel and is shocked by the exploitation of the hotel's black workforce. Robbie is sufficiently inspired by memories of cross-racial organization in New York to propose forming a union (352); those memories also make Robbie open to the possibility that Oscar Jefferson might prove an exception to white southern workers' possessive investment in whiteness over and above class solidarity with their black colleagues. Though black and white southerners alike associate Robbie's pro-union activism with New York (353, 394), the germinal organization and resistance comes from a combination of blacks with experience beyond Crossroads (Richard, Robbie, and union organizer Jim Collins) and local workers both black and white (especially Joe and Oscar). Amid this incipient cross-racial and cross-generational activism, Joe is shot dead after again confronting foreman Mack for swindling him out of his full salary. Yet the closing scene of the novel depicting Joe's funeral is figured not as a tragic ending but rather a collective beginning: the politically engaged preacher Ledbetter declares that "Joseph Youngblood lives in all of us.... His spirit lives in the National Association for the Advancement of Colored People... and the cause of freedom" (471). It is an eerily prescient finale to a novel published in the same week as the May 1954 *Brown v. Board of Education* decision.

A skeptic might object that rather than foreshadowing the Civil Rights movement, the closing images of cross-racial solidarity—especially the scene when Oscar crosses the color line to give blood to the dying Joe—obfuscate the failure of labor organization in the South during the Depression and after World War II. From this perspective, the conclusion of *Youngblood* might seem to exemplify Fredric Jameson's definition of a "symbolic act," in which "real social contradictions, insurmountable in their own terms, find a purely formal resolution in the aesthetic realm."[20] Christopher Bigsby has charged that *Youngblood*'s "[b]elief in the possibility of an alliance between 'the hundreds and the thousands' of southern Negroes 'and the decent thinking white people' seems to owe more to left-wing optimism than to reality as depicted in the novel itself."[21] Killens was well aware of the chasm between white and black southern labor: working as a bellhop at Macon's Dempsey Hotel during the early 1930s, he witnessed firsthand how "Macon's virulent racism" ensured that "most black workers felt no personal allegiance to white workers, who frowned on interracial labor activism even though it promised to improve working conditions for everyone."[22] *Youngblood*'s publication also followed the failure of Operation Dixie, the Congress of Industrial Organizations' (CIO) concerted drive between 1946 and 1953 to unite and unionize black and white southern workers. The Killens family home in Macon served as a local base for Operation Dixie, but the campaign foundered on the recalcitrant rock of white southern racism. Killens recalled in "Downsouth-Upsouth" how "our experience had grimly taught us that the white workingman clung to his whiteness far more desperately than he did to his Christianity and his so-called revolutionary tradition." The white southern worker was "one of the *obvious* reasons that the C.I.O. 'Operation Dixie' failed in its noble undertaking to organize the Southern unorganized, the most exploited working class in the country."[23] By the time that essay was published Killens had, as Wald notes, lost "his confidence in the capacity of the Euro-American working class to discern its own self-interest, although he admired a few heroic white martyrs in the civil rights movement."[24]

Yet Wald is also right to insist that Killens's overt embrace of "a revolutionary form of Black nationalism" in the 1960s remained "informed by his long-held vision of socialism" dating back to the late 1930s and 1940s.[25] I will have more to say about these ongoing links between socialism and black nationalism in Killens's life and work. But already in *Youngblood*, if black southern consciousness is struggling to be born within the eponymous family and wider black community, it cannot be separated from either the possibility of class-based solidarity across the color line or the emphasis on black solidarity across the Mason-Dixon line. For Killens, the formation of a (neo-national) black southern consciousness was not an end in itself. The political maturation of black southern workers like Joe and Robbie is inextricable from the experience of racism and economic exploitation that Robbie and Richard have encountered in the urban North. So too the successful organization of this black political consciousness—be it in the Depression timeframe of *Youngblood*'s main events or in the post–Operation Dixie, pre–Civil Rights movement moment of publication—requires the involvement of national organizations like the NAACP and the CIO.[26] This is not to suggest that Killens offered a vulgar relativist viewpoint that racial and economic exploitation in the North and South were simply the same. As he later stated, "Of course one must say now emphatically, the North is not the South. New York is not Mississippi."[27] But in *Youngblood* and the writings that followed, Killens revealed that the supposed differences between New York and Mississippi or Brooklyn and Macon were more "superficial" than they seemed; indeed, the Civil Rights movement reaffirmed Killens's sense that black southerners' political struggle was crucial to black consciousness nationally—and internationally.

"This Is the Place Where the New World Is":
And Then We Heard the Thunder

In the eighteen months following the publication of *Youngblood*, Killens's attention was kept focused firmly on the South by the *Brown* decision, the emergence of the Civil Rights movement, and his impassioned response to William Faulkner's notorious comments on desegregation. But Killens "reached an activist crossroads" as the limits of focusing on regional racism and the shaky prospects of cross-racial activism came up against his growing interest in global (especially African) freedom struggles.[28] By 1963—the year he published *And Then We Heard the Thunder*—Killens was telling the *Muhammad Speaks* newspaper that "When I wrote *Youngblood* . . . I was not as nationalistic in my beliefs as I am now." Journalist Joseph Walker noted that Killens "listed incidents throughout the South and the emerging African nations (many of which he has visited) as influences on his development" as a black nationalist.[29] Yet Killens did not simply shape-shift from class-based integrationism to race-based nationalism. Wald remarks that "Killens was by no means a recent convert to black nationalism in the 1960s" and points to Killens's approving assessment of Harry Haywood's Black Belt Nation thesis in his first-ever publication, a 1949 review of Haywood's book *Black Liberation* (1948).[30] In a draft of that review, Killens began to work through Haywood's argument that "[t]he Negro people are a nation particularly because they possess all of the attributes required for nationhood. An historically evolved stable community of language, territory, economic life and psychological make-up manifested in a community of culture." In the late 1940s, this community remained centered in the Black Belt South, which, despite the demographic revolution wrought by the Great Migration, was "still the living quarters for one third of the Negro people."³¹ As we have seen, Hurston too—albeit from a different political perspective—focused on the black folk who remained in the South. But for both Haywood and Killens, their emphasis on black southern "national freedom" was also entirely compatible with cross-racial, class-based liberation politics in the South. It was necessary to focus first on black agricultural workers because of the formidable power of Jim Crow, "the weapon the bosses use to keep the working class divided." The achievement of black southern national solidarity would be the prerequisite for liberating the southern working class more generally: "The white worker today has everything to gain and nothing to lose by the self-determination of the Negro nation in the South."³² As Wald observes, "The primary concern of Killens, like Haywood, was the evolution of national consciousness on the part of the African American population in the South as the means of access to a socialist future."³³

Equally striking is Killens's stress on how, "[i]n Haywood's words, 'the shadow of the plantation falls upon the Negro in Harlem, in Chicago's South Side, in the hundreds of urban "Black Belts" throughout the country.'" Killens glosses Haywood's emphasis on the racial and economic ligatures between urban North and rural South in terms that anticipate his own definitions of downsouth and upsouth: "Jim Crow is as hard and as fast in Stuyvesant as in Mississippi or Georgia. Oh how the plantation does cast its shadow. The plantation psychology has become the rule rather than the exception throughout this democracy of ours."³⁴ For Killens as for Haywood, such homologies between North and South were material as well as mental: much as New York's Stuyvesant Town housing project "is owned and operated by the Metropolitan Life Insurance Company, one of the biggest plantation owners in the Black Belt," so the southern "plantation is owned lock, stock and barrel by Northern capital. The Morgans, Rockefellers, duPonts, Mellons are the real plantation slave drivers. It is they who perpetuate the Jim Crow, semi-slavery Black Belt. As Haywood points out, their banks maintain the credit structure without which the plantation could not live."³⁵ This plantation-ghetto complex was a national rather than regional phenomenon.

What *did* change in Killens's worldview between the late 1940s and late 1950s was his younger self's utopian hope for solidarity with the white southern working class; such hope was less sustainable following the failure of Operation Dixie and whites' massive resistance to the Civil Rights movement. In the early 1960s, Killens turned to "the emergence of Third World revolutionary movements in the former colonies of the Western nations."³⁶ Yet this too was not an entirely new development in Killens's thinking. Gilyard demonstrates that Killens's interest in African anticolonial movements emerged not in the early 1960s but during the late 1940s, following Henry Wallace's failed presidential campaign.³⁷ Moreover, Killens first encountered Haywood's thesis and an important internationalist mentor, fellow Georgia native Alphaeus Hunton, at Howard during the 1930s. By 1950, Hunton was conceptualizing black solidarity at national *and* global scales:

> [W]e have to be concerned with the oppression of our Negro brothers in Africa for the very same reason that we here in New York or in any other state in the Union have to be concerned with the plight of our brothers in Tennessee, Mississippi or Alabama.... Racial oppression and exploitation have a universal pattern, and whether they occur in South Africa, Mississippi or New Jersey, they must be exposed and fought as part of a worldwide system of oppression, the fountain-head of which is today among the reactionary and fascist-minded ruling circles of white America. Jim-Crowism, colonialism and imperialism are not separate enemies, but a single enemy with different faces and different forms.[38]

In 1952 Killens helped Hunton and the Council on African Affairs (CAA) organize a New York protest against apartheid, picketing the South African consulate with a sign bearing the legend "American Labor Supports Freedom for South Africa."[39]

As books like Penny M. Von Eschen's *Race Against Empire* (1997) and Cheryl Higashida's *Black Internationalist Feminism* (2011) make clear, Hunton and Killens were hardly alone among black intellectuals of the period in making such internationalist gestures. Higashida stresses that "mainstream African American politics had adopted a global perspective on domestic civil rights as a result of World War II, the dawn of independence throughout the Third World, and the end of formal, direct imperialism."[40] In *F.B. Eyes: How J. Edgar Hoover's Ghostreaders Framed African American Literature* (2015), William Maxwell reveals how, "[w]orried by wartime black internationalism," the FBI intensified its surveillance of black writers. Killens's FBI file, which eventually ran to 194 pages (one page longer than Claude McKay's), was opened in 1941 (one year before Richard Wright's) while he was working for the National Labor Relations Board and suspected of being "a tool on [*sic*] the Communist Racial Equality State."[41] Only with the exponential growth of anticommunism during the late 1940s and early 1950s, as well as black liberal delinking of the domestic Civil Rights movement from postcolonial struggles during the latter part of the 1950s and early 1960s, did this global perspective wane. But it did not expire: black leftists in groups like the Harlem Writers Guild, which Killens cofounded and chaired, ensured the endurance and development of "black nationalist internationalism." This worldview "held that self-determination for oppressed nations would bring about socialism for the working classes of all nations"—commensurate with the Black Belt Nation view of the U.S. South—*and* "linked the struggles of African Americans in the United States to struggles for national self-determination in the Caribbean, the Americas, Africa, Asia, and Australia."[42]

The influence of such postcolonial struggles on Killens's creative work is already evident in *Lower Than the Angels*, a play completed in 1960 but never produced. Killens's manuscript for *Angels* was based on a section of *Youngblood* that he temporally relocated to the present, thereby allowing the drama to speak to and about black southern political agency in the activist era of regional "leaders like Martin Luther King and Rev. [Fred] Shuttleworth and [Ralph] Abernathy and Daisy Bates and Robert Williams." But in the second act, protagonist Jim Kilgrow Jr. cognitively remaps his local situation in south Georgia in relation to "that great new world where black men and women walk in dignity. Dreamed all those powerful places with those beautiful names. Ghana—Mali—Songhay—Gao—Timbuctu—GreatGodAlmighty! Nigeria and Senegal—That's the happiest dream I ever dreampt. Everybody everywhere called me brother. I can't stay in this place much longer—I'll go crazy if I do."[43] In 1961 Killens himself visited Africa for the first time, traveling some twelve thousand miles through more than a dozen nations including Nigeria, Mali, Ghana, Liberia, and Senegal; he subsequently recalled thinking "'Outside Africa... the old world of the West is dying.' Inside Africa, a New World is a-borning." Killens's experiences in Africa confirmed his conviction that the continent's postcolonial revolutions were relevant to the movement in the U.S. South: "The tides of freedom are lashing against the beachheads from Montgomery to Johannesburg."[44]

In spring 1962 Killens experienced another milestone: his first meeting with Malcolm X. Since the 1955 Bandung conference, Malcolm too had been energized by anticolonial struggles in Africa and Asia. In July 1959 Malcolm undertook his first trip to Africa (Egypt) before proceeding on to the Middle East (Saudi Arabia). In a letter home published by the *Pittsburgh Courier*, Malcolm anticipated Killens's language almost two years later: "Only yesterday, America was the New World, a world with a future—but now, we suddenly realize Africa is the New World—the world with the brightest future." For Malcolm as for Killens, this was "a future in which the so-called American Negroes are destined to play a key role."[45] Increasingly stymied by the political conservatism and passivity of the Nation of Islam (NOI), Malcolm became correspondingly more interested in black leftists' engagement with global revolutionary struggles in and beyond Africa. When Killens, Julian Mayfield, Robert Williams, and others formed the Fair Play for Cuba Committee in April 1960, "Malcolm and the NOI watched from a distance," but in September 1960 Malcolm met Fidel Castro during the latter's controversial stay in Harlem while Killens joined thousands of cheering African Americans in the street outside Castro's hotel.[46] Killens came to see Malcolm as (in Gilyard's words) "an Up South complement to King," and by late 1963 Malcolm and Killens were collaborating on "an agenda of African American political empowerment connected to a conception of the African American struggle as part of worldwide rebellion against oppression."[47]

It was within this vibrant political atmosphere that Killens's second novel appeared in January 1963. Although *And Then We Heard the Thunder* is a semi-autobiographical account of black soldiers' experiences in the U.S. Army during World War II, it has mostly been read as reflecting wider political debates during the years prior to publication—especially Killens's embrace of black nationalism. Paul R. Lehman locates the "development of a Black psyche" in *Thunder* and Killens's overall career along a linear trajectory of stages in which "The Rise of Black Nationalism" stands as the most advanced stage yet achieved.[48] Bigsby reads *Thunder* much more skeptically as exhibiting the conspicuous failure of Killens's attempt to balance a "double vision" in which his "present convictions" (a black nationalist eschatological turn to "racial cataclysm") are "constantly haunted by the ghosts of old ideologies" (earlier, more optimistic liberal-left dreams of "working-class unity" across racial lines).[49] Even Wald privileges the period of *Thunder*'s production: "The ideological climate of the late 1950s and early 1960s in which Killens's novel was written is the critical ingredient."[50] However, there are serious limitations to considering *Thunder* primarily within the context of 1960s black nationalism. First, it oversimplifies Killens's *simultaneous* engagement from the late 1940s until the early 1960s with both leftist hopes for cross-racial solidarity between southern workers (which Killens never entirely abandoned) *and* black nationalist internationalism. Second, periodizing *Thunder* in the early 1960s displaces both the novel's *temporal* focus on World War II and its *spatial* turn from the U.S. South to the Global South: from south Georgia to the South Pacific theater.

As Jennifer C. James observes, because "the curiously little scholarship existing about *Thunder* tends toward a single issue: whether Killens' evisceration of the Jim Crow military leads him to adopt a stance more 'nationalist' or 'integrationist,'" "the author's years in the South Pacific" have been reduced to "an interesting biographical detail when they are mentioned at all."[51] Yet this aspect of Killens's biography is clearly significant, given his own emphasis on "the forty-one months I spent in the service of my country during World War II," not least the "twenty-seven of them island-hopping, ducking bullets in the South Pacific." This three-and-a-half-year period (July 1942 to December 1945) was the crucible in which Killens's career was forged: in the South Pacific he decided he wanted to be a writer and recalled "soaking up material for my second novel, *And Then We Heard the Thunder*."[52] A notebook in the Killens Papers at Emory University features a letter drafted at the "11th Replacement Depot, Tokyo," on November 4, 1945, in which Killens responds to a racist missive published in an unnamed magazine: "We didn't go through all of this hell over here to come complacently back home to face Jim Crow, discrimination, racial and religious bigotry. We fully intend that America will be a better country, a freer nation, a more democratic place in which to live. We will settle for nothing less." The same notebook features a draft fragment for a novel called "They Never Come

Back" that opens on May 3, 1945, in the Philippines and focuses on U.S. soldiers leaving for home after "[t]hirty nine months of service in the Pacific." As they prepare to depart, white soldiers taunt uncomprehending Filipino fishermen: "Goodbye, all of you monkey-faced sonofabitches." The white American narrator "felt ashamed" to witness such blatant racism and responds by reaching out to an African American soldier, Jim, suggesting that they team up to integrate the respective hatches on the ship; Jim responds by saying that such efforts will do little to resolve institutional racism.[53] As this tentative early foray into fiction suggests, *Thunder* "is the novel Killens was bursting to write when he reentered civilian life in 1945."[54] But whereas James locates *Thunder* within its wartime context and as the culmination of a larger literary history of African American war writing, I want to focus on how the novel resituates the U.S. South and its historically racialized labor regimes in relation to both upsouth and Global South geographies. Through *Thunder*'s narrative migrations—from Georgia via California and the Philippines to Australia—we can also discern more clearly the wartime genesis of Killens's vision of a "New World" in which not just regional but also national and global racism can be overcome.

And Then We Heard the Thunder opens in Harlem where Solly Saunders, a black southern migrant "all the way from Dry Creek, Georgia," is preparing to leave for military training at Fort Dix in New Jersey.[55] Solly is encouraged by his wife, Millie, to "[b]e an American instead of a Negro, and concentrate on winning the war" (6), but at Fort Dix another soldier, Joseph "Bookworm" Taylor, declares his intention to "[b]uck myself right out of this white man's Army" (16). Solly responds by affirming a combined racial *and* national cause: "If Hitler conquered America, the Negro would be a hundred times worse off than he is now. Furthermore we're American citizens and the country is at war and they need us, and when we get back we won't let them forget that we fought like everybody else" (17). Solly, Bookworm, and the rest of their company are soon sent from New Jersey to south Georgia to continue their training at Camp Henry military base, near the small town of Ebbensville. Recalling Richard Myles's migration from New York to the "foreign country" of Crossroads, at Camp Henry, Solly feels a profound sense of displacement from the nation to which at Fort Dix he committed himself: "Millie and New York City hundreds and hundreds of miles away, in another country, it seemed. Maybe it was in another world" (43). Bookworm feels even more acutely disoriented, seeing the South as the region that proves the pervasive reality of white racism and precludes *any* sense of affiliation with the nation: "*Our* country.... I bet goddammit you bet not let any of these Georgia pecks hear you claiming this country" (46). Bookworm also notes approvingly that "Tojo is kicking gobs of crackers' asses!" (43), to which Solly retorts that the Japanese emperor is anything but a heroic figure of resistance to racism:

> There is no need of your Bee-Essing yourself about Tojo just because he's colored. Look at all the Chinese people he's killed. This is not a racial war. This is a war of democracy against fascism pure and simple, and if you're for Tojo, you're for Hitler....
> ... Hitler and Tojo and the governor of Georgia are on the same damn team. All three of them're against you and me. (47–48)

In *Youngblood*, black union organizer Jim Collins locates the power of Georgia governor Eugene Talmadge at the local scale, depicting Talmadge as metonymic of the local elite's manipulation of poor whites (405–6). Solly situates Talmadge's tyranny on a global scale, linking the Georgia governor and his regional demagoguery to foreign fascists—though he makes this rhetorical move partly to shore up his own wavering faith in U.S. national identity and the patriotic cause.

Solly's rhetoric dovetails with the "Double V for Victory" campaign, initiated by the *Pittsburgh Courier* and premised upon the belief that African American support for military success against international fascism would facilitate victory over racism within the nation's borders. As one black worker put it, "The first V for victory over our enemies, from without, the second V for victory over our enemies from within. For surely those who perpetuate these ugly prejudices here are seeking to destroy our democratic form of government just as surely as the Axis forces."[56] But when Bookworm is beaten by local white military police, Solly begins to lose faith that American democratic ideals will trump "southern" racism and global fascism. Worrying that he has become a "new-styled slicked-up uncle tom" who "wanted to be accepted in the World of White Folks" (60–61), Solly now identifies fascist racial ideology not just with a "Georgia peck" like Talmadge but the nation—and nation-state apparatus—as a whole: "There's Americans who believe in *Herrenvolk*. The American Army is based on *Herrenvolk*" (71). Discussing the "military fictions" of Killens's fellow Georgian Carson McCullers, Stecopoulos notes that "the U.S. military didn't so much reflect as exacerbate the many tyrannies of the Jim Crow South" as "thousands of African American men reported to army installations throughout the South and found themselves confronted by an extraordinarily hostile white military." At the Fort Benning army base near McCullers's hometown of Columbia, such hostility was expressed through strict segregation and violence, including an on-base lynching; thus the South "wasn't so much an exotic elsewhere" for black troops in training "as an uncanny space that both mirrored a proximate Jim Crow regime and recalled the horrors of Nazi Germany."[57] At Camp Henry, Solly has a similar disturbing sense that both regional racism and international fascism are converging at the strictly disciplined local scale of a military base run according to national military policy.

But if Solly now identifies the U.S. military with the Nazis' "*Herrenvolk*," the regional South remains especially *unheimlich*. This is partly because of Solly's repeated encounters with racism both on and off the base, but it is also because he regards Georgia as "the foreign country of his birth" (117). Amid this "eerie feeling of strangeness and at-homeness clashing and merging," Solly looks to his local lover, Fannie Mae Braxton, to provide a sense of place and past. He muses that "maybe I knew her when I was a little boy in Georgia and she was a little biddy girl," and ponders how "[s]he made him feel he had been on a long long journey and had come back home at last" (78). Like many of Jean Toomer's nonsouthern male characters throughout *Cane* (1923), Solly figures a black southern woman in overtly physical and sexual terms. Fannie Mae's "body warm and black and brown as dark-brown toast and slim and sweet as sugar cane" becomes an objective correlative for that "sweetish kind of nostalgia" Solly occasionally feels for his own southern ancestral roots; Fannie Mae's corporeal presence allows him to feel "as if he had traveled along this road once before in life" (103). It is notable, then, that the narrative depicts Fannie Mae as considerably more politicized than Solly. Fannie Mae is a far more fervent believer in Double V: as Bookworm notes, she "says she's an anti-fascist. Down here [the U.S. South] and over there [Europe]" (53). When Fannie Mae herself points out that "[y]ou folks have the Double-V in New York. Victory against the fascists overseas and against the crackers here at home," she rhetorically remaps Bookworm's "down here" and Solly's southern "road" down "home" to include activism in the urban North. Solly demurs because "[h]e did not want to discuss the war or politics or Double-V or NAACP," but Fannie insists: "A fascist is a fascist and a cracker is a cracker. The war is everywhere we find it" (79). Stubbornly unwilling to fully acknowledge that the realities of racism within the nation (not just Talmadge's Georgia) might validate Fannie Mae's Double-V worldview, Solly tries to explain away her activism by displacing it onto "her Southern background"; quarantining it within her "bitter" regional experience of racism (82); and neutralizing her political insight by reducing her to a "pretty little country wench" (154). This gendered, sexualized southernization of Fannie Mae's body allows Solly to, in Duck's terms, "displace fundamental questions about political affiliation ... concerning the nation-state" via the familiar strategy of "associating the nation with democracy and change and the region with racism and tradition."[58]

Thunder's title, epigram, and the subtitles of all four sections derive from Harriet Tubman's observations about the assault on Fort Wagner by the Massachusetts 54th Infantry in July 1863, thereby invoking a longer history of heroic black struggle by both black male soldiers and black female activists. The subtitle and imagery of the novel's first section, "The Planting Season," serves to locate the racism and containment experienced by black soldiers at Camp Henry within the regional history of plantation slavery. This history was evident in the material landscape of Fort Benning, which "was named for a local

Confederate general and used a former plantation home as its HQ."⁵⁹ In *Thunder*, soldiers in other companies from Solly's regiment begin to figure the white southern colonel Rutherford as a neo-planter and the black soldiers under his command as "Rutherford's Slaves." Another soldier, Jerry "Scotty" Scott, scathingly critiques the division of labor among the black troops, telling Solly that "[y]ou're like the slave that lived in the Big House. I'm a field hand" (88). The increasingly disillusioned Solly proposes writing to the black press with an exposé of "how Negro soldiers are fighting these cracker [*sic*] for democracy down in Camp Johnson Henry in Ebbensville, Georgia . . . Tell[ing] the whole world about Charlie's plantation" (94). Gilyard argues that in *Thunder* "many African Americans occupy neoslave status and that the South itself is where you find it."⁶⁰ This is true, but only up to a point: again, downsouth cannot be separated from upsouth. Though Solly is granted his wish to "get out of this foreign country where he was an alien, and never a citizen . . . where he was born and lived as a boy, but could never grow up to become a man" (118), there is no easy ascent up north from neoslavery. When the black soldiers' letter is published, Rutherford exacts revenge by sending the soldiers on to California, knowing full well that they will soon be sent on to combat in the South Pacific.

The second part of *Thunder*, set in California, is entitled "Cultivation": Killens thus maintains the neoslavery metaphor but mobilizes it beyond the U.S. South to stress the production of black war labor as part of a national (to cultivate the plantation metaphor further) military-agricultural complex. In September 1941 a critical report authored by William Hastie, civilian aide to Secretary of War Henry Stimson, stated: "The traditional mores of the South have been widely accepted and adopted by the Army as the basis of policy and practice affecting the Negro soldier."⁶¹ In *Thunder*, Solly and his fellow black soldiers find that the racial segregation so familiar from Camp Henry is also practiced at Fort Ord in Monterey Bay. As such, Solly can no longer displace the experience of institutional racism onto the South: "Here we are supposed to be fighting against the racist theories of Hitler and we find the same theories holding forth in our own so-called democratic Army" (219). Solly contemplates deserting the army and nation altogether: "he would fake some papers and steal a jeep and take off for Mexico and Guatemala and eventually South America" (226). Instead, he and the rest of the regiment are shipped out of San Francisco for "the Southern Seas," and the third section of *Thunder* follows their voyage.

Even upon arrival in the South Pacific, the historical echoes of racial slavery resound as the black troops are restricted to manual work: "there were no Japanese to fight . . . there was only the labor battalion at the waterfront. Tote dat barge and lift dat bale" (271). Following a Japanese bomb attack and while preparing to invade an island in the Philippines, Solly desperately recasts his failing belief in the military cause and American exceptionalism ("No land has ever had the potential that was yours still is yours" [274]) to envision a brave new postracist world extending from the Jim Crow South to apartheid South Africa: "a world after the war, in which he was walking everywhere in his country and through the whole world from Mississippi to Stalingrad to Calcutta to Johannesburg" (288). However, further incidents of racial tension between black and white U.S. soldiers sour such utopianism: "The white Yankees told the Filipinos not to sleep with the black Yankees because they would rape the women. The black Yankees told the Filipinos, 'Them crackers ain't no good. We colored folks got to stick together'" (336). Learning about the history of U.S. imperialism in the Philippines (339) further erodes Solly's faith in abstract notions of fighting for "Freedom and Democracy" (288); so too does an uncanny sense of solidarity with Filipino farmers that triggers the return of his repressed familial and racial ties to that "foreign country of his birth," the U.S. South. Observing the Filipino "menfolks in the fields behind their ploughs," Solly ponders "his own, the Negro people, standing deep in the corn and cotton fields of Georgia and Mississippi with nowhere to go and not a damn thing to look forward to. War or no war, it would make no difference to them, except for those who gave their sons up in noble sacrifice to the great bloodletting in the name of peace and freedom" (311).

Despite Solly's growing disillusionment, *Thunder* gestures to the stubborn possibility of class-based connections across the color line. In the Philippines, Solly becomes friendly with a group of white anti-aircraft gunners from Kentucky, one of whom declares that "I didn't have no goddamn freedom down on the farm where I come from. I worked from sunup to sundown and didn't never get nowhere" (327). However, the friendship is cut short when a Japanese bomb "atomized everyone of Solly's coffee-drinking Ack-Ack buddies from the bluegrass country" (337). Solly is also drawn to and repelled by the views of a "self-proclaimed Black Nationalist from New York City and Trinidad," Geoffrey Grant, who "pictured the Japanese as the champions of the colored race" (257). Circa 1963, the violent death of the white southern gunners could be read as a symbolic expression of Killens's lost confidence in the white working class, while the charged characterization of Grant might have reminded Killens's contemporary readers of historical antecedents for global visions of "colored" solidarity, such as Marcus Garvey's United Negro Improvement Association and the esoteric pro-Japanese groups that appeared in African American communities during the 1930s. Solly is somewhat sympathetic to Grant's worldview, which he knows derives partly from Grant's experiences of racism as a Caribbean immigrant to the United States (328); however, he again repudiates the whitewashing of Japanese imperialism. But Grant's flawed notion of transnational "colored" solidarity prompts Solly to start more seriously envisioning his own alternative vision of a future beyond the boundaries of American exceptionalism: "Solly wanted General Grant to say that Asia and Africa were the New World—the brand-new hope for all mankind" (259).[62]

For the remainder of the novel, it is this inchoate vision of a brave New World defined by global nonwhites that Solly inclines toward. As critics have noted, this reflects Killens's own investment in black nationalism, postcolonialism, and pan-Africanism in the years that he was writing *Thunder*. Solly's New World dream recalls not only Killens's epiphany in Africa circa 1961 but also Malcolm X's similar vision of a "New World" two years earlier. Nevertheless, Solly's encounters with white American racism from the U.S. South to the South Pacific, as well as his growing alertness to global forms of oppression and resistance, must also be considered in the context of World War II. *Thunder* can be historicized via accounts of racial strife in the U.S. Army's South Pacific operations—accounts that were repressed at the time and remain little known today. After a beach battle in the Philippines during which Solly is wounded and kills a Japanese soldier, he is transported to the Australian city of "Bainbridge" to convalesce. The fourth and final part of *Thunder* is set in Bainbridge, a thinly veiled version of Brisbane, where Killens himself was stationed briefly in 1944 and where, between March 11 and 20, 1942, a series of serious conflicts took place between black and white U.S. soldiers. *Thunder* culminates with a rendition of those conflicts. In a November 1963 pitch to *True* magazine, Killens outlined his plans for an article that would capitalize on the relative success of *Thunder* by detailing the historical incident: "It was practically unknown throughout the rest of the civilian world. It was, in the words of Ted Poston of the New York Post, 'one of the best kept secrets of World War Two,'" even though "when I arrived there a few months later ... [a]ll Australia was still in shock and still buzzing about the infamous BATTLE." Killens declared: "The climax of my new novel, AND THEN WE HEARD THE THUNDER, is based on this actual BATTLE ... the entire structure of my novel was dictated by this final confrontation which I knew would take place in Australia."[63]

The final section of *Thunder* uses the experience of African American soldiers in Australia to meditate on issues of race, class, labor, and the dialectical tension—not least in Killens's own career—between socialist internationalism and black nationalism. Based in Bainbridge, Solly and his fellow black troops discover that U.S. military policy in Australia, as in California and the Philippines, reproduces "the traditional mores of the South." As historian Kay Saunders observes, "formal internal segregative policies and practices employed in the U.S. were transferred to and refined in Australia."[64] Bookworm reports that though the first wave of black soldiers in Brisbane were treated well by Australians—"They were heroes and color didn't mean a goddamn thing"—the situation changed with the arrival of "them Southern peckerwood divisions": at that point, the U.S. military began "putting places off limits to colored soldiers all over everywhere. The MPs worse than they are in Georgia" (374). When members of the 913th suffer sustained abuse from white southern soldiers and de facto segregation imposed by Army authorities, even their white captain,

FIGURES 5 AND 6: Competing views of the U.S. military presence in the South Pacific. A cartoon from the *Sydney Sun* newspaper depicts Uncle Sam helping an Australian soldier defend his country from a racialized, bestial Japan (apparently depicted as a gorilla). By contrast, the September 8, 1945, edition of the African American *Chicago Defender* newspaper anticipates Killens's novel by stressing, first, the U.S. military's exportation of "southern" racial structures (represented by the ship *Mississippi*, the whip-holding slaver-like white figure of authority, and the segregation of black and white soldiers); and second, a sense of affiliation between African American "liberators" and "Asiatics" in a white-supremacist world. Figure 5 courtesy of the Australian War Memorial; Figure 6 courtesy of the *Chicago Defender*.

Robert Samuels, complains that "the peckerwoods in this Jim Crow Army [are] turning Bainbridge into Georgia" (414)—a succinct indictment of what Stecopoulos calls the "racial assumptions informing the state's role in making domestic southern and global southern spaces."[65] These conditions generated the conflict between black and white U.S. soldiers during March 1942, after which U.S. General Patrick J. Hurley was moved to declare that "I have never seen the racial problem brought home so forcibly as it is here in Queensland."[66]

However, the familiar U.S. (southern) "racial problem" was complicated by the Australian context. The official Army report on the events of March 1942 emphasized white American soldiers' resentment of "negro troops entering dance halls and skating rinks patronized solely by white people," and their "association with white girls on the streets of Brisbane and in houses of prostitution, the latter without definite segregation." But the report also registered that the relatively welcoming attitude of locals toward black GIs—"Negro soldiers were invited into the homes of white Australians, were taken on rides and tours around the city"—contradicted Australia's official policy of white supremacy. In 1942 General Douglas MacArthur observed that "[t]heir policy of 'white Australia' is universally here": as Kay Saunders remarks, this White Australia policy facilitated "a double process of segregation—one operating internally in the U.S. armed forces and another maintained by Australian civilian authorities."[67]

Killens portrays social (including sexual) interaction between black Americans and white Australians as well as the legal-political reality of white Australian supremacy. Solly becomes romantically involved with Celia Blake, a nurse and war widow from Bainbridge, while he and other black soldiers drink with working-class white Australian soldiers at the Southern Cross pub. None of these Australian troops object to his relationship with Celia; instead, they interrogate *American* racism. One of the Australian soldiers, Hank Dobbs, decries Samuels's belief that "the U.S.A. is going to have progressive capitalism after the war" because "our capitalists can afford to give our working people the highest standard of living in the world." Dobbs asks Samuels: "What can you afford to give your Negroes? That's what I bloody well would like to know" (386). Dobbs's friend Steve charges that "You blokes carry your white supremacy everywhere. You swaggering bawstards, you come over here and try to impose your own sick policy on your allies . . . most of you white Yankees swagger like the Nazis . . . act like they're occupying Australia. And if I were an American Negro I'd tell you all to go to blazes" (387–88). At one level, this exchange dramatizes Stecopoulos's point that "[w]hite racism and white racist violence were by no means limited to the South or to a 'dixified' U.S. military"; they were also expressed abroad via the "incipient 'empire of bases'" that included the war's Pacific theater.[68] On another level, however, Dobbs's claim to speak for the "American Negro" against "white supremacy" conveniently elides institutional racism in Australia itself. By this point, Solly and his fellow black soldiers know all too well that "dixified" U.S. military policy has been reconstructed in Australia: Solly tells Celia that "[t]he bloody MPs threw me out of two places today right here.... Not in Mississippi or Georgia—right here in dear old darling Queensland" (410). But the African American troops are also acutely aware of their host nation's "White Australia" policy, which was especially evident in Queensland, "the state with the most rigid internal segregation of Aboriginal people in the Commonwealth."[69] Yet when Samuels challenges the Australian soldiers—"What about your White Paper? What about your own colored people?"—Dobbs responds disingenuously: "That wasn't a race problem at all.... That was a labor problem" (388). Though Solly initially resists getting sucked into an argument between white American and Australian soldiers, he eventually declares that "I'm putting my money on that large minority known as colored people, three quarters of the world's population" (392). This prompts Steve to turn his fire on Solly: "You're not a Socialist. You're nationalistic and you're anti-white and you're reactionary" (392). This tense exchange can be read as a reflection of disputes over socialism and black nationalism during the early 1960s. But it also suggests how Killens's experience of a dual form of white supremacy during World War II—Jim Crow segregation in the U.S. Army and the "White Australia" policy—alerted him to the limits of an international socialist worldview, articulated by white men, that subordinated race to class, *and* the potential of a transnational antiracist, anticolonial front among "colored people."[70]

Despite being banned by the U.S. Army from socializing in Bainbridge, Solly and the other black soldiers return to the Southern Cross because, in Bookworm's words, "Goddammit, this ain't Mississippi" (425). Dobbs and other Australian soldiers declare their support for the African American troops in terms of resistance to the United States' neocolonial "occupying" of Australia: "This is still our country, I hope" (426). In a confrontation with U.S. military police, black soldier Jimmy Larker is arrested; after the black troops organize to liberate Jimmy from jail, the situation degenerates into an armed battle between a "White Army" and a "Black Army" (466–67). As James notes, this climactic sequence is comparable to a slave rebellion—the culmination of the novel's neoslavery metaphor, though the rebellion is supported by Captain Samuels (*Thunder*'s equivalent of Oscar Jefferson crossing the color line) and a select few white Australians.[71] Scotty, Grant, Bookworm, and Larker all die during the battle.

On the penultimate page of *Thunder*, in the immediate aftermath of the battle, two "Dixiefied" white troops approach Solly without weapons and declare: "We just sorry about the whole damn thing. Colored folks ain't never done us nothing" (484). For Bigsby, this scene bolsters his claim that the ideological "contradiction" already apparent in *Youngblood* becomes patently obvious as the "apocalyptic implications" of the battle "are immediately subverted by a resulting [cross-racial] brotherhood which ... seems little more than a gesture toward the Killens of 1954." That *Thunder* "ends as southern white soldiers apologize for their racist brutality" proves that "Killens cannot accept the reality of his own vision."[72] But Killens's embrace of black nationalism cannot be so easily separated from his enduring hope for interracial solidarity: as we have seen, both viewpoints can be traced back to Killens's earliest published work. Nor is an apocalyptic eschatology unique to 1960s black nationalism: it is central to the Christian theology underpinning the African American jeremiad from Frederick Douglass to Martin Luther King. Also, as Manning Marable deftly demonstrates, Malcolm X recast the "urgent emphasis on the coming apocalypse" in "the Nation of Islam's theology" to his post-Nation *political* emphasis on global "class struggle."[73] What is more, the white southern soldiers' apology is *not* the end of the scene or novel. After the two white southerners "sat down near them but apart," Solly reimagines once more his vision of a postwar "new world" by doing away with racial, regional, and national designations altogether: he envisions "build[ing] something new that was neither East nor West nor North nor South, but something new, superior to anything that ever was" (484–85). But Solly also recalls Grant's "righteous anger" and belief in colored peoples: "Perhaps the New World *would* come raging out of Africa and Asia, with a new and different dialogue." Finally, five African American soldiers approach and Solly invites them to "Sit down, mates, and make yourself at home. This is the place where the New World is" (485).

If we read postbattle Bainbridge as the "New World," it appears bitterly ironic: this world is less new (or utopian, as Gilyard sees it) than the dystopian endpoint of those racial practices that have followed Solly and his fellow black soldiers from the U.S. South to the South Pacific theater, where Jim Crow meets White Australia.[74] However, if this brave New World refers to a group of battle-scarred African Americans resituating themselves in relation to the revolution "raging out of Africa and Asia," then it mediates in more optimistic fashion the embrace of postcolonial and pan-African struggle by African American activists during the period in which the novel was written. If we consider too that the black soldiers are accompanied in battle by white Australian troops and a New York Jewish captain (Samuels) who saves Solly's life, it suggests that "Killens's 1960s spin on liberation" might yet include a "multiracial and socialist" dimension.[75]

From "Downsouth-Upsouth" to *Black Southern Voices*

In the tumultuous years following the publication of *Thunder*, Killens continued to explore the dialectic between interracial class-based solidarity and global black liberation. In May 1964 Malcolm X returned to New York from a five-week trip to Egypt, Saudi Arabia, Nigeria, Ghana, Morocco, and Algeria; the following month Malcolm officially launched the Organization of Afro-American Unity (OAAU) and asked Killens to coauthor the OAAU's "Statement of Basic Aims and Objectives."[76] By now Malcolm's worldview cleaved closely to Killens's own vision of black nationalist internationalism: following Malcolm's break with the Nation of Islam and *hajj*-inspired embrace of "the possibility of solidarity with white allies," the OAAU was also "pointedly anticapitalist and more global." As Gilyard notes, there are clear correspondences between *Thunder*, the OAAU statement, and some of the essays that Killens included in *Black Man's Burden*, published on New Year's Day 1966.[77] *Black Man's Burden* reaffirmed in nonfictional form Killens's emphasis on black diasporic struggles at regional (downsouth), national (upsouth), and transnational (Global South) scales. Bookended by essays emphasizing how "Africa and Asia got up off their knees and threw off the black man's burden" of "slavery and colonialism," *Black Man's Burden* figures "the Freedom Movement" in the United States as part of this global, postcolonial struggle because it "will tear the fences down and bring this country into the family of mankind. This, too, is a part of the Black Man's Burden." But Killens also reiterates his hope for cross-racial solidarity at the regional scale: "the poor white Southerner will have everything to gain on that great-getting-up-morning and nothing to lose, save his 'whiteness' ... the poor white man and his black brother will be able to come together and demand a higher standard of living for everybody."[78] Notwithstanding Harold Cruse's attack on Killens's "contradictory" and "middle-class, Left-tinged conformity" in *The Crisis of the Negro Intellectual* (1967), Killens himself saw no inherent contradictions between his support for Black Power, his enduring hope for downsouthern solidarity between working-class whites and blacks, and his belief that "the American Negro can be the bridge between the West and Africa-Asia."[79]

In February 1965 Killens himself turned south again to become writer-in-residence at Fisk University. Killens organized numerous conferences on black issues and mentored a new generation of black southern authors, most notably Knoxville native Nikki Giovanni. At Fisk, Killens also finished both *Black Man's Burden* and his third novel, '*Sippi* (1967). Though a lesser work than *Youngblood* and *Thunder*, '*Sippi* sustained Killens's emphasis on the simultaneously regional, national, and global scales of the black liberation struggle. The novel begins with a prologue set in Wakefield County, Mississippi, during the immediate aftermath of the May 1954 *Brown* decision but stresses too *Brown*'s significance for world-historical change "[f]rom Johannesburg to Birmingham, from Rangoon to Ouagadougou, from Timbuktu to Lenox Avenue."[80] Because '*Sippi* spanned the years after World War II to the present of the novel's publication, critics have seen it as "virtually a sequel" to *Youngblood*; Killens's third novel also recalled his first by moving back and forth between the rural South and urban North.[81] Like *Youngblood*, *'Sippi* sometimes emphasizes a sense of spatial and temporal dissonance between North and South, especially as experienced by protagonist Chuck Othello Chaney: "New York City seemed a million miles away in time and space. He should have gone there and forgotten 'Sippi" (373). Yet Chuck comes to believe, like Jim and Johnny Kilgrow in *Lower Than the Angels*, that the rural South is ground zero in a *national* "revolution" for civil rights and Black Power. Chuck's position here contrasts with Cruse's contemporaneous view that "the final solution of the race question in the United States will be in the North not the South. True revolutions are never settled in the hinterlands, or more precisely, the more backward regions of any nation."[82] As before in Killens's work, upsouth and downsouth cannot be so easily separated: resolving to return to Wakefield County to help locals organize, the university-educated Chuck tells black bourgeois New Yorker Sherry Kingsley that "you and I both will be in the midst of the volcano when it erupts. You in New York City, and me in Mississippi" (327).

In another echo of *Youngblood*, *'Sippi* explores how southern racial demagoguery divides and conquers black and white labor. State senator Roger Johnson declares that "If you admit a nigger is your equal, then you got to give him equal pay for equal work. You take away the poor peckerwood's white superiority, and you got to give him some other kind of compensation.... Can you imagine how powerful the damn labor unions would be in Mississippi if niggers and peckerwoods got together? How come you think all that new industry is coming down here from the North?" (311–12). But by the mid-1960s, even paternalist white planter Charles Wakefield can see what Solly Saunders, a fellow "war hero" (3) of the Pacific theater, perceived twenty years earlier: the potential strength of global nonwhites. Wakefield counsels Johnson: "It's world power we're negotiating now.... Africa, Asia.... We need markets, man. We need political influence on a world scale. And the world is colored, therefore we got to at least pretend to be fair to our colored people." Yet Wakefield remains confident that the power of the white southern ruling class can be sustained beneath the superficial appearance of reform because the nation itself offers a model of institutionalized inequality: "[M]ake the South like the North. And niggers sure haven't got any power up there, and everybody knows it" (312–13). As *'Sippi* concludes, it is the activist vision of local black leader David Woodson—an apotheosis of Killens's black male heroes and a cross between Malcolm and Martin Luther King—that emerges as the clearest challenge to this white supremacist changing same. Woodson is "Northernized" and has "been to Mother Africa, the land of their ancestors" (108) but remains rooted as a "black son of Mississippi," poised to radicalize blacks downsouth and upsouth. Woodson gestures to the possibility of labor-based cross-racial solidarity but relates it to a "renaissance of black consciousness" (411) in the rural

South: "White poor folks have everything to gain from our struggle for Black Power, because one of our aims is to fight a last-ditch struggle with poverty" (419). Like the post-*hajj* "Brother Malcolm... our black Messiah" (413), Woodson welcomes the contribution of those "tremendous white folks in the Movement" but insists that "the main thrust must come from the black and disinherited," "the black brotherhood from Watts to Mississippi" (358). The novel climaxes with Woodson's assassination in Wakefield County: a more explicitly "apocalyptic" conclusion than to either *Youngblood* or *Thunder* and an eerie foreboding of King's murder in Memphis in April 1968. The brief epilogue, like the *Brown*-invoking prologue, situates local events on a "world scale" as Woodson's death prompts "[o]utraged demonstrations everywhere, especially in the colored nations of black Africa and brown Asia." It also generates "[p]itched battles between black and white Americans in the rice paddies of Vietnam" (431)—a bleak reprise of the Battle of Brisbane/Bainbridge, and a premonition of the violence that broke out between black and white U.S. soldiers in Vietnam following King's assassination.

Killens's later novels moved in other directions. His Pulitzer-nominated satire *The Cotillion* (1971) takes place in New York among the black bourgeoisie; he published young-adult novels about Denmark Vesey (1972's *Great Gittin' Up Mornin'*) and John Henry (1975's *A Man Ain't Nothing But a Man*); and he worked for many years on a novel about Alexander Pushkin (*Great Black Russian*) that appeared posthumously. The FBI continued to monitor Killens, registering his continuing interest in a distinctly downsouthern version of black nationalism: a July 1972 FBI report remarked that Killens had sent a hundred dollars to "the Republic of New Africa for deposit in the New African Prisoner of War Fund in Jackson, Mississippi." The New Orleans–based RNA, the report warned, sought "to establish an independent black nation within the United States, demanding the States of Alabama, Georgia, Louisiana, and Mississippi, and $10,000 per black citizen for reparations."[83] At the time of his death, Killens was working with Jerry Ward on the anthology *Black Southern Voices*, including an introduction which reiterated that "Macon, Georgia, where I was born is downSouth, New York City, to which I escaped, is upSouth. And the only difference is the sugar-coating"; Killens also continued to emphasize the cultural links between the U.S. South and the wider world, especially black southerners' "African roots." For all Killens's various attractions to labor-based cross-racial activism, black nationalism, pan-Africanism, and postcolonialism, he consistently insisted that "[a]s the South goes, so goes the nation," and that "Black Down-Southern Voices" could and should "broaden and deepen the literary picture of this nation, [and] promote a deeper understanding of... the world at large."[84] Killens's unjustly neglected body of work still has much to teach us about "the nuanced inseparability of North and South"—as well as U.S. South and Global South—"in any fruitful model of American cultural studies."

CHAPTER 4

The North–South Axis of Race, Class, and Migration in Russell Banks's Fiction

In a 2007 article, Anthony Hutchison offered this opening gambit: "Aside from William Faulkner it is difficult to think of a white twentieth-century American writer who has negotiated the issue of race in as sustained, unflinching and intelligent a fashion as Russell Banks."[1] It might seem an inflated claim when, as J. J. Wylie observed in a 2000 interview with Banks, "there doesn't seem to be much scholarly attention being paid to your work." Even following the 1997 film adaptations of Banks's novels *Affliction* (1989) and *The Sweet Hereafter* (1991), there was only a moderate upturn in scholarship. This relative paucity of critical attention hardly testifies to the range and power of Banks's output during a remarkably prolific career. Banks himself speculated "that the main problem was—and it may still be—that I didn't fit into any easy categories or niches that were the conventions at the time for studying fiction."[2] Certainly reviewers and critics have struggled to schematize Banks's vast and varied oeuvre: although during the 1980s Banks's fiction moved away from the experimental postmodernism that characterized some of his earliest stories and novels, it continued to subvert the conventions of realism. But scholars have also failed to fully account for the extent to which the drama and drive of Banks's writing derives from his conviction that "the collision of races, Africans and Europeans, colliding on the American continent" constitutes the "master story" of not just the United States but the hemisphere as a whole.[3] In pursuing this master story, Banks's literary geography has ranged across the United States and the (black) Atlantic world, from New England via Florida to Haiti, Jamaica, and (in 2004's *The Darling*) Liberia. Such expansive shifts across and between regional and national boundaries, within and between books, have stymied critical attempts to locate Banks as, for example, a "New England writer": a tempting designation, given that Banks was born in Newton, Massachusetts, and grew up in New England. Tellingly, though, Banks's books have repeatedly returned to the U.S. South—especially Florida—as a kind of ground zero for "the collision of races" with which his work is so concerned. Hence, though Banks is even less obviously a "southern writer" than a New England one, his work and worldview is especially germane to *Where the New World Is* and my project of resituating the U.S. South at various transregional and transnational scales.

By the mid-1990s, some reviewers and interviewers were beginning to discern the geographical heterogeneity of Banks's fiction. Rob Davidson put it to Banks that his collected fiction was "not a Yoknapatawpha County. It's New York, New Hampshire, Florida, Haiti, Jamaica, and the Caribbean ... a 'global village.'" Banks acknowledged that "most of it is set in the far northeastern part of the United States, or the Caribbean and south Florida" before elaborating that, rather than following "the east-to-west flow of culture from Europe to North America," his work moved along a "north–south axis." Banks stressed that "the flow has changed, to Hispanic-American and Caribbean-American culture moving north and south. You can see it. It's not just reflected in the culture and language, it's reflected in the economics, too." He pointedly added that this orientation "is not unfamiliar to Latino-American writers" or "African-American writers, either, that north–south axis.... Toni Morrison has got a lot more in common with Carlos Fuentes and Gabriel García Márquez than with the novelists of Eastern Europe."[4] Banks's attention to this intertextual, hemispheric "axis" recalls Fuentes's famous affirmation that Faulkner "is both yours and ours, and as such, essential" to Latin American writers.[5] It echoes too Édouard Glissant's insistence that Faulkner's fiction is connected within "the compass of Creolization" to that of García Márquez and Alejo Carpentier as well as Morrison and Alice Walker: a constitutive part of that "poetics of Relation" permeating the postplantation cultures of "the southern United States, the Caribbean islands, the Caribbean cost of Latin America, and the northeastern part of Brazil."[6] Yet despite Banks's suggestive remarks, no critic has properly considered the role of this "north–south axis" in his life and work, or the location of the U.S. South on that axis.

In this fourth chapter, I assess Banks's engagement with the U.S. South not as an exceptional region but rather via a (partly autobiographical) poetics of relation to both the nation and the "extended Caribbean." I concentrate primarily on *Continental Drift* (1985), especially its representation of Florida's liminal location on a north–south axis extending from New Hampshire to Haiti. In particular, I unpack the novel's depiction of transregional and transnational patterns of migration to Miami and how, as Jessica Adams puts it in *Just Below South* (2007), the "history of interactions between Caribbean islands and southern states" has continued with "twentieth- and twenty-first-century Haitian migration to southern cities like ... Miami."[7] By the early 1980s, Banks was convinced that Miami had become "the center of the New Immigration, and the resulting collision among cultures, languages, races, and classes will characterize and eventually define American life in the next century."[8] But rather than pursuing the comparisons with Faulkner—also noted by poet Dave Smith in a blurb claiming that *Continental Drift* was "a Southern novel by a Yankee"⁹—I seek to demonstrate how Banks can be read in (a poetics of) relation to another writer who explored Florida on a north–south axis and hemispheric scale: Zora Neale Hurston. Through *Continental Drift*'s vivid depiction of Haitian migration to Florida, Banks extends Hurston's earlier emphasis on the migratory routes between the U.S. South and the Caribbean; there are further echoes of Hurston in Banks's depiction of working-class southward migration to Florida from *within* the United States. First, however, it is worth adumbrating Banks's own encounters with the U.S. South and Caribbean, and their impact on the hemispheric shift in his fiction prior to *Continental Drift*. Relevant here is Banks's most autobiographical novel, *The Book of Jamaica* (1980), the book that, as Banks later noted, "makes clear what direction I'm going to go in for the rest of my career" and serves as an intriguing intertext to Hurston's *Tell My Horse: Voodoo and Life in Haiti and Jamaica* (1938).¹⁰

Russell Banks's North–South Axis:
From New England via Florida and North Carolina to Jamaica

Following a fraught upbringing in a fractured New England working-class family, Russell Banks spent his defining years in the U.S. South. In 1958 eighteen-year-old Banks "hitchhiked south from [his] mother's home in Massachusetts" with a course set for Cuba: he was determined "to join Fidel Castro and Che [Guevara] ... and put my poor shoulder to the wheel of revolution."¹¹ But beatnik Banks got no further than St. Petersburg and suburban Lakeland, where he worked as a furniture mover, department store window-dresser, and shopping mall shoe salesman. Following a brief spell in Boston, Banks turned south again to a trailer park on Islamorada Key and a rooming house in Key West, "a Caribbean kind of town ... a last jumping off place before you got into the Caribbean."¹² If not revolutionary in the Cuban sense, these formative experiences in Florida began to shape Banks's understanding that race defined the "master story" of U.S. history: "travelling into the South in my teens to Florida" made it "transparently obvious that we are a racialized society in an inescapable way."¹³

This became even more evident to Banks following his enrollment at the University of North Carolina in 1964: "It wasn't really until Chapel Hill that race became a meaningful part of my sense of self and sense of American history."¹⁴ As Banks recalled during a return to the UNC campus in 2000: "When I walked into Chapel Hill I walked into the middle of the civil rights movement.... [I]t was very hard, especially if you were in the South, not to get caught up in the civil rights movement." Chapel Hill was also the crucible in which Banks's fledgling career as a writer was forged as students rebelled against the English Department's emphasis on "people who were (it looked like to us) Southern writers for one thing, and formalists for another"—apparently a reference to the influence of erstwhile Agrarian converts to the New Criticism. Initially, Banks's exposure to "Southern writers" in the classroom and the Civil Rights movement outside served to compound his sense of regional difference. In an early story entitled "The Adjutant Bird," the narrator muses that "I'm a New Englander here in the South with my wife who also happens to be Southern.... I'm thinking to myself how she doesn't know how different we are." Banks later observed that though this apprentice story retreated into "a regional identification... exacerbated, perhaps, by living in the South at that time," it prompted him "eventually to reject the identification of myself in regional terms, or in strictly—and parochially—narrow cultural terms."[15] Never again would Banks identify only as "a New Englander" or figure southernness as simply "different" or distinctive: though his mature fiction focuses on local and regional identities, it consistently situates them at national or transnational scales.

After graduating from Chapel Hill in 1967, Banks returned to New Hampshire and established himself as a teacher and writer. But Banks's personal history of southward migration was far from finished: in 1975 he finally made it to the Caribbean. Following two short visits to Jamaica, he returned with his family for a prolonged residential stay (from May 1976 to September 1977), funded via various grants and fellowships. Banks explained this move to Jamaica as an enactment of his increasing "north–south orientation" but admitted that while "I found myself absolutely fascinated by the people who surrounded me... I couldn't penetrate. I couldn't eliminate my whiteness, my American-ness, my middle-class-ness."[16] Banks was forced to recognize that such profound differences of race, class, nationality, economics, and culture could not be overcome: shucking off one's "regional identification" as a "New Englander" in North Carolina was one thing, but shedding one's white male American privilege in Jamaica was another. Yet precisely this "gradual slow accumulation of understanding about race and racial difference and class" compelled him to interrogate the effects of such social categories, not least the power of (his own) whiteness within "a color-defined society [where] we are invited to think that white is not a color."[17] This process of recognition transformed Banks's fiction: he later identified "an evolutionary jump between *Hamilton Stark* [1978] and *The Book of Jamaica*" because "I couldn't avoid being implicated by race and that's one of the themes" of the latter book: "you can't escape your skin color in a racialized society, even if you're white."[18]

Black/White/Southern/American Visions:
Hurston's *Tell My Horse* and Banks's *The Book of Jamaica*

The Book of Jamaica traces the experiences of a white American writer and professor at "New England College" after he moves to Jamaica in the mid-1970s.[19]

His first stay, from December 1975 to February 1976, is initially as a "tourist" with his family, having "read two or three travel books" about Jamaica.[20] But already during this first visit he becomes interested in "investigating the living conditions and habits of the Maroons" (3), a remote community in the Cockpit country around "Nyamkopong" that originated in the late seventeenth century with runaway slaves' resistance to British rule, and endured through the two Maroon wars of the eighteenth century. Returning to Jamaica in April 1976, the writer is distracted by the local legend of American movie star Errol Flynn's possible involvement in the murder some years previously of a black Jamaican woman: the myth of "Captain Blood" becomes the focus of the first of four sections that make up the writer's "book of Jamaica."[21] He and his family return to Jamaica again in fall 1976, funded by a "large private foundation" to "continue your work in the writing of fiction" (202); by this point, however, the writer has become disillusioned with his unfinished novel and considerably more enthused by his investigation of the Maroons.

The writer at first believed it would be possible to transcend transparent differences of nationality, race, and economics. He wryly recalls how "I told my wife and children, we will not be tourists. This time we will not even have to *see* any tourists! We will see only the *natives*! They will be black, of course, and mostly slender, smiling, and poor—but when they learn that we are not tourists, they will be honest, and they will like us, because even though we are rich and white, we are honest and we like them." The family's obvious differences from the "natives" are expressed in their rental of a luxury house near Montego Bay through the writer's connection with Upton West, an American friend from "our days at Chapel Hill" (74). West's father is "a retired British army captain" while his mother "dabbles in real estate" in Jamaica and "trains the help in her own house" (75). The symbolically named Wests, who embody the continuity of British colonial and American neocolonial exploitation of Jamaica, had in turn put the narrator in touch with the Churches, owners of the rental property. The Church family "had done exceptionally well . . . because from 1965 to 1975 there had been a building boom along the north coast of Jamaica, as increasing numbers of Americans and Canadians decided to invest capital in the construction of three- and four-bedroom villas that could be rented to other Americans and Canadians" (76). As Robert Niemi has observed, the writer is initially "willfully obtuse about his accommodations" at a time when Prime Minister Michael Manley's socialist government "had determined to eliminate . . . capital and capitalists" through policies that "destabilize[d] a 300-year-old status quo based on, in the narrator's words, 'relentless racial oppression and economic exploitation.'"[22] The writer's first interactions with "the *natives*" are with "the help": the Churches' black housekeeper and driver (78), and only after witnessing verbal abuse of a black waiter during a dinner party at the West home does the writer decide to "despise the Wests and the

Churches and all the people who resembled them, and to love a people [the Maroons] I might never understand and definitely would never become" (122). Yet even on his return trip in April 1976 to study the Maroons, the writer still, "like most Americans, believed more in the essential sameness among people than in their difference. I thought I could learn to know what it was like to be a Maroon. I could not then see any conflict between that belief and my ambition to replace a point of view with a vision" (26).

It is worth considering this white American male writer's "vision" alongside Hurston's perspective on Jamaica and the Maroons in *Tell My Horse*. For if (as we saw in chapter 1) scholars have both censured and celebrated Hurston for situating black southern folk culture in relation to the Caribbean, in *Tell My Horse* her subject positions as black, southern, female, folklorist, and author are inseparable from, and perhaps superseded by, her identification with U.S. neocolonial power. Hurston begins by observing that because pocomania—"a mixture of African obeah and Christianity enlivened by very beautiful singing"—is "important to a great number of people in Jamaica, so perhaps we ought to peep in on it a while."[23] From the opening, then, Hurston's point of view interpolates the reader: that "I" so soon segues into "we" is an early sign of how, as Leigh Anne Duck notes, "Hurston identifies herself insistently with non-Caribbean readers, configuring herself as the agent of an outsider group's gaze."[24] When Hurston adumbrates the British colonial history of Jamaica, and especially the country's alien (to her) system of racial classification, her subject position as an *African* American outsider comes to the fore. She admits that Jamaican racial categories constitute "a curious spectacle to the eyes of an American Negro" and that her own use of "the word black ... in the American sense" does not accord with that of her Jamaican hosts (7)—a subtle gesture of recognition that the "one-drop" model of U.S. racial classification, which (as we saw in chapter 2) spread from the South to become "the nation's definition, generally accepted by whites and blacks alike," is not easily applicable beyond U.S. borders.[25] That Hurston's (African) American identity distinguishes her from the people she invites her fellow outsiders/readers to "peep in on" is also evident in the second chapter, during which she recounts her participation in a curry goat feast on the Magnus banana plantation in St. Mary Parish. Here Hurston's national-racial difference is compounded by her gender as she stresses that the locals "did something for me there that has never been done for another woman. They gave me a curry goat feed" (11); she also recounts the misogynistic view of "American women" advanced by "a young man of St. Mary's" the following morning (16). Yet it is precisely Hurston's privileged status as an American, above her more marginal identity as a woman, that facilitates her presence at the plantation feast in the first place.

In the third chapter, Hurston's identity as American becomes not merely apparent but ascendant. She recounts her time spent with the Maroons in the village of Accompong, culminating with a hog-hunting expedition. Here especially we see how, to adapt Rosemary Hathaway's observations about *Their Eyes Were Watching God*, Hurston's book "becomes the reader's Baedeker (or travel guide) to the unfamiliar; the author ... becomes the tour guide."[26] This is immediately evident from the second-person address of the chapter's opening sentence: "If you go to Jamaica you are going to want to visit the Maroons at Accompong" (21). To be sure, Hurston expresses respect and awe for the proud history of Maroon culture: "Here was the oldest settlement of freedmen in the Western world, no doubt. Men who had thrown off the bands of slavery by their own courage and ingenuity. The courage and daring of the Maroons strike like a purple beam across the history of Jamaica." But Hurston then turns her gaze (metaphorically if not literally—she seems to be looking south rather than north) away from this proud Maroon history to another even more awesome force: the modernity and manifest destiny of the United States:

> And yet as I stood there looking into the sea beyond Black river from the mountains of St. Catherine, and looking at the thatched huts close at hand, I could not help remembering that a whole civilization and the mightiest nation on earth had grown up on the mainland since the first runaway slave had taken refuge in these mountains. They were here before the Pilgrims landed on the bleak shores of Massachusetts. Now, Massachusetts had stretched from the Atlantic to the Pacific and Accompong had remained itself. (22)

John Lowe argues that here Hurston enacts not only "a wry displacement of the myth of the Puritan origins of the American self, but also an attempt to rupture the artificial chronological boundaries of the Americas."[27] However, this simultaneously temporal and geographical shift in Hurston's gaze, from the "very primitive" Maroon settlement to a metonymically modern and expansive (rather than colonial-era and Puritan) Massachusetts, is implicated in the worldview of a U.S. neo-imperialism that stretches "from the Atlantic to the Pacific" and beyond, including both Jamaica and—as we see in the second section of *Tell My Horse*—Haiti, which was occupied by the U.S. military from 1915 to 1934. Hurston's subsequent move, as she goes from observing authentic Maroon customs to actively designing and directing the construction of Accompong's first stove, also seems like a distinctly colonial gesture (23). Eve Dunbar argues that *Tell My Horse* renders the Maroon community as "a failed civilization that has made little progress beyond its early freedom" whereas Hurston herself personifies the "modernity" of the United States, and that the stove-building scene exhibits that "unmistakable amount of U.S. nationalism and ethnocentrism" which critics usually identify with *Tell My Horse*'s much longer section about Haiti.[28] Hurston could not always extricate her anthropological participant observation from how, as John Muthyala puts it, "Europe and North America have historically defined ... the exotic and barbaric native and the 'third world'" as "in need of progress and modernization."[29]

Hurston concludes the chapter by recounting her participation in the hog hunt, a traditional Maroon custom that she instigates herself: "I kept on talking and begging and coaxing until a hunting party was organized" (31). Describing the hunt, Hurston seems to enact another shift from ethnographic observation of the custom to participant immersion in it: she goes from "stumbl[ing] along with my camera and note book" (32) to recounting how on "the second day ... I lost my Kodak somewhere. Maybe I threw it away" (33). In a southern literary context, this scene anticipates Ike McCaslin removing his watch and compass as "he relinquished completely" to the wilderness in Faulkner's "The Bear" (1942).[30] By this point, though, Hurston's identity as an (African) American outsider and tour guide—albeit an unusually engaged and perceptive one—is too pronounced to be sloughed off in the "monstrous" landscape of Cockpit country. As we saw in chapter 1, much of Hurston's writing during the 1930s revealed previously understudied continuities between the black diasporic cultures of the U.S. South and the Caribbean. However, in Hurston's book of Jamaica and Haiti, her "vision" as a black southern female participant-observer in and of the New World's African diaspora is inextricable from another identity as "American": a citizen of that "mightiest nation" represented by the hard power of Massachusetts, rather than the softer, syncretic cultural forms of south Florida or New Orleans.[31]

In *The Book of Jamaica*, the white male writer's more sustained engagement with the Maroons at Nyamkopong (a thinly veiled fictionalization of Accompong) forces a recognition of how *his* privileged identity as American profoundly mediates—and both enables and disables—his relationship to and representation of Jamaica. Before his first visit to Nyamkopong, Banks's narrator begins to relate his rudimentary research into the Maroons to his ideological rationale for "going as a social scientist, to collect evidence that would support my own idea about history, race and economics." He asks himself: "Why can't I simply *see* them, talk to them, engage myself with them the same as I do with my neighbors in New Hampshire?" (87). The writer resolves to "neutralize the effects of my training somewhat" to "destroy my point of view, all my points of view" and "replace a point of view with a vision" (26). This attempt to strip away his academic gaze inverts Hurston's declaration in *Mules and Men* (1935) that only by taking up "the spy-glass of Anthropology" under the scholarly guidance of Franz Boas could she both "see myself like somebody else" and fully discern her "native surroundings" in south Florida.[32] But unlike Hurston in Eatonville, the writer in Jamaica has not grown up with "these people" as his "neighbors"; like Hurston in Accompong, he remains an outsider.

Both in his everyday life in Jamaica and in his book of that life, the writer initiates various narrative strategies to circumvent his sense of not being able to "see" his Jamaican "neighbors." As a skilled reader as well as writer, he discerns that a popular history, Carey Robinson's *The Fighting Maroons* (1969), is unreliable because it is "by a white Jamaican for an audience of white readers" (81): less an account of its titular subjects than "the historical, racial and economic superiority of the people the Maroons had fought against" (86). Figuring himself as a reader once again—or as a kind of postmodern geographer—he tries during his first journey to Nyamkopong to read the landscape itself on the premise that "topology expresses its own geologic past and can be read as a text." Initially he admits that "this text was backward to me" because "the land forms were the expression of female forces" rather than "male processes" resulting from "eruption or penetration" (92–93). Yet the writer subsequently celebrates this gendered vision of (in Annette Kolodny's seminal phrase) "the lay of the land" as evidence that he has moved *beyond* a masculinist-tourist's gaze: "for me to perceive it [the 'female' topology] as 'natural' required an enormous shift in what had seemed natural up to now, natural and therefore inevitable. The tourist in me took another step backward, and the traveler came forward one" (93).[33]

The writer's own text takes on various points of view in its formal attempt to negotiate the national, racial, and economic dynamics that complicate his relation to the nation and its people. The first two sections are told mostly in the first person, but the second section briefly shifts into the second person, requiring the reader to imaginatively identify with a Maroon father whose daughter's partner yearns to "go up to Virginia and pick apples for six weeks and earn enough cash money to ... break this terrible cycle. He doesn't want to be a subsistence farmer like you all his life" (141–42). As Niemi remarks, "Though Banks's professor is conversing with his alter ego, the reader can scarcely avoid being interpolated into the narrative by the force of the direct address, *you*."[34] Such a socially conscious second-person address seems to contrast with Hurston's interpolation of her non-Jamaican reader as a potential tourist, yet such hypothetical scenes and characters—the anguished father, the daughter-*cum*-single mother, the migrant worker, the frustrated subsistence farmer—retain the "abstract" typology of social science (or ethnography) that the writer is trying to overcome. In the third and fourth sections, the narrative shifts again, from the first to the third person. This formal shift in perspective may serve to obviate any suspicion that the writer's own "book of Jamaica" has thus far been received as "by a white [American] for an audience of white readers." The writer is acutely aware that despite his musings on "vision" transcending "point of view" and becoming a "traveler" rather than a "tourist," the first-person narrative form may have encouraged "touristic reading" of the Maroons. (As we saw in chapter 1, this is Hathaway's term for "the fallacious practice whereby a reader assumes, when presented with a text where the writer and the group represented in the text are ethnically different from herself, that the text is necessarily an accurate, authentic, and authorized representation of that 'Other' cultural group."[35]) As it turns out, the third and fourth sections of *The Book of Jamaica* cannot formally transcend the writer's own racial and national subject position. Like Hurston's self-identification as an "American" or "American Negro," the repeated third-person references to the writer as "the American" and "the white American" amplify his difference from the Maroons, who refer to him as "Johnny": not his real name, but a generic sobriquet they apply to "all nice white men" (275). The Maroons may accept and utilize "Johnny's" presence, but their nickname reminds the writer and his readers that he is still an outsider.

Echoing Hurston's journey to Accompong, the writer's account of his first visit to Nyamkopong reveals that his "vision" remains distinctly American. However, it also reveals his *white* American anxieties about racial identity as well as his attempts to work through disturbing homologies between a putatively "innocent" American "point of view" (47) and a neocolonial gaze more often associated with European history and culture. Entering the Maroon village for the first time, the writer compares himself with Paul Gauguin in Tahiti, E. M. Forster in India, and Isak Dinesen in Africa. But in contrast to those twentieth-century European artists, apparently negotiating colonial contexts with (complacent) self-assurance about their own superiority vis-à-vis the natives, Banks's writer experiences both an anxious form of blindness and an eerie sense of his own invisibility. Like Hurston, he attributes this sensation to an uncanny *difference* from U.S. race relations; in this case, however, it is the conspicuous *absence* of African Americans that accentuates the white male's sense of displacement from the United States, even as he recognizes that his fearful perception of the Maroons is deeply rooted in American racial attitudes:

> I saw and heard it all, and yet, throughout, it seemed that I saw and heard nothing... they did not see me and hear me the way a black American would. Even so, I could not stop viewing them as if I were in... Detroit or Roxbury or Watts. And that is why I was afraid, afraid the way only a white American can be afraid and the way Gauguin and Forster and Dinesen were never afraid. They may not have known precisely where they were when they found themselves in Tahiti, India or Africa, but they knew that they were not in Paris, Cambridge or Copenhagen.... A white American, I was blind, and lost. (99)

This eerie entry into Nyamkopong is eased when the writer meets Terron Musgrove, a Maroon and Rastafarian who has lived and worked in Montego Bay and Port Antonio, "where the banana boats of United Fruit were loaded" (4), and who can "tell me what to 'see,' as if I could not see on my own" (101). Gratefully receiving Terron as visual and verbal translator nevertheless involves recognizing that certain neocolonial binary oppositions remain operational, and to which a "white American" is *not* innocently exceptional: "He was black and I was white; he was a Jamaican and I was a foreigner ... he was a Maroon and I a direct descendant of their enemies" (14). Terron guides the writer to the Maroon chief, Colonel Martin Luther Phelps, and a meeting that echoes Hurston's encounter with Accompong's leader, Colonel Rowe. Much as Hurston finds that she is following in the footsteps of fellow Boas mentee Melville Herskovits and "some one else [who] had spent three weeks to study their dances" (22), Banks's writer comes across "the name and address of the Canadian professor who had preceded me by about six weeks" (99). Much as Hurston describes the dispute between Rowe and the Maroon medicine man who "wanted to be the chief" and so "seized the treaty that was signed long ago between England and the Maroons" (25), Banks's writer details the "split" (131) between Phelps and "secretary of state" Colonel Wendell Mann, who jealously carries a copy of the same treaty. But the most significant comparison between *Tell My Horse* and *The Book of Jamaica* is the way in which interactions with the Maroons amplify their narrators' privileged status as Americans. Indeed, to the degree that Banks's white northern male northern writer is aware that his privileged subject position compels examination of (his own) U.S. power, he may be indebted to the black southern female author who, in *Mules and Men* and *Tell My Horse*, pioneered the deconstruction of "the 'scientific' model of anthropology" through a "more 'performance-based' model" that dramatized her role as an observer *and* participant. *The Book of Jamaica*'s reflexive meditations on the relationship between academic participant-observer and native subject, and on the relationship between fiction and nonfiction, dovetailed with anthropology's postmodern turn; Hurston, however, "seemed to recognize the fictiveness of ethnography and the ethnographic possibilities of fiction decades before the likes of [Edward] Bruner, Clifford Geertz, and James Clifford."[36] Still, those innovations—inextricable from Hurston's alertness to her own subject position as a black southern woman—did not prevent her gaze from becoming imbricated with U.S. power in and over Jamaica or Haiti.

Despite earnestly immersing himself in Maroon life, the writer/Johnny comes up against the limits of his earlier belief "more in the essential sameness among people than in their difference." Alarmed by the tension in Nyamkopong between assimilationists like Phelps "who wished to accommodate themselves with the larger, national identity" and traditionalists like Mann "who saw the Maroon people as a separate polity in Jamaica" (131), the writer and Terron travel to other Maroon villages to try to heal historical divisions. The writer dares to begin believing "with a certain arrogance" that he is no longer a "tourist," and that he has successfully dissociated himself—formally signaled by the shift to the second person—from that "white American traveling with you and Terron" (198). However, subsequent tragic events reveal not only the depth of the divide between the various Maroon villages and factions but also the failure of the writer's own (experiential and narrative-formal) attempts to detach his participation in those events from his "white American" subject position. Transporting Maroon leaders from Gordon Hall to Nyamkopong for a summit leaves "the white American's eyes... wet with tears" (248), but any chance of reconciliation between the two villages recedes as Phelps fails to greet his guests appropriately. The Gordon Hall contingent then becomes aware of Phelps's complicity with the national police when they witness the seizure and beating of a Rastafarian resident of Nyamkopong (a flagrant infringement of the treaty with the British that guaranteed the Maroons semi-autonomy, especially in matters of justice). The situation rapidly degenerates as Phelps is murdered, Terron's friend Benjie is framed, Terron warns the writer that rumors also implicate "the white American" (280), and the writer's wife ends their marriage and returns to the United States with their children in tow.

The writer's involvement with the Maroons ends in chaos when he severs a man's hand on a final ill-starred mission to Gordon Hall: conceding "I've seen everything I wanted to see" (335), he departs on a "one-way ticket for the six-fifteen flight to Miami" (336). It is a vivid, violent culmination to the way in which, as David Roche has noted, "the novel deconstructs [the writer's] universalist vision."[37] Johnny has learned just how hard it is (to quote Banks again) to "escape your skin color in a racialized society, even if you're white"—though precisely this white American privilege facilitates Johnny's escape to Miami. Here it is worth returning to the writer's earlier interest in the legend of Errol Flynn. For if the writer's prevailing identity as "the American" hinders his full immersion in Maroon life and culture, it also enables him, like Flynn, to escape the consequences of a violent act. Johnny evades justice and escapes to Miami despite severing a man's hand with a machete; in 1952 Flynn was not even questioned by the authorities about his alleged involvement in the sexual abuse and murder of the local black woman. Johnny tries to fathom Flynn's power: "This was true magic, I thought, this was obeah. The distance between the world of the wealthy and the world of the poor was so great that he who had wealth was truly a magician" (57). It is a striking image: a wealthy white American rather than a poor black Jamaican is metaphorically associated with the practice of "primitive" magic of African origin. Discussing *Tell My Horse*, Annette Trefzer argues that Hurston shows how Haitian "voodoo functions as a metaphor" so that "spirit possession" becomes an indirect verbal and performative expression of "political and revolutionary potential."[38] When the writer ponders Flynn's power in *The Book of Jamaica*, obeah functions as a metaphor for other, rather less revolutionary but no less political forms of "possession": the possession of whiteness, wealth, and neocolonial power. Like *voudon* or obeah these forms of possession appear "magical" but are in fact mystified; they serve to "distance" Flynn from Jamaican "ordinary men and women" even as he exploits them—whether through his control of land and labor or alleged sexual abuse and murder. Like the Wests and Churches of the writer's own experience, Flynn twenty years earlier was "[t]he modern epitome of the colonial ruling class."[39] Symbolically enough, Flynn's ranch was built on "the remains of [an] old sugar plantation" (52) surrounded by what Terron—a former employee of the United Fruit Company, profiting from the global trade in bananas grown on Jamaican plantations—"called 'slavery walls,' not because they had been used to pen slaves but because they had been built by slaves" (36). Johnny distances himself from the "first world" of white Jamaicans and American expatriates by invoking his "class status" as the son of "working people" (114–15), but in Johnny's departure from that world and escape to Miami, we see how he too can call upon the "magic" of wealth, whiteness, and Americanness. Banks's next novel about the north–south axis would develop the metaphorical richness of possession (and dispossession) associated with New World black faiths to critique the malignant "spirit" of an American capitalism newly centered in nominally "southern" cities like Miami.

Obsession, Possession, and Global Migration: The Narrative Form and Scales of *Continental Drift*

In 1998 Banks recalled: "Having gone through the same experiences, literally and imaginatively, that the protagonist in *The Book of Jamaica* experiences, I began to flyn my life more consciously and aggressively in racial and class terms, laying the ground on which I stood a few years later when I wrote *Continental Drift*." He added that "my obsession extended out into the entire Caribbean, including Haitian religion, history, and culture generally."[40] The genesis of *Continental Drift* can be traced more specifically to October 1981. Banks was working on a novel about the friendship between Nathaniel Hawthorne and Franklin Pierce but confided in his diary: "Facing a crisis in my work unlike any in the last 5–6 years, as I realize how politically insipid it is, how self-centered, effete, safe it all is." He asked himself: "Who *needs* such a book, especially now at the end of the 20th century?"[41] Banks was already "thinking about a novel about *refugees* . . . Set in Haiti and southern Florida" and focusing on an American who "traffics in illegal aliens" with "a charter boat out of Islamorada," when he read an article in the *New York Times* about Haitian migrants drowning off the Florida coast: the boat on which the victims were being smuggled into the United States had traveled via "an unidentified Baham island" before striking a reef and capsizing in four-foot waves. Thirty-three people died, their bodies washing ashore near Fort Lauderdale, while another thirty-four reached the shoreline only to enter a "Federal detention facility for illegal aliens."[42] Banks developed a second narrative strand that would follow a young Haitian woman as she, accompanied by her baby and teenage nephew, leaves north Haiti aboard a boat supposedly bound for south Florida. In the published novel, Vanise Dorsinville's northward migration to Miami from Haiti includes numerous traumatic experiences and detours via the Caicos Islands and Bahamas before a tragic end to the journey off the south Florida coast, as the U.S. Coast Guard spots the boat on which she and her fellow Haitians are being smuggled into Florida by the boat's white American captain, Bob Dubois. Dubois and the Jamaican mate, Tyrone James, panic and cast their human cargo overboard; Vanise is the sole survivor. This basic plot built on both the October 1981 *New York Times* story and Banks's research into the April 1980 manslaughter conviction of a Florida boat captain and Bahamian mate who, when pursued by the coast guard, forced a Haitian mother and her five children to jump into the sea off Palm Beach.[43]

However, Banks was also writing out of the larger sociopolitical context of contemporary U.S.-Caribbean relations, especially immigration. As Gilbert Muller observes, "Banks establishes the historicity of his novel at the precise time when Florida's shores were receiving armadas of boat people from Cuba and Haiti."[44] Since the 1960s, a steady flow of Haitians fleeing the presidential regimes of François "Papa Doc" Duvalier (1957–71) and his son, Jean-Claude "Bébé Doc" Duvalier (1971–86), had been entering the United States. Immigration and Naturalization Service (INS) statistics indicated that 41,670 Haitians entered the United States legally between 1972 and 1979, with an estimated 40,000 to 50,000 arriving illegally between 1972 and October 1981.[45] In spring 1980 the United States began jailing Haitian exiles or deporting them back to Haiti, where the younger Duvalier's staunch anticommunism dovetailed with U.S. Cold War foreign policy: Alex Stepick notes the glaring contrast between the "deportation of Haitians" and the "welcoming of Cubans" fleeing Fidel Castro's regime via a similar seaward route to south Florida.[46] Between October 1980 and October 1981, U.S. authorities apprehended 11,258 illegal immigrants from Haiti; as one of the *New York Times* stories that Banks used put it, "[t]he Federal Government's position is that the Haitians are economic immigrants, not political refugees."[47] Local political antipathy in Miami toward the influx of Haitians played a role too: "The INS thereafter began to expend a greater effort in controlling the flow of Haitians than was expended on nearly any other group of illegal immigrants." Many Haitians were incarcerated "in Krone detention center, described by many as a concentration camp in the middle of the Everglades swamps," and in September 1981 "the Reagan Administration ordered the Coast Guard to interdict Haitian boats loaded with illegal aliens on the high seas and return them to Port-au-Prince, the Haitian capital."[48] Banks marked a passage in another *Times* article from November 1981 reporting how "Haitian officials said relations with the United States improved greatly after an agreement was reached in September that allows American Coast Guard vessels to intercept boats suspected of carrying

Haitian émigrés to the United States and to return undocumented aliens in Haiti."⁴⁹

Banks was acutely aware of the problems involved in representing his Haitian characters: like *The Book of Jamaica*, *Continental Drift* foregrounds the narrator's subject position and its mediation by race, class, gender, and nationality. The opening "Invocation" identifies the narrator's perspective as that of "*a white Christian man*" obsessed "*with race and sex and a proper middle-class American's shame for his nation's history*." But the white American male "vision" familiar from Banks's previous novel is mediated further by the invocation of the *loa* Legba to help tell this "*American story of the late twentieth century*": "*you don't need a muse to tell it, you need something more like a loa, or mouth-man.... Let Legba come forward, then, come forward and bring this middle-aging, white mouth-man into speech again.*"⁵⁰ This narrative strategy reveals the influence of Banks's life "when I was in Jamaica and spending a lot of time in the back country with the Maroons":

> The chief had a person he called his mouth-man... the mouth-man had all the responsibility to speak.... He was a rapper. I loved the idea, I thought, now that's what I want; I want a mouth-man....
>
> With *Continental Drift* I said, OK, I'll invoke a narrator the way you invoke a loa in Haitian Voudon. Which is to say, I'll allow myself, if I can, to be in a sense possessed... so that opening invocation is literally an invocation to bring into existence, into the book the loa Legba to speak for me, Russell Banks, through the book.⁵¹

Despite this conceit of a white American male narrator becoming "possessed" by Legba, it does not resolve the problem that both the narrator and Legba might in turn "possess" Vanise's voice or colonize her consciousness; indeed, the deleterious effects of Vanise's possession by *voudon* loas becomes a theme later in the novel. But in terms of narrative form, Banks's alertness to the mediating roles of race, class, gender, and nationality resulted in a respectful distance from the interiority of a protagonist so radically different from himself and his "white Christian" narrator: "when I wrote about her [Vanise], I just tried to describe her behavior from the outside and not interpret it. I deliberately avoided that, because it seems to me that to write about the interior life of a Haitian woman is a presumptuous thing for an American white male to do."⁵² Banks's dilemma was a familiar one in U.S. southern literature: Alice Walker remarked that fellow Georgian Flannery O'Connor "retained a certain distance... from the inner workings of her black characters" and that this "seems to me all to her credit, since, by deliberately limiting her treatment of them to cover their observable demeanor and actions, she leaves them free, in the reader's imagination, to inhabit another landscape, another life, than the one she creates for them."⁵³ By contrast, Glissant charges that "Faulkner does not try to enter 'into' the mind of Dilsey" in *The Sound and the Fury* (1929) but ameliorates his criticism that "Faulkner's Blacks are conventional silhouettes" by way of a question: "Is this a way of respecting the opacity of the Other or is it the beginning of a system of apartheid?"[54] In the controversial essay "If I Were a Negro" (1956), Faulkner himself observed: "It is easy enough to say glibly, 'If I were a Negro, I would do this or that.' But a white man can only imagine himself for the moment a Negro; he cannot be that man of another race and griefs and problems."[55]

Yet it is not only Vanise whose story is told from the "outside" in *Continental Drift*. In the opening chapter, "Pissed," the novel shifts to a third-person, neo-realist form to convey Bob Dubois's deep frustration with his working-class life in Catamount, New Hampshire, "a community closed in by weather and geography" (5). Though Banks has stated that the chapters focused on Vanise are "complemented by the chapters about Bob Dubois, where it's very much a third-person subjective narrative and you're inside his experience," in a basic formal sense the third-person point of view remains "outside" Bob's consciousness too.[56] Bob's white working-class New Hampshire background does correlate with Banks's own, and moments of free-indirect discourse do take us "inside his experience." Nevertheless, any sense of being "inside" Bob's consciousness may have less to do with narrative form than the subject position of readers who are themselves white, male, and/or American, and so predisposed to empathize with Bob more than Vanise.

Banks's experimentation with narrative form and perspective is also apparent during the second chapter, "Battérie Maconnique," which begins with an extraordinary sequence that, as Muller notes, "subvert[s] the strict conventions of realistic and naturalistic fiction."[57] The point of view shifts from Bob and Elaine's decision to relocate to Florida (at the end of "Pissed") to a global perspective on migration:

> It's as if... millions of them travelling singly and in families, in clans and in tribes, travelling sometimes as entire nations, were a subsystem inside the larger system of currents and tides, of winds and weather, of drifting continents and shifting, uplifting, grinding, cracking land masses. It's as if the poor forked creatures who walk, sail and ride on donkeys and camels, in trucks, buses and trains from one spot on this earth to another were all responding to unseen, natural forces, as if it were gravity and not war, famine or flood that made them move. (34)

As reviewer John Leahy noted, here is the novel's "dominant metaphor" for "a phenomenon of human geography: the migrations of politically and economically oppressed individuals and groups across continents to seek refuge."[58] The narrator depicts migration at a global scale via a truly omniscient worldview that perceives demographic movements as analogous to "natural" meteorological or geological "forces." Yet almost immediately the narrator undercuts the analogy, identifying himself with a privileged gaze that implicates the reader, and warning against the temptation to see nonwhite, non-Western migration as "natural" rather than as the result of social, historical, and economic processes:

> Seen from above, then, the flight of a million and a half Somali men, women and children with their sick and dying beasts out of the drought- and war-shattered region of Ogaden in the Horn of Africa would resemble the movement of the Southwest Monsoon Current.... The movement of the Somalis would seem inevitable, unalterable and mindless; and because we would have watched it the way we watch weather, it would seem tragic. We could not argue over who was at fault or what should have been done; ideology would seem a form of vanity, a despicable self-indulgence. (35)

Abjuring such environmental determinism, the narrative shifts focus again: much as *The Book of Jamaica* interpolates its narrator and reader ("you") with a Jamaican migrant worker in Virginia, a switch in the referent of the pronoun ("we") morphs the narrator *and* reader into a member of an impoverished Pakistani family hoping to earn money guiding "rich Afghans down from the passes to the refugee camps" (37). The narrative then shifts continents back to the Americas, homing in on Haiti, where the first-person plural now refers to a local family anxiously anticipating a hurricane in the northwest coastal settlement of Allanche. This is the family of Vanise Dorsinville, and for the remainder of the chapter the narrator becomes Vanise's sister-in-law, the closest that *Continental Drift*'s form comes to conveying Vanise's own voice and vision. By making the character narrator "a poor, middle-aged woman with five children living in a daub-and-wattle cabin in the hill country of Haiti . . . with a husband gone off to America in a boat" (41), Banks also requires his readers to relate to the experience of Caribbean blacks connected to the United States through migrant labor patterns. Yet the "tourists from America" mentioned by Vanise's sister-in-law serve to remind readers of the pitfalls of "touristic reading": the danger that a "white American" reader receives this first-person part of the novel as (to quote Hathaway again) "necessarily an accurate, authentic, and authorized representation of that 'Other' cultural group."

Banks has commented that "I'm much more interested in humanity on a larger scale and humanity on a one-to-one scale; nothing in between seems to be able to engage my imagination."[59] The narratological and geographical shifts of the first two chapters manifest this dual concern as *Continental Drift* moves between the individual scale of Bob and Vanise's respective journeys to Florida and the global scale of (Asian and African) mass migration. But as the second chapter concludes with Vanise, her baby, and Claude departing Allanche and heading for the coast to secure passage in a fishing boat to Florida, so too the narrative begins to move along a "north–south axis." I want to turn now to the

Haitians' northward migration along that axis via a kind of circum-Caribbean "middle passage" replete with further intertextual echoes of Hurston.

The South–North Middle Passage and Crossroads: Hurston's Extended Caribbean Revisited

In her *New York Times* review of *Continental Drift*, Michiko Kakutani complained: "Because Vanise's inner life is never delineated with the care lavished on Bob's, the reader sometimes feels the author straining to use her as a metaphor for the yet unspoiled American dream."[60] Yet it is not Vanise but Claude who hastily exchanges his Haitian identity for a new faith in the American dream. Leaving Allanche aboard the fishing boat, Claude "turns away from the south and faces north" and casts aside his doubts by declaring "now we are going to America" (107). Vanise is less convinced that the United States will compensate for the loss of her life in Allanche. As the boat sails northward, Vanise perceives the physical geography of Haiti as more than merely receding: "First the village of Le Môle at the base of the green hills is devoured, then the low slopes checkered with cane fields and coconut palms go under, gone to where the dead abide, and at last the familiar dark green hills succumb. There is no known place peering back at her from the horizon, and now she faces only a point on the compass, an abstraction called south, *Adonai*, that refuses to speak to her in any voice but her own" (106). Tracing Vanise and Claude's northward journey, the narrative pans out again, spatially and temporally, to situate their migration within New World history. Vanise is wryly aligned with Christopher Columbus and Juan Ponce de León as people "who have sailed this passage north of Hispaniola"; the reader also encounters pictorial representations of what human geographers Peter Gould and Rodney White call "mental maps."[61] Columbus's colonialist mental map features "his Cathay" in the west, with Spain looming large in the east (107); it is juxtaposed with Vanise's map, in which Haiti to the south is figured as bigger than the United States (metonymically represented by Florida, much as Massachusetts stood for Hurston's "modern" and "mightiest" nation) to the north. Vanise's mental map suggests her continued sense of Haiti as home, albeit one that is ominously dematerializing into "an abstraction called south." Yet Vanise adapts her map to the contingencies of the harrowing process of northward migration. When Vanise, Claude, and the baby are left by the traffickers on North Caicos, some six hundred miles south of Florida, Vanise has the resources to remap the situation: "As she walks, her map gets extended ahead of her to the horizon.... Her map is a living, coiling and uncoiling thing ... a process, the kind of map you must keep moving into, if you want to read it" (114). Vanise enacts another cartographic practice, stopping at a crossroads and drawing a compass in the dirt: "to the east, *À Table*; to the west, *Dabord;* in the north, *Olande*; and in the south, *Adonai*." Like the narrator in the opening invocation, Vanise invokes the spirit of "old Papa Legba to help them," and Claude, like the "outside" reader, is privy to Vanise's previously hidden belief in *voudon*: "He did not know that his Aunt Vanise possessed so much *rada* knowledge, that she was a *mambo*" (117). Claude is even more astonished when Legba appears in the form of a yellow, three-legged, talking dog.

Banks renders the scene in which the canine manifestation of Legba guides Vanise and Claude in much the same neorealist prose that he used to depict Bob's everyday life in the opening chapter. But the depiction of Legba also recalls Hurston: Edward M. Pavlić has attempted to "make readers attuned to West African cultural traditions" and the coded presence of the trickster deity Esu-Elegba at key moments in *Their Eyes Were Watching God*. Pavlić argues that the reference during Joe Starks's funeral to "[t]he Little Emperor of the cross-roads ... leaving Orange County as he had come—with the outstretched hands of power" is not only "an ironic tribute to the pomp and failure of Joe Starks' modern identity" but also a sly gesture to Elegba, also called (as Hurston notes in *Tell My Horse*) "Barron Carrefour, Lord of the Crossroads" (128).[62] Pavlić invokes Louisiana poet Yusef Komunyakaa's essay "Crossroads" (1996): "The crossroads is ... a place where negotiations and deals are made with higher powers. In the West African and Haitian traditions of Legba, it is a sanctified place of reflection.... There is an accrued bravery here."[63] Komunyakaa's gloss on the crossroads as a black diasporic chronotope chimes with Vanise's decision to call on the higher power of Legba; her "accrued bravery" at the North Caicos crossroads contrasts with Claude's growing fear as she deals with the dog by offering it some of their ham as a trade for its guidance. The scene's intertextuality with *Their Eyes* extends if one considers Pavlić's further claim that the rabid dog which bites Tea Cake is another manifestation of Esu-Elegba: because "Tea Cake isn't willing or able to make proper sacrifices to Esu-Elegba"—a point supplementing my own observation (in chapter 1) that Tea Cake instead submits to the possessive authority of white southern landowners—the deity exacts his revenge in the form of the rabid dog, leaving Janie to "[w]onder where he come from."[64] By contrast with Tea Cake, Vanise humbly offers herself and the ham to the *loa*. The effect of Legba's intervention is ambiguous, however: the dog leads them to sanctuary with a local man, George McKissick, who subsequently exploits Vanise sexually.

The sixth chapter traces Vanise and Claude's brutal experiences during the next stage of their northward journey, from North Caicos to Nassau: a kind of "middle passage" (188).[65] Both Vanise and Claude are raped by white and black men alike: English and Jamaican sailors as well as fellow Haitian migrants. Amid such brutality, Vanise draws ever more fervently on *voudon* to sustain her. Exemplifying Joan Dayan's point that, "for the possessed," *voudon* "is not a loss of identity but rather the surest way back to the self, to an identity lost, submerged, and denigrated,'" Vanise begins to embrace "*les Morts* from the dark side, Ghede and Baron Cimetière" (198).⁶⁶ In the Bahamian village of Elizabeth Town, which includes a shantytown populated by Haitians employed in the Nassau tourist industry (208), Vanise is pressed into prostitution by local businessman Jimmy Grabow. Rescued by the increasingly resourceful Claude, Vanise immerses herself still further in *voudon:* the chapter ends with Vanise participating in a ceremony during which she is possessed by Agwé, "the Lord of the Sea, a powerful loa, dark and masculine" who wears "the very face of history" (215). Her nephew, by contrast, adheres more firmly to his faith in the United States:

> Claude could never forget America. Not now, not after all he'd suffered.... There was an exchange that had taken place, and he'd come out with a vision.... [W]hile Vanise still looked to *les Invisibles* for definitions she could not provide herself, he was beginning to look to America for that. The loas had moved around from in front of him to the back, and in their place *America* had come forward, insisting, like the loas, on service and strategy, promising luxury and power, scolding, instructing and seducing him all at once, and in that way, as the loas had done before, creating him. (201)

The spatial metaphors of this passage echo the earlier image of Vanise and Claude departing Haiti, Claude gazing northward and "forward" to the United States while Vanise looks longingly southward and "back" to their homeland as a worldly locus of the *loas*. But the passage also stresses the parallel between Vanise's immersion in *voudon* and Claude's blind faith in his "vision" of the United States. Embarking near Nassau on the final leg of their journey to Florida, Claude and other Haitian migrants believe that they will be "realized" when they possess commodities in the United States: "[T]hey will own all the things that Americans own—houses, cars, motorcycles, TV sets, Polaroid cameras, stereos, blue jeans, electric stoves. Their lives will soon be transformed from one kind of reality, practically a nonreality, into a new and, because superior, an ultimate reality. To trade one life for another at this level is to exchange an absence for a presence, a condition for a destiny" (301). Where Vanise is possessed by the *voudon* spirits of Ghede and Agwé, Claude and the other Haitians are possessed by the idea of possession: by the commodity fetishism that is the spirit of American capitalism.

Strangers in a New World:
Southward and Northward Migration to Florida

I want to shift back now to the other pole of *Continental Drift*'s north–south axis: the Dubois family's southward migration from New Hampshire to Florida. The family's arrival in central Florida also recalls Hurston's writing: for all the apparent changes in the material landscape of trailer parks and superhighways, Florida's racialized labor relations in *Continental Drift* recall *Mules and Men*, *Their Eyes*, and Hurston's unpublished 1950s manuscripts. Bob and Elaine are shocked to witness groups of blacks "working in gangs in the orange groves, riding in the backs of trucks, mowing lawns, striding along the highways and sidewalks." Cécile Accilien has noted that "Haitian migrants have shaped the cultural landscapes of Miami and Atlanta. Yet their presence in the South remains 'strange.'"[67] Bob and Elaine's stunned exposure to immigrant black labor epitomizes a broader white southern *and* American blindness to demographic and economic realities—a willfully blinkered "vision" that continues to make "strange" the substantial presence of Haitian and other Afro-Caribbean workers. Bob and Elaine are as "blind and lost" in south Florida as the narrator of *The Book of Jamaica* was upon entering Accompong; but whereas "the white American" in Banks's previous novel could at least compare with "the way a black American would" see and be seen by him, Bob and Elaine cannot distinguish African Americans from Afro-Caribbeans. This conflation of native- and foreign-born blacks compounds the *unheimlich* sense that *they* are not merely transregional migrants but immigrants to another country: "the American blacks in the department stores and supermarkets, the Jamaicans and Haitians in the fields, the Cubans in the filling stations—these working people, who got here first, belong here, not Bob and Elaine Dubois" (55). Eerily unmoored from a regional or national sense of place, the couple, confronted by the "composite culture" of a multiethnic, circum-Caribbean population, seeks refuge in what Glissant calls the "atavistic dream" of a "homogenous population."[68] Or to put it another way—and to quote Paul Gilroy in another context—they "seek salvation by trying to embrace and inflate the ebbing privileges of whiteness." Though Bob and Elaine are themselves "working people," they sense that "racialized identification is presumably the best way to prove that they are not really immigrants at all but somehow already belong to the home-space in ways that the black and brown people against whom they have to compete in the labor market will never be recognized as doing."[69] Hence Elaine's rhetorical effort to reassert Americanness *as* whiteness, thereby redeeming Florida as a national "home-space" while rendering the black workers foreign and strange once more: "All those black people working in the fields and everything, they're not really Americans, right?" (56).[70]

That Bob and Elaine have difficulty perceiving "American blacks" as "really Americans" is partly attributable to their small-town northern background: Bob grew up in Catamount "without having known a single black person well enough to learn his or her name" (55). A few months later, working as a clerk in his brother's liquor store near Winter Haven, Bob still "hasn't yet learned to tell them [Haitians, Jamaicans, and Cubans] apart from the black Americans" (67). Hence Bob projects on to George Dill, a shy black clerk from Macon, his generalized, racialized fear that machete-wielding, ganja-smoking Jamaican gangsters are planning to rob the store and kill him (70). Yet Bob is also drawn to George's daughter, Marguerite. Bob tries to fathom this burgeoning attraction through regional and racial categories that exoticize Marguerite's otherness: he marvels that "he, Bob Dubois of Catamount, New Hampshire, has fallen in love with Marguerite Dill of Auburndale, Florida, by way of Macon, Georgia, where she was a Southern black woman married to a Southern black man" (98). Bob's imaginative poverty is also evident in his extended metaphor for their first sexual encounter: "he has a quick vision of himself as a white boat, a skiff or maybe a flat-bottomed Boston whaler, sliding easily onto the hot golden sands of a tropical beach, with dark, lush jungle ahead of him, the burning sun and endless blue sky above, and behind him, the sea, surging, lifting and shoving him up and forward onto the New World" (96). If the colonial, racial, and sexual tropes of this "vision" are predictable, it is nevertheless telling that Marguerite has been transfigured into something more than black and southern: she is now the "hot golden" breast of the New World. For Bob, sexual penetration and possession of Marguerite become a way to metaphorically *and* corporeally counter his emasculating fear that members of the black diaspora, rather than white migrants from New Hampshire, "belong" in a southern state that seems more Afro-Caribbean than Anglo-American.

Muller notes that Bob's aspirations "are cast by Banks as part of a larger demographic movement of the citizens of the Northeast seeking a new life in the nation's Sun Belt." Bob himself, however, knows only that he is "pissed" with his life in New Hampshire and believes—wrongly, it transpires—that his older brother Eddie and one-time best friend Avery Boone have remade themselves successfully by going south before him. So, though Bob may exude "working-class angst in the era of late capitalism," he never fully understands it as such.[71] Bob is skeptical about "the old life-as-ladder metaphor" that "everyone in America seems to believe in" (13), but his own southward migration reveals a residual faith in that metaphor. Hence Bob's profound frustration when his economic status and class position remains much the same in Florida as it was in New Hampshire—but now bedeviled by racial anxieties too. It is grimly ironic that the first time Bob feels any kind of connection with a black person other than Marguerite is during a holdup at the liquor store, a moment that otherwise encapsulates all of Bob's fears concerning the racial Other: "He and the man with the shotgun, the man who will kill him, are alike, Bob thinks" (102). Bob ends up killing the robber, a turn of events that bleakly foreshadows his brief encounter and connection with Haitian immigrant Claude Dorsinville.

After reencountering Boone, Bob agrees to move his family further south. Based in the Florida Keys, Bob begins to run fishing trips for northern tourists on Avery's boat, the *Belinda Blue*. Bob's enduring belief in the American dream's "life-as-ladder metaphor" is apparent when he assents to Avery's insistence that they can "get rich" (176) if Bob takes part ownership of the boat. Eventually, though, Bob discovers that Avery is heavily in debt and can only turn a profit by running drugs and smuggling Haitians into the country. Belatedly, Bob begins to see through his own ongoing faith in the dream of "trading" one life and place for another:

> even if he hadn't followed his older brother to Oleander Park and hadn't followed Ave on down to the Keys ... he'd still end up one night just as he is now, his life a useless, valueless jumble of broken plans, frustrated ambitions, empty dreams. He'd end up with nothing to trade on.
> ... It's dreams. And especially the dream of the new life, the dream of starting over. The more a man trades off his known life, the one in front of him that came to him by birth and the accidents and happenstance of youth, the more of that he trades for dreams of a new life, the less power he has. Bob Dubois believes this now. (283)

Bob perceives that Eddie and Avery too traded their lives in New Hampshire for the dream of going south to a new place and life. However, hemmed in by his dire economic situation, Bob agrees to Avery's half-baked plan to smuggle a boatload of Haitian immigrants into the Keys from the Bahamas. Here the north–south trajectory of Bob's life intersects decisively with Vanise and Claude's south–north equivalent.

As we saw in chapter 1, Janie's southward migration from Jacksonville to the Everglades gradually facilitated a circum-Caribbean connection between black southern and Bahamian migrant workers. Bob's southward migration from Oleander Park to the Keys, and his fateful journey farther south to collect the Haitians from New Providence, achieve no such connection. When Tyrone first brings the Haitians aboard the boat, Bob reflexively registers their otherness: "how astonishingly black they were, *African*, he thought.... Why do they throw away everything they know and trust, no matter how bad it is, for something they know nothing about and can never trust?" Bob fails to recognize the resemblance to his own migratory imperative in departing New Hampshire for Florida: "The way he sees himself ... he is their opposite" (305). Bob does continue to ponder the Haitians' situation, albeit through racist conceits about their primitive intuition: "He can't stop himself ... from believing that these silent, black-skinned, utterly foreign people know something that, if he learns it himself, will make his mere survival more than possible" (307). Bob comes closest to understanding the Haitians' situation and perspective when trying to communicate with Claude. Fleetingly Bob sees himself in the Other, a fellow migrant similarly seduced by a New World dream:

> Like me, Bob thinks. Like my father and Eddie too ... like all of us up in our crow's nests keeping our eyes peeled for the Statue of Liberty or the first glint off those

gold-paved streets. *America! Land, ho!* Only, like Columbus and all those guys looking for the Fountain of Youth, when you finally get to America, you get something else. You get Disney World and land deals and fast-moving high-interest bank loans, and if you don't get the hell out of the way, they'll knock you down, cut you up with a harrow and plow you under, so they can throw some condos up on top of you or maybe a parking lot or maybe an orange grove. (311–12)

It seems to be a moment of insight, one that may even go beyond those situations in *The Book of Jamaica* where the white American narrator's "gaze becomes inverted, with himself, a white man, as its object": here the white American migrant looks at a black Haitian immigrant and sees himself.[72] Yet almost immediately after Bob's apparent epiphany, the U.S. Coast Guard spots and pursues the *Belinda Blue*. Whereas Janie and Tea Cake try to save Nassau native Motor Boat from the hurricane and resulting flood, Bob and the Jamaican mate Tyrone cast their Haitian human cargo overboard to save themselves. Only one of the fifteen Haitians survives: not Claude, but his aunt Vanise.[73]

(Dis)possession, Voodoo Economics, and the Spirit of American Capitalism

I proposed earlier that whereas Vanise seeks sustenance in being possessed by the *loas* Ghede and Agwé, Claude is "possessed" by the spirit of American capitalism: a bad faith that commodity culture will enable a new identity and the (re)possession of oneself, "to exchange an absence for a presence" (301). We have subsequently seen that Bob's southward migration, "trading" his "known life" in New Hampshire for a new one in south Florida, arose out of much the same faith. Yet it is neither Claude nor Bob who most succinctly articulates the perils of possession by the spirit of capitalism. Shortly before committing suicide at his suburban house in central Florida, Eddie Dubois confesses to his younger brother: "If I can't come up with the money [to pay off his crippling debts], I'll be gone too. Repossessed, just like the fucking house and the boat and the store and everything. You didn't know that, probably. There's people can repossess people" (260). Pondering "the United States as a locus of possession—by which I mean an admixture of ownership and what we might call spirit possession," Jessica Adams posits: "Possession expresses a complex of money, fetishism, and being owned, in a sense, by what you own."[74] Eddie's expression of existential anxiety is bound up with this complex, but it can also be historicized with reference to "voodoo economics," the notorious concept coined in 1980 by Ronald Reagan's then-rival for the presidency, George H. W. Bush. Speaking the year before Banks began *Continental Drift*, Bush was scathingly critical of Reagan's advocacy of tax cuts to liberate the "free" market—though, as Keith Cartwright has observed, this model of "voodoo 'trickle-down' economics became mainstreamed as both Bushes continued the

Reagan-Thatcher free-market approach to flows of global capital increasingly unregulated and untaxed by the nation-state."[75] In Banks's novel, we encounter various characters experiencing a kind of voodoo-economic-*cum*-existential crisis in which they are so possessed by the pursuit of capital and commodities that they end up "repossessed"—dispossessed of not just what they own but of their sense of selfhood. In a telling moment aboard the *Belinda Blue*, Bob compares Claude's migrant dream with his own and concludes: "It's never a fair exchange... here I am. Only it's not me anymore" (312). Bob too has been (re)possessed, and his direct role in the death of fourteen Haitian boat people only exacerbates his alienation. That Bob is possessed by a spirit more sinister than Agwé, the Lord of the Sea, is suggested when Elaine realizes that her husband was involved in the Haitians' drowning: Elaine looks on horrified as "Bob's face comes up as if from the bottom of the sea, white, bloated, and whiskery, eyes like holes, mouth a bloodless slash" (347).

In the final chapter, Bob seeks to redeem or repossess himself by tracking down the sole survivor among the Haitian boat people. Bob turns south one last time, traveling through the Everglades to Little Haiti, "a forty-block section of the city squeezed on the west by Liberty City," the largest African American community in Miami. Decades after Hurston discovered Bahamian music and dancing in Liberty City and told Langston Hughes that Bahamian "folk lore definitely influences ours in South Fla.," the transformation since the 1960s of a previously Anglo blue-collar neighborhood into Little Haiti represents "the ongoing history of the New World" (351).[76] Having learned of Vanise's whereabouts from five Haitian-born youths, Bob tries to hand Vanise the blood money he received for transporting her and the other Haitians from New Providence: Bob hopes that, in return, Vanise can help him repossess his identity by "nam[ing] him to himself." But Vanise turns away, leaving Bob to confront the five young men who, brandishing knives, gesture for him to hand over the cash. Instead, Bob again becomes possessive of—and possessed by—the blood money: as the gang "pounce on him, stabbing at him until he falls," Bob's final words are "No! This money is *mine!*" (363).

At the end of *Continental Drift*, then, both Bob and Vanise remain "possessed" in different ways: Bob by money and Vanise by Ghede, the "dark and malicious loa of death and regeneration" (320), whom Vanise believes intervened to save her from drowning off the south Florida coast. Like Claude, his fellow believer in the spirit of capitalism, Bob dies; Vanise survives. This is not to suggest that *Continental Drift* figures *voudon* as a more authentic cultural formation that retains relative autonomy from the cash nexus. In Little Haiti, Vanise's brother Émile must pay forty dollars for the services of the local *houngan* who promises to "take her to Ghede" (323), while "Ghede" is presented as both authentic *and* artificial: "This is surely, truly, he, Brav Ghede, Baron Cimetière. This is the loa himself.... And it's a very good Ghede, too. Convincing" (326). That a subsequent exchange between the two *loas* is depicted as a theatrical dialogue—"mounted" Émile and the *houngan* taking on the roles of Agwé and Ghede respectively—enhances the sense of *voudon* as performative. There are also disturbing signs that while *voudon* provides Vanise with sanctuary, it also damages her subjectivity and agency. In Elizabeth Town, Vanise's faith in (and fear of) the *loas* facilitates her objectification and enslavement by Grabow: when Claude asks Vanise why she does not try to escape, she replies that "[t]he loas are angry with me.... So I must stay here" (205). At the end of the novel, it remains unclear whether Vanise—who has lost her baby son and nephew to the sea and who is "possessed now clearly by Ghede himself" (329)—will ever be more than "sad and empty, a shell" of the person she was (328). *Continental Drift* neither sensationalizes nor valorizes *voudon*, situating Vanise's faith in social, racial, and economic contexts:

> When you have even partial control over your destiny, you're inclined to deny that you do, because you're afraid the control will go away. *That's* superstition. But when, like Vanise, you have no control over your destiny, it's reasonable to assume that someone or something else does, which is why it's reasonable, not irrational, for Vanise to believe that the bizarre fact of her survival, her destiny now, is due to a loa's intervention, and because of the particulars, it's reasonable for her to assume that the loa is Ghede. (320–21)

When the narrator elaborates on how *voudon* "makes an impoverished, illiterate black woman's troubles the pressing concerns of the gods" (209), there is a distinct echo of *Tell My Horse*'s observation that poor Haitians utilize the spirit of Papa Guedé to bolster their own circumscribed power: "Gods always behave like the people who make them. One can see the hand of the Haitian peasant in that boisterous god, Guedé, because he does and says the things that the peasants would like to do and say" (219). Like Hurston, Banks challenges readers to rethink whatever stereotypical attitudes they might hold about voodoo/*voudon* and other non-Christian forms of spiritual faith. In 2000 Banks stated, "I wanted to redeem voudon, if I could, and take it back from the sensationalists and the racists and those who have eroticized it"; he noted further that "a Southern Baptist service," regarded as "perfectly normal" from one perspective, "from another point of view ... can look really bizarre."[77] Banks's suggestion that U.S. southern religious rituals are no more inherently "normal" than Haitian ones resonates with Trefzer's observation that in "comparing voodoo with Southern Protestantism, Hurston challenges Americans' assumptions about their own culture."[78] Hurston stressed that rituals in black southern Protestant and sanctified churches shared elements with Haitian *voudon* ceremonies: for example, the practice of "shouting" was "nothing more than a continuation of the African 'Possession' by the gods."[79]

As we have seen, however, *Continental Drift* also juxtaposes Vanise's possession by *loas* with Bob, Eddie, and Claude's possession by the spirit of capitalism, a form of possession that *dis*possesses these men of their "social memory—call it a 'spirit'": that matrix of social, historical, and cultural consciousness which ensures that, as Joseph Roach puts it, "a body [is] in some sense possessed of itself."[80] *Continental Drift*'s suggestion that white male American citizens as well as black female Haitian illegal immigrants can be "possessed" by voodoo economics also resonates with Patricia Chu's reading of how in U.S. cultural history the ultimate horror of "zombification" is when it imperils "white male subjectivity" and citizenship—when white men fear that they too have become alienated, automated victims of "regimes of modern labor" resembling "premodern" racial slavery.[81] The horror that Bob experiences when Vanise turns away may include a shock of recognition that he is not merely "pissed" at a life of blue-collar labor but "possessed" by money in a way that cannot be redeemed. By contrast, Vanise may yet find (in Dayan's formulation) "a way back to the self." *Continental Drift* invites readers to contemplate which form of possession is "really bizarre": possession by *loas* or by the spirit of American capitalism ascendant from New Hampshire via Florida to Haiti.

Coda:
The Extended North–South Axis
in *Rule of the Bone*

The Book of Jamaica and *Continental Drift* were the first two of "at least four books" that Banks has written "about the African diaspora from the white point of view."[82] In 2005 Banks reiterated his long-held belief that New World slavery and its legacies constituted "the central drama in the history of race in the United States, and in the entire hemisphere, really": "What I'm really interested in, in the long haul, is trying to enter that history of race from different points of view, from different periods, and in a sense write different chapters in it. *The Book of Jamaica* deals with it in the Caribbean, *Continental Drift* in some ways deals with it as it collides in Florida and in the Southern part of the United Sates in contemporary time, and *Rule of the Bone* deals with it from the point of view of an American boy in the 1990s."[83] *Rule of the Bone* (1995) is narrated by Chappie, a troubled white working-class teenager from upstate New York. Having been sexually abused by his stepfather and fallen into an increasingly itinerant life of petty crime and drug abuse, Chappie encounters I-Man, a devout Rastafarian eking out a self-sufficient existence while squatting in a derelict, immobilized bus. I-Man had "come up from Jamaica in April with a crew of migrant farmworkers"; "the same crew was supposed to go to Florida on a bus and cut sugarcane all summer for a different company and come back north in the fall and pick apples," but I-Man quit once it became apparent "that he wouldn't be able to practice his religion here in spite of America being a free country."[84] I-Man's status as an "illegal alien escapee" (333) in the U.S. North echoes the experience of runaway slaves and gestures to historical-geographical continuities in the exploitation of black labor throughout the nation as a whole, from Florida to New York. Chappie is intrigued by the apparent commonality between I-Man's situation and his own ("I was an outlaw too") and enthusiastically embraces the Rasta's belief that "every free man" should shuck off his "slavery name" (156), reinventing himself as "Bone" and traveling with I-Man to Jamaica.

In Jamaica, Bone reconnects with his biological father, a shady doctor based in Montego Bay, and becomes an associate of the Accompong Maroons. At this point in Bone's first-person narrative, Terron and other Maroons from *The Book of Jamaica* reappear. Bone insists that "[i]t wasn't like I wanted to be made into an honorary Negro or anything" (314), but like Johnny before him Bone learns through a violent sequence of events that the possession of whiteness and Americanness puts him at a privileged distance from black Jamaicans. When I-Man is murdered following a murky dispute over a drug deal, Bone is spared because—in the words of the American drug lord involved in the ambush—"We shouldn't do a white kid anyhow, man.... Too much trouble, especially since he's American. The tourist board'll go nuts" (338–39). Bone himself becomes "twisted up by" the realization that his "[w]hiteness... saved me from being blown away" (342), pondering "what a little turd I was for trying not to be white when all the time I'd been enjoying the benefits of the white race, like still being alive for instance" (344–45). Bone eventually resolves to "light out for the marina" (377) in Montego Bay, where he meets "Captain Ave from Key West, Florida originally who ran this charter boat called *Belinda Blue*" (378), the vessel once piloted by Bob Dubois. The novel concludes with Bone aboard Avery Boone's boat off the coast of eastern Jamaica, assisting Bob's former partner with a "month-long surf-and-turf family vacation" (380) for a wealthy New York family. Though the novel ends with Bone in seaborne limbo, gazing at the stars for guidance, it seems that, like Johnny, Bone will escape back to the United States via south Florida.

Banks's continuing fascination with Florida is also evident in *Lost Memory of Skin* (2011), set in the fictional south Florida city of Calusa and plumbing the complex relationship between a convicted sex offender and an Alabamian professor of sociology. But *The Book of Jamaica* and *Continental Drift* retain their privileged role within Banks's body of work as the pair of novels that initiated his engagement with forms of relation between the United States—especially its "Southern parts"—and the Caribbean. For Banks, the geographic scales of Florida are simultaneously southern, American, and circum-Caribbean. In its constantly shifting demographics, Banks's literary cartography of the state is, like Vanise's mental map, "a living, coiling and uncoiling thing... a process, the kind of map you must keep moving into, if you want to read it." This relational spatial poetics, in which Florida is viewed vis-à-vis New Hampshire and Haiti, or New York and Jamaica, has defined Banks's sense of himself among "north–south writers," a successor to Faulkner and a contemporary of Morrison.[85] Banks is no "southern writer," but his explorations of a hemispheric "north–south axis" across interlinked novels extend Faulkner's and Hurston's own multivolume endeavors to re-scale the U.S. South.

CHAPTER 5

Workings of the Spirit, Spirit of the Workers

Migration, Labor, and the Extended Caribbean in Erna Brodber's Louisiana

Louisiana (1994), the third novel by Jamaican author Erna Brodber, signifies to dazzling effect upon the life and writing of Zora Neale Hurston and does so more directly and deliberately than Russell Banks's novels of the previous decade. This has not gone unnoticed by critics: Vera Kutzinski, Shirley Toland-Dix, and Samantha Pinto have offered valuable readings of *Louisiana*'s intertextual engagement with Hurston. As Kutzinski notes, already in the prologue *Louisiana* "encourages [the reader] to recognize Zora Neale Hurston as a model" for the black woman who is both the primary author and protagonist of the text that follows.[1] This prologue is presented in the form of an "editor's note" to a rediscovered manuscript by one Ella Townsend, a Columbia-trained anthropologist who traveled to south Louisiana in 1936 under the auspices of the Works Progress Administration (WPA) "to retrieve the history of the Blacks of South West Louisiana using oral sources." We are told that Townsend subsequently "disappeared leaving a blotch on her name."[2] The main text is Ella's own newly discovered narrative, which reveals that the young scholar's search for "oral sources" concentrated on interviews with Sue Ann King (also known as Mammy), an aged resident of St. Mary Parish whom "the white people" from the WPA had identified as a rich repository of "important data" about "the history of the struggle of the lower class negro" (21). However, the interviews took an unexpectedly "personal and certainly unscholastic" (22) turn: as Ella tried to extract the appropriate "data," Sue Ann was in psychic contact with her late Jamaican friend Louise (also known as Lowly). Together Sue Ann and Louise anointed Ella as the conduit or "horse" through which they "communicate with each other telepathically not only across space...but from terrestrial to extra terrestrial" spheres (60). Ella was shocked to discover evidence of Sue Ann's telepathic conversations with Louise on the tape of their interviews; even more startlingly, she discovered her own voice periodically interjecting the refrain "Ah who sey Sammy dead," from a Jamaican folk song of which Ella had no conscious knowledge. The recording ruptured Ella's faith in social-scientific objectivity, and when she became possessed during Sue Ann's funeral she realized that "I was going to be, if I was not already, a vessel, a horse, somebody's talking drum" (46). Ella abandoned her academic work for the WPA and moved with her partner Reuben Kohl to New Orleans, where the couple took up residence in a boarding house run by a psychic called Madam Marie and populated by migrant workers from the Caribbean. Ella eventually completed the painstaking transcription of the interview tapes, which became the first part of her manuscript; she also wrote about her psychic experiences and efforts to uncover the lives of Sue Ann and Louise. Ella died in January 1954 and was buried in "St Mary, Louisiana, New Orleans style" (165).

Even this reductive overview of Ella's adult life and narrative should give some sense of how it echoes Hurston's career. As discussed in chapters 1 and 4, Hurston conducted extensive anthropological research into black southern and Caribbean culture; like Ella, Hurston was employed for a period by the WPA. Ella's shaken faith in academic objectivity recalls how Hurston's adoption of "the spy-glass of Anthropology" did not always dovetail with her formulation of a pioneering subject position as an active participant in, as well as observer of, the black southern "crib of negroism."[3] Ella's removal to New Orleans in 1936 and participation in the city's subterranean spiritual culture recalls Hurston's exploration of and immersion in "hoodoo" in New Orleans during 1929, which she wrote about in the essay "Hoodoo in America" (1931) and part 2 of *Mules and Men* (1935). Ella's status as a "horse" for Sue Ann and Louise also evokes the title and subject matter of *Tell My Horse* (1938).[4] We saw in those earlier chapters how Hurston expanded her exploration of black folk culture by turning south of the U.S. South to the Bahamas, Jamaica, and Haiti; as Toland-Dix notes, both "Hurston and Brodber explore cultural legacies of the U.S. South and the Caribbean through an African diasporic lens."[5]

Given the intertextual echoes of Hurston's take on New Orleans as "the hoodoo capital of America," a place where "rites vie with those of Hayti in deeds to keep alive the power of Africa," it is not surprising that critics have focused on the way Ella's tale too emphasizes "the hegemony of the spirit" (98) in the U.S. South and Caribbean.[6] Like *Mules and Men* and *Tell My Horse*, *Louisiana* probes the conscious—and unconscious—formed from what Joseph Roach calls a circum-Caribbean "cultural politics of memory" that is "realized through communications between the living and the dead."[7] It is worth stressing here Roach's focus on cultural *politics*. As I noted in chapter 4, *Tell My Horse* emphasizes that poor Haitians express *political* meaning through their worship of Papa Guedé: as "the deification of the common people," the loa Guedé "comes as near a social criticism of the classes by the masses as anything in all Haiti."[8] Pinto helpfully draws out Hurston's subtle demonstration of how the "possessive audience" of Haitians "is shown to *labor* before, during, and after a possession"—a reminder that Guedé's "social criticism" involves interrogating the way that labor itself structures the difficult relations between the masses and the upper classes.[9] According to Toland-Dix, Brodber also "boldly depicts the revolutionary potential of active connection with the spirit world.... Like Hurston, she identifies spirit possession as a strategy of resistance to oppression as it constitutes a realm that colonial powers cannot control."[10] Yet critics have said little about *Louisiana*'s profoundly political emphasis on the historical and material conditions of blacks in Louisiana from Reconstruction to the eve of the Civil Rights movement—not least their strategies of resistance to racist and capitalist exploitation of their own *living and laboring* bodies. Even Pinto qualifies that *Louisiana* is "[p]ossessed more with alternative knowledges than political acumen."[11]

I want to suggest that while (to borrow a phrase from Houston Baker) "workings of the spirit" have become hegemonic in criticism of *Louisiana*, other more worldly forms of work are equally important to a fuller understanding of the novel. Spiritual and psychic forms of knowledge, or "[c]elestial ethnography" (61), help uncover—in fact themselves constitute—a historical and "political unconscious" of black U.S. southern and Caribbean labor struggle. The novel's "cultural politics of memory" cannot be comprehended without attending to either its remarkably rich narrative cartography of black (especially black female) migration during the late nineteenth and early twentieth centuries or its excavation of the ways in which black labor in Louisiana during that period resisted economic exploitation and racist oppression. Rendered in a form that registers the hidden, unwritten nature of black southern labor history, Ella's narrative gradually reveals black workers' struggles in both rural and urban areas: in the canefields of St. Mary's and on the waterfront of New Orleans. Ella excavates how the Great Migration to the North in the late nineteenth and early twentieth centuries resulted at least in part from violent white repression of black workers' efforts to strike and unionize; however, she also records ongoing attempts during the 1920s and 1930s to organize black labor within the South. Ella's manuscript also shows how links between black southerners and Caribbean (especially Jamaican) migrant workers were informed by a flourishing belief in Garveyism as an organized "strategy of resistance to oppression" by capitalism and racism. In this chapter, then, I seek to demonstrate that critical readings of Brodber vis-à-vis Hurston should extend into an aspect of *Louisiana* that has received insufficient attention: the material world of black southern and Caribbean labor previously mapped in *Jonah's Gourd Vine* and *Their Eyes Were Watching God*. But Brodber's depiction of how capitalist labor relations and conventional gender roles generate deleterious forms of spirit (dis)possession also echoes Banks's *Continental Drift*, while Reuben's coda to Ella's narrative gestures to a jumping of scales from the U.S. South and Caribbean to postcolonial Africa and the Global South.

Circum-Caribbean Commonalities and Migrations

The editor's note announces the inauguration of "the Ella Townsend Foundation for the study of commonalities in African America and the African Caribbean in the period between the World Wars" (5)—itself likely another sly acknowledgment of Hurston's pioneering work between 1929 and 1939 on the U.S. South and the Caribbean. Throughout Ella's manuscript, such "commonalities" are often apparent not only in the parallels between Ella and Zora but also in onomastic overlaps that again intone Hurston's work. For example, Sue Ann is from St. Mary Parish, Louisiana, while both Ella and Sue Ann's dead friend Louise are from the vicinity of a village called Louisiana in St. Mary, Jamaica. St. Mary is both the region of Jamaica that Hurston depicts in part 1 of *Tell My Horse* (see chapter 4) and the home of Brodber herself. By 1944, Ella has come to see herself as the embodied spirit of two people, Louise and Sue Ann, and two places: Louisiana in St. Mary, Jamaica, and St. Mary Parish, Louisiana.[12] Ella also renames herself "Louisiana" in honor of New Orleans' status as the circum-Caribbean "link between the shores washed by the sea" and as a playful sign that she now "join[s] the world of the living and the world of the spirit.... In me Louise and Sue Ann are joined. Say Suzie Anna as Louise calls Mammy. Do you hear Louisiana there?" (124). Here we see how, to adapt Emily Apter's observations about Édouard Glissant's homonymic strategies in *Faulkner, Mississippi*, Brodber "uses place-names" as well as character names "to translate the world of the American South into the language of Caribbean worlds"—and vice versa.[13]

However, such "commonalities" are not only expressed at the spiritual and onomastic levels. *Louisiana* also maps the material geography of migration. This encompasses various transregional and transnational routes: the familiar Great Migration of black southerners to northern metropolises; a form of reverse migration from the U.S. North to the U.S. South; and hemispheric movements between the Caribbean and the United States. Born in Jamaica, Ella grew up in New York as the daughter of immigrants who were part of a broader exodus from the Caribbean that, as Heather Hathaway has remarked, both compounded and complicated "the 'Great Migration' of African Americans from the southern United States."[14] In New York, Ella's mother and father consciously sloughed off their Caribbean heritage, which explains Ella's initial failure to recognize the source of the phrase that she hears herself speaking on the tape: "I now know that it is the refrain of a folk-song from home [Jamaica] but I didn't know the song, having left there at an early age and my parents, wishing to dissociate themselves from some aspect of their past did not / would not have sung such a song nor would they have kept company with people who would sing such a song" (31). Indeed, the denuding of Ella's Jamaican identity is such that, when she sets out on her "voyage from north to south,

New York to Louisiana," she is, as Reginald Khokher argues, "firmly situated as American" rather than Jamaican.[15]

Gradually, however, Ella's triangular movements from Jamaica via New York to Louisiana facilitate a fuller comprehension of the "commonalities" between African American (especially black southern) and Afro-Caribbean cultures, not least the role of migration. Arriving in southwestern Louisiana and interviewing Sue Ann enables Ella to begin confronting "how little she knows of the land of her parents" (19); in New Orleans, the sound of "Sammy Dead-O" being sung by the "West Indian crew" (87–88) is the catalyst for a personal and spiritual epiphany, as the song triggers Ella's repressed memories of her grandmother's death and funeral in Jamaica. In chapter 1, I noted how Hurston adapted the term "great migration" to describe the arrival in New Orleans "of Haitian and Santa Dominican Negroes after the success of [Toussaint] L'Ouverture." In *Louisiana*, Madam Marie intones the mythical voodoo priestess Marie Laveau, who (as Cynthia James notes) likely "arrived in New Orleans after the Haitian revolution in 1809."[16] The modern-day sailors at Marie's boarding house extend this Caribbean great migration to New Orleans into the mid-twentieth century: "The port of New Orleans is a very active one. There are ships and sailors from every conceivable part of the world. Madam was acutely interested in those who looked most like us. The banana boats from the West Indies had a fair share of such sailors. These made up the bulk of Madam's clientele" (78). By 1946, Ella has inherited Madam Marie's customers and so is ministering spiritually to both locals and foreigners, "having a great deal of difficulty in separating my West Indians from my Americans" (129). Ella also travels mentally and spiritually back and forth across the sea with the sailors: "when the boats to the West Indies sound off, they take me with them and I am sitting right here in New Orleans, Louisiana, yet searching grave-stones, stringing duppy bead, going into caves, eating mangoes and jackfruit there" (123). Ella never returns physically to Jamaica; however, her combined archival and spiritual work with the tapes and as Sue Ann and Louise's "horse"—Ella's "anthropology of the dead" (61)—take her back in time to uncover a history of regional, national, and hemispheric migration that is intimately bound up with black labor struggle.

Labor Struggle in the Louisiana Canefields

After her move to New Orleans in 1937, Ella listens once again to her WPA-sponsored interviews with the late Sue Ann King. Ella is surprised to find new "material" on the recordings in which Sue Ann refers to her mother: "Read about the caneworkers strike on the Teche, my child? That's my Mamma's strike" (113). In 1949 Ella learns more about this mysterious strike, which she dates to 1878 based on a newspaper report headlined "Disturbance in the canefield" (139). By 1952, Ella/Louisiana can describe Sue Ann's mother's role in "organizing [caneworkers] towards wresting a better deal from sugar planters. The focus of action of Mrs Grant and her co-conspirators was better pay and the modification of a system of remuneration in which workers were forced to spend their wages in the company stores owned by the same plantation owners and from which debts were deducted before the pay reached the hand of the worker. . . . It is the general assumption that she was disposed of by the planters because of her political activities" (151). Through Ella's necessarily elliptical narrative of Sue Ann's mother's life and her death during the Teche Strike, Brodber deftly references the conflicts between sugar planters and workers in southern Louisiana during and after Reconstruction. That this history is subtly sedimented within Sue Ann's oral narrative (and mediated through Ella's machine and analysis) may be less surprising to readers aware that for Brodber herself, "[t]he reconstruction period in the South of the USA became my special paper for my honours history degree."[17] The period's sugarcane conflicts have been explored by historians William Hair, Thomas Becnel, and John C. Rodrigue, whose *Reconstruction in the Cane Fields* (2001) provides the most thoroughgoing analysis. Where cotton was king elsewhere in the South, sugar had ruled southern Louisiana since the mid-1790s when, in a prime example of the links between plantation economies in the U.S. South and the Caribbean, production was revolutionized "using techniques imported by slave and freeblack refugees from Haiti."[18] But in 1862 New Orleans and the rest of Louisiana fell to Union forces, and General Benjamin Butler required planters to start paying slaves for their work. It is notable then that Ella identifies 1862 as the year that Sue Ann's mother was born (150)—one might say that she symbolizes the birth of free wage labor for blacks in Louisiana.

Between 1862 and 1877, south Louisiana caneworkers asserted their new political and economic rights—not least in St. Mary, the parish that according to the 1860 census had the highest population of slaves. The formal abolition of slavery by Louisiana Unionists in September 1864 and the formation of the Freedmen's Bureau in 1865 facilitated the emergence of a free labor market, and former slaves took full advantage. While freedmen could do little to prevent the perpetuation of a plantation economy (the result of a compromise between planters and moderate Republicans), they repeatedly demanded decent wages and went on strike when planters tried to withhold part of their pay or enforce restrictive contracts. Throughout St. Mary and the rest of the sugar region, wages rose as freedmen asserted their labor value and planters began to compete with one another for the best workers. In 1869 a St. Mary newspaper editor claimed: "We doubt if there is a spot in the whole South where they are as well paid as in this parish." Many sugar planters went bankrupt by refusing or failing to adjust to the emerging free labor market. Others tried uniting against the "labor problem": in both 1875 and 1878, St. Mary planters met to fix wages and end the growing practice of full cash payment to black workers. Each time, however, individual planters reneged on the deal in their quest for profit. Freedmen proved adept at exploiting the situation: in 1877 a St. Mary journalist grumbled that sugar workers "strike as they commence rolling cane [the most delicate part of the season for planters] and demand higher wages."[19] But sugar workers also exercised their new legal freedom and labor power by becoming migrants: like Sue Ann's mother, who briefly left St. Mary for New Orleans (where she met Sue Ann's father, a black sailor), some sugar workers went to the Crescent City to find different forms of employment. Others traveled north as part of the famed "Kansas Fever."[20]

The novel's dating of "the Teche Strike" to 1878 also has a symbolic resonance: this was year zero following the death knell of Radical Reconstruction, the 1877 election of President Rutherford B. Hayes, who promised federal withdrawal from the South. Already by 1876 the South had been largely "redeemed," with Louisiana, South Carolina, and Florida the exceptions. Sugar workers in south Louisiana who earned (and struck for) cash wages remained considerably better off than the many "free" blacks who were becoming mired in sharecropping elsewhere in the South, but for the first time since the Civil War, the region's sugar planters could call on the Louisiana state militia to repress labor protests by violent means. The planters' renewed power over workers was demonstrated during the events leading up to the Thibodaux Massacre of 1887. Though this labor conflict culminated in Thibodaux, in Lafourche Parish, St. Mary was once again a focal point as south Louisiana workers garnered support from organized labor. In a meeting with the St. Mary branch of the Louisiana Sugar Planters Association (LSPA), the Knights of Labor requested an increase in rolling-season wages; the LSPA refused, so the knights continued organizing sugar workers in the area. On November 1, 1887, between six and ten thousand sugar workers along Bayou Lafourche and Bayou Teche went on strike. As with the 1878 Teche Strike in Brodber's novel, so in 1887 sugar workers were striking for "better pay and the modification of a system of remuneration in which workers were forced to spend their wages in the company stores owned by the same plantation owners": planters had introduced scrip, "causing much disaffection among sugar workers."[21]

In response to the November 1 strike, planters called on the state militia and paramilitary groups: strikers were evicted from their cabins, arrested, and replaced with hired white hands. Tensions increased on November 5 when strikers in St. Mary shot at white workers who had replaced them on the Pharr plantation; whites exacted retribution by killing strikers in Pattersonville. The violence reached a grim conclusion eighteen days later when strikers in Thibodaux fired on white deputies. Whites responded by killing at least thirty black strikers; perhaps hundreds more perished but were unaccounted for. In *Louisiana*, Sue Ann situates her mother's murder during the Teche Strike and relates it directly to a northward exodus of black southern workers decades before the Great Migration: "Til now nobody seen the body, they tell me. Nobody know if that be the woman lynched down in Louisiana that have this state with Mississippi flying off to Chicago city" (113). Rodrigue describes a similar scene of terror and confusion in 1887: "Because many black people fled the area altogether, never to return, it was impossible to determine how many died." What is clear is that the violent repression of the strike dealt a devastating blow to the cause of free black labor in south Louisiana: "With the Knights of Labor crushed, no attempt was made to organize workers on sugar plantations until the mid-twentieth century."[22] By dating *Louisiana*'s Teche Strike to 1878, Brodber amplifies the symbolic nature of Sue Ann's mother's life *and* death: if black workers' rights as free laborers were born in 1862 with Butler's requirement that planters pay wages to their slaves, they were violently repressed in the decades following the end of federal Reconstruction in 1877.

Labor Struggles in New Orleans

Brodber's novel stresses that despite the violent repression of sugar workers, black labor in Louisiana did not simply submit; rather, the focus of struggle shifted from rural areas like St. Mary to New Orleans. Sue Ann followed her mother's example of "punished resistance" (151), and of rural-urban migration within the state, by becoming involved in a longshoremen's strike in New Orleans. Again the elliptical form of Ella's narrative, combined with the difficulties she encounters trying to uncover black southern labor history, means that Sue Ann's activism in New Orleans is only gradually revealed to the reader. By March 1938, Ella has discerned that "the 'pre-Chicago days of Sue Ann Grant-King'" require more research into "the longshoreman's strike" (108) mentioned by Sue Ann in the original WPA interview (18). But it is not until 1952 that Sue Ann and her husband, Silas King, communicate psychically to Ella that they met in Chicago after Sue Ann had "the foresight to flee Louisiana" following her involvement in "that waterfront strike" (146). Later the same year Ella/Louisiana documents a slightly more detailed version of this story: "The incipient labour movement of the pre–World War I days was Mammy's stage, her chance to perpetuate the family tradition. She became involved in New Orleans in the longshoreman's strike" (152) until news "of the shooting and jailing of the strikers" (155) prompted her to flee to Chicago.

Here again *Louisiana* dramatizes the historical struggles of free black southern labor. In November 1887 black longshoremen in New Orleans declared their solidarity with caneworkers in St. Mary and Lafourche parishes by protesting the recent massacres in Pattersonville and Thibodaux. Organized labor in New Orleans was much stronger than in the sugar region, not least due to an impressive level of solidarity across the color line despite the ascendance of

Jim Crow. Historian Eric Arnesen observes: "During the 1880s and early 1890s, [New Orleans' waterfront workers'] unprecedented experiment in interracial cooperation provided a sharp contrast to rural repression, intensifying urban segregation, and racial exclusion."[23] Since the end of the Civil War, black waterfront workers had been organizing and striking—sometimes on their own, but often with whites—for better wages and working conditions. Black longshoremen founded their own union in April 1872—a year before white workers established a separate union—and went on strike every year between 1872 and 1875.[24] September 1880 witnessed the first truly interracial strike of black and white waterfront workers, and the founding of the Cotton Men's Executive Council (CMEC) that same year "inaugurated a new era in the history of New Orleans labor" by establishing "a network of institutionalized solidarity." During the 1880s, the CMEC "wrested control of the labor supply from their employers" and secured "probably the highest longshore wages in the country." Interracial solidarity was formalized in 1901 with the founding of the Dock and Cotton Council, and the following year black and white screwmen agreed to divide all work equally "[t]o prevent employers from playing one race off against another."[25] Two major strikes by waterfront workers in 1903 and 1907 were particularly successful in strengthening interracial solidarity and union "control over the waterfront labor process." Cotton planter and Louisiana senator C. C. Cordill fulminated that "[t]his is the worst nigger-ridden city in the South," while a steamship agent denounced New Orleans as the "worst labor-ridden city in the country." Such rhetorical links between race, class, and organized labor were telling. By contrast, the president of the black longshoremen's union was quoted in the *New Orleans Picayune* declaring that "the whites and Negroes were never before so strongly cemented in a common bond and in my 39 years on the levee, I have never seen such solidarity."[26]

This intensive union activism in New Orleans between 1901 and 1908 tallies with *Louisiana*'s representation of Sue Ann's involvement in the "labour movement of the pre–World War I days." Moreover, Sue Ann's subsequent flight from New Orleans to Chicago symbolizes the wider Great Migration of black workers from Louisiana. In 1916 New Orleans' *Item* newspaper remarked that on the docks, "where negro labor is much depended on, workmen are becoming more scarce every day. To such an extent has the labor supply been drained by the North that steamship men find it a considerable problem to facilitate the loading and unloading of cargoes."[27] Paranoid white politicians and businessmen believed northern industries were employing agents to entice away black workers. The reality was that despite the struggles of black labor on the waterfront, workers were discovering (often from friends and family already relocated to Chicago or Detroit) that they could earn more, and find better housing and schools, in the urban North. As Hurston put it in *Jonah's Gourd Vine*: "Do what they would, the State, County and City all over the South could do little to halt the stampede. The cry of 'Goin' Nawth' hung over the land like the wail over Egypt at the death of the first-born."[28]

Grassroots Garveyism in Louisiana

After migrating to Chicago, apparently just before the outbreak of the First World War, Sue Ann meets both Jamaican expatriate Louise Grant (Lowly) and Silas King, her future husband and fellow labor organizer. Sue Ann, Silas, and Louise soon become involved in Marcus Garvey's United Negro Improvement Association (UNIA), which "gave them a framework within which to do concrete [political] work." But rather than stay in Chicago, Sue Ann and Silas "returned to St Mary, Louisiana, where she and perhaps he as well, did organisational work" (153). Thus Sue Ann returns to St. Mary through a reverse migration from the urban North. But this is not because Brodber—to recall Hazel Carby's critique of Hurston—"discursively displaces the urban migration of black people in the continental United States" by stressing the "continuity" between black southern culture and "beliefs and practices in the Caribbean."[29] Rather, the emphasis on Garveyism constitutes *Louisiana*'s primary narrative "commonality" between Caribbean and African American *political* activism, supplementing rather than supplanting those spiritual connections between the Caribbean and the U.S. South already identified by scholars such as Toland-Dix and Kutzinski.

Already in the transcript of Ella's first WPA interview with Sue Ann, there is a buried allusion to UNIA organization in St. Mary: while communicating psychically with Louise, Sue Ann refers to Silas and herself as "two aging blooms, [with] three units to set up" (11). Ella also transcribes without really registering Sue Ann's approving observation that "[t]hey rebellious folks, them Jamaican racemen. One feisty fighting lot" (20). It is not until 1952 that Ella fully understands why Sue Ann "came to be of interest to those looking for the history of South West Louisiana": "Mammy was a Garvey organizer and a psychic." Ella glosses that while she "had long known about the latter," she is astonished to learn that Sue Ann was also "[a] black nationalist. Well, well, well." Using Ella as his horse, the long-dead Silas recalls Sue Ann's activities in St. Mary's parish: "Organising in the dead of night, sneaking here, setting up meeting there, carrying all those quarters people on [her] head" (148). Even after Silas's death Sue Ann had "continued her political work intertwining it with her psychic work, a combination which served to make her a legend" (153). Ella now knows that Sue Ann always gave her spiritual and political labor equal weight: no "hegemony of the spirit" here. Sue Ann's workings of the spirit were counterbalanced by the spirit of the workers: the sugarcane workers she organized in St. Mary and the waterfront workers of New Orleans.

First-time readers could be forgiven for not registering that the editor's note already identified Ella's narrative as a text which, in its unorthodox and polyphonic form, combines spiritual *and* social analysis: "*Louisiana* is a mixture of social history and out of body experiences, perhaps a new field of study" (4). True to this paratextual promise, Ella's manuscript uncovers (to recast Toland-Dix's phrase) "the revolutionary potential" of spirit possession *and* organized labor. Still, its depiction of Garveyite activism in Louisiana may surprise some readers: after all, the stunning popular success of the UNIA in the United States during the late 1910s and 1920s is usually associated with the urban North and especially New York, where the first U.S. branch of the UNIA was founded in 1917. Already in 1918 Garvey moved the UNIA headquarters from Kingston to Harlem: it made sense "that he should be tempted by Harlem, the most highly politicized black community in the world," at a time when the influx of southern-born blacks and West Indian immigrants considerably expanded his potential audience.[30] In chapter 3, we saw that in John Oliver Killens's *Youngblood* (1954) migrants "from South Carolina and Georgia and Mississippi and Barbados and Trinidad and other points south" meet at the Myles family's Brooklyn apartment; among their subjects are the "conditions of the Negro north and south and praising Marcus Garvey and damning Marcus Garvey."[31] The UNIA's impact among African Americans who remained in the South is less well known, but in a 2002 interview Brodber stated her belief that "African Americans of the South were very important to the Garvey movement." Brodber learned from Tony Martin's pioneering study of Garvey and the UNIA "that Louisiana had more Garvey units than anywhere else in the world."[32] In *Race First* (1976), Martin cited rediscovered UNIA files which revealed that circa 1926 Louisiana had no fewer than seventy-four UNIA branches; the states with the next largest number of UNIA branches were Virginia, with forty-eight, and North Carolina, with forty-seven. Martin deduced that "if the number of branches in a given area can be taken to indicate the extent of UNIA penetration, then the southern United States was the most thoroughly UNIA-organized area in the world," with Louisiana "far and away the most thoroughly Garveyite state."[33] In *The Continent of Black Consciousness* (2003), Brodber again cited Martin's work and noted that in the 1920 census "only 1225" of Louisiana's 700,275 "negroes" were of West Indian origin: hence the members of Louisiana's seventy-four branches "must have been more than the 1225 West Indians." Brodber also drew on Jeanette Smith-Irvin's research for a roll call of black southern Garveyites that included women like Queen Mother Moore, born in New Iberia in 1898 and a UNIA member as late as 1972, and Madam de Mena, "one of the UNIA's international organisers, who was born in New Orleans, Louisiana."[34]

Building on Martin's work, other historians have since conducted important research into "grassroots Garveyism" in the U.S. South. Claudrena Harold has argued that the initial success of the UNIA between 1918 and 1922 demonstrated "the southern black majority's determination to play a crucial role in the making of a New Negro modernity" and a desire for "the essential attributes of modernity: self-possession, economic independence, cultural capital, and political power." Though the procapitalist and self-help dimensions of Garvey's philosophy are not obviously compatible with leftist labor struggle, the rise of the UNIA in Louisiana provided a vital organizational focus for black southerners "routinely marginalized in the American labor movement."[35] Brodber argues that Garvey was able to reach the black masses because, in contrast to socialists and communists, "Garvey waited for no foreign mind" to define black political thought and action; "like an applied anthropologist," Garvey preferred to rely on his own "participant observation" of black life. Consequently, Garvey "did not ... see Jamaicans as different from Alabamans; neither the Jamaicans nor the Alabamans needed to change their nationality" to become citizens of Garvey's "continent of black consciousness."[36] Mary Rolinson observes that during the 1920s "Louisiana blacks, particularly in the river parishes in southern Louisiana, universally embraced the UNIA," partly because "there was a marked West Indian heritage there."[37] This enthusiasm was not only a rural phenomenon: the New Orleans division of the UNIA grew exponentially between February and October 1921 as membership rose from seventy people to some four thousand.[38] Garvey himself "visited the Crescent City several times, and his presence had an enormous impact."[39] Crucially, however, the UNIA moved beyond a cult of personality or narrow political perspective to develop what Harold calls "*local Garveyism*": a grassroots strategy that included collaboration with New Orleans' extant and "vibrant world of black labor activism," which "provided institutional support" to the UNIA. For example, the Negro Longshoremen Hall operated as the main base for UNIA meetings and activities, while the longshoremen and other black unions provided local leadership.[40] There is then a bleak irony that New Orleans, "the gateway to the Caribbean," was the city from which Garvey was deported back to Jamaica in December 1927. Rolinson identifies 146,689 Garvey sympathizers in the South between 1923 and 1927 who either attended mass meetings or signed petitions demanding Garvey's release from jail; of that number, 57,576 came from Louisiana. That "[f]ive thousand loyal followers were on hand at New Orleans to listen to Garvey's farewell address from the deck of the vessel taking him to the Caribbean" suggests the level of support that the UNIA continued to command in New Orleans and Louisiana more generally.[41]

Given the scale of this UNIA presence in Louisiana, one begins to understand that a Garveyite activist like Sue Ann King, operating in St. Mary parish during the 1920s, is not the anomaly she may seem. Rolinson's emphasis on "grassroots Garveyism" and Harold's attention to "local Garveyism" dovetail with Pinto's point that in *Louisiana* "[i]t is not Garvey himself but his organization's ability to locally distribute power and diasporic literacy to Mammy or Jamaican-born Lowly that is significant."[42] Or as Brodber herself has put it, "Garvey's originality and his contribution to history" is "that he inspired black people towards the creation and operation of the UNIA."[43] Beyond the local scale, an activist like Sue Ann would have been in the vanguard of UNIA organization nationally and hemispherically: her friendship with Louise, who left Chicago after the 1919 race riots and returned to her homeland to continue UNIA work (156), makes Sue Ann especially alert to the potential for establishing political ties between blacks in the South and the Caribbean. The local strength of the UNIA in Louisiana, combined with its circum-Caribbean ties to Jamaica, also elucidate Madam Marie's special interest in the banana boat workers at her guesthouse. Ella quickly recognizes that Marie is attuned to the *cultural* commonalities between the Caribbean and African American tenants: "Her West Indian friends, Jamaican, I think, told her about Anancy, the spider. Where we here talk about Brer Rabbit, their talk was about Anancy" (78). But it is much later that Ella realizes Marie too was a UNIA organizer. Both Sue Ann and Marie saw the possibility of forging *political* links between Caribbean and U.S. southern blacks: "even after Mr G [Garvey] left" the United States in 1927, the two women continued their organizational work, "wanting to pull the sides of the sea together, wanting to set them little islands together and tack them on to New Orleans" (148).

Some readers may remain puzzled that Ella registers the UNIA legacy in New Orleans circa 1952, twenty-five years after Garvey was deported and long after his organization's popular success. Cynthia James posits that "*Louisiana* conflates and mythicizes successive time-waves of American West Indian migration, treating the importance of Garveyism as a unifier of the diaspora between the world Wars, long after the movement had failed."[44] Yet as Rolinson emphasizes in the first sentence of her book: "Garveyism did not disappear after Marcus Garvey's deportation from the United States in 1927."[45] Harold shows that the New Orleans UNIA's grassroots strategic emphasis on "local issues" and "community outreach programs" sustained Garveyism long beyond the departure of Garvey himself. Though institutionally the New Orleans UNIA suffered a "precipitous decline" during the 1930s, the legacy of "local Garveyism" resonated with later generations of New Orleans activists and authors: see, for example, Kalamu ya Salaam's 1978 poem "Whirlwind Storm Warning UNIA."[46]

World War II also regenerated northward "great migration" across the extended Caribbean to New Orleans. Ella observes circa summer 1943: "The men are coming back. More men than before. Not just sailors now, employees of the United Fruit Company as well as farmworkers.... [T]hese new West Indian men, we hear, are being invited to come here to help with the war effort.... They come, paid for we think, by our government. They plough as is right. They weed the plants; they cut cane; they pick apples" (116). In spring

1943 the U.S. government's Emergency Wartime Labor Program reached an agreement with the British colonial authorities in Kingston to recruit tens of thousands of Jamaican agricultural guest workers. The arrangement had political benefits for both sides. The United States secured immediate, nonpermanent foreign labor deemed vital to the war effort, not least to replace African Americans recruited into the U.S. Army and (as we saw in chapter 3) sent to fight as far away as the South Pacific. Meanwhile, Jamaica's largely white elite could temporarily export thousands of unemployed and increasingly militant working-class blacks who, already battered by the Depression, were suffering from the wartime disruption of overseas trade, which particularly affected small peasant farmers trading perishables like bananas. With Jamaica's first democratic election on the horizon in 1944, the American guest worker program appeared to many members of the colony's elite as an "ideal way to curry favor with [a] soon-to-be black electorate" that was agitating for the prospective agreement. Historian Cindy Hahamovitch writes: "As news of the 'U.S. farmworker programme' spread by newspaper, radio, and word of mouth in the spring of 1943, thousands of Jamaicans began sending letters of inquiry to the Jamaican Department of Labor and to the United Fruit Company"; even the Maroons formed a delegation to demand their inclusion in the scheme.[47]

Initially the Jamaican colonial secretary's ambivalent support for the program came with a significant caveat: that the colony's black British subjects should not be sent to the U.S. South. Yet when the first Jamaican participants arrived on American shores in summer 1943, they often "docked in the first U.S. port they could reach. This meant that guestworkers disembarked in the South." Many were processed through New Orleans and Camp Pontchartrain, "a staging area for African American army personnel shipping out to join the nation's still segregated military," before traveling on to farms in the North and West. The colonial secretary soon bowed to pressure from the War Food Administration, and Jamaican agricultural workers began to arrive on U.S. Sugar's plantations in Florida. Here they experienced the "Jim Crow Creed" in full effect: though the guest workers' status as citizens of a U.S. war ally supposedly protected them from the abuse meted out to black southern workers, "race trumped citizenship" as Jamaican arrivals were herded into labor camps surrounded by barbed-wire fences. During the winter of 1943–44 "the importation program expanded to include other southern states and other southern employers," and "Jamaicans discovered that conditions weren't better elsewhere in the South"—including labor camps in Louisiana.[48] As if anticipating the sequence in *Continental Drift* when Vanise Dorsinville's northward migration from Haiti to Florida replays slavery's "middle passage," Ella depicts Caribbean workers' perilous wartime circumstances as "[a]nother middle passage as unfathomable as the first, a middle passage that you consent to taking" (118). But with British and U.S. companies like United Fruit continuing to control most of Jamaica's cultivated land, and their impoverished rural families relying on remittances, guest workers kept on consenting. As Ella observes in December 1943, "the men have to move. Coast people make their living from the sea. More still, the thing in the sea [i.e., German submarines] stops traders from taking food to their islands. Now they come, not excited at having travelled by their wont, but tired and wrought from crossing a great divide in search of that food" (118). As I noted in the introduction, the Emergency Labor Importation Program was supposed to conclude with the end of the war; instead, the immediate postwar period saw an increase in the number of guest workers arriving from Jamaica and other Caribbean countries. These Caribbean "non-immigrant" workers "were not slaves, [but] neither were they free": they were the inadvertent vanguard of that "quintessentially modern form of international migrant," which then as now exists "in a no man's land between nations."[49] They would also become, as we saw in chapter 1, the subjects of Hurston's unpublished 1958 essay on migrant labor in Florida.

Spirit Possession as a Political and Historical Unconscious

By focusing on the more historical-geographical materialist dimensions of *Louisiana*, I do not mean to diminish the value of those critical readings that stress "the hegemony of the spirit" in Brodber's novel. I trust too that my critical approach does not simply recapitulate the narrow worldview of the WPA authorities who used Ella to gather information about the "history of the struggle of the lower class negro that they want to write" (22). Rather, I have been trying to show that Brodber depicts the spiritual *and* material dimensions of black life and labor in Louisiana during the late nineteenth and early twentieth centuries. Strikes by and union organization among southwestern Louisiana caneworkers and New Orleans longshoremen are pivotal to the narrative, as is the role of grassroots Garveyism in engendering solidarity among black southerners and Afro-Caribbeans alike. Pinto is the only critic to have apprehended that "Garvey-as-possessor" of the text's diasporic black consciousness constitutes "a means to more names, more dates, more history, and a deeper genealogy of Caribbean and U.S. connections, especially for working-class and feminist histories."[50] But even Pinto does not investigate that "deeper genealogy" of labor action by cane cutters and waterfront workers before Garveyism "possessed" rural Louisiana and urban New Orleans. *Louisiana*'s formally opaque rendering of "revolutionary black resistance" via union and UNIA organization gradually reveals subterranean histories often overlooked in studies of black southern life, but which scholars within the "new labor history" such as Arnesen and Robin D. G. Kelley have helped bring into focus.[51] Harold pointedly remarks that "new southern studies" too should "devote more attention to the incredibly rich history of southern Garveyism," given that "[l]ong before terms such as *Global South* captured the imagination of the scholarly community," UNIA members and labor activists in New Orleans performed "a decisive role in the struggle" versus "racial oppression, dehumanizing labor practices, and colonial subjugation."[52]

To be sure, there is a danger of overstating the significance of Garveyism in the U.S. South: for example, Martin extrapolates from the files concerning the UNIA's southern branches to make the grandiose claim that it "was not only the organization of newly urbanized Afro-Americans. It was also the organization of the great mass of black peasants all over the South, Southwest and elsewhere."[53] This is reminiscent of communist Harry Haywood's overheated claim that the Black Belt Nation Thesis which influenced Killens (see chapter 3) was not only "an indigenous product, arising from the soil of Black super-exploitation and oppression in the United States," but also "expressed the yearnings of millions of blacks for a nation of their own."[54] Brodber is careful to avoid idealizing the U.S. South as a site of black nationalist, diasporic, or class consciousness. Ella comments on how her partner Reuben responds to black life and culture in St. Mary Parish on his first visit in 1936. Born in the Congo but brought up in Antwerp before moving to New York, Reuben apparently personifies the *routed* "transnational and intercultural" black Atlantic experience theorized by Paul Gilroy.[55] But Reuben is also a "man wandering in search of a connection" and as such primed to romanticize the rural South as an authentic black community in which he will find a *rooted* racial identity. As Ella wryly remarks, "[H]e was so set on finding himself in the new world of Negroes that if he was told that coloureds barked, he would gladly bark" (42). Ella acknowledges that Reuben feels rejuvenated by his contact with the music he hears in St. Mary Parish but also recognizes that he is fetishizing the canefields as a more natural, unconscious source of black expressive culture than either the Congo (where his identity has always been complicated by his biracial parentage and upbringing in the colonial center of Belgium) or the urban North: "In St. Mary Louisiana, he was wallowing in it [blackness] ... he was strutting, strumming, learning to jazz and getting acquainted with the blues. Not that he was a total stranger to these two latter, for he had met them in Europe and had ferreted out every music making spot there was in New York. But these products there were processed. In this Louisiana canefield sounds and styles were coming hot out of the oven" (53). Reuben's notion that black music from the rural South is more authentic than the "processed" jazz and blues of New York recalls Hurston's proposition that Bahamian music is "genuine Negro material" whereas African American "neo-spirituals" are adulterated, commercialized, and thus inauthentic.[56] Ella's alertness to the fallacy of authentic "racial" cultural expression recalls the more nuanced outlook of *Their Eyes Were Watching God*, where (as we saw in chapter 1) Hurston more subtly identifies the cultural chasms as well as commonalities between African American and Bahamian migrant workers on the muck.

Still, both Ella and Reuben discover in New Orleans a thriving circum-Caribbean circuit of cultural exchange which persuades Ella that, with caveats, "Reuben was right: he had found his family" (79). Appropriately, Ella and Reuben enter this circum-Caribbean (and by extension, pan-African) culture via Congo Square. Roach and other scholars have explored the storied past of dancing, African-language singing, and voodoo rituals that characterized Congo Square; in *Louisiana*, the square is depicted as a space in which black expressive forms remain vibrant and fluid. Even the understated Mrs. Forbes tells Ella of "her days and nights watching Count X and King Y" play jazz in Congo Square. Moreover, the mutation of such black expressive forms—"deeply indebted to Africa yet no longer of it," in Roach's formulation, and best defined as "Afro-Caribbean" according to jazz scholar Christopher Washburne—extends from the public square into ostensibly private spaces, informing encounters between native southern blacks and their Caribbean counterparts.[57] Recounting how "the singing in my parlour of the U.S.–West Indian men has more than once been the inspiration for a jazz work" (130), Ella traces a transnational genealogy of jazz in New Orleans reminiscent of Gilroy's delineation of the development of hip-hop in the Bronx, emerging "out of the cross-fertilisation of African-American vernacular cultures with their Caribbean equivalents."[58] In New Orleans, Ella and Reuben immerse themselves in a hybrid, historically contingent, and routed circum-Caribbean expressive culture, rather than romanticizing one rural southern community as a rooted repository of authentic blackness.

In *The Political Unconscious* (1981), Fredric Jameson posits that "history is *not* a text, not a narrative, master or otherwise, but that, as an absent cause, it is inaccessible to us except in textual form." In *Louisiana*, such "prior textualization" of history, "its narrativization in the political unconscious," is largely unavailable to Ella Townsend, except in an occasional old newspaper article.[59] Instead, Ella encounters the narrativization of history—the history of black and Caribbean workers—in the oblique form of WPA-sponsored oral accounts by Sue Ann Grant-King or the psychic messages transmitted posthumously by Sue Ann and her fellow UNIA organizers Louise and Silas. *Louisiana*'s heady mix of the sociohistorical and the spiritual, of the profane and sacred, and of the vernacular-traditional and technological-modern (Sue Ann's oral history recorded on the WPA's tape machine) has been termed "magical realism" and "postmodern marvelous realism."[60] The antimimetic form of the novel, especially its representation of spirit possession and psychic communication, might be understood as an attempt to represent a *double* absence, whereby the first-degree absence of history itself (as described by Jameson) is compounded by a more specific second-degree absence of textual records concerning black southern labor. The ways in which spirit possession and psychic communication facilitate Ella's awareness and understanding of a larger (and largely unrepresented) extended-southern history of labor struggle suggests that the "hegemony of the spirit" in Ella's life and narrative is homologous with, rather than antithetical to, a profoundly historicized "political unconscious."[61]

Discussing voodoo rituals and Mardi Gras Indian observances in New Orleans, Roach observes that "[a] body possessed of its social memory—call it a 'spirit'—is a body in some sense possessed of itself."[62] Roach here ventures that spiritual communication with and possession by the dead is inextricable from social, historical, and political consciousness among the living. This echoes Hurston's emphasis on how the "possession" of the poor by the spirit of Papa Guedé facilitated social critique: "They needed a spirit which could burlesque the society that crushed him.... The spirit of Guedé is Baron Cimeterre with social consciousness, plus a touch of burlesque and slapstick."[63] *Louisiana* develops this sense that spiritual possession facilitates sociopolitical self-possession: a way of being in the (material) world that enables social memory, consciousness, and resistance. Already in Brodber's previous novel *Myal* (1988), workings of the spirit were linked to the material world of work. In *Myal*, which takes place partly in the United States but mostly in Jamaica, Musgrave Simpson meditates on the ways in which imperialism and capitalism have been guilty of "[s]eparating people from themselves, separating man from his labour." If this recalls Karl Marx's classic analysis of the worker's alienation from his own production, Reverend Simpson indicts capitalist exploiters with another term: "Spirit thieves!" Simpson's analogy between spiritual dispossession and capitalist exploitation of the worker's labor is later extended as the psychics Dan and Willie—aliases for Reverend Simpson and another character called Ole African—figure the imperialist-capitalist "theft" of the (slave) worker's labor as a form of zombification: "They split man from his self. A working zombie."[64] There are distinct echoes here of Banks's *Continental Drift*, particularly Eddie Dubois's fear of being "(re)possessed" by voodoo economics (see chapter 4).

However, much as *Louisiana* refuses to romanticize black southern folk culture, neither does it shy away from dramatizing the gendered implications of Ella's spirit possession. While spirit possession may engender self-possession in the terms outlined by Roach, it also threatens to dispossess Ella of her worldly identity as a professional woman. Ella's loss of authority over her own body and identity throughout her eighteen years as a "horse" is at times deeply disturbing; in her journal she asks herself, "[W]ho am I? I merely listen and transcribe. After this, a blank. Nothing more" (113). In linking the living and the dead as well as the U.S. South and the Caribbean, Ella becomes not merely a "passage" but a "hole" (124). Kutzinski remarks on the conundrum of Ella's "lack of agency" during the New Orleans section of the narrative; Pinto notes how Ella "finds herself unable to bear children or even sustain her own material body" while she is confined to a traditional "gender-role status as the kept wife with no sense of the world beyond her immediate doorstep." Yet Ella's domesticated life also facilitates her diasporic sisterhood with the dead (Sue Ann and Louise) and enables her to see and embody "the link between the shores washed by the Caribbean sea" more clearly than she ever could have as an anthropologist in New York. As Pinto puts it: "Staying put and staying *home* . . . can be read as diasporic acts—feminist engagements with the global." Less persuasive perhaps is Pinto's more general claim that "both tradition and modernity . . . offer limited scripts for gendered agency, leaving black women subjects out of history and their present political moment": as we have seen, *Louisiana* uncovers the worldly, historical forms of union and UNIA activism practiced by women like Sue Ann, Lowly, and Marie.[65]

There are, then, two forms of spiritual experience in Brodber's fiction. First, there is the process of being *dis*possessed, transformed into a zombie, by an exploiting "spirit." As in *Continental Drift*, that exploiting spirit might be a malevolent god, slavery, or capitalism. Second, there is the process of being "possessed" by a spirit that bolsters selfhood through social memory and social consciousness—Roach's self-possession. *Myal* focuses on the former while *Louisiana* emphasizes the latter, as Ella is possessed by spirits who provide her with a previously obscured social memory, a hidden history, of African American and Caribbean labor. But such possession is not unambiguously positive: it sometimes evacuates rather than engenders selfhood, and there are uneasy parallels between Ella's "blankness" and the way that Vanise Dorsinville too becomes a "shell" of her former self, more "hole" than whole.[66] Ultimately, though, workings of the spirit do help Ella—and readers of her politically (un)conscious narrative—to perceive the worldly spirit of those workers who organized in the canefields and on the waterfront.

Around the time of Ella/Louisiana's death in early 1954, Reuben adds an epilogue articulating his sense of why Sue Ann "would not tell the president nor his men" from the WPA—or even Ella—her story: "[I]t was not hers; she was no hero. It was a tale of cooperative action; it was a community tale" (161). With its emphasis on political organization among rural Louisiana caneworkers, Sue Ann's "community tale" recalls another key text of U.S. southern and African American literature: Ernest Gaines's *The Autobiography of Miss Jane Pittman* (1971). In Gaines's novel, the eponymous protagonist's account of her life from the 1860s to the 1960s also becomes a "community tale" of how African Americans on Louisiana sugarcane plantations endured the rollback of Reconstruction and decades of Jim Crow before seizing the overtly activist moment of "cooperative action" that was the Civil Rights movement. As the young historian who edits Jane's narrative observes, "there were times when others carried the story for her. When she was tired, or when she just did not feel like talking any more, or when she had forgotten certain things, someone else would always pick up the narration."⁶⁷ Something similar happens in *Louisiana*, except that in the seventeen years since Ella conducted her WPA interviews with Sue Ann, the "community tale" is extended through other media and into other places.⁶⁸ These alternative forums include Ella's private diary entries, finally published to a wider audience by the Black World Press in Miami; Ella's public contacts with Caribbean sailors in New Orleans; her psychic communication with Sue Ann, Louise, and Silas across temporal and spatial borders; and finally Reuben's epilogue, which suggests that the political spirit embodied by Ella/Louisiana will be extended to encompass not just the U.S. South and the Caribbean but the African diaspora more broadly conceived. Reuben first pays his respects by visiting Ella's homeland of Jamaica (165–66); then, pausing to note the return of black protest to New Orleans with the Civil Rights movement ("There is marching again here"), Reuben readies himself to join the Mau-Mau revolution versus Belgian colonial rule: "I am hearing of Kasavubu and Lumumba. I am beginning to think that I must put down my spade in the Congo where I was born. The prospect is exciting. That would be an extension of the community" (166). These final observations circa April 1954, a month before *Brown v. Board of Education* and the publication of *Youngblood*, anticipate Killens's linkage of the civil rights struggle downsouth and postcolonial revolution in the Global South. They also move *Louisiana* beyond Gaines's more "rooted" Louisiana fiction to extend across the (black) Atlantic the kinds of "routed," migratory, and diasporic communities that Hurston mapped throughout her life and work.

CHAPTER 6

Neoslavery, Immigrant Labor, and Casino Capitalism in Cynthia Shearer's *The Celestial Jukebox*

Cynthia Shearer's novel *The Celestial Jukebox* (2005) reworks a familiar southern literary theme: the transformation of a rural, agricultural community—the fictional Mississippi Delta hamlet of Madagascar—by capitalist modernity. What makes Shearer's novel so powerful is its complex engagement with the social and demographic shifts generated by contemporary economic globalization and immigration. Prominent strands of the narrative focus on the arrival of immigrants from both south of the U.S. South (Honduras and Mexico) and across the Atlantic (Mauritania in northwest Africa): people whose lives are, in Matthew Guterl's words, "marked by polylingual, transnational, and economic connections to a global South running from ... Asia to Africa to Latin America."[1] However, *The Celestial Jukebox* does not figure these shifts simply as global-southern breaks with a rooted, place-based, regional-southern past. Shearer's novel also assesses the uncanny continuities between the employment and exploitation of immigrant workers in the twenty-first-century South and the labor practices that characterized the region during and after slavery.

To disentangle the interwoven threads of *The Celestial Jukebox*'s wide-ranging engagement with economic globalization, migration, and labor in the contemporary South, this chapter is divided into four sections. I begin with the immigrant narrative of Angus Chien, sole owner and proprietor of Madagascar's Celestial Grocery. The story of the Chien family, which in some ways is metonymic of the "Mississippi Chinese" experience more generally, represents an earlier case of immigration to the South that anticipates the influx of Hondurans, Mexicans, and Mauritanians in the narrative present. Moreover, the novel dramatizes how the changing socioeconomic status of the Mississippi Chinese throughout the twentieth century both challenged and reinforced the region's rigid racial structures. In the second section, I turn to *The Celestial Jukebox*'s representation of the shift in rural delta land use since the 1940s, especially in relation to the globalization of agriculture at the turn of the millennium. This "jumping" of geographic scale from the local to the global connects with the ways in which two local farmers, Dean Fondren and Aubrey Ellerbee, employ gambling metaphors. These metaphors express not only the difficulties of farming locally in an era when agricultural production and competition has gone global, but also the complexity of living within the wider economic system of "casino capitalism." The proliferation of casinos in and around Madagascar provides the novel's most vivid metaphor for—and material example of—this casino capitalism. But rather than representing a radical break with earlier modes of agricultural production based on slavery and sharecropping, casino capitalism references and recalls those regional structures. In the third section, I demonstrate how *The Celestial Jukebox* explores the eerie echoes resounding between the regional history of slavery and the "neoslavery" labor formations of the globalized South in the twenty-first century. The legacies of plantation slavery resonate at casinos performing a simulacrum of the Old South while employing new arrivals from Africa and in the arduous fieldwork undertaken by immigrants from Latin America.

In the fourth and final section, I focus on Boubacar Traore, a fifteen-year-old immigrant from Mauritania. Boubacar's story encapsulates the ambiguities and ironies arising from the intersection of slavery's legacies with contemporary African immigration. Moreover, Boubacar's own experience of slavery in Mauritania—a country that outlawed slavery as recently as 1980 and where bondage yet endures—invites us to consider the specter of the "peculiar institution" not as a distinctly U.S. southern legacy but in comparative, transatlantic perspective. Finally, I show how *The Celestial Jukebox* traces another kind of transnational ligature between Africa and the U.S. South: Boubacar's experience of music as a fluid and hybrid expressive form that, circulating across the black Atlantic, affirms the continuities between African and African American cultures.

Global Southern Sojourners and Settlers: The Mississippi Chinese

The hamlet of Madagascar is in many ways an identifiably southern (literary) community, constituted as it is by "a small handful of people out in the middle of nowhere who had learned to look out for each other."[2] Yet the narrative's core trio of long-term residents collectively embodies complicated racial histories and demographic shifts that predate the novel's primary focus on globalization, immigration, and labor in the twenty-first-century South. This trio comprises a white small farmer, Dean Fondren; a black agricultural entrepreneur, Aubrey Ellerbee, once Dean's protégé but now Madagascar's most prominent individual landowner and employer; and Angus Chien, the Chinese-born proprietor of the Celestial Grocery, home of the eponymous jukebox and the hub of the hamlet for some sixty years.

Early on the narrator remarks: "The Celestial was the last of a constellation of Chinese-run country stores that used to exist in almost every river town between Memphis and New Orleans" (31). Historian James W. Loewen observes that the first Chinese grocery opened in Mississippi as early as 1872 or 1873. However, as I noted in the introduction, the Chinese presence in the delta goes back to the late 1860s, when primarily Cantonese workers from south China began to arrive at the instigation of cotton planters seeking to solve the labor upheaval that followed Emancipation and Confederate military defeat. Already in 1869, Frederick Douglass noted that the planters had introduced "a kind of Asiatic slave trade" intended "to supplant the black laborer in the South"; in this regard, "coolie" labor also anticipated the importation of Caribbean agricultural "guest workers" during and after World War II (see chapters 1 and 5).³ Loewen and Moon Ho Jung have shown that after 1870, planters hoped that Chinese immigrants would bolster "white political power by displacing voting Negroes" enfranchised by the Fifteenth Amendment.⁴ When native black southerners reacted to the "Redemption" of the white South by migrating themselves, as during the 1879 "Kansas Fever," delta planters turned again to Chinese immigrant labor to keep their plantations functioning. But the Chinese refused to accept their assigned lot as the solution to the postbellum crisis of southern labor. The earliest arrivals from China saw themselves not as migrants but "sojourners, temporary residents in a strange country, planning to return to their homeland when their task [earning money to send back home to their families] was accomplished."⁵ Moreover, Chinese immigrants were unwilling to remain as plantation workers: an increasing number became merchants, in the process cannily exploiting the South's rigid biracial social structures by establishing businesses in black neighborhoods that white businessmen deemed beneath them. As more Chinese prospered as grocers, they also became settlers rather than sojourners. Though the 1882 Chinese Exclusion Act stymied immigration—as David M. Reimers notes, it "marked the first time Congress banned a specific nationality group"—Chinese "black-oriented groceries" in the delta were for decades sufficiently prosperous "to encourage male relatives to come in from China and from other parts of the United States."⁶

In *The Celestial Jukebox*, Solomon Chien and his son Angus arrive in Madagascar in 1938 as refugees from the atrocities committed by Japanese soldiers in Nanking during the second Sino-Japanese War. Strictly speaking, this is historically anomalous: the Chinese exclusion acts were not repealed until 1943, following the wartime alliance between China and the United States against Japan. Nevertheless, the Chiens' arrival in Madagascar brings into focus the longer Chinese history of immigration to the Mississippi Delta that anticipates the arrival of African and Latin American immigrants in the narrative present; what is more, their establishment of the Celestial Grocery symbolizes a shift in local land use. Loewen notes that after about 1940 "the commissary on the plantation and the plantation store in town ... practically vanished," and because the social strictures of Jim Crow disallowed white merchants from filling the niche, "the field [was] open to the Chinese." Between the early 1940s and the late 1960s Chinese groceries were more commercially successful than ever: by 1970, over "90 percent of all Chinese families in Mississippi now operate[d] groceries."[7] *The Celestial Jukebox* captures this sociospatial shift in the delta economy by situating Solomon Chien's new store on the site of a former plantation commissary: "When the Chiens first arrived in America [in 1938], there was a faded tin sign over the store, ABIDE PLANTATION" (284). Yet if the Coca-Cola sign that replaces it symbolizes the ascendancy of consumer capitalism, Solomon Chien invests it with his own nonmonetary meanings. For Solomon, the "big red circle on the Coca-Cola sign" has less to do with sexualized commodification ("The painted woman lifted the drink with a knowing leer") than his own transnational familial trauma: the red circle reminds Solomon of the symbol at the center of the Japanese flag and "the bad things that had happened to his [Angus's] mother and his sister" during the Nanking Massacre (285). Solomon's solution is to remove the sign "to the side of the store" (286) and reintroduce the original commissary sign as elaborately redesigned by Marie Abide, a local artist and descendant of the plantation owners who sold the commissary to Solomon. Decades later, "there was a new Coca-Cola sign above the door," but Angus still honors his late father's grief by covering the red circle with "the Chinese character that represents *long life*" (287).

Delta Land Development and Casino Capitalism

The conversion of the Abide commissary into the Celestial Grocery foreshadows the intensified redevelopment of former plantation land up to the narrative present. Most immediately, part of the plantation was divided into small farms. As I have discussed elsewhere, during the 1930s the Nashville Agrarians figured the small farmer (rather than the planter) as the South's man at the center and celebrated the small farm (rather than the plantation) as the region's rooted bulwark against modern U.S. finance capitalism.[8] But Dean Fondren's small farm is no neo-Agrarian haven; neither is Dean, *pace* Neil Segars's dubious claim, "a Delta planter fallen from grace."[9] Dean's farm does not predate or preclude modern capitalist development, originating as it does from speculation in former plantation land: Dean "purchased from a Memphis holding company the tract of land on which the old Abide house, her [Marie Abide's] grandfather's, still stood like a marooned riverboat" (14). By the turn of the twenty-first century, agricultural competition in the Global South threatens the farm's future, and Dean articulates his awareness of this perilous situation in the form of a rhetorical question: "Why buy a Mississippi strawberry when you could get it for a fraction of the cost in South America, where the government supplied the overseers and there was no minimum wage?" (326). This rhetorical question also captures the cognitive "jumping" across geographic scales that Neil Smith suggests is required to fathom how and why capitalism's globalized search for ever-cheaper labor can impact at the most local, personal level.[10] But even more strikingly, Dean also figures farming as a form of gambling: "It was not the first time in his life Dean had borrowed more money than he could comprehend. And it was not the first time in his life everything he'd ever worked for was wagered on a certain six weeks in which it might rain too much or not enough. It was an old knowledge in his bones now: he could lose the land beneath his feet sixteen ways from Sunday, depending on several floating variables of rain, sun, and the federal government" (98).

Dean here relates the "wager" of small-scale farming to both natural phenomena (the land and the weather) and socioeconomic factors, including competition from cheaper labor elsewhere in the globalized agricultural economy. However, the correlation between farming and gambling gains considerable extra resonance from the latest form of delta land development: the construction of huge casinos in and around Madagascar. While both Angus's store and Dean's farm result from the small-scale commercial redevelopment of former plantation land, they are dwarfed by the Lucky Leaf Casino, built in "Israel Abide's main cotton field, which had been so large it had taken six cotton pickers at the time to work it" (181). Another casino development threatens to uproot long-established members of the Madagascar community: Angus receives a letter with an offer to buy his land from an "outfit calling itself *Futuristics*, with a riverfront address in Memphis" (31). Angus subsequently learns from Aubrey, who has received a similar letter, that Futuristics is a "*[g]ambling company*," and when Angus asks Aubrey if he intends to sell his land to the casino, Aubrey's response amplifies Dean's connection between farming and gambling: "*Hell, I'm already gambling everything I got, every day. I gamble that the rain will come. I gamble that the sun will shine. I could lose it all, kapow, just like that*" (37).

The speculative development of casinos in and around Madagascar indicates how, as Tara McPherson observes, casino gambling has become "one of the region's new tourist industries."[11] In June 1990 the Mississippi state legislature passed the Gaming Control Act, following Nevada's model of low taxes on casino profits and a level of support from the Mississippi Gaming Commission that "defined their role as promoting the casino industry, not just regulating it." By 1996, there were twenty-nine non–Native American casinos in the state; by 2004, casinos—primarily located on the Gulf Coast and in Tunica County in northwest Mississippi—were generating $2.8 billion in gross revenues and employing between 28,000 and 30,000 workers. Fully 78 percent of that revenue came from tourists or visitors.[12] Such radical transformation has prompted poet Natasha Trethewey to observe that "the casinos are now the creators of the dominant economic narrative" in Mississippi and that their "corporate narratives can prevail, cross-written over the small-town story."[13]

More than that, though, the casinos provide a compelling metaphor for "casino capitalism" as a wider (indeed, worldwide) socioeconomic phenomenon. In *Casino Capitalism* (1986), political economist Susan Strange wrote: "The Western financial system is rapidly coming to resemble nothing so much as a vast casino. Every day games are played in this casino that involve sums of money so large that they cannot be imagined." Strange remarked that while this deregulated, technologically mediated, and increasingly decentered "global casino of high finance" had moved beyond the control and decision-making of nation-states, it impacted profoundly on the everyday life of ordinary people—people like Dean, Aubrey, and Angus: "A currency change can halve the value of a farmer's crop before he harvests it.... A rise in interest rates can fatally inflate the cost of holding stocks for the shop-keeper.... [W]hat goes on in the casino in the office blocks of the big financial centers is apt to have sudden, unpredictable and unavoidable consequences for individual lives."[14] In *The Celestial Jukebox*, the materialization of casino capitalism in the form of the Lucky Leaf occasionally recalls the Agrarians' jeremiads against the destruction of "place" and "community" by finance capitalism and land speculation. When Boubacar first arrives at the Memphis airport, he meets an African American soldier who helps him locate his Mauritanian relatives in Madagascar. The soldier asks, "*How your people come to be in that place? It ain't even a place no more, just kind of pass it on the way to the casino*" (20). Here one might discern an echo of Robert Penn Warren's assertion circa 1936 that the "abstract" property relations of finance capitalism destabilize "the relation of man to place."[15] There are moments too when operations at the Lucky Leaf recall Strange's observations about the intensification and acceleration of casino capitalism through the ceaseless 24/7 operation of the global financial markets: as "a big bunker with no windows" that is open night and day, the Lucky Leaf is shrewdly designed to ensure that its customers "*lose track of time*" (182).[16] At such moments Shearer's novel figures casino capitalism as an invasive, distinctive, and debilitating socioeconomic formation that appears to usurp Madagascar's traditional, natural, rural, and agricultural southern way of life. Here *The Celestial Jukebox* has something in common with *Yonder Stands Your Orphan* (2000), the final novel by Shearer's former teacher Barry Hannah. As Scott Romine has shown, *Yonder Stands Your Orphan* depicts a rural southern "home," Eagle's Lake, Mississippi, imperiled by "the surrounding dystopian terrain of Big Marts, bad restaurants, tourist traps, and Vicksburg casinos, the last described by one character as 'math become a monster.'" Romine notes that Hannah's novel mourns the loss of "a shared social space" eroded by "an abject terrain of casino capitalism and pawn shop culture."[17]

Yet *The Celestial Jukebox* also challenges and complicates oversimplistic oppositions between the southern agrarian tradition and (post)modern land speculation; between a nostalgic sense of place on the small farm and a dystopian sense of displacement in the capitalist casino. Dean, Aubrey, and Angus are not neo-Agrarian small farmers and shopkeepers helplessly swamped by globalization; rather, they are both subject to and complicit with casino capitalism. When Aubrey declares to Angus that "*I'm already gambling everything I got, every day*," he signals a connection rather than a contrast between his daytime existence as a farmer and his nighttime status among the "clients" at the Lucky Leaf. Like Dean, Aubrey knows that farming itself has become enmeshed in a speculative system where a "currency change can halve the value of a farmer's crop before he harvests it." Hence there is a certain logic in Aubrey's path from farm to casino: "Each night he lay down to sleep having wagered every dime he owned on the next day, on the wayward variables of rainfall, the fluctuations of government subsidies, plus the migratory flights of Hondurans. It was one such night that he first went to the casino" (199).

Aubrey and Angus conform in other ways to the speculative logic of casino capitalism. Strange emphasizes the prominent role of speculation in "financial futures" throughout the contemporary capitalist system, describing such speculation as a rarified and highly abstracted form of gambling: "A speculative market can be defined as one in which prices move in response to the balance of opinion regarding the future movement of prices, as distinct from normal markets in which prices move in response to objective changes in the demand for, or supply of, a usable commodity or service. In this respect, a speculative market most resembles a racecourse, where there is a market for bets on the horses (or dogs) that will win or get a place." Within such a market, speculators/gamblers look to "anyone with ready access to the opinions of operators [who] will have better information."[18] In Angus's case, a cousin in New York advises him to invest in (or gamble on) stocks. Strikingly, Angus gambles on Futuristics and the Arkansas-based grocery chain Dixie Barrel, even though these are the very companies that threaten to uproot Angus from his land and store (87, 393). In the capitalist casino where, as Strange remarks, "futures trading in commodities has been completely overtaken by trading in financial futures," the suitably named Futuristics seems a safe bet to Angus's cousin because the firm retains a speculative interest in that most valuable of material commodities: the land on which it builds its casinos (though as Fredric Jameson remarks, even land value is "intimately related to the credit system, the stock market and finance capital generally" in that all are forms of "fictitious capital" derived from the expectation of "future profits").[19] Meanwhile, Aubrey tries to assuage a sense of "his own weightlessness" as his farm melts into debt: "he'd get up out of bed and get on the Internet and search for himself, look himself up on the NASDAQ as if to reassure himself he'd not yet been buried alive"

(199). In a technologically mediated speculative financial system which fulfills Strange's prediction that "the moment is rapidly approaching when for all financial dealing, there will no longer be 'financial centers' in the old sense, but one widespread global market in financial futures," it is disturbingly apt that Aubrey, gambling in the stock market from rural Mississippi, seeks his identity in stocks that are doubly abstracted by the constant online operation of the global capitalist casino. The threat of repossession means that farmland provides Aubrey with no secure sense of self or "relation of man to place": like Eddie Dubois in Russell Banks's *Continental Drift*, Aubrey senses that to be "repossessed" is to lose not merely one's property but one's very identity.[20]

Immigrant Labor and Neoslavery in the Globalized South

Yet rather than enacting a radical break with a (mythic) southern past rooted in farming the land, casino capitalism in *The Celestial Jukebox* draws on that past—or rather a simulacrum of it. The Lucky Leaf Casino plugs into what McPherson refers to as "the romanticized history of the plantation" perpetrated by "the nostalgia industry." Besides being built on the site of the former Abide plantation, the casino features "mindless murals of the old moss-draped *trompe l'oeil* plantations on the walls, while uniformed overseers stood stationed like sentinels at discreet intervals" (183). Plantation tourism is thus yoked to the twenty-first-century rise of casino tourism: as McPherson remarks, "[a]ll over the South, 'heritage' tourism has been enjoying a resurgence in popularity, fueled by the growth of casino gambling."[21] To adopt Romine's terms, the Lucky Leaf "produces locality in ways that are recognizably archaic" by utilizing "a distinctively late-capitalist set of tools."[22] But as a simulacrum of the Old South, the Lucky Leaf is hardly "the reflection of a basic reality"; rather, in Jean Baudrillard's distinction, "it masks the *absence* of a basic reality"—the regional history of slavery.[23] Southern heritage industries reproduce romantic myths of the plantation even as they "must necessarily repress the memory and legacies of slavery."[24] At the Lucky Leaf, the conspicuous presence of "uniformed overseers" signifies on while simultaneously evading the ambiguous status of the casino's black employees as costumed neoslaves; similarly, the casino's internal currency, a "pseudo-money, something resembling old plantation scrip" (185), gestures to yet never explicitly acknowledges the postslavery exploitation of black sharecroppers. (Dean can still remember "the arpeggio of sharecropper shacks that had once belonged to the big house" [14] on the land the casino now occupies.) Such selective commodification of southern plantation imagery is also apparent at Madagascar's new Dixie Barrel: the chain store charges visitors to its "*souvenir shop*" a price of "*three dollars for one cotton boll wrapped in a little baggie*" (36). Jessica Adams posits that "both the slave and the commodity fetish are things for sale in which people have been obscured by the processes of production." If Dixie Barrel's bagged cotton bolls are commodity fetishes for an idealized plantation South, they also suggest how "slavery shrinks into a memory of leisure anchored by recommodified things."[25]

However, the legacies and memories of slavery cannot be entirely repressed. Their return is triggered by the employment in the delta of nonwhite immigrant workers from Africa and Latin America. As Adams notes, in the contemporary South "[t]he image of the plantation as an uncomplicated site of white achievement" is juxtaposed with and challenged by "landscapes irrevocably shaped by industrialism and globalization" and increasingly populated by immigrant workers.[26] Much as Dixie Barrel's King Cotton fetishism is facilitated by the "*three shifts of Mexicans*" (36) who built the new store, the Lucky Leaf's corporate owners in Nevada rely on low-wage immigrant workers like Boubacar's Mauritanian uncles to sustain the day-to-day operation of their neoplantation. This generates eerie historical resonances: entering the casino for the first time, Dean is struck that the presence of dark-skinned employees intones the gaudy history of slavery: "Liveried valets from Africa and Arkansas loitered in purple coats with golden epaulets under a splendid fringed purple awning. The Africans spoke English with French accents, murmuring in exaggerated politeness to squinting senior citizens debarking from buses that could double as ambulances. Mississippi had not seen such tasteless excess since before the Civil War. Everybody knew the sad outcome of *that*" (181).

Dean has entered the casino in order to extricate Aubrey from further gambling debts, and there is a grim irony that Aubrey, a descendant of slaves, has become subject to the casino's neoplantation economy. However, Shearer does not push the analogy between slave plantation and capitalist casino too far, and for good reason: the complexities arising from the intersection of local southern history and a modern global economy mitigate against easy transhistorical equivalences. As the largest local agricultural landowner, Aubrey can hardly be characterized only as the oppressed descendant of slaves. One might be tempted to argue that Aubrey's entanglement with the Lucky Leaf demonstrates the power of (casino) capitalism to "enslave" even the shrewdest workers and that the casino's "clients," rather than the African employees, are the true neoslaves, subject as they are to the gaze of "muscled overseers standing on what once had all been cotton fields" (185) and the rigged circulation of "casino scrip" (182). However, such an argument would be susceptible to the pitfalls of relativism that imperil any attempt to compare the modes of production and forms of labor in slave-based and "free" market systems. Adams observes that for "Karl Marx, capitalism has the ability to enslave." But when Marx wrote in *Capital* that workers must guard against "selling themselves and their families into slavery and death by voluntary contract with capital," was he speaking literally or metaphorically of capitalism as slavery?[27] Was Marx suggesting that "free" wage labor was equivalent to racialized chattel slavery, a system that still existed in the U.S. South? Historian David Roediger has traced how among U.S. labor leaders "instances of comparison between wage labor and chattel slavery between 1830 and 1860 were... both insistent and embarrassed" as "the stunning process by which some white workers came to call themselves slaves" was undermined by "the tendency for metaphors concerning white slavery to collapse." There were various reasons for this, but "a consistent lesson taught by abolitionism was that chattel slavery was a category of oppression much harsher than any other."[28] Meanwhile, native white southern contemporaries of Marx like George Fitzhugh compared slave and free labor but did so in order to assert the moral superiority of racial chattel slavery in the South over "wage slavery" in the urban North.

The shade of these antebellum debates and metaphors looms over contemporary loose talk about global, neoliberal capitalism *as* slavery. When Dean imagines his wife Alexis asking, "[W]hy would he want anyone else to be enslaved to the same piece of land he'd been a slave to most of his life?" Dean responds mentally "*Everybody has to be a slave to something*" (107). Dean's phlegmatic worldview is admirable, given that he has recently borrowed from a bank "an amount of money that was incomprehensible to him, in order to get his crops in the ground" (97), but the slavery metaphor jars when one recalls that Dean's land was once, like the site of the Lucky Leaf casino, worked by black slaves. The intersection of local southern history and a modern global economy, and the accompanying discourse of (neo)slavery and casino capitalism, is further complicated when one turns to the novel's representation of immigrant labor. As Dean recognizes, the Lucky Leaf's employment of African workers recalls a larger regional tradition of racialized labor exploitation. Boubacar's Mauritanian uncles dare not leave work to welcome him to the United States in case they lose their jobs to other new arrivals: "A worker had taken time off for his wife to give birth, so his uncles had said, and found himself replaced that very day by another Mauritanian, someone from his same street back in Nouakchott" (17). Yet these immigrants are not simply passive victims of a timeless southern practice of exploiting dark-skinned workers. They affirm their social and economic agency, and they do so at a transnational scale. The African American soldier who assists Boubacar at the Memphis airport is bemused to discover that this black boy is going south to Mississippi. Having sketched the northward trajectory of the Great Migration, the soldier declares: "*See, everybody else all the time trying to get the fuck out, and here you go, trying to get the fuck in*" (24). While Boubacar knows nothing about the regional history of racial strife, he understands that "*[c]asino money is very good in my village*" (23) back in Mauritania. As I noted in the introduction, Global South workers are often well aware that under neoliberal capitalism, wages remain far higher in a hegemon like the United States: while at the national scale wages in the South remain "well below the U.S. average... in the broader global context the

South has become a high-wage region."²⁹ This may staunch the influx of foreign corporations looking for ever cheaper labor, but it makes Mississippi attractive to immigrants like Boubacar and his relatives because wage remittances to Mauritania are a crucial source of income.

A further complexity arises from Aubrey's exploitation of nonwhite immigrant labor. Aubrey complains that he cannot hire Africans because "[t]*hey all want to wear them tuxedoes over at the casino*" (35), yet he considers "the migratory flights of Hondurans" part of his "wager" in the global capitalist casino. Writing about the role of Mexican migrant labor in the contemporary South, anthropologist Sandy Smith-Nonini observes: "In agriculture, a labor-intensive industry that depends on land—a non-exportable resource—labor relations become paramount." Cheap, mobile transnational labor is especially crucial within the "competitive climate" of a globalized agricultural market where strawberries can be produced in South America at "a fraction of the cost" in the U.S. South.³⁰ By hiring illegal Honduran migrant workers from the mysterious Hispanic contractor Tomás Tulia, Aubrey is effectively gambling on cheap migrant labor offsetting the fierce competition that he (like Dean) faces from a putatively "modern" global agricultural economy that, south of the U.S. South, retains the exploitative labor practices of plantation America ("the government supplied the overseers and there was no minimum wage"). Aubrey addresses criticism that he is exploiting the Honduran workers with the cynical retort that "*the whole country would go under if we all paid real wages*" (135).

For other characters, however, Aubrey's willfully ignorant contract hiring of Honduran workers from Tulia recalls a southern history of labor exploitation that encompasses not only slavery but also the postplantation exploitation of native blacks and nonwhite immigrants. Dean warns Aubrey: "*They got laws now, for what you got to give your workers. Otherwise, these folks come in from these other places and just drag in the same old troubles we got over a long time ago, start up the same old mess all over again*" (208). Though well intentioned, Dean's attempt to remind Aubrey of the local history of racialized labor relations is freighted with ambiguity. Dean could be alluding to Reconstruction or the Civil Rights movement, but he draws on a distinctly *white* southern discourse that figures outside agitators as the agents of (rather than activists against) racial "trouble." Moreover, by using the plural pronoun "we," Dean rhetorically co-opts Aubrey to a simplified vision of cross-racial southern community. Similar ambiguities are apparent in the ways that nonwhite, nonsouthern characters relate the region's racial history to Aubrey's present-day status as the largest local agricultural landowner. The young black photographer Peregrine Smith-Jones, the daughter of Princeton professors, perceives Aubrey as an unscrupulous neoplanter whose spiraling debts to the casino constitute a kind of comeuppance: "*There's a kind of justice in this, don't you think?... I mean, the big daddies could finally lose their plantations, right?*" (186). But Dean defends Aubrey, in turn accusing Peregrine of perverting the legacy of her southern slave ancestors by working part-time as a waitress at the Lucky Leaf, which he again figures as a modern-day plantation: "*You know there's more'n one way to be a slave to white men*" (187). Once more the barely repressed legacy of plantation slavery returns at the casino but does so in the overwrought rhetoric of a southern white man telling a nonsouthern black woman that she is a voluntary slave.

Angus Chien's subject position within this fraught discourse of slavery and neoslavery is perhaps the most complicated. This arises partly from Angus's unusual status as an earlier immigrant to the South, and partly from amorous feelings for his new employee, Consuela Ramirez. Consuela too is an immigrant: born in Honduras and naturalized as an American citizen in Texas, she has recently arrived in Madagascar with her migrant worker sons, who are contracted through Tulia to work in Aubrey's fields. Motivated by a clumsy chivalry toward Consuela, Angus confronts Aubrey about Tulia's abusive treatment of Ramirez family members: "*That Tulia is a bad bird, Aubrey. Bad doings. He's buying and selling his own kind.*" In sarcastic self-defense Aubrey invokes the southern history of whites enslaving blacks: "*As opposed to buying and selling them that ain't your kind?*" (135). Exasperated, Angus tries to claim empathy with Aubrey's ancestral history by gesturing to his own heritage as a Chinese immigrant: "*Look, I didn't ask to come here, and your people sure as hell didn't ask to come here, but nevertheless we all here now*" (136). Aubrey refrains from pointing out the difference between the African slave trade, which brought "his people" to Mississippi, and the voluntary arrival of the Mississippi Chinese (or in Angus's family's case, as refugees from the Japanese invasion of Nanking). Angus recapitulates his reductive equation between African American slavery and the delta Chinese experience when he confronts Tulia himself: "*You doin' the same thing to those people [Consuela and her family] that was done to my people and to Aubrey's a long time ago. . . . You was telling those men they got to buy their food only from you, cause you the boss*" (203). For all the righteous fervor fueling Angus's indictment of Tulia's labor practices, the implication that the earlier exploitation of Chinese immigrants is comparable to African American slavery remains problematic. As we have seen, even the earliest Chinese arrivals in the late 1860s quickly left the cotton fields; moreover, having arrived in 1938, Angus himself has no more ancestral connection to those first immigrants than Helga Crane does to the black southern "folk" in Nella Larsen's *Quicksand*.

An even more loaded exchange occurs when Aubrey enters the store during Angus's showdown with Tulia. Angus vents his fury at Aubrey's complicity with the contractor by using the most loaded epithet of all: "*Get out of my place of business, nigger*" (204). Angus's racial slur signals the depth of his anger at the exploitation of Consuela's family, but it also suggests something of the delta Chinese's peculiar situation within the slowly shifting racial structures of the post-1945 South. In 1927 the Supreme Court's *Lum v. Rice* decision upheld racial segregation in Mississippi schools by defining the "Mongolian or yellow race" as part of the "colored races"; in the next few decades, many Mississippi Chinese worked hard to distinguish themselves from the African American population with whom they had been legally classified: "The Chinese ... began to take seriously white Mississippi's low placement of them. They then worked systematically to eliminate the causes of that treatment, in order to rise from Negro to white status." Writing in 1971, Loewen remarked: "For a time they were considered neither white nor black" but "are now viewed as essentially 'white.'"[31] But in a more recent study of Asian Americans' "racial interstitiality" within an otherwise strictly segregated South, Leslie Bow observes that however successful Mississippi Chinese businessmen became, they were still perceived by powerful whites as "partly colored."[32] Angus's actions over the course of three decades exhibit the profound ambiguities involved in negotiating this racial interstitiality. On one hand, there is a striking flashback to 1974 in which Angus takes a stand for and with Aubrey after local white farmers "threaten Aubrey for becoming a landowner." According to Segars, here "Angus most clearly subverts [Robert Seto] Quan's depiction of Chinese in the post Civil Rights era as being deferential to whites and wary of blacks."[33] On the other hand, the novel also casts back to a scene circa 1971 (not cited by Segars) in which Angus aligns himself with local whites. That year Aubrey's father, Raymond Ellerbee, was killed in Vietnam and his body brought back to Madagascar. Dean was powerfully affected by the death of this local soldier but realized that he barely knew Ray due to racial segregation; this prompted Dean to start questioning Jim Crow and to act by helping dig Ray's grave. But as a Chinese immigrant, Angus did not dare challenge Madagascar's racial mores, instead anxiously reaffirming his difference from blacks by telling Dean that "*They got their own world.... They don't tell us their business. You know that*" (189). Though Angus did provide Dean with a shovel to dig Ray's grave, his possessive, pronominal investment in whiteness illustrates the restrictive nature of identity formation in a society defined by the racial binaries of black and white, and how, as Bow notes, "[t]he immigrant will to incorporation" sometimes "manifests itself as a learned racism against the African American."[34] In two scenes thirty years apart, Angus's use of the word "business" suggests the ethical as well as economic implications of Delta Chinese efforts to elevate themselves socially: his reaffirmation of racial difference ("*They don't tell us their business*") segues into the expression of a decidedly familiar form of racism ("*Get out of my place of business, nigger*"). The fact that, circa 2001, Aubrey is now far wealthier than the Chinese man whose grocery he integrated three decades earlier is momentarily obscured by the recrudescence of the old racial slur; the historical baggage hanging on

Angus's use of the n-word complicates Segars's claim that Angus's "insulting powerful men of the community" (Tulia and Aubrey) is "all for the sake of the oppressed Hispanic workers."[35]

Angus may have evaded the Civil Rights movement in 1971, but in 2001 his feelings for Consuela draw him inexorably into the Hondurans' struggle for better living and working conditions. Initially his involvement in this struggle is unwitting: dreamily enamored with Consuela, he does not realize that local residents believe he is helping her whole family to unionize. It is Dean who alerts Angus: "*They sayin' you helpin' the Hondurans put a union together.*" Such gossip has potentially serious implications: "In that isolated part of Mississippi the phrase [labor union] is used quietly, in the same manner one would raise the possibility of a deadly contagious disease" (125). When Angus subsequently addresses these rumors to Consuela, she explains that her missing son, Hector, has been helping organize migrant workers with "*money from the people in Florida. Immokalee pickers*" (128). Here *The Celestial Jukebox* alludes to one of the most significant efforts to organize Latino/a workers in the contemporary South, though one that again has historical resonances. As detailed by Zora Neale Hurston between the 1930s and 1950s (see chapter 1), south Florida has long experienced an annual influx of intraregional and transnational migrant workers each harvesting season. However, since the 1980s fruit and vegetable picking in the area has been increasingly dominated by Latino/a immigrants working in exploitative and abusive conditions for middlemen contractors employed by agribusiness corporations, supermarkets, and fast-food chains. As I noted in the introduction, attempts to ameliorate and resist such conditions prompted the formation of the Coalition of Immokalee Workers (CIW) in Collier County, Florida, in 1993. Before the CIW's successful campaigns against McDonald's and Taco Bell, pickers in Immokalee earned as little as forty cents for each thirty-two-pound bucket of tomatoes, working conditions that prompted a Justice Department official to call south Florida "ground zero for modern slavery."[36]

Another dimension of this "modern slavery" is the trafficking or smuggling of young Latina women, "some as young as fourteen, into the United States" with promises of domestic and agricultural work; having paid substantial smuggling fees to cross the border, thousands of women have been "held in sexual slavery."[37] In Shearer's novel, Consuela reveals to Angus that her niece was sent from Honduras to work in the United States but has been pressed by "*Tulia's people*" into prostitution. Consuela's son Hector, who has pursued the disappearance of his cousin, has vanished too. Consuela indicates to Angus that this is not so much because Hector knows about the sexual slavery—Consuela's niece has been recovered and anyway "[e]*verybody knows about the girls.... They got many girls. Nobody cares about them*" (134)—but due to his wider efforts, supported by the CIW, to organize migrant labor against exploitative contractors like Tulia. In a tour de force chapter entitled "Nocturne, with Black Escalade," the narrative tracks the movement through Madagascar and north along Highway 61 of the black car in which a captive Hector is transported before being beaten, bound, and thrown off a bridge in Helena by local gangsters operating in the pay of Tulia.

By the turn of the twenty-first century, evidence of involuntary servitude in agricultural labor camps across the rural South had become so pronounced that the government's attempt to pass the Victims of Trafficking and Violence Protection Act in 2000 included a proposed "federal felony charge for holding people in involuntary servitude, updating the Thirteenth Amendment's prohibition of slavery to take into account the combination of debt peonage and psychological coercion that characterize modern slavery."[38] In *The Celestial Jukebox*, Dean ponders the bleak living conditions of Aubrey's Honduran employees and recalls "rumors of work camps so far back from the river roads that nobody knew what went on there, and nobody had the nerve to ask" (102–3). From such dire accounts and grim rumors, it is all too feasible to compare the so-called *nuevo* New South with the plantation-based Old South. Guterl identifies historical continuities between the exploitation of African American slaves, Chinese coolies, Caribbean cane-cutters, and Central American agribusiness workers: "Like slaves and coolies, these men and women were (and are) 'nobodies'; and, as was the case in the age of the American Mediterranean, the United States is utterly dependent on their unfree, 'slavery-like' labor."[39] In the introduction, I showed how since 2006, numerous new southern studies scholars have expressed variations on Houston Baker's point that the "squalid subsistence-living conditions [that] are frequently the norm for Mexican and Central American farm workers" in the contemporary U.S. South "mirror in dark ways chattel slavery's worst deprivations of body and spirit."[40] *The Celestial Jukebox* anticipated such scholars by tracing the historical ligatures between African slavery in the antebellum South and the exploitation of Latino workers in today's globalized South: oppressive labor structures that seem distinctly "southern" even as they result from different eras of economic globalization. But Shearer refrains from figuring today's "modern slavery" as equivalent to antebellum chattel slavery; she refuses to render—to quote Yogita Goyal in another context—"slavery as a metaphor" in such a way that "the historical specificity of slavery as a transnational system of labor disappears from view."[41] Shearer's novel tracks less a "continuous thread" than what Michael P. Bibler calls an "irregular continuum" of racialized exploitation that reappears throughout southern history. Shearer shows how "even as we acknowledge the seeming repetition of events from slavery to the present," so "we should also quickly recognize that such comparison diminishes the unspeakable atrocities of African slavery and ignores the specificity of twenty-first century racism and poverty."[42]

Commodities and Cultural Continuities across the Black Atlantic

Just as Boubacar has begun to forge a new life in Madagascar by securing unpaid work in Angus's store, his situation is transformed once again by the arrival of the Wastrel, an Arab "Sufi master whose father had owned the boy's father's family" (113) back in Mauritania. Karyn H. Anderson notes that "[i]n an attempt to replicate the social stratification of Mauritania, the Wastrel assumes authority over Boubacar."[43] In doing so, the Wastrel also provides a running critique of U.S. capitalism, not least that native black southerners descended from slaves remain subject to false desires generated by commodity fetishism: "*They are not free.... They are owned by what they are driven to possess*" (371–72). Once again, then, the definition and meaning of "slavery" is recalibrated in complex ways: the Wastrel's view that African Americans are voluntary slaves to U.S. capitalism is (to put it mildly) problematic given his own family's ownership of slaves back home. The Wastrel also requires Boubacar to identify which people back in Mauritania were "[*b*]*izan* [free] *or harutine*." As Kevin Bales notes in *Disposable People: New Slavery in the Global Economy* (2000), Haratines are the class of ex-slaves or descendants of slaves, often the offspring of Arab masters and Afro-Mauritanian slave mothers, who traditionally "form a middle layer in Mauritanian society"—the "name literally means 'one who has been freed.'"[44] Boubacar himself believes that such categories are "complicated": of one "obscure old woman" named by the Wastrel, Boubacar recalls that she was well loved despite her "*harutine*" status, so "did it matter?" (372). Bales notes that under the "old slavery" system that endures in Mauritania, and in which "race matters intensely" in ways that recall "the nineteenth-century American South," there sometimes exists "a deep emotional link between master and slave." Bales terms this "the paradox of Mauritanian slavery," noting that despite its often "brutal" and extremely restrictive nature, some kinder masters treat "their inherited slaves almost as their own children" and that "[m]any slaves think of themselves as members of their master's family."[45] This recalls the paradoxical ideology of paternalism that, as Eric Foner remarks, allowed U.S. southern "slaveowners to think of themselves as kind, responsible masters even as they bought and sold their human property—a practice at odds with the claim that slaves formed part of the master's 'family.'"[46]

Mauritanian slavery has endured despite its official abolition in 1980, but Western criticism of the practice has involved a sizable dose of moral hypocrisy. Boubacar's grandmother was once paid by a French television crew to "lower her veil and look into their cameras" while an interviewer smugly declared: "*Look into the eyes of the Western world.... Let them see the face of slavery*" (22). As Amira Jarmakani has argued, at least since the 1979 Iranian

Revolution "the veil had functioned in the United States as shorthand" for a larger "narrative of Muslim women's oppression" which "implies that patriarchal oppression is inherent to Islam" and employs "a simplistic equation of being uncovered (unveiled), or revealed, with being modern and emancipated." Jarmakani suggests that "the symbol of the veil serves important purposes for the project of U.S. imperialism" (like French colonialism before it) by justifying political and military intervention in predominantly Arab and/or Muslim nations.[47] Yet "just as the Confederacy had a powerful friend in Great Britain, who needed the South's cotton," so the survival of slavery in Mauritania has been "supported by France [Mauritania's former colonial ruler] and the United States, who need help to stop the spread of Islamic fundamentalism."[48] Hence the "liberation" of oppressed nonwhite women is advocated, or the endurance of racial and sexual slavery tacitly accepted, depending on exigencies of U.S. foreign policy in a given time or place. Moreover, we have already seen how Shearer's narrative emphasizes the endurance of neoslavery within the United States' own borders: hidden in plain sight in "work camps" on "back roads," barely obscured by the veil of the "free" market.

Nevertheless, it remains that the Wastrel's claim that black southerners are still "*not free*" is conveniently detached from his own familial history of owning people. The Wastrel also fails or refuses to recognize the agency of minority groups, be they native black southerners or African immigrants. Nor does the Wastrel's view that African Americans are possessed by their desire for possessions—another moment resonating with *Continental Drift*'s focus on characters possessed by the spirit of capitalism—allow for the relative autonomy of cultural forms that are also commodities. Music emerges as the expressive form that encapsulates the widening chasm between the respective worldviews of Boubacar and the Wastrel. When Boubacar confesses that "*I am liking American music, the Johnny Cash, the B. B. King,*" the Wastrel responds witheringly: "*To L'Américain, everything is commodity. Even his misery. His misery is his music. He sells shares of it in the stock market. 'Futures,' he calls it*" (116–17). The Wastrel's view that "American music" is merely a "commodity" generating artificial desires in duped consumers tallies with his dim view of black Memphians "*owned by what they are driven to possess.*" But the Wastrel also echoes Theodor Adorno's older Marxist argument that popular music is the cultural logic of capitalist "standardization," thinly obscured by the "halo of free choice" that characterizes "pseudo-individualization."[49] By contrast, Boubacar figures popular music as a fluid and hybrid cultural form that both retains a relative autonomy from commodification and, circulating *as* a commodity throughout the black Atlantic, reaffirms the links between African and African American cultures.

In *The Black Atlantic*, Gilroy traces "the plural richness of black [musical] cultures in different parts of the world in counterpoint to their common sensibilities—both those residually inherited from Africa and those generated from the special bitterness of new world racial slavery."[50] Boubacar's story vividly dramatizes such pluralities *and* commonalities. *The Celestial Jukebox* depicts New World blues being transmitted "back" to Africa, long before Boubacar himself migrates—with his Salif Keita and Stella Chiweshe cassette tapes in tow—to the Mississippi Delta. Boubacar's appreciation of "American music" began with his discovery of "a John Lee Hooker tape in perfect condition" in a dustbin behind a tourist hotel in "the barren tent city of Nouakchott" (116), the capital of postcolonial Mauritania. Exploring the "transatlantic route[s]" of African American music, Gilroy notes how in the late nineteenth century Nashville's Fisk Jubilee Singers embodied "the passage of African-American folk forms into the emergent popular-cultural industries of the overdeveloped countries."[51] More than a century after the Jubilee Singers' European tours, Boubacar's discovery of music by Clarksdale-born, Memphis-bred Hooker exemplifies the passage of black southern cultural forms as commodities (such as cassette tapes) to so-called underdeveloped African countries via the global tourist industry. As Wanda Rushing emphasizes, "[G]lobal flows of technology and communication have carried Memphis music from its 'place' of origin to a receptive global audience"—though given that Boubacar discovers the tape while foraging in the hotel's waste, one might also say that Hooker's blues songs become (in Gilroy's phrase) "a variety of found sounds."[52]

Boubacar's engagement with black southern music while in Mauritania ensures that upon arrival in Mississippi he is already attuned to sonic links between the musical traditions he has inherited in Africa and the music he hears—and eventually plays—in the delta:

> Boubacar soon learned where to set his dial on the radio on Sunday nights to catch the live broadcasts from the churches in Clarksdale or the DJs spinning gospel tunes. He listened furtively in the dark, eavesdropping on the *kaffir*. Mississippi church music was a bright, brassy contretemps that reminded him a bit of Nigerian highlife sometimes, and *soukous* at others. He listened attentively for the moments when the women in the church would clap their hands in complicated contrapuntal rhythms, like the Senegalese. *Kaffir* music did not seem the danger that his grandmother had told him about. (291)

To the Wastrel, however, Boubacar's love of American music constitutes a kind of brainwashing that imperils the boy's duty to sustain the supposedly organic oral tradition of "*your father's songs*" (117). Though Boubacar stresses cultural and racial continuities between Africans and African Americans—"*Muddy Waters was a black man.... He looked a lot like Tariq Haifez, the Moroccan who used to come to Nouakchott to buy the scrap metal*" (150)— the Wastrel holds unyieldingly to his anticapitalist, anti-American, and anti-Semitic view of blues and rock.[53] Boubacar's embrace of American music is metonymized in the National Steel guitar that he first sees in the window of the Blackjack Zion Rescue Mission in Madagascar. For Boubacar, the National Steel is not simply a commodity but something sacred: "He would never smash the silver guitar, if Allah blessed him enough to own it. To smash an instrument was to destroy the spirits it harbored" (51). Boubacar's yearning to possess the guitar is secondary to its possession by spirits; he figures the guitar not as a commodity fetish (though it is that too—a gift bought for Boubacar by the Clarksdale blues musician Cornelius "Steakbone" Booker) but as a fetish in an earlier and notably African sense. As Melanie Benson remarks, "[T]he fetish originally denoted a man-made object perceived to have supernatural or religious significance and transformative power, particularly for the so-called primitive cultures of Egypt and Africa in collision with European Christianity in the sixteenth and seventeenth centuries."[54]

Boubacar learns to play the National Steel properly when he overcomes his residual "fear" of the "kaffir" (293) and their "infidel music" (295) to see the Mighty Sons of Destiny play live. When the African American musicians arrive, Boubacar observes "the differences in their faces. He could see the whole continent of Africa there, Kenya to Morocco" (294). The Mauritanian immigrant discovers that "Black *kaffir* music in America was a party of holy ghosts. It was like the bullets in the dry bones of the old slave believers, some of whom had surely been Sufis. No matter that the music was buried in the levees, on nights such as these it was seeping back to the surfaces in the churches, and it had spilled into the river of rock-and-roll" (300). In the imagery of bullet-ridden slave bodies and sound buried down by the river, another legacy of slavery resurfaces within the novel's contemporary global southern landscape: another version too of Patricia Yaeger's "reverse autochthony," that bleak regional history of black people being "hurled into water or earth without proper rituals, without bearing witness to grief, without proper mourning" (see also chapters 1 and 2).[55] But the South's barely repressed history also returns or "seeps back" in music that expresses what Gilroy calls the "slave sublime": though "generated from the special bitterness of new world racial slavery," this music reaches back and forth across time and space.[56] Boubacar can relate to this cultural legacy; indeed, at a later benefit for the Latino/a workers held at the Celestial Grocery and featuring the Mighty Sons of Destiny, even the Wastrel puts aside his prejudices about the commodified inauthenticity of American music: "There was a loud bump at the door, and all looked up in time to see the Wastrel, bringing in his big Wolof drum. The boy loved him then: that he would sit down with the *kaffir* to play, because it was kindness, it was the right thing to do for the Latinos who came from far away to make the roads and the buildings because *L'Américain* didn't like hard work anymore" (344).

However, such scenes of transnational cultural connection are soon overshadowed as Boubacar and his countrymen experience the immediate repercussions of 9/11. As Muslims and immigrants, Mauritanians come under suspicion in Mississippi and beyond: "A woman from Nouakchott who now lived in Kentucky phoned to say that her husband had been taken, as had all the Mauritanian men there" (412–13).[57] In this fraught climate of suspicion toward dark-skinned Muslims, Angus and Dean take Boubacar to Memphis to see the immigration judge whom he has been told "to contact if there was trouble" (17) and watch Boubacar "vanish into the crowd" (416) on Main Street. Boubacar seems to be following the bad example of the "boy from his neighborhood" who "had simply vanished, into the godless streets of Memphis" (18). But the narrative follows Boubacar as he walks through Memphis and into a branch of Tower Records where he "could hear African drums. It sounded very much like the Wastrel.... It was most definitely African drumming, probably Wolof" (417).

In fact, Boubacar is listening to "Sing, Sing, Sing," a Benny Goodman song featured on "a big band compilation"; as a Tower employee explains: "*We're supposed to be playing all this old war music*" (417) in the wake of the terrorist attacks. Both Goodman and Gene Krupa, the drummer on "Sing, Sing, Sing," were white jazzmen: Boubacar identifies Goodman as "the Jew" (418) who, according to the Wastrel, "*stole from the blacks, the whites, the classical composers*" (374). On the surface, then, the moment seems saturated by aesthetic, ethnic, and commercial inauthenticity: the "African drums" are in fact played by a Jewish-American musician on a commercial recording from an earlier age of mechanical reproduction, now recast in the era of late capitalism as a post-9/11 signifier of patriotism. Moreover, Boubacar experiences the moment in a chain record store located within a mixed-use development on the edge of the "Beale Street Historic District," a site that critics have dismissed as "just another theme park in a landscape of consumption ... a 'Disneyfied,' sanitized, contrived entertainment district for white tourists in a themed metropolis that is no longer considered a real place."[58] Yet it is a powerful experience for Boubacar, a kind of apotheosis of his immersion in "American music" as a creolized cultural form that resounds throughout the black Atlantic.

In this pivotal scene, *The Celestial Jukebox* diverges radically from Andrew Lytle's clarion call in *I'll Take My Stand* (1930) to preserve the (white) South's authentic, organic, and distinctly oral culture: "Throw out the radio and take down the fiddle from the wall."[59] There is too a striking departure from Fred Chappell's 1980 short story "Blue Dive," which depicts a jukebox in the eponymous North Carolina nightclub as a sinister symbol of modernity, churning out "machine music" that threatens to consign the songs of traveling bluesman Stovebolt Johnson to the dustbin of southern cultural history.[60] Boubacar's epiphany while listening to "Sing, Sing, Sing" in Tower Records recalls his earlier rapturous encounter with the Rock-ola jukebox in Angus's Celestial Grocery, "the most beautiful thing he had seen in all his fifteen years" (45), until he finds the National Steel guitar. Given Shearer's emphasis on transatlantic cultural and demographic continuities as well as the titular significance of "jukebox," it is entirely appropriate that Lorenzo Dow Turner (one of Zora Neale Hurston's teachers at Howard University) traced the word's etymology back through the Gullah word *jug* or *juk*, meaning "infamous, disorderly," to the Wolof word *jug*, meaning "to lead a disorderly life."[61] But while Angus's jukebox facilitates Boubacar's embrace of American music, the Rock-ola's playlist draws almost entirely from a biracial South that predates the boy's own immigrant experience: because the Rock-ola has "not been serviced since the riots in Memphis the night Martin Luther King died," it features only songs "released before April of 1968. Johnny Cash, Otis Redding, Carl Perkins, Percy Sledge, Slim Harpo, Wilson Pickett" (33). The Rock-ola's only concession to an immigrant South beyond the familiar black-white binary is "a torch song by Lydia Mendoza" and a 1920s Mexican *corrido* about deportation, "Los Deportados," sung by the Bañuelos Brothers, "left over from some summer past when there were more Mexican faces in the fields than black ones" (90). In "godless" Memphis on September 11, 2001, it is instead a chain record store that becomes Boubacar's own celestial jukebox, a magical multicultural space that enables the Mauritanian teenager to connect Jewish jazz musicians to Wolof drummers; where the sacred mingles with the profane (or *jug*); where spirit possession segues into commodity fetishism; and where creative love supersedes cultural theft: "The living and the dead were all here, in this place that was like a jukebox of all spirits. They had collected each other's songs, kept them safe, made new ones by stealing old ones" (418).[62]

As the novel ends, Boubacar is on the road again, playing Mauritanian songs on Beale Street before buying a bus ticket to New York: the latest in a long line of dark-skinned musicians to migrate north via Memphis, but also an African and Muslim who, in the charged aftermath of September 11, is gaining a double-edged "second sight in[to] this American world."[63] The power of *The Celestial Jukebox* as a narrative of casino capitalism, immigration, and labor in the globalized South is that it gives readers that second sight too.

CHAPTER 7

Southern Transpacific
Narratives of Asian Immigration, 1965–2015

The trajectories of transnational migration to and sometimes from the U.S. South upon which *Where the New World Is* has focused are primarily hemispheric (the Caribbean and Latin America in Hurston, Banks, Brodber, and Shearer) and transatlantic/black Atlantic (Europe in Larsen; Africa in Shearer and Brodber). Within transnational American studies, however, there has been increased attention to the transpacific. In his contribution to *Imagining Our Americas: Toward a Transnational Frame* (2007), Rob Wilson called for another recasting of "José Martí's North–South reformulations" to encompass the relationship between the United States and "the transnationalizing Pacific Rim." If Wilson is right that "the U.S. geopolitical imaginary" has been "transformed at both the global-transnational and local-subnational levels," what then of the relationship between the Global "East" and the subnational U.S. South?[1] In 2008 Harilaos Stecopoulos noted that "[w]hile hemispheric relations have been fruitfully examined in the new southern studies, the region's relations with other parts of the world remain largely unanalyzed," and proposed "the South's connection to China" as a promising line of enquiry.[2] The following year, Jaime Harker pointedly observed that "[t]he Pacific Rim, so far, has not figured prominently in . . . larger discussions of the global South and the 'new' Southern studies." Harker suggested that prioritizing plantation slavery and its legacies has meant that the new southern studies' vision of a putatively "global South is largely defined by the Caribbean and the Americas."[3] Furthermore, evidence that the Quentissential fallacy endures in southern (literary) studies can be found in the field's muted response to relevant texts by Asian American authors. As Leslie Bow remarks in *Partly Colored: Asians Americans and Racial Anomaly in the Segregated South* (2010), "Asian American literature is 'foreign' to the [sic] southern literature" because writers ranging from V. S. Naipaul to Susan Choi "who set Asian American prose narratives in the South or inscribe southern Asian American characters, are not widely recognized to be 'southern' writers."[4]

As in the cases of Larsen, Banks, and Brodber, I am not concerned with claiming these and other Asian American authors as "southern" or integrating their writing into an expanded southern literary canon. On one hand, attending to the demographic ligatures between Asia and the U.S. South facilitates the kinds of "multiethnic disruptions to the region's black-white binary" that Melanie Benson Taylor suggests have yet to register fully within the new southern studies, where "reductive racial contours" remain stubbornly persistent.[5] So if this chapter shifts our attention from the hemispheric to the transpacific, in certain ways it also circumvents those familiar black-white contours in ways that the circum-Caribbean focus of chapters 1, 4, and 5 could not. (After all, whether from the Bahamas, Haiti, or Jamaica, Afro-Caribbean migrants are "black" by conventional U.S. racial classification.) On the other hand, I share Bow's concerns that Asian Americans and their stories may be "all too readily incorporated into newer versions of the imagined South" as "multicultural, cosmopolitan, globally connected" that conveniently "serve to rebrand southern studies."[6] Having said that, literary representations of "Asians in the South" or southerners in Asia (see chapter 3) can help us "think globally and comparatively about the region" while simultaneously revealing the residual power of "southern" racial categories or structures of feeling.[7] For Bow, Asian American narratives are valuable precisely because they both "connect the region to circuits of economic globalization and transnational migration" *and* reconfigure (rather than transcend) the enduring significance of "the struggle central to southern literature... the tension between blacks and whites."[8]

Yet even when recognizably "southern" realities impinge upon the lives and labor of Asian immigrants, they do not necessarily define them. Indeed, the main claim of this chapter concerns "the South" as a scale of analysis. In two of the three works of fiction about Asian (Chinese and Vietnamese) immigration on which I focus, "the South" is not a scalar unit through which the protagonists understand their experiences. Though readers, especially those trained as "southernists," may be tempted to see these books as being about "Asians in the South" or as representative texts of a newly multiethnic southern literature, the central characters in Lan Cao's *Monkey Bridge* (1997) and Ha Jin's *A Free Life* (2007) do not regard themselves as being either "Asian" or in "the South"—let alone "southern." I begin this chapter, though, with *Bitter in the Mouth* (2010), Monique Truong's brilliantly observed novel about a South Vietnamese orphan, Linda Hammerick, adopted by a white southern family in small-town North Carolina. Because Linda (the narrator as well as protagonist) is integrated into both the family and the wider white community, she does grow up understanding herself as "southern"; moreover, Linda's self-fashioning and her narrative are saturated with intertextual references to seminal southern coming-of-age novels. Though the second half of *Bitter in the Mouth* subverts such familiar scripts, "the South" remains present throughout the novel as a scale through and against which Linda can formulate her identity.

In some ways, *Monkey Bridge* clearly resembles *Bitter in the Mouth*: like Truong's Linda, Cao's character-narrator Mai Nguyen is part of the "1.5 generation" of immigrants who spent part of their childhood in South Vietnam before the fall of Saigon in 1975.[9] But in stark contrast to Linda, neither Mai nor her mother, Thanh, register their new surroundings in suburban Virginia as "southern": the scale of "the South" is largely irrelevant to the Nguyen women and the rest of the "Little Saigon" community in Falls Church. Despite scholars' attempts to read *Monkey Bridge* and its other South (South Vietnam) through familiar southern literary-critical "senses" of place and history, such tropes are at best tenuous, not least because the characters themselves invoke U.S. *national* scales and mythologies to locate their immigrant identities. In the third and final novel discussed in this chapter, *A Free Life*, Chinese-born protagonist Nan Wu arrives in metropolitan Atlanta following periods studying and working in Boston and New York. While Nan encounters disturbing examples of anti-Asian and antiblack racism, he is only slightly more engaged than Mai Nguyen by the scale of "the South"; like Mai he tends to figure his immigrant experience through myths and metaphors of Americanness. Taken together, these three novels—especially *Monkey Bridge* and *A Free Life*—help us see that in a region that is also part of a globalized world, you do not (*pace* Quentin Compson) "have to be born there"; indeed, you might not "*tell about the South*" at all.[10]

Historian Ira Berlin has identified the 1965 Hart-Celler Immigration and Nationality Act as even more significant than the Voting Rights Act, famously passed earlier that year in response to the Selma to Montgomery march and the police violence it generated. Like the Civil Rights movement, Hart-Celler "initiated a transformation of black America" but also reinvented immigration and the nation's broader ethnic makeup at a time when the percentage of foreign-born peoples in the United States was at its lowest ever ebb.[11] As we saw in the introduction and chapter 6, Chinese immigrants and their descendants had been present in the South ever since white planters fantasized that "coolies" could replace blacks as plantation laborers after the Civil War. However, the notorious 1882 Exclusion Act severely restricted Chinese immigration to the United States for decades. Only after Hart-Celler abolished the national origins quota system (overriding widespread opposition from white southern politicians) did immigration from China and other Asian nations rise dramatically, bringing unprecedented numbers of "global Easterners" into the U.S. South. By 1980, there were about half a million Asian immigrants living in the region; over one million by 1990; and more than two million by 2000, approximately 2 percent of the South's total population.[12] Of course, such statistics are inherently problematic, conflating as they do different nationalities (Koreans, Chinese, Japanese, Indians, Pakistanis, Bangladeshis) as well as ethnic, linguistic, or religious identities. If globalization and transnationalism challenge the conventional borders of "the U.S. South" or "the United States," so too "the quasi-stable 'field-imaginaries' of area-studies-based frames like 'Asia' or 'East Asia' or 'the Pacific'—or 'Japan,' 'Korea,' or 'China,' for that matter—no longer exist in the same bounded, monolingual, or homogeneous way."[13] Nevertheless, among these variegated forms of "Asian" immigration, it seems fairly clear that the influx of Vietnamese following the failed U.S. war for South Vietnam (the Republic of Vietnam) had the most striking demographic impact on the U.S. South—and on recent fiction about the region.

By the turn of the new millennium, of the one-million-plus Vietnamese and Vietnamese Americans living in the United States, nearly 160,000 resided in the South. In Georgia, the number of Vietnamese Americans increased by almost 400 percent between 1990 and 2000.[14] Going back to the late 1970s, Vietnamese workers and entrepreneurs have been prominent in the Gulf Coast fishing sector, though, as Vy Thuc Dao notes, "they are actually the third major group of immigrants to work closely with the seafood industry" in Biloxi, following the Poles who arrived in the late nineteenth century and the Croats and Serbs who came in the early twentieth century.[15] Frank Cha has explored how the presence of Vietnamese shrimpers in Biloxi and other coastal areas generated both conflict and cooperation with native white workers: 2003 saw the formation of the Southern Shrimp Alliance (SSA), "a cooperative partnership between white and Vietnamese American shrimpers to combat what they viewed as unfair business practices by foreign seafood companies." As Cha shrewdly explains, the SSA constituted a self-conscious recasting of "the *southern* shrimping industry" as "a multiethnic enterprise."[16] But in "Relic," a story from Robert Olen Butler's Pulitzer Prize–winning collection about Vietnamese immigrants in Louisiana, *A Good Scent from a Strange Mountain* (1993), the Vietnam-born businessman narrator figures his entry into the shrimp industry through a classic *national* mythology: "America is the land of opportunity." He prophesizes: "In ten years people from Vietnam will be the only shrimp fishermen in the Gulf of Mexico.... [W]hen this is so, I will be making even more money."[17]

The narrator of "Relic" could not have anticipated that a perfect storm of economic globalization (the growing importation to the United States of cheaper shrimp from elsewhere, including Vietnam) and a natural catastrophe compounded by political failings (Hurricane Katrina in August 2005) would severely erode Vietnamese investment and employment in Gulf Coast shrimping. One result of this confluence is that, like so many others, "the Vietnamese have gravitated toward finding work in the recovering casino and gaming industry."[18] When Natasha Trethewey wrote (see chapter 6) that "the casinos are now the creators of the dominant economic narrative" in Mississippi, she also observed that although this narrative ostensibly dovetails with the "more liberal narrative" of a multiethnic "new Mississippi" which welcomes immigrant workers, ultimately the only color that matters is "money green."[19] Before and after Katrina, Vietnamese American communities in New Orleans and along the Gulf Coast have been exploited and ignored while struggling to make their own narratives heard.[20] Dao demonstrates that long before the hurricane hit, the gaming industry was encroaching on Biloxi's Vietnamese neighborhoods, while Cha shows how Katrina "threatened to displace Vietnamese Americans once again"; at the very least, the repercussions of the storm "further marginalized" a group "already accustomed to being overlooked by regional and national policymakers alike" who viewed them "as an insular immigrant community." More optimistically, Cha also details how "the Vietnamese American residents of New Orleans East and East Biloxi" have since Katrina "striven to reinvent themselves as a socially conscious and politically assertive community that plays a proactive role in the cross-racial, (multi)cultural regeneration of the Gulf South"; as Eric Tang too has shown, this has involved considerable collaboration with black neighbors.[21]

Looking "Asian in the South": Passing, Intertextuality, and the Solitary Foreigner in Monique Truong's *Bitter in the Mouth*

In 1998 Michael Kreyling claimed that "the central historical referent for southern identity is no longer the Civil War but Vietnam." The resulting "radical change [that] can be felt in the foundations of southern society and literature" may now have less to do with depictions of the Vietnam War in the 1980s fiction of native white southern writers like Barry Hannah and Bobbie Ann Mason than the more recent rise of literature about Vietnamese immigrants on U.S. southern ground.[22] Monique Truong's superb second novel, *Bitter in the Mouth*, offers a self-reflexive recasting of the southern gothic bildungsroman for a post–Hart-Celler era in which the latest U.S. military intervention in Asia has, in demographic terms, blown back to even the most provincial of small southern towns. *Bitter in the Mouth* is the coming-of-age story of narrator-protagonist Linda Hammerick, the seemingly biological scion of a white Southern Baptist family whose wealth and social standing in Boiling Springs, North Carolina, derive from ancestral ownership of a slave plantation. It is no accident that this bildungsroman form and theme echo seminal post–World War II southern coming-of-age novels such as Carson McCullers's *The Member of the Wedding* (1946), Faulkner's *Intruder in the Dust*, and Truman Capote's *Other Voices, Other Rooms* (both 1948). Truong herself has acknowledged the "inspiration" of Capote's debut novel and located *Bitter*'s genesis in her own childhood encounter with surely the most popular southern bildungsroman of all: Harper Lee's *To Kill a Mockingbird* (1960).[23] *Bitter in the Mouth* signals its southern literary intertextuality from the *Mockingbird* epigram, via the opening scene's introduction of Linda's great-uncle "Baby" Harper Evan Burch (a textual heir of Cousin Randolph from *Other Voices, Other Rooms*), to Linda's participation in a freshman Yale literature seminar, "Dysfunctionalia: Novels of Misspent Southern Youths and their Social Context, 1945 to the Present." (All that in the first dozen pages.) But *Bitter* is hardly mere homage. Truong has said that "[w]hile re-reading *Mockingbird*, I began to think more about what it means to set a novel in the American South, and how I could contribute to a genre [the southern gothic] that had already given readers so many of the defining narratives of the region" (292). Truong's publisher resisted such genre-bending because, according to the dictates of "mainstream U.S. publishing" (and echoing Bow's critique of southern literary studies), she was "an Asian American author and not a Southern writer."[24] Halfway through the narrative, we encounter Truong's singular twist on the southern gothic: the deferred revelation that Linda is South Vietnamese, which "Linh-Dao Nguyen Hammerick" (158) herself only fully comprehends after hearing that name called during her Yale graduation ceremony.

Part of *Bitter in the Mouth*'s formal innovation thus derives from the way its deferred revelation of Linh-Dao/Linda's origins in another "South" explores and then explodes the way readers have conventionally experienced earlier southern literary comings-of-age as white (Ann Moody or Alice Walker notwithstanding). However, Linda's epiphany regarding her ethnicity also retrospectively reveals how the white citizens of Boiling Springs conspired to repress the challenge that her presence—in particular, her highly visible bodily difference—might otherwise have posed to the town's hegemonic whiteness. Only gradually does Linda (and with her, the reader) uncover the repressed archaeology of knowledge concerning her arrival in Boiling Springs circa 1975 after being transracially adopted by lawyer Thomas Hammerick and his wife, DeAnne. Not until 1998 does Linda learn from the by-now widowed DeAnne that Thomas met and fell for Mai-Dao, a South Vietnamese woman, while studying at Columbia Law School in 1955: "Young Thomas told her that he was from the South. She told him that she was from the South too. He, unlike many Americans at the time, knew that her country had been partitioned into North and South just the year before" (268). Twenty years later, following the fall of Saigon to the Viet Cong, the evacuation of U.S. troops, and the reunification of North and South Vietnam, Mai-Dao, her academic husband Khanh, and their seven-year-old daughter Linh-Dao arrived in Chapel Hill as refugees, at which point Mai-Dao renewed contact with Thomas. Already severely traumatized by the war and resulting upheaval, and plagued by jealousy after discovering his wife's hidden personal history, Khanh killed Mai-Dao and himself, leaving Linh-Dao an orphan as well as a refugee.

In the second half of *Bitter*, Linda recalls how in New Haven and New York "complete strangers" had asked her "what it was like to grow up being Asian in the South," as if recasting Shreve McCannon's famous question to Quentin, "*Tell about the South. What's it like there.*"[25] Linda pointedly responded: "You mean what was it like growing up *looking* Asian in the South" (169). Yet this notion of being only optically "Asian" is not quite right either: Linda subsequently avers that she "willed away" her "Asian" body and "few in Boiling Springs seemed to *see* anyway" (170). In the introduction, I referenced James Peacock's observation that in much modern southern literature "the less diverse southern setting accentuates the foreigner as standing out."[26] In chapter 6, I cited Bow's concept of "racial interstitiality": the anomalous subject position of those "Asians in the South" who complicated the "powerful visual iconography" of racial segregation by appearing "to stand outside—or rather, *between*" black and white, "within the space between abjection and normative invisibility."[27] Yet in *Bitter* the adult Linda realizes that, due to a disingenuous "pact" among the white citizenry that amounts to "an act of selective blindness" (170–71), her childhood self stood out rather less than might be expected. Linda's conspicuous corporeal difference was literally overlooked as through the Jim Crow "system's ready but inconsistent accommodation of ambiguity," she becomes—due to her privileged status as a singular adoptee within a prominent family—less "partly colored" than an "honorary white."[28]

Tellingly, Linda observes that only the local Piggly Wiggly's black women workers "actually saw me." These women are accustomed to being defined by the "visual economies of race" underpinning what Tara McPherson terms the South's "lenticular logic of racial visibility"—a segregationist worldview that a racial anomaly like Linda would otherwise disrupt.[29] To be sure, the second half of Linda's narrative does acknowledge, in classic return-of-the-repressed fashion, moments from her childhood when the "open secret" of her ethnicity became painfully evident. She recalls the shock of recognition that the white "children of Boiling Springs ... were never fooled by my new name" and would "silently mouth 'Chink' or 'Jap' or 'Gook' at me"—epithets "intimately connected to how the children saw my body" (171–72). She later adds that at "the age of fourteen, I had figured out that I was neither a Chink nor a Jap" because her ninth-grade history textbook references her namesake, Nguyen Van Thieu, former president of South Vietnam (216). Nevertheless, Linda's integration into southern whiteness was sufficiently immersive that "only in passing" did she encounter the "parallel adult world in my hometown": Boiling Springs' black community (170). Linda's word choice here is unwittingly revealing, however, for it is the white community's disingenuous "blindness" that facilitates her childhood "passing" as white. The theme of passing is formally expressed by the way in which the first half of *Bitter* leaves the reader unaware that Linda is (also) Linh Dao. Here Truong's technique is reminiscent of the daring opening to Nella Larsen's *Passing* (1929). As George Hutchinson has observed, "Riffing brilliantly on the nature of passing in the novel's very exposition," Larsen "withholds any mention of race or color until well into Chapter 2."[30] Yet the manner in which Linda's visible difference remains like "Boo Radley, not hidden away but in plain sight" (171) deviates from what Werner Sollors describes as the usual conceit about the "racial passer as 'impostor'": that the passer's nonwhiteness would eventually be exposed by "visible or otherwise detectable signs" of her "real" racial identity.[31] Because the "white Christian citizenry" has consciously overlooked Linda's visibly detectable ethnic difference, Linda only becomes aware of it herself when it is "seen" during "passing" encounters with black adults or named (pejoratively) by white children.[32]

The moment of "revelation" when Linda hears her given name at the Yale graduation ceremony also generates the second half of the narrative. Here the reader is required to reenvision not only the first half's deceptively soft-pedaled memoir of a white Southern Baptist girlhood but also the sociopolitical connotations of Linda's South Vietnamese origins vis-à-vis U.S. hard power in the wider world. First, in a passage that intones almost a century of U.S. military intervention in "the East," Linda wonders what might have happened if her adolescent "Asian" body had been more fully subject to Boiling Springs' white southern male gaze: "how many of the men would remember the young female bodies that they bought by the half hour while wearing their country's uniform in the Philippines, Thailand, South Korea, or South Vietnam?" (171). Linda's heightened awareness of this orientalist, global-eastern history of U.S. state power also anticipates and informs her understanding of how a regional-southern religious denomination has come to wield significant global southern clout. This power is visible due to the arrival in Boiling Springs of other nonwhite foreign bodies: the town's Gardner-Webb Baptist College has morphed into Gardner-Webb University, "complete with out-of-state students and even some from overseas, mostly from small Third World countries where the Southern Baptist Convention International Mission Board was most active" (199).

As a young adult, Linda also becomes attuned to the contemporary realities of rather less privileged migrants from the Global South. In February 1998 Linda takes a Greyhound bus back home from New York for the funeral of Baby Harper and his partner, Cecil Brandon, victims of a plane crash off the west coast of Colombia. Of her first bus journey in twelve years, Linda comments:

> The demographics of long-distance bus travel hadn't changed, except that there were now men from Central and South America, in their twenties, thirties, and forties, who looked uniformly exhausted, as if they knew that every state of the union would be the same for them: New York or North Carolina, apples or tobacco, produce fields or slaughterhouses. Their migration was a peculiar form

of travel. Peculiar in that it was travel that took them nowhere. Wherever they landed, it was exactly the same. (Immigration was migration fueled by faith that *this* wasn't so.) (210)

This suggestive summary of the political economy experienced by migrant workers moving from the Global South to the Global North (within which, as in Banks's *Rule of the Bone*, southern states are interchangeable with "Yankee" New York) is vividly juxtaposed with Linda's thicker description of Baby Harper's tourist trips to South America. From Harper's first literary pilgrimage to Cartagena in 1990—inspired not by *Mockingbird* or his own "high camp" favorite, *Gone with the Wind* (258), but Gabriel García Márquez's *One Hundred Years of Solitude*—"foreign travel" to "a different South" helped Harper come to terms with his queer sexuality, through his late-blooming romance with traveling companion Cecil. As Truong herself has observed, South America triangulates the "two poles" of "South Vietnam versus the Southern U.S." and is the place "where Baby Harper gets to... be the person he could not be in his own South." Similarly, critic Rachael Price observes that Harper "finally finds a 'South' that expands, rather than limits, his horizons."[33] But there is a world of difference between Harper's liberating literary-themed journeys to Santiago (José Donoso), Montevideo (Eduardo Galeano), Rio de Janeiro (Clarice Lispector), Buenos Aires (Manuel Puig), and Bogotá (Márquez again) and the migrant workers' "peculiar form of travel" by bus in and around a uniformly United States of exhausting manual labor. Here *Bitter in the Mouth* seems less interested in "what it was like to grow up being Asian in the South" or even "growing up *looking* Asian in the South" than in adumbrating the base economic realities and inequalities underpinning the hemispheric links between the U.S. (South) and the Global South.[34]

For all the transnational resonance of such moments, *Bitter in the Mouth*'s meditation on being or looking "Asian in the South" focuses on an individual in a relatively isolated small-town locale. Linda lives, as Truong remarks, "in a community where there is no other Asian American or Vietnamese American."[35] It is this unique status that makes Linda's childhood "passing" possible and resembles Helga Crane's status as the singular and thus ambiguously accepted "*Sorte*" among white Danes in the Copenhagen section of *Quicksand* (see chapter 2). *Bitter in the Mouth* also resembles Susan Choi's exquisitely rendered *The Foreign Student* (1998), which similarly focuses on an individual Asian immigrant's experience in the South as a consequence of U.S. military intervention in Asia. In Choi's novel, South Korean refugee Chang Ahn—previously a translator with the United States Information Service during the Korean War—arrives alone in Sewanee circa 1955 to study at the University of the South.[36] Like *The Foreign Student*, *Bitter in the Mouth* bolsters Sharon Monteith's point that even more recent "fictions about migrants and exiles have focused on individual protagonists in stories of solitary foreigners who arrive in the post-war South"—the war may be different, but the singularity of the immigrant character remains the same.[37] Let us turn, then, to a novel that offers a vivid narrative cartography of Vietnamese characters' lives within a larger immigrant community in another southern state.

"It Hardly Mattered":
Souths, Exiles, and Immigrants
in Lan Cao's *Monkey Bridge*

Like Monique Truong, Lan Cao left Vietnam as a young refugee in 1975: she and her family settled in Virginia, and her debut novel *Monkey Bridge* traces a similar immigrant trail. The narrative is structured through the first-person account of a teenager, Mai Nguyen—like Linh-Dao, part of the "1.5 generation"— and the private writings of her mother, Thanh. Mai arrives in Connecticut in February 1975, ahead of the infamous U.S. withdrawal from Saigon, and is taken into the care of a U.S. colonel who was a family friend in South Vietnam. Thanh follows in April, initially spending "four months in Fort Chaffee, an Arkansas army camp used as a refugee-resettlement center" before settling with Mai in Falls Church, part of "the Vietnamese community [that] tended to cluster in Arlington and Fairfax counties, Virginia."[38] Citing the familiar image of the U.S. South "as a ghost-ridden culture still grappling with defeat in the Civil War," Monteith and Nahem Yousaf claim that "[t]he ghosts of Vietnam that haunt *Monkey Bridge* fuse with Confederate ghosts that linger in Virginia."[39] This is to overstate the case: such Confederate ghosts are mentioned only once, and for Mai they are hardly as powerful as the "stubborn back-looking ghosts" that haunted Quentin in *Absalom, Absalom!*; they are not even as vivid as the specters of those Confederate and U.S. Army soldiers who trouble traumatized Vietnam veteran Ray Forrest in Hannah's *Ray* (1980).[40] Mai recalls how her mother chose to move to Falls Church "because it was a mere thirty minutes away from Washington, D.C., capital of the United States and of the Free World." The sense (however fallacious) of federal governmental protection this location provides to Thanh is such that "[i]t hardly mattered that all around us ghosts of a different war lingered, the Battle of Fredericksburg, the Battle of Bull Run, Confederate victories secured by Robert E. Lee's Army of Northern Virginia" (30–31).

"Northern Virginia's Little Saigon" is a substantial "world in and of itself, a world that census takers had documented, one hundred thousand and growing." However, exemplifying Ha Jin's definition in *The Writer as Migrant* (2008) of the dislocated "exile" who is mired in a melancholic obsession with his or her homeland (more about which below), much of Little Saigon's population is seduced by "the sheer seductive powers of nostalgia" (204) for their former lives, families, and ancestors in South Vietnam.[41] Mai refers to "my mother's Little Saigon community" as "a cordial and modest grouping of exiles intent on maintaining the steady rhythm of the old along with some new practical twists to usher them into the demands of a new American life" (133). Thanh figures herself as "*an exile many times over*": as her private writings gradually reveal, even before the upheaval of her removal from Vietnam via Arkansas to Virginia, she had moved one hundred kilometers *within* South Vietnam when she married Mai's father, a university professor, an uprooting she tellingly describes as being forced "*at fifteen to immigrate*" (54). Mai bemoans how her mother and other Little Saigon residents "continued to live in a geography of thoughts defined by the map of a country that no longer existed" (66), South Vietnam, while treating Falls Church "as a mere way station"; it seems to Mai that Thanh "had no claim to American space, no desire to stake her future in this land" (91). There is a clear contrast here with the way Mai conceptualizes her own acculturation: only "eight weeks into Farmington," Connecticut, "the American Dream was exerting a sly but seductive pull" (37). Thanh in turn complains that Mai has been too easily seduced by the "*American sense of invincibility*" and faith in "*Manifest Destiny*," which she indicts as the "*antithesis*" of "*Karma*" (55). For Thanh, Mai's American Dream constitutes a form of false consciousness: she believes that Mai is less acculturated than "*lost between two worlds*" (53).

Yet as *Monkey Bridge* proceeds, Mai herself admits the limits of her assimilation, confessing (in the narrative, not in person to her mother) "my fear of the wide-open space, my inability to feel connected to the American soil" (192). Mai is increasingly drawn to the specter of her family's past in South Vietnam, and especially the mystery surrounding the absent figure of her maternal grandfather, Baba Quan. In Mason's *In Country* (1985), seventeen-year-old Kentucky teenager Sam Hughes is haunted by her absent father, Dwayne, who died before her birth fighting for the U.S. Army in Vietnam. Eventually Sam discovers and reads letters that Private Dwayne Hughes sent home, achieving a connection with her father even as she learns disturbing information about his actions on the battlefront. Mai's discovery of her mother's private writings in their Falls Church apartment plays a similar structural and revelatory role in *Monkey Bridge*. However, there is a significant divergence in Cao's novel from the fiction of Hannah or Mason: the haunting ghost is Vietnamese, rather than a white U.S. southern soldier-victim of the war. In Falls Church, Mai has perceived Baba Quan through the haze of firsthand childhood memory and her mother's idealized reminiscences about a virtuous Mekong Delta tenant farmer who cultivated a Confucian faith in and connection to "the ancestral land and the village burial ground." Convinced that Baba Quan's "continuing devotion was to the past, not the future," Mai has been encouraged to believe that her grandfather would not be willing or able to come to Virginia even if she could somehow circumvent the U.S. embargo to contact him. Put another way, Baba Quan's deep faith in "the transmigration of the ancestral spirit" (159) apparently precludes his transnational migration to the United States.

The "parallels" between "[t]he centrality of place, family, and the past" in traditional southern literature and *Monkey Bridge*'s South Vietnam has prompted Maureen Ryan to argue that "Allen Tate's famous 'backward glance,' the South's fascination with a lost war and a romantic antebellum past, is for Vietnamese refugees a visceral connection back to Vietnam, to familial lands and the very real spirits of honored ancestors."[42] If there is some sort of southern literary parallel in *Monkey Bridge*, it is an extremely dark one. In a twist that recalls not only the wartime atrocities revealed in Dwayne Hughes's letters home from the war in Vietnam but also the familial secrets and turmoil that wrack Faulkner's Sutpen clan against the backdrop of the Civil War, Mai discovers in her mother's writings that Baba Quan was no simple farmer tending to ancestral lands and spirits. Having prostituted his wife, Tuyet, to a local landlord, Uncle Khan, who fathered Thanh, Baba Quan joined the Viet Cong as a secret agent to exact personal revenge, eventually murdering Khan on the same day that Tuyet died. The harrowing legacy of having thus witnessed her supposed father murder her biological father finally causes Thanh to kill herself in Virginia. Yet the grim irony is that her mother's suicide may be what liberates Mai from a debilitating, melancholic obsession with the familial past in Vietnam, so that she can again embrace an American future by creating "[a] brand-new slate ... unmarred by any undercurrents or tremors of Saigon or even of Falls Church, Virginia" (257). Even Thanh, for all her skepticism toward Mai's assimilation, expresses in her final missive the "*hope that my act of sacrifice will give you the new beginning that you deserve*," unburdened of "*our family history of sin, revenge, and murder*" (252–53). *Monkey Bridge* ends with Mai about to embark on "the openness of an unexplored future" (260) by leaving Virginia to study in Massachusetts, though it remains unclear whether she will be more successful than Harvard student Quentin Compson in sloughing off a war-torn and tragic familial past.

For all the supposed (literary) parallels between U.S. southern and southern Vietnamese obsessions with "place, family, and the past," *Monkey Bridge*'s immigrant characters never *register or explore* such parallels. Unlike the Vietnamese fishermen of the Southern Shrimp Alliance, the Little Saigon community makes little effort to engage with (the idea of) "the South" or to make it multiethnic. Thanh and her best friend Mrs. Bay, owner of Little Saigon's Mekong Grocery, produce Vietnamese foodstuffs for sale only to other "Old World exiles" in Falls Church; in doing so, they "massage the bittersweetness of nostalgia into hard cash" (224). Moreover, as we have seen, both Mai and Thanh conceptualize their immigrant experience (whether positively, ambivalently, or negatively) through recognizably national or western rather than "southern" mythologies: the American Dream, Manifest Destiny, wide-open spaces, and a *"new frontier"* (56). Whatever their other differences, for Mai and Thanh "the South," with its (white) lost causes and Confederate ghosts, is simply not relevant. Here I would second Ryan's observation that "the Vietnamese perception of the new world to which they must become acculturated is that it is, simply, America." I am less persuaded, however—at least in the case of Cao's novel—by Ryan's qualifying corollary: "If these Vietnamese characters themselves demonstrate no conception of living in a culturally unique region of the United States, the authors who place them in Virginia, Maryland, Louisiana and Texas do." For unlike Truong in *Bitter in the Mouth*, Cao in *Monkey Bridge* offers no sly intertextual gestures to the southern literary tradition, to possible parallels between South Vietnam and the U.S. South, or to "the self-conscious myth of the South as burdened by past and place."[43] Though Monteith and Yousaf postulate a "rhizomorphic South" in which the "southern literary tradition does not atrophy" but is sufficiently "permeable" to accommodate immigrant narratives, in *Monkey Bridge* regional identity has little if any meaning: "the South" is not, contra their recasting of Robert Penn Warren's formulation, "the setting but also the *theme*" of Cao's novel.[44]

We might instead return to the concept of geographic scale and Jon Smith's observation (quoted in the introduction) that "'the South' increasingly appears to be an unhelpful scalar unit." *Monkey Bridge* operates at both "a larger scale" (transpacific immigration between South Vietnam and northern Virginia, via Connecticut and Arkansas) and "smaller one[s]" (the macroscales of Thanh and Mai's apartment, Little Saigon, or Thanh's ancestral village, Ba Xuyen, in the Mekong Delta). Cao's rich debut, largely set in "the South" but not self-consciously of or about it, may be a case study for the applicability of Duck's "southern studies without 'the South.'" The same can be said for the next novel I want to discuss: Ha Jin's *A Free Life*.

"My Problem in the South": Exiles and Immigrants in Ha Jin's *A Free Life*

When Chinese immigration to the U.S. South resumed after Hart-Celler, the newcomers' class background and destination contrasted markedly with the previous century's plantation "coolies." As Reimers remarks, "The first Chinese who moved to Atlanta after new immigration policies went into effect in the 1960s were highly educated; some 80 percent had 'professional degrees with advanced training.'"[45] The metropolitan Atlanta area has remained something of a mecca for Chinese immigrants. In the long novel *A Free Life*, by Chinese-born Ha Jin—the pen name of Jīn Xuěfēi—well-educated protagonist Nan Wu moves alone to the United States in 1985, severs his ties with Communist China following the 1989 Tiananmen Square massacre, and, by way of Boston and New York, settles with his family in the northeastern Atlanta suburb of Lilburn. There Nan's former political activities and ongoing literary ambitions are supplanted by the more immediate imperative of securing economic stability for his family by buying the Gold Wok, a Chinese restaurant. In Boston, Nan worried that blue-collar jobs undermined his dreams of becoming a scholar or author and "had turned him into a semi-coolie"; in Lilburn, he consciously reinvents himself as "a laborer now, a professional cook," work that leaves him too "exhausted" to write.[46]

In depicting the Wu family's relocation to suburban Atlanta, *A Free Life* dramatizes how hackneyed notions of southern literature's "sense of place" and obsession with (the burden of) history no longer hold. In *The Writer as Migrant*, Jin writes: "For most migrant writers today, displacement makes them more vulnerable and their existence more haphazard, since they cannot fall back on any significant past and must struggle to survive in new places." He also approvingly quotes Salman Rushdie's novel *Shame*: "Roots, I sometimes think, are a conservative myth, designed to keep us in places."[47] In *A Free Life*, the displaced, uprooted Nan conceives of himself as something like the opposite of the firmly located, history-saturated southern literary protagonist: Nan imagines himself as "an immigrant without a noteworthy and burdensome past" (356). Not that Nan shows any *interest* in situating himself within or against traditional models of U.S. southern identity. Rather, like Cao's Mai Nguyen, Nan defines himself as an "immigrant" within *national* tropes and traditions; moreover, he does so against those "exiles" who remain inextricably identified with the Chinese homeland. Throughout *A Free Life*, Nan develops a firm conviction to live "not as an expatriate or an exile but as an immigrant" (125) and contrasts himself with the New York–based scholar Manping Liu, "an exile, whose life had been shaped by the past and who could exist only with reference to the central power that had banished him from China" (356). Liu embodies Jin's view that "nostalgia is associated mostly with the experience of a particular type of migrants, namely, exiles": "The present and the future have been impaired by their displacements, and their absence from their original countries gives them nothing but pain."[48] If Thomas Wolfe's well-worn maxim that "you can't go home again" has a very literal meaning for political exiles like Liu, a self-styled immigrant like Nan sees this less as a burden than as an opportunity. Nan is more than "willing to accept the immigrant life as the condition of his existence so as to become a self-sufficient man. He felt grateful to the American land that had taken in his family and given them an opportunity for a new beginning" (356). The Wus want to "put down roots here" in Georgia partly because they have "no recourse to a place they could call home" back in China (297). Nan does take a short trip from Atlanta back to Beijing and Harbin (his hometown in northeast China and the nation's tenth biggest city) after securing U.S. citizenship but experiences only a tenuous connection to his parents (especially his staunchly Communist father) and witnesses corruption among local officials (some of whom are old friends). This leads Nan to conclude: "Clearly a person like him wouldn't be able to survive here [in China]. Now he wanted all the more to live and die in America. How he missed his home in Georgia" (568). Exemplifying what *The Writer as Migrant* calls "the truth of the relationship between oneself and one's native land after a long absence from it," Nan has discovered that "[s]ince most of us cannot go home again, we have to look for our own Ithakas and try to find ways to get there."[49]

Nan's gratitude to "the American land" also typifies his tendency to "place" himself in national rather than regional terms. Pondering a move from Boston to the Atlanta area, Nan does note economic differences between the U.S. North and South: "He'd heard that some Chinese restaurants in Georgia, Florida, Mississippi, and Alabama were quite affordable." For a while, the region's enduring reputation for exceptional racism counterbalances such financial benefits: "The crux of the problem was whether they'd be willing to go to the Deep South, where they had heard that racial prejudice was still rampant" (165–66). Having made the decision to move to Atlanta anyway, Nan does encounter moments of thinly veiled racial prejudice. Native white residents of their Lilburn subdivision veto the prospect of Nan's friend Shubo Gao—who has a PhD in sociology from the University of Georgia but has had to take on restaurant work—buying the house next door to the Wus. One of these white neighbors disingenuously declares that "there're too many Chinese in the neighborhood already" and that "we need diversity": "We don't want this subdivision to become a Chinatown" (411). Bow argues that "the Asian individual's resistance to interpreting his place in southern culture if it threatens the inviolability of his subjectivity" sometimes involves a willful blindness regarding not only white racism toward African Americans but also the possibility that such racism might be turned on himself.[50] Yet while Nan experiences the reality of white southern racism, he and other Chinese immigrants more often discuss and define their "place" and subjectivity through a predominantly national imaginary that tends to deemphasize racial and regional prejudice. When Mr. Wang, the previous owner of the Gold Wok, pitches his restaurant to Nan, he downplays the enduring specter of the Ku Klux Klan and figures metropolitan Atlanta as a kind of immigrant frontier in which Nan can make himself over into a pioneer: "there were thousands upon thousands of Asian immigrants living in the Atlanta area, which, he [Mr. Wang] claimed, was almost like virgin land just open for settlement" (166).

Initially, Nan's achievement running the restaurant suggests a more successful acculturation than Mai Nguyen's ambivalence about her new homeland's "wide-open spaces." When Nan's poet friend Dick Harrison visits the Gold Wok, which is "thriving" partly due to the patronage of Mexican construction workers (229), Dick declares: "This is impressive. I can see that you're becoming an American capitalist.... [Y]ou're on your way to realizing your American dream, aren't you?" Nan defensively tells Dick that "I just want to be independent" (260) but gradually comes to doubt his focus on securing economic stability. Echoing the role of "possession" and zombification in *Continental Drift* and *Louisiana* as metaphors for capitalist exploitation of the worker's labor and identity, Nan comes to see his own work at The Gold Wok as that of the unfree undead: he has become "a walking corpse." Like Banks's Bob Dubois, Nan now concludes that "the whole notion of the American dream was shoddy, a hoax," not least because that dream has displaced his aesthetic ideals: "It seemed that he had forgotten his goal and gotten lost in making money. Why hadn't he devoted himself to writing poetry?" (418–19). Strikingly, Nan imagines writing anglophone poetry in spatial terms as "claiming his existence in this new land ... becoming a truly independent man who followed nothing but his own heart" (472). But this claim on space is metaphorical rather than material, individual rather than regional, and the South's supposed "sense of place" holds no meaning for Nan: "He knew that, living in Georgia, he couldn't possibly present that kind of landscape in his poetry" (515). This distinctly literary sense of displacement may have something to do with the fact that Nan's suburban life and labor in Lilburn hardly facilitate the southern pastoral of lore—the kind of bucolic vision fleetingly felt by Choi's Chang Ahn at Sewanee during the 1950s and now sought some four decades later by Nan's old acquaintance, the artist Bao Yuan, in Tennessee's Blue Ridge Mountains. But Nan also refutes the seductive fallacy posited by other Chinese immigrants: that "the climate in the South" is desirable because it "was similar to that in their home provinces back in China" (166; see also 261, 343). By contrast, Nan states explicitly that "*This is my problem in the South. I can't blend myself into the landscape. Always at odds with the flora and fauna here*" (455).

If Nan finds no muse in the southern landscape, neither does he—in contrast to Truong's Linda—turn to southern literature. Instead, Nan draws on Alexander Pope to express the complex sense that while "he wasn't completely at home here," nevertheless "he felt that his feet were finally standing on solid, independent ground" (189); he absorbs V. S. Naipaul's novel *A House for Mr. Biswas* for its resonant portrayal of "the struggle the protagonist waged for having his own shelter in his own corner of land" (227). Unlike his old friend Danning, who visits Oxford, Mississippi, as part of an official delegation of Chinese writers (592), Nan feels no obligation to make a pilgrimage to William Faulkner's hometown. It is therefore ironic that just after Danning departs for Oxford, Nan, depressed by his inability to write, encounters a passage from Faulkner that articulates the gnawing sensation that "his pursuit of the American dream ... his devotion to making money" has been misguided. After reading Faulkner—the relevant passage begins "The writer must teach himself that the basest of all things is to be afraid"—a distraught Nan destroys the restaurant's God of Wealth statue and sets "aflame a whole sheaf of banknotes" (604–5). It is telling that the words are from Faulkner's Nobel Prize address: they foreground the kind of "old universal truths," rather than regional shibboleths, that appeal to Nan's own abstracted, individualized, and deterritorialized identity. But if Faulkner's famous words register most immediately for Nan as a critique of his reductive focus on "becoming an American capitalist," they may also appeal to Nan's residual antipathy for Chinese communism. As Deborah Cohn has demonstrated, Faulkner's rhetoric during and after the Nobel Prize speech, in the service of U.S.-state sanctioned cultural diplomacy, "was deeply intertwined with that of the totalitarianism paradigm": the use of ostensibly apolitical modern literature as (in Lawrence Schwartz's words) "an instrument of anti-Communism and an ideological weapon with which to battle the 'totalitarianism' of the Soviet Union." The focus of Nan's anti-Communist ire may be China rather than the defunct Soviet Union, but his post-Tiananmen determination to "be a free individual" (619) and live "a free life" as an artist dovetails with the discourse of a U.S. State Department official who interpreted Faulkner's speech as "the free world's challenge to all forces that would enslave the human spirit" and a "summing-up of free man's determination to stay free."[51]

Nan resolves to sell the Gold Wok and take a night clerk position at a Korean-owned motel on Buford Highway to give himself more time for reading and writing. The penultimate page of *A Free Life* features a poem to his long-suffering wife, Pingping, which ends "My love, I've come home" (620); "home" is also the final word of the novel (621). However, home here refers less to a specific locus than to a kind of existential and linguistic form of self-placement. All too aware that he can't go home to Harbin again, Nan has come to believe that any connection to home, land, and place must necessarily be contingent for an immigrant like himself. As his poem "Homeland" puts it, "Eventually you will learn: / your country is where you raise your children, / your homeland is where you build your home" (635). It is decidedly not Dixie for which Nan takes this stand: he is only moderately more engaged by the idea of "the South" than Mai Nguyen. This is not to downplay the Wus' experience of racism in metropolitan Atlanta, though given that *A Free Life* begins with Nan's time in Massachusetts and New York, we know that such racism is not exceptionally "southern": while working as a nightwatchman at a Watertown factory, Nan is called a "gook" (32). My point is that purportedly "southern" structures of feeling remain more germane in *Bitter in the Mouth* where, "in the absence of other Vietnamese Americans in Boiling Springs," the singular figure of Linda has more clearly "internalized racial hierarchy" in familiar black and white terms.[52] The relevance of "the South" as a scale is rather less distinctive or defining to the Vietnamese and Chinese immigrants of *Monkey Bridge* and *A Free Life*. The question of whether Nan Wu's life is a "southern story" is irrelevant to

Nan's own tale of two continents. In Jin's 660-page novel, the geographic scales at which the immigrant protagonist strives for "a free life" are less regional than local (the Gold Wok, suburban Lilburn, metropolitan Atlanta); national (well-worn but, for Nan, meaningful metaphors of virgin land and the American Dream); and global (his escape from China and determination not to be defined as a Chinese "exile").

Southerners in Asia: White Expatriates in Brittani Sonnenberg's *Home Leave*

Despite his extensive education at Chinese and American universities, Nan Wu (like his friend Shubo) remains bound on Buford Highway to the kind of service-industry position so often occupied by immigrant labor. But as I noted in the introduction, scholars including Sawa Kurotani, Donald Nonini, and Sayuri Guthrie-Shimizu have stressed that as "the South meets the East," the "formation of new transnational circuits made up of labor migrants, businesspeople, [and] professionals" has generated a significant "urban, internationalized, middle-class" of white-collar Asian employees in areas like North Carolina's Research Triangle. These "cosmopolitan professionals" moving in and through such transnational circuits also include native U.S. southerners going in the opposition direction.[53] This is a central theme of *Home Leave* (2014), the debut novel by Hamburg-born Brittani Sonnenberg, which follows the family of corporate executive Chris Kriegstein as his work takes them back and forth between the U.S. South, Asia, and Europe. The novel opens circa 1977 in familiar southern (literary) territory: Vidalia, Mississippi, a small town transformed by post-*Brown* white flight, and the birthplace of Chris's future wife, Elise Ebert. That same year, Elise meets Chris (who grew up in Indiana) in Athens following a University of Georgia basketball game; by 1981, Chris and pregnant Elise are living in Germany: "Moving to Hamburg also meant leaving Mississippi again: putting another country, another culture, between the delta and herself."[54] In 1992, after a second spell in London and five years in Atlanta, the Kriegsteins—Chris, Elise, and their two daughters, Leah and Sophie—move to Shanghai. Here the family live (almost inverting Nan Wu's approach to life in suburban Atlanta) less as immigrants than as expatriates: they remain largely confined to a bubble shared by fellow anglophone corporate families. When venturing into the city, the children of these families from the United States, New Zealand, and Australia practice a globalized version of white privilege (137), remaining as "unaware of and unconcerned with the regional economic disparity" within Shanghai as Japanese corporate families in the unevenly developed Research Triangle.

During this alienating period in eastern central China, Elise and the children recall the Atlanta era (1987–92) as the "good years" (100, 109). Living in Little Five Points, Elise had "relaxed back into her southern accent, visited her mother and [sister] Ivy once a month in Mississippi, dropped in on her brothers now and then in Little Rock . . . and could hardly remember being anywhere or anyone else" (102). Hence Atlanta—which I have characterized elsewhere as a postsouthern "international city," a global capital of capital and immigrant hub that subverts familiar narratives about the South's "sense of place"—becomes, for this cosmopolitan and partly southern family, the closest they have to a stable "home." This is especially the case for Leah, Sophie, and Elise (who is constrained by the conventional role of trailing spouse and housewife wherever the family resides) when they begin to take summer vacations back in the United States without Chris: "This habit of home leave will cement Atlanta as 'home' in their minds, since they always fly back to the Atlanta airport" (109). A comforting sense that not just Atlanta but the U.S. South more generally offers a residual (albeit more routed than rooted) sense of homeplace is solidified between 1993 and 1995 by summer "home leave" at the Ebert family cabin in North Carolina's Great Smoky Mountains (143–44). Yet within the context of Chris's career, these various southern sites—Vidalia, Little Rock, the Smokies, and even Atlanta, where Chris took an extended career break—are diversionary nodes on the periphery of a global corporate matrix that in 1996 takes the Kriegsteins from Shanghai to Singapore.

In August 1996 thirteen-year-old Sophie dies in Singapore from a congenital heart defect, and Elise and Leah's nostalgia for Atlanta deepens. But by the time Leah is old enough to go to college back "home" in the United States, she figures herself in the first-person plural among those "repatriated global nomads" who return each summer, on a kind of reverse "home leave," to their expatriate existences in Asia and elsewhere. Newly and acutely self-conscious of their privileged separation from native populations, including the servants who perform their domestic labor (208), Leah and other well-heeled "third-culture kids" become "enamored of postcolonial theory and literature" as they guiltily ponder "how different were we in Singapore / Ghana / Martinique in 1996 . . . than the French in Algeria in 1890?" This literary-theoretical self-reflexivity regarding one's own globalized subjectivity is evident when Leah qualifies the historical continuities between colonialism (in E. M. Forster's *A Passage to India*) and contemporary corporate globalization (in her own life): "Absorbed in guilt and self-deprecation, we do not pause to consider the condescending implications of this assumption: namely, that certain modernized, independent nations are as helplessly victimized and subjugated by global business now as they were by colonialism in the late nineteenth century" (211).

Leah's narrative ends circa 2011 in Berlin, where she is working as a voice actor doing "African-American accents" for a recording of *A Raisin in the Sun*

(220). In a back-cover blurb, Ha Jin remarks that Sonnenberg's novel "describes migrations as a contemporary existential condition"; we might add that, like his own *A Free Life*, *Home Leave* suggests how the U.S. South is now more than ever inseparable from the "new transnational circuits" of migration. The difference is that "labor migrants" like Chris and Leah Kriegstein are of a different economic status, ethnicity, and nationality than Nan Wu, and that they still benefit—as suggested by Leah's postmodern minstrelsy as a voice actor, and despite signs of a burgeoning post-American world—from a transnational form of white privilege.[55] It is one more reminder that for all Nan's utopian yearning to lead "a free life" in a purely aesthetic realm, unconstrained by either capitalism or communism and at least relatively autonomous from the "racial prejudice" so associated with "the Deep South," (U.S.) whiteness retains power from the global "East" to the global West (and global North) of which the "subnational" U.S. South is a part.

EPILOGUE

Transnational American Studies with "the South"

Morrison, Matthiessen, Eggers, and Lalami

Throughout *Where the New World Is*, we have seen how numerous authors born outside the U.S. South (Nella Larsen, Russell Banks, Cynthia Shearer) and the United States (Erna Brodber, Monique Truong, Lan Cao, Ha Jin, Brittani Sonnenberg) have followed a seemingly familiar Faulknerian imperative to *"tell about the South."* Notwithstanding the Quentissential fallacy that "you would have to be born there," these writers have been narrating "the South" since modern southern literature was invented via the fabled Faulkner-led "Renascence" (often dated to the 1929 publication date of *The Sound and the Fury* but also the year after Larsen published *Quicksand*). However, alongside two native-born black writers, Zora Neale Hurston and John Oliver Killens, these authors have radically resituated "the South" at an array of other geographic scales: from the local, intraregional, and national to the hemispheric, transatlantic, transpacific, and global southern. Within this eclectic constellation of authors, Hurston, for so long excluded from southern literary history, emerges as a key figure for her pioneering representations of an extended South; indeed, Hurston becomes a precursor for some of the later authors in ways that both parallel and diverge from Faulkner's role as the major figure of the Southern Renaissance. But if Hurston, Larsen, Killens, Banks, Brodber, and Shearer all relocate "the South" at various transnational scales, some of the authors discussed in the final chapter do not really tell about "the South" at all. Established models of southern (literary) regionalism are insufficiently "scale-sensitive" to an assessment of *Monkey Bridge* or *A Free Life*, novels featuring Vietnamese and Chinese immigrant protagonists in suburban Virginia and Georgia for whom "the South" is an unknown *and* unhelpful scalar unit. Hence, to the degree we read such novels through a "southernist" lens, we may also need to practice Leigh Anne Duck's "southern studies without 'the South.'"

Relatedly, we cannot really claim the likes of Cao and Jin (or Larsen and Brodber) as "southern writers" and should resist the temptation to reinvent southern literature via a vulgarly additive strategy of appending "multiethnic" novels to an existing canon. Rather, I have tried to show that the literary texts discussed in this book bear out Suzanne Jones's point that "international writers and writers who are new immigrants to the South," together with select southern-born and nonsouthern U.S. authors, "can help us think globally and comparatively about the region."[1] (Hurston, Larsen, and Killens were already doing just such thinking more than half a century ago.) But if we have been witnessing the development of a more materialist new southern studies without "the South," then American studies may yet benefit from paying *more* attention to the region as something other than its own fantasy of "the staid, backward Other": as integral to the United States in a globalized world, and American studies' own oft-debated "futures."[2]

In this epilogue, I want to parse the seemingly paradoxical notion of southern studies without "the South" and transnational American studies with it. In doing so, I turn to texts by four more authors widely seen as major *American* writers: Toni Morrison, Peter Matthiessen, Dave Eggers, and Laila Lalami. On one hand, that reviewers and scholars generally regard these writers as leading figures of contemporary American literature may further erode the categorical relevance of "the South" and "southern literature." On the other hand, precisely because "the South" is not the scalar unit at which these texts were conceived or received, they can "help us to think globally and comparatively about the region" at various local, national, and global scales. Assessing Morrison's *Tar Baby* (1981), Matthiessen's *Shadow Country* (2008), Eggers's *Zeitoun* (2009), and Lalami's *The Moor's Account* (2014) benefits from a southern studies without "the South" still being read as a distinctive "region" but sensitive to how such texts depict continuities between slavery, convict labor, and the exploitation of immigrant workers in the contemporary neoliberal era of "globalization." But these books also call for an American studies with "the South": a critical praxis alert to the ways in which such abusive labor relations are less exceptionally "southern" than identifiably American. Moreover, by collectively ranging across some six hundred years of history as well as hemispheric, transatlantic, and black Atlantic geographies, the four books also drive home that "present-day forms of immiseration" are linked to "previous phases of globalization."[3]

Negotiating "Southern Small-Town Country Romanticism" and Black Diasporic Cosmopolitanism:
Toni Morrison's *Tar Baby*

It seems appropriate to begin with perhaps the most important American author of the last fifty years and the United States' only living Nobel Prize–winning novelist. There are innumerable ways of reading Toni Morrison's work, but in *Race and White Identity in Southern Fiction* (2008) John Duvall notes a critical tendency "that sometimes places Toni Morrison in the context of southern literature": "so the argument goes, since her parents migrated from the South, Morrison was raised with southern structures of feeling, and her fiction sometimes has southern settings."[4] A recent version of this argument can be found in *Southscapes: Geographies of Race, Region, and Literature* (2011), in which Thadious M. Davis posits that Morrison's life and writing reach "backward in time and into the South to claim a history" and articulate "the regionality of the black self." *Southscapes* situates Morrison's major works *Song of Solomon* (1977) and *Beloved* (1987) among an array of texts by African American authors that represent "the recovery of a later modern black identity that is rooted in the South as grounded manifestation of the ever-desired formative 'homeplace.'" Moreover, Davis argues that such texts run "counter to the exilic imagination and migratory identity often apparent in the displaced writers of color from the Caribbean, South America, [and] Africa."[5] The invocation of Morrison to argue that a rooted, regional black sense of (home)place supersedes more routed, transnational ways of being in and writing about the world is also evident in Christopher Lloyd's *Rooting Memory, Rooting Place* (2015). Lloyd posits that Morrison's short novel *Home* (2012) reverses "transnational and postsouthern" turns in southern studies by reaffirming a "rooted sense of Southern place" that exemplifies not only "Morrison's regional roots" but also a more general "desire in contemporary Southern fiction to return to the South." Despite *Home*'s depiction of "global routes" via Frank Money's traumatic tour of duty in Korea, Lloyd stresses Frank's "roots in the South"; though the novel is set in the early 1950s and Frank's memories of life and labor in Lotus, Georgia, are conflicted, Lloyd stresses that "*Home*'s journey South establishes regionalism as a continuing and potent force for contemporary African-American identity."[6]

Yet the Morrison book that mostly thoroughly contemplates (and complicates) the role of an ostensibly "rooted" U.S. South in relation to "global routes" is *Tar Baby*. In this relatively overlooked fourth novel, Morrison meditates on the legacies of New World slavery and black rural life in both the U.S. South and the Caribbean vis-à-vis contemporary forms of black "being in the world."[7] This meditation proceeds mainly via the fraught romance between Jadine Childs, a light-skinned cover model, Sorbonne graduate, and recent resident of Paris and Rome, and William "Son" Green, a former soldier and itinerant sailor born and raised in the tiny town of Eloe, Florida. Jadine and Son meet in inauspicious circumstances on Isle des Chevaliers, a remote Caribbean island near Dominique (a former French colony) largely owned by white American candy tycoon Valerian Street; Valerian employs Jadine's "Philadelphia Negro" uncle Sydney and aunt Ondine as his butler and cook respectively. The notion that Morrison's fiction features "southern structures of feeling" has sometimes been advanced by comparing it to Faulkner's. But if shades of Faulkner's Mississippi appear in *Tar Baby*, they are, as in *Absalom, Absalom!*, connected to what Édouard Glissant calls the "configuration of the Plantation" complex "from northeastern Brazil to the Caribbean to the southern United States."[8] Though based in Philadelphia, the Street family firm's profits were partly derived from the sale to southern blacks in "Maryland, Florida, Mississippi" of cheap candies named "Valerians"; Valerian's uncles considered "manufactur[ing] a nickel box of Valerians in Mississippi where beet sugar was almost free and the labor too" (51) until the Great Migration evacuated the state of black workers *and* consumers. L'Arbe de la Croix, Valerian's house on Isle des Chevaliers, was designed by a Mexican architect on land cleared by "laborers imported from Haiti" (9), recalling the French architect and slaves from Haiti or Martinique who built Sutpen's Hundred. More generally, the association of Valerian with "sugar and cocoa"—pondered by Son during a dramatic showdown around the dinner table on Christmas Day (202–3)—personifies the wider history of white mastery throughout the New World plantation system.

The first six chapters of *Tar Baby* take place on Isle des Chevaliers; in chapter 7, the newly coupled Jadine and Son relocate to New York, to which the former responds in terms that recall Helga Crane's arrival in and return to Harlem: "This is home, she thought with an orphan's delight; not Paris, not Baltimore, not Philadelphia. This is home" (222). But for Son, New York's "prestressed concrete and steel" constitutes a kind of objective correlative for his conviction that Jadine's way of being (black) in the world is fake; it also strengthens Son's "insist[ence] on Eloe" (223) as a site of the authentic blackness that New York allegedly lacks. This privileging of Eloe is reliant on a romantic vision of rural black southern womanhood that uncannily anticipates how, during the decade following the publication of *Tar Baby*, "vernacular" African American literary criticism became invested in what Madhu Dubey has described as a feminized "southern folk aesthetics." As we saw in chapters 1 and 2, Houston Baker lauded Hurston over Larsen, whose work lacks "the southern, vernacular, communal expressivity of black mothers and grandmothers." But interestingly, Baker also identified an "expressive cultural succession" between "Zora's conjure woman" and Morrison, discussing Morrison's work (though not *Tar Baby*) in terms of its emphasis on black "village values" maintained by "venerable women."[9] Certainly, Son's Florida hometown echoes Hurston's all-black Eatonville—"There are ninety houses in Eloe. All black. . . . No white people live in Eloe" (172)—and he remembers it as a feminized exception to the imperialist, masculinist "sticky-red" U.S. nation mapped out (quite literally) by a Mexican crewmate: "That separate place that was presided over by wide black women in snowy dresses and was ever dry, green and quiet" (167–68). Moreover, since meeting Jadine, Son has fantasized about "manipulat[ing]" her so that she will share his "dreams" of Eloe, which foreground "the southern, vernacular, communal expressivity of black mothers and grandmothers": "dreams he wanted her to have about yellow houses with white doors which women opened and shouted Come on in, you honey you! And the fat black ladies in white dresses minding the pie table in the basement of the church and white wet sheets flapping on a line, and the sound of a six-string guitar plucked after supper while children scooped walnuts up off the ground and handed them to her" (119).

Son eventually persuades Jadine to join him on a journey south, and chapter 7 ends with the couple leaving New York "hand-in-hand for Eloe" (230). Chapter 9 begins there: it is the only chapter of *Tar Baby* set in the U.S. South, which may crudely explain why even critics interested in Morrison's "southern ethos" have overlooked the novel.[10] However, Jadine's firsthand encounter with the town does not involve nourishing immersion in black southern matrilineal community. Son's old friends Soldier and Drake regard her, when they are not "ignor[ing] her" (246), as "his prize woman ... like she was a Cadillac he had won, or stolen, or even bought for all they knew" (253). When the "neighbor women" visit Jadine, they too figure her as "Son's Northern girl" (250), echoing Helga's experience of being defined as "dat uppity, meddlin' No'the'nah" and Reverend Pleasant Green's wife.[11] Though Son's aunt Rosa greets her as "daughter" (252), Jadine regards the designation as restrictive rather than regenerative: "No, Rosa. I am not your daughter, and he is not your son" (262). In chapter 9's central and most surreal scene, Jadine has a nighttime vision in which various older women from her own and Son's lives are "crowding into the room" at Rosa's house: "each pulled out a breast and showed it to her" (258). The "night women" (262) represent a threat to Jadine's status as a sexually liberated, cosmopolitan, working woman: they are "taking away her sex like succubi" (258) and appear "all out to get her, tie her, bind her. Grab the person she had worked hard to become and choke it off with their soft loose tits" (262). Jadine concludes that "[t]he women in the night had killed the whole weekend. Eloe was rotten and more boring than ever. A burnt-out place. There was no life there. Maybe a past but definitely no future and finally there was no interest. All that Southern small-town country romanticism was a lie, a joke, kept secret by people who could not function elsewhere" (259).

To be sure, Jadine, like Helga, has her own prejudices about "Southern small-town country" life, and her sense of the natural environment around Rosa's house as "the blackest nothing she had ever seen" may be read as a barely repressed projection of anxieties about her own (lack of) racial and regional authenticity: "It's not possible, she thought, for anything to be this black" (251). Maternal, fertile black women associated with not only Son's South but also the Caribbean and Paris sometimes leave Jadine feeling "[l]onely and inauthentic" (48).[12] In *Home*, it is the older black women who "took turns nursing Cee," Frank's sister, back to health in the "timeless time" of Lotus, Georgia.[13] Similarly, in *Tar Baby*, the older black women of Eloe seem to exhibit those "sacred" and "ancient properties" that Jadine is said to have "forgotten" (305), which are lauded in the novel's dedication, and which some critics believe the book itself celebrates. Yet the trip to Eloe seriously undermines Son's gendered assertion of rural, rooted southern blackness over Jadine's transnational, routed subjectivity. After returning to New York, Jadine redoubles her earlier drive to move beyond national and racial categories defined by white European *or* black U.S. southern men: "I want to get out of my skin and be only the person inside—not American—not black—just me" (49). By contrast, Son holds stubbornly to his idealized vision of women "out of north Florida" and so remains unable to comprehend Jadine's own dream of "equality, sexual equality" (268): their relationship is torn asunder, and Jadine leaves Son to return to Isle des Chevaliers.

Son's romantic privileging of (his own) southern roots precludes him from acknowledging that Jadine is, like Helga, an orphan raised in northern cities with no ancestral, matrilineal connection to the rural South. But it also prevents Son from recognizing that he and Jadine are *both*, despite their different social circles and circumstances, mobile members of a modern, multidimensional black diaspora. Already as a teenager Son had fought "all over Vietnam" (224), and upon fleeing Eloe in 1971 he "joined that great underclass of undocumented men ... an international legion of day laborers and musclemen, gamblers, sidewalk merchants, migrants, unlicensed crewmen on ships with volatile cargo, part-time mercenaries, full-time gigolos, or curbside musicians. What distinguished them from other men (aside from their terror of Social Security cards and *cédula de identidad*) was their refusal to equate work with life and an inability to stay anywhere for long" (166). Son's working life as a sailor—Paul Gilroy's emblematic black Atlantic figure—took him from "off the coast of Greenland" (131) to "close to Argentina"; his closest friends on board were Mexican and Swedish (167). Though Son often boasts to Jadine that his identity remains rooted in Florida—"Anybody ask you where you from, you give them five towns. You're not *from* anywhere. I'm from Eloe"—he also, when it suits him, insists that he can be just as global and adaptable as her: "I've lived all over the world, Jadine. I can live anywhere" (266). As Yogita Goyal has shrewdly observed, whereas "Jadine's mobility has frequently been censured by literary critics, who suggest that Morrison portrays her as insufficiently black *and* as insufficiently female," a closer reading reveals that "[e]ven Son, who is interpreted [by some critics] as the symbol of stability" and as "invested in the image of stable black Southern culture, is constantly on the move." Goyal quite rightly stresses that "both Son and Jadine appear as representatives of migration or mobility at different points in the novel."[14]

Tar Baby further challenges expectations about who and what is rooted or routed by tracing the transnational migrant lives and labor of other ostensibly provincial or "primitive" black characters. At L'Arbe de la Croix, white and black residents alike (Valerian, his wife Margaret, Sydney, Ondine, and Jadine) all refer to a black domestic worker by the diminutive "Yardman," but it transpires that Gideon (his real name) has been traversing national boundaries across the Americas for decades. Gideon moved first to Quebec, where he worked for "a Canadian farmer," before marrying "an American Negro" (109) and spending twenty years in the United States. Despite "the humiliations of immigrant life which U.S. citizenship did not change," this hemispheric mobility facilitated Gideon's employment by Valerian: "all of his forty years of immigrant labor paid off when an American who owned a house on Isle des Chevaliers came to stay and needed a regular handyman/gardener with boat skills, English and a manner less haughty than that of the local Blacks" (110). Hence both Son *and* Gideon personify a contemporary version of that "cosmopolitanism from below" theorized by Ifeoma Nwankwo: a way of being in the world derived from African-descended slaves who, while enduring white masters' "hegemonic cosmopolitanism, exemplified by the material and psychological violence of imperialism and slavery," nevertheless envisioned themselves as subjects rather than objects.[15] In the late-1970s setting of *Tar Baby*, hegemonic cosmopolitanism has mutated via Valerian's decaying neoplanter capitalism into economic globalization's exploitation of "that great underclass of undocumented men" of which Son and Gideon have been part. Here it seems telling that *Tar Baby* was published in 1981, the year that, according to Paul Giles, "the multidimensional effects of globalization" were just beginning to propel the United States, as well as its literature, into a new "transnational era" dominated by "global networks of exchange."[16] However, a counterhegemonic cosmopolitanism from below is practiced by *Tar Baby*'s "undocumented men": subjects without citizenship, permanent residence, or work permits who, through "their refusal to equate work with life," will not be reduced to mere laboring bodies.

Still, if Son and Gideon practice a bottom-up cosmopolitanism, it does not follow that jet-setting Jadine has been co-opted to an elitist top-down cosmopolitanism. Such an opposition would be just as reductive as figuring Jadine as "northern" to Son's "southern"; "city girl" (171) to his "country boy" (158); rootless high-fashion model to Eloe's rooted "fat black ladies"; or "little white girl" (121) to Son's authentic black manhood. In resituating the region at hemispheric, diasporic, and (black) Atlantic world scales rather than recapitulating the South (or north Florida) as Son's "separate place," Morrison interrogates such binaries, even while dramatizing their perniciously enduring power. In the process, *Tar Baby* reconfirms that, as in the writing of Hurston and Banks, Florida is a key site for thinking about the South at various national and global scales—particularly through the prisms of race, migration, and labor.

Neoslavery and U.S. Empire in South Florida: Peter Matthiessen's *Shadow Country*

Though the temporal focus is on an earlier era—the late nineteenth and early twentieth centuries—Florida plays a similar role in *Shadow Country*, Peter Matthiessen's epic novel about Everglades entrepreneur Edgar J. Watson. Weighing in at well-nigh nine hundred pages, *Shadow Country* won the National Book Award and was lauded as "a great American novel" (*New York Review of Books*, *Miami Herald*) and "a touchstone of modern American literature" (*Publishers Weekly*).[17] But at least one reviewer remarked the Faulknerian-southern resonances, especially in the Sutpen-like figure of Watson. Tom LeClair deemed *Shadow Country* "a deeper South *Absalom, Absalom!*" that "[t]o the tragic dignity of Faulkner's novel . . . adds the ironic indignity" of Watson's story initially being "recounted by the laboring folk that he, like Sutpen, dominated."[18] In the preface to *Shadow Country*, Matthiessen himself defined his "new rendering of the Watson legend" as "one man's obsessive self-destruction set against the historic background of slavery and civil war, imperialism, and the rape of land and life under the banner of industrial 'progress'"—all themes with which Faulkner engaged deeply.[19] If *Shadow Country* follows *Tar Baby* by inviting comparison with Faulkner's depiction of the South's location within plantation America, it also depicts the region's relationship to distinctly modern forms of American capitalism and neo-imperialism.

Edgar Watson's identity as both the scion of a South Carolina slave-owning clan—Edgar's grandfather owned sixty-eight slaves (499), while his father fought for the Confederacy—*and* a pioneer planter in late nineteenth-century Florida vividly captures the continuities between slavery in the Old South and postbellum forms of labor exploitation. Early on Watson's apprentice Erskine Thompson recalls how Watson (like Sutpen) "[w]orked his crew like niggers and worked like a nigger alongside of us" (12); Watson himself is frank about employing and exploiting "drifters of all colors from the shantytowns and saloon alleys of Ybor City and Key West" (680–81).[20] That southwest Florida is initially figured as an anachronistic remnant of the late Confederacy also seems to confirm its "southern" identity. Though there are a few French and Spanish immigrant settlers living alongside (but largely segregated from) Mikasuki Natives, Erskine observes that "[m]ost of our old Glades pioneers was drifters and deserters from the War Between the States who never got the word that we was licked" (11). However, the narrative also repeatedly references the "western" mythology of the frontier. Watson first visits Florida's "virgin land" (561) in 1871. On his more permanent return in 1894—a year after "[t]hat professor," Frederick Jackson Turner, reaffirmed the view of the 1890 U.S. Census that the frontier was closed—he is driven by "the prospect of so much virgin coast awaiting man's dominion. . . . This Everglades frontier was a huge wilderness to be tamed and harnessed" (640–41). Yet beneath these "southern" and "western" identities, the rural Florida landscape reveals a longer history of colonial settlement and genocide. Watson builds his Chatham Bend plantation on Calusa Indian shell mounds (298, 642); his other house in Fort White is on "the former site of a seventeenth-century Spanish mission destroyed by the British when they came to north Florida from Charlestown at the start of the eighteenth century and butchered every Spaniard and Indian they could lay their hands on" (704). Watson describes "Cape Sable, the long white beach where Juan Ponce de León and his conquistadors went ashore" (645), and an eccentric earlier settler called Jean de Chevelier reminds him "that "France had conquered Florida back in the 1590s . . . had it not been for the Louisiana Purchase, France's rightful territories would include most if not all of North America" (664). This colonial history predates the invention and consolidation of "the South" in the decades before the secession of the Confederate States; that Watson occupies the land once squatted by Chevelier—he also finds and buries the Frenchman's corpse—symbolically personifies the Anglo-American (rather than simply white southern) succession to French and Spanish colonialism in Florida.

At the same time, though, the "Watson legend" traces the rise on Native, colonial, and neo-Confederate ground of distinctly modern modes of capitalism and (neo-)imperialism. With the outbreak of the Spanish-American War in 1898, Watson declares that "he will never salute the Stars and Stripes. . . . [T]he South, he says, was the first conquest of the Yankee Empire, and Cuba and the Spanish colonies will be next" (77). Edgar's view here anticipates historian C. Vann Woodward's influential argument that the (white) South was the nation's original "colonial economy" as well as George Handley's more recent claim that "[t]he South essentially was the first colony of U.S. imperial expansion" subsequently practiced on "an international scale."[21] However, Edgar himself is known locally as "the Emperor" Watson "because of his grand ambitions for the [Ten Thousand] Islands" (60, 665). Watson's sugarcane operation at Chatham Bend and ambitious plans to develop "modern agriculture across the state" using prison "[s]lave labor" (193)—articulated in "some long-range proposals for the Everglades, 'the last American frontier'" (828) to his friend Napoleon Broward, governor of Florida from 1905 to 1909—are less the Old South redux than a prototype for the industrialized agribusiness later practiced in south Florida and throughout the hemisphere by U.S. Sugar and the United Fruit Company. Watson is keenly aware that, despite the official abolition of slavery, "the commerce in human beings which had made our nation great was by no means dead. Chinese coolies and other illegal immigrants would gladly pay enterprising captains to set them ashore in Florida, where most wound up as indentured labor for the new railroad companies, resort hotels, large-scale drainage schemes, and development enterprises seeking to bring both of Florida's wild coasts into the modern world" (646). Here *Shadow Country*'s literary cartography depicts a version of the "coexistence of modes of production in narrative form" that Fredric Jameson identifies in Faulkner's fiction.[22] The unevenly developing west and east coasts of Florida appear at this hinge in history as respectively a remote, even precapitalist "frontier" sparsely populated by Confederate refugees and Natives living off the land and largely outside a money economy, *and* as a privileged locus for the transnational circulation of capital and labor in "the modern world." Watson notes the vivid contrast between his own southwest Florida, which he so yearns to develop, and the emergence of Key West as a bustling "port city, with eighteen thousand immigrants and refugees of color" (646).

But Edgar's "Emperor" sobriquet suggests another neo-imperial and "international scale" to this emergent capitalist modernity. Local acquaintance Owen Harden recalls Watson's excitement over "his grand plan" to develop southwest Florida leading seamlessly into his declaration "that the U.S.A. was bringing light to the benighted, spreading capitalism, democracy, and God across the world" (99). Watson himself moves within four short paragraphs from observing "the epochal economic changes taking place in America at the approach of the new century" via his own position "as a stern supporter of the capitalist system" to remarking after the outbreak of war in Havana and Manila that "the nations of Europe were establishing huge colonies in Africa and Asia and the U.S.A. would do well to grab its share of colonial territories and resources while the grabbing was good" (672–73). As Harilaos Stecopoulos has demonstrated, during the Spanish-American War white-supremacist southerners like author Thomas Dixon "found appealing the president's [McKinley's] vision of a world in which the United States treated the territory and markets of people of color as their own." For all his grumbling about "the Yankee Empire" extending itself from the Confederacy into Cuba, Watson, like Dixon, supports U.S. imperialism and its racialized vision of the world. Though Edgar insists that there remains an unexploited "last frontier" *within* the United States, his ambitions as "Emperor" of the Everglades are entirely compatible with what Stecopoulos identifies as the belief that "[o]verseas expansion provided Americans with a way of extending the logic of the frontier into the new century."[23] Thus *Shadow Country* dramatizes the links between a "southern" history of exploiting slave and neoslave labor, the local fin de siècle rise of capitalist "Emperor" Watson, and the hemispheric and global expansion of a neo-imperial United States as it enters the "American Century."

As it turns out, Watson's "grand plan," like Sutpen's "design," consumes its progenitor. Watson bitterly observes that Governor Broward instead backs "John D. Rockefeller's partner Henry Flagler," who utilizes "the brute labor done by... thousands of unknown men" to complete the Florida East Coast Railway. Watson sourly remarks the hypocrisy and injustice of his reputation on the opposite coast as a tyrannical planter who kills rather than pays his cane-cutters, claiming that his own "field hands were better housed and fed than the immigrants and Caribbean blacks and crackers who perished" on the job for Flagler. He also notes not merely the state's but the nation-state's complicity in such practices: "Nobody wanted to investigate all that dying, least of all the U.S. government, because Flagler was opening up south Florida for development, commerce, and big investors. 'The kind of red-blooded American who made this country great'—that's what the newspapers called Flagler. There was red blood, all right, but it wasn't his" (829). Much as previously loyal worker Wash Jones kills "Kernel" Sutpen, so in October 1910 "Emperor" Watson is murdered by "the laboring folk that he, like Sutpen, dominated." Yet in the longer view, Watson's design for southwest Florida succeeds as "the start of this whole new sugar industry" that made "fortunes for other men" (281) like *Tar Baby*'s Valerian Street and the white "boss" who employs Janie and Tea Cake on the Everglades "muck" in *Their Eyes Were Watching God*. Years later, Edgar's proto-environmentalist son Lucius is left to ponder the consequences of such development: "tons of chemicals dumped into the pristine waterlands, the wretched slave camps for the migrant workers—the price of progress, Papa would have called it, celebrating any and all such evidence of the Twentieth Century cavalcade" (415). Bill House, Edgar's former neighbor, tells Lucius in the 1920s that "Big Sugar don't care nothing about workers' rights or the damn risks so long as they're rakin in big profits. Know who got convicted on a slavery charge just lately? United Sugar! U.S.A! *Slavery!* In the Twentieth damn Century! That what they call progress?" (440). As we have seen, Hurston investigated such "progress" in her unpublished 1958 essay on Florida's agricultural migrant workers; labor abuses continued through four more decades in which Florida's sugar industry was the nation's biggest employer of H-2 guest workers. Matthiessen would have been well aware of the historical-geographical continuities between his "new rendering of the Watson legend" and the twenty-first-century exploitation of Caribbean migrant workers that led the U.S. Justice Department to declare south Florida "ground zero for modern slavery."[24]

Angola South:
Post-Katrina, Neoplantation New Orleans
in Dave Eggers's *Zeitoun*

When Hurricane Katrina hit the Gulf Coast in August 2005, the familiar, often favorable discourse of New Orleans exceptionalism—the city's French/Spanish/Creole/Caribbean distinctiveness from both the rest of the U.S. South and the nation as a whole—took a dubious turn into what Karin H. deGravelles terms "the third world-ing of New Orleans": the pervasive use of "a language of Otherness in which New Orleans became 'not America' in a wide range of contexts and media."[25] The post-Katrina hypervisibility (via the news networks' camera eye) of black residents *cum* "refugees" in and around the Superdome was coupled with a discursive displacement of the hurricane's victims beyond both region and nation: as Jennifer Greeson observes, "the term 'Third World' was resurrected from the dustbin of outmoded parlance, as aghast onlookers and media commentators made the diagnosis again and again. 'This doesn't look like America,' ran the refrain. 'It looks like the Third World down here.'"[26] DeGravelles points out that such language revealed a national unwillingness to recognize, and a rhetorical urge to relocate, "the level of poverty and vulnerability" that Katrina had exposed "within one of the wealthiest and most powerful countries in the world."[27] Though in contemporary discourse "the Cold-War era terms 'First World' and 'Third World'" are more usually substituted by the supposedly "descriptive, nonhierarchical geographical designations" of "global North" and "global South," it is telling that, as Stecopoulos notes, post-Katrina news reports also "often drew analogies between this portion of the domestic South and other places in the global South such as Rwanda and Bangladesh."[28]

The aftermath of Katrina in the city long celebrated (and consumed) as "America's European Masterpiece" and the capital of "America's Caribbean Coast" revealed intersections of the Global North and Global South in ways that were more than merely rhetorical.[29] As I noted in the introduction, the relocation of Katrina "refugees" to points west and north within the nation was followed by the arrival of large numbers of foreign workers recruited and often exploited by contractors involved in rebuilding New Orleans and other Gulf Coast cities. Furthermore, immigrant residents and their second-generation families, including (as observed in chapter 7) the Vietnamese Americans of New Orleans and East Biloxi, also suffered disproportionately from Katrina and its sociopolitical aftereffects. Dave Eggers's *Zeitoun* explores the post-Katrina trials experienced by an individual representative of another immigrant demographic from the Global South: Middle Easterners. Eggers's nonfiction account maps the dystopian landscape of New Orleans after the flood through the eyes of Syrian immigrant Abdulrahman Zeitoun; in the process, *Zeitoun* (like *The Celestial Jukebox*) also elucidates the post-9/11 tribulations of Muslims in the United States. There are continuities here too with Eggers's larger body of work: his previous book, *What Is the What* (2006), explored both the trauma of the Sudanese civil war that began in 1983 and the African immigrant experience in Atlanta. *Zeitoun* itself emerged from interviews conducted for the oral history project *Voices from the Storm* (2005), published by Eggers's McSweeney's imprint. *Zeitoun* extends *What Is the What*'s textual mapping of transnational migration from the Global South to the U.S. South (as part of the Global North) even as it interrogates "outmoded" but recrudescent binary oppositions between Third and First World.

Before casting back in time to Valentino's traumatic childhood uprooting from his home in southern Sudan, *What Is the What* begins with the adult Valentino living as an alienated refugee in Atlanta. Through this "framing device," Eggers foregrounds "the many unforeseen struggles of his [Valentino's] life in the U.S.," including fraught encounters with black Atlantans who see him not as a fellow "African American" but rather "one of those Africans who sold us out" during the transatlantic slave trade.[30] *Zeitoun* opens with a similar form of temporal and spatial framing as Abdulrahman happily recalls his upbringing in northern Syria from a position "[t]hirty-four years later and thousands of miles west": August 26, 2005, in New Orleans, three days before Katrina hits the city and throws his life into turmoil. From these opening paragraphs, the narrative stresses that Zeitoun's Syrian family were well-educated cosmopolites despite living in the modest fishing town of Jableh. The sailor's life of Abdulrahman's brother Ahmad brought him (like Morrison's Son) into contact with various cultures: "He wanted to guide great vessels around the world, to speak a dozen languages, to know the people of every nation."[31] This seafaring cosmopolitanism is also conveyed through photographs of Ahmad posing in various global port cities. One 1978 image shows Ahmad at what appears to be the intersection of Burgundy and Canal Streets, intoning New Orleans's history as a port city that, in A. J. Liebling's famous description, "resembles Genoa or Marseille, or Beirut or the Egyptian Alexandria more than it does New York.... The Mediterranean, Caribbean, and Gulf of Mexico form a homogenous, though interrupted, sea."[32] The image of Ahmad also foreshadows Abdulrahman's own arrival in the city circa 1994 as a world citizen rather than "Third World" refugee, after ten years sailing between "the Persian Gulf, Japan, Australia, and Baltimore... Holland and Norway" (145), and "by way of Houston and Baton Rouge and a half-dozen other American cities" (6).

Like Ha Jin's *A Free Life*, *Zeitoun* offers a variation on that mythic American theme of the immigrant's self-made success: in the eleven years since coming to New Orleans, Abdulrahman has built up a successful business, Zeitoun A. Painting Contractor LLC, and acquired "six properties with eighteen tenants" (14). However, this recognizable American story of ascent and assimilation is defamiliarized by the way in which Zeitoun's fair-wage policy derives from the Koran—"He always quoted the Prophet Muhammad: 'Pay the laborer his wages before his sweat dries'" (40)—and the emphasis on his transnational labor force: "Zeitoun had hired men from everywhere: Peru, Mexico, Bulgaria, Poland, Brazil, Honduras, Algeria.... Many workers were transient, intending only to spend a few months in the country before returning to their families" (19). What is more, before Katrina but after 9/11 there are ominous signs that Middle Eastern and/or Muslim immigrants are experiencing ethnic and religious prejudice. The Zeitouns hear about a history teacher at a local high school harassing "a tenth grader of Iraqi descent" by calling Iraq a "third-world country" and suggesting that "the student would 'bomb us' if she ever returned to Iraq" (45). This incident is freighted with dramatic irony given that, after Katrina, "[t]he media consensus was that New Orleans had descended into a 'third-world' state" (109). Romanian-born, New Orleans–based author Andrei Codrescu critiqued such Third World–ing of his adopted home—in George W. Bush's words, "that part of the world"—by connecting the Bush administration's response to Katrina with its 2003 intervention in Iraq. For Codrescu, both Baghdad and New Orleans had been rendered "part of a world that . . . has to be secured by armies, not saved through compassion."[33] It is grimly ironic, then, that after losing contact with Abdulrahman, his Syrian family, watching events unfold from afar on television, try to compassionately save the New Orleans Zeitouns. Abdulrahman's siblings implore his white, Baton Rouge–born wife, Kathy: "How can you live in that country? . . . You need to move back here. Syria is so much safer, they said" (183). Here Kathy is rhetorically detached from her homeland ("that country") and refigured as a native or citizen of Jableh ("back here"), a town she has only once visited. At such moments, *Zeitoun* disrupts post-9/11, post-Katrina discourses about the relative status and imagined geography of the "First" and "Third" worlds.

More than that, though, Eggers's text constructs a counternarrative to the "media consensus" about how and why the Crescent City "descended into a 'third-world' state." Kathy witnesses "the hyberbolic and racially charged news coverage" featuring "images of African American residents wilting in the heat" and "standing on rooftops waiting for help" (109). Anxiously awaiting information about her husband's whereabouts, Kathy watches press conferences and *Oprah* interviews by Mayor Ray Nagin and the city police chief that give credence to rumors of baby rape in the Superdome and citizens being reduced to (in Nagin's words) "this almost animalistic state." But in *Zeitoun* it is not the supposedly bestial behavior of traumatized, uprooted, nonwhite "refugees" that makes post-Katrina New Orleans seem suddenly part of the "Third World." Rather, it is the brutal mistreatment of citizens like Zeitoun himself, taken into police custody while helping to rescue fellow residents left stranded by the storm. Abdulrahman is incarcerated in a hastily converted Greyhound station and subsequently a maximum-security "correctional center" in St. Gabriel, Louisiana. This "dizzying series of events—arrested at gunpoint in a home he owned, brought to an impromptu military base built inside a bus station, accused of terrorism, and locked in an outdoor cage"—is so bewildering that "[i]t surpassed the most surreal accounts he'd heard of third-world law enforcement" (218).

If here the "Third World–ing of New Orleans" is slyly recast to critique authoritarian police actions, there is also a long regional history of law enforcement rife with just such abuse of nonwhites. For the bus station prisoners and guards alike, the local reference point for incarceration is Louisiana's notorious state penitentiary, Angola, "the country's largest prison... an eighteen-thousand-acre former plantation once used for the breeding of slaves" (310). Jessica Adams has noted that when the Louisiana Corrections Board purchased the Angola plantation in 1901, "[p]lantation labor and the penitentiary were set to converge." A century on, in the wake of post-9/11 "homeland security" hysteria about Muslim terrorist "sleeper cells" within the United States and post-Katrina fears of a "Third World" internal other, the ways in which "[t]he penitentiary performs the plantation's disciplinary function" take a further twist: as Zeitoun later discovers, Camp Greyhound was partly built by inmates from Angola (310).[34] Christopher Lloyd has rightly remarked that here "Eggers is illuminating the historical resonances of this prison's (and the South's) treatment of labor and work.... Zeitoun's captivity is made explicitly to dialogue with this tangled notion of the Southern past."[35]

However, at the global scale of the "war on terror," the ad hoc jail resembles nothing so much as that most notorious locus of the post-9/11 military-disciplinary complex: Guantánamo Bay in Cuba. Initially, Abdulrahman naïvely reaches for more benign local points of reference: "[I]t was not unprecedented. During Mardi Gras, when the local jails were full, the New Orleans police often housed drunks and thieves in temporary jails set up in tents." But soon he recognizes that the jail "looked precisely like the pictures he'd seen of Guantánamo Bay" (218–19). Even the guards and soldiers "referred to it as Angola South, but far more were calling it Camp Greyhound": after all, "just like Guantánamo, all prisoners could be seen by anyone, from any angle," and "with the orange [prison] uniforms completing the picture, the similarities were too strong to ignore" (229, 227). Another Camp Greyhound prisoner cites the then-recent specter of the war on terror's turn to the Middle East itself following the Bush administration's invasion of Iraq, Syria's eastern neighbor: "Someone in Zeitoun's cage mentioned Abu Ghraib, wondering at what point they'd be asked to pose naked, in a vertical pyramid, and which guard would lean into the picture, grinning" (228). This invocation of the notorious U.S. military abuse of Iraqi prisoners at what was previously Saddam Hussein's main incarceration and torture facility marks a kind of culmination to *Zeitoun*'s dismantling of complacent distinctions between the U.S. South and U.S. nation-state; First and Third Worlds; and in George W. Bush's infamous formulation, "us" and "the terrorists."[36]

The (Native) South as "The North": Colonialism, Slavery, and Protoglobalization in Laila Lalami's *The Moor's Account*

Laila Lalami's extraordinary neoslave narrative *The Moor's Account* imagines seismic historical events as they were experienced by perhaps the first black

African to arrive in the New World. Moroccan-born and raised Lalami hereby reminds us that the region we know today as the South "has always been globalized" and that an "earlier transnational history virtually created the historical South."[37] *The Moor's Account* vividly dramatizes how the first wave of European colonial exploration (and exploitation) of North America occurred not in Massachusetts or Virginia but Florida; that the Native population in Florida and further west had a profound influence on the would-be colonists; and that in Mustafa ibn Muhammad ibn Abdussalam al-Zamori, the Moroccan slave protagonist known to historians as Esteban Dorantes, a Muslim presence in "the South" may have predated the likes of Abdulrahman Zeitoun by almost half a millennium.

The Moor's Account opens with Mustafa telling "The Story of La Florida" from the moment in 1527 when a Castilian expedition of some six hundred men arrived "at the edge of the known world"—almost certainly Tampa Bay.[38] As historian Robert Goodwin observes, this expedition, led by and later named after the military leader and Caribbean slave trader Pánfilo Narváez, mired its dwindling band of survivors in an "almost interminable peregrination through the swamps of Florida, the seas of Alabama, the waters of the Mississippi, [and] the lagoons and prairies of Texas" before their return to Spanish rule in modern-day Mexico.[39] But in Lalami's variation on "cosmopolitanism from below," Mustafa's narrative also moves back in time and space to encompass his earlier life in northern Africa and initial enslavement in southern Europe. We learn that Mustafa was raised in the Moroccan city of Azemmur, where his promising career as a trader (including, with coruscating dramatic irony, his purchase and sale of three slaves) was ruined by a Portuguese siege of the city; desperately seeking to support his family, Mustafa sold himself into slavery.[40] Transported to Seville in southern Spain, Mustafa was, in an archetypal act of colonial onomastics, rechristened Esteban (109); in Seville and subsequently in La Florida, Mustafa's identity is further diminished by his master, Andrés Dorantes de Carranza, who refers to him by the diminutive Estebanico (149) and the nicknames "El Moro, El Negro, El Arabe" (49). Mustafa's own "account" thus constitutes a counternarrative to both colonialism's everyday discourse and the official "Joint Report" of the "three Castilian gentlemen" (3)—Dorantes, a nobleman called Alonso del Castillo Maldonado, and treasurer Álvar Núñez Cabeza de Vaca—who survived the expedition. It challenges too Cabeza de Vaca's celebrated travelogue *Chronicle of the Narváez Expedition*, which made only passing reference to "[t]he fourth [survivor] ... Estevanico, an Arab Negro from Azamor" (324).[41] By tracking Mustafa's forced migrations as a slave and cog in colonial expeditions, *The Moor's Account* maps the routes connecting the early (black) Atlantic world of which "the South" and its slave economy subsequently became a part.

In the opening sentences of Mustafa's account, 1527 is recast as "the year

934 of the Hegira"; the Atlantic is rendered as "the Ocean of Fog and Darkness"; and "La Florida" (as it had been designated by Ponce de León) becomes, in accordance with the "naming conventions" of "my people" in Morocco, "the land of the Indians" (5). These are all manifestations of Mustafa's belief, developed during his traumatic experiences of enslavement and forced Catholic conversion, that "[a] name is precious; it carries inside it a language, a history, a set of traditions, a particular way of looking at the world" (7). Mustafa proceeds to detail the expedition's initial encounters with unknown Native tribes, including the first armed conflict in which, "in the middle of a battle between two foreign peoples" (23), he fights alongside his Castilian masters and kills an Indian in self-defense. Following further conflicts, disease, and starvation, the surviving expedition members embark on a lengthy (and, for many, deadly) voyage via makeshift barges from "the Bay of Oysters"—now Apalachee Bay in Alabama—along the Gulf Coast to present-day Galveston Island, Texas. Mustafa recounts the "calamity that befell the Capoques" (174) as a virulently infectious bowel disease contracted from the colonists decimates the tribe. Yet it is by listening to the Capoque women that Mustafa first begins to learn their language, leading him into the more liminal (if still limited) role of interpreter between the surviving Castilians and various Native tribes on whom the explorers become almost entirely dependent. Though Mustafa fears "the prospect of an endless exile" (211) and dreams of returning to Morocco as a free man, he and the Castilians go native, adopting tribal dress and marrying Indian women. Moreover, Mustafa's apparent medical skills impress the shaman of the Avavares (another tribe based in present-day Texas), and he and the three white men become nomadic healers to and between numerous tribes.

In this process, the European colonial discourse of master and slave, civilization and savagery, breaks down. Mustafa's observation that the Avavares refer to himself and the Castilians collectively as "the Children of the Sun" because they are "strangers from the east" (243) suggests how Native perspectives radically undermine conventional understandings of what constitutes "the West" and "the East," Old World and New, white and black, and—temporally as well as spatially—"the South."[42] Mustafa's detailed renditions of his experiences with the Apalaches, Capoques, Carancahuas, Yguaces, Avavares, and other Native tribes bear out Eric Gary Anderson's point that what scholars now call "the Native South" existed "prior to the invention of the South as a distinct and heavily mythologized U.S. region most often regarded as biracial rather than multicultural." As Anderson notes, this Native South "is vastly older, vastly different in its ways of inhabiting both space and time, vastly more diverse"; it is in fact "a place that has been Native for vastly longer than it has been southern," a redefinition that did not occur "until quite late in its twelve-thousand-year history."[43]

Mustafa's situation changes drastically once again in 1536, when he and the three Castilians encounter Spanish soldiers and are taken to the settlement at Compostela in New Galicia (present-day Mexico), where the governor is enslaving the Natives and seeks the survivors' help to map the uncharted Indian territories. Mustafa, Dorantes, Castillo, and de Vaca proceed further south via Guadalajara to the former Aztec city-state of Tenochtitlán, where the "Official Report" of the expedition is compiled (and from which Mustafa is excluded). While the Castilians slough off their connections to Native culture and reintegrate themselves into the Spanish colonial worldview—"they were seeking royal grants, or getting married [to Spanish women], or acquiring estates, forgetting everything that we had been through in the north" (303)—Tenochtitlán's notorious conqueror, Hernán Cortés, tries to secure Mustafa as a guide "for whatever mission he was planning to the north" (292); so too does Cortés's rival, the viceroy of New Spain, Antonio de Mendoza. To liberate himself from Dorantes, Mustafa takes up Mendoza's offer. Departing Tenochtitlán in 1538 and separating from the expedition's Spanish leader "on an advance mission to the north" (310), Mustafa sheds his "Castilian clothes" (311) and warns the Zuni (a Pueblo tribe based near the Zuni River in what is now New Mexico) that the Spanish rule "the territories south of here" (319) and are seeking to extend their dominion. Mustafa then fakes his own death at the hands of "the fierce Indians of Hawikuh" (thereby playing on Castilian prejudice about Native savagery) to escape Spanish slavery and join his wife on "our journey home to the land of the Avavares": "Esteban would be laid to rest. But Mustafa would remain, free to live a life of his own choosing" (320).[44]

In its temporal and spatial span—forty-one years and thousands of miles across three continents—Mustafa's cosmopolitan-from-below account dramatically resets the coordinates of the South within the longer *durée* and larger geography of European colonial exploitation of Africa and the Americas. "The South" encountered by Mustafa and the three other survivors of the Narváez expedition is, from the perspective of Spanish rule in Tenochtitlán, the unknown world to "the north": a periphery populated by Natives not yet conquered and enslaved, and shrouded in enticing rumors about the fabled Seven Cities of Gold. As Goodwin notes, the "knowledge of the previously unexplored north" garnered by Esteban and the three Castilian survivors "made them important players in the politics of Mexico City and the Spanish Empire."[45] *The Moor's Account* is then a dramatic cognitive remapping of that more common psychogeography of "southern distinctiveness" through which the U.S. South is contrasted with the U.S. North. That our own disciplinary discourse struggles to articulate such radical (albeit in this case colonial) reorientations without retaining the usual rubric is evident not only in a term like "Native South" but also the subtitle of one of the historical sources for *The Moor's Account*: Goodwin's *Crossing the Continent, 1527–1540: The Story of the First African-American Explorer of the American South* (2008). Cited in Lalami's acknowledgments,

Goodwin's history similarly traces the Narváez expedition via an emphasis on the previously elided Esteban. But for all that Esteban may have been the first black person to arrive in "La Florida," neither he nor his Castilian masters would have conceptualized this territory as "the American South": as Goodwin remarks, Florida was "the name the Spanish gave to the whole of the American south, from Georgia and Florida to modern New Mexico." Nor was Esteban/Mustafa "African American" in our conventional understanding of that term.[46]

If we compare the literary geography of scale in *The Moor's Account* to other recent novels focusing on contemporary immigration, such as *Monkey Bridge* or *A Free Life*, Lalami's novel stresses that "the South" was once not merely what Jon Smith calls "an unhelpful scalar unit" but an unknown one. It was—to refashion Michael Kreyling's titular phrase—the South that wasn't there yet.[47] Yet this needs qualifying, given that Lalami's novel brilliantly dramatizes the coalescing nexus of European colonialism, transatlantic (forced) migration, and slave labor that would forge "the South" that constitutes our disciplinary known world. As a historical novel projecting back to a time and space *before* that "fixed, defined society" we thought we knew, *The Moor's Account* is, like *Shadow Country*, germane to thinking through the ways in which contemporary globalization, including immigration and labor exploitation, represent historical-geographical breaks and continuities with "the South."[48] Reading Lalami's novel may be a kind of case study for "southern studies without 'the South,'" but it also compels an American studies *with* the South—or a *transnational* American studies with the *Native* South. Ultimately, (new) southern studies and (transnational) American studies would benefit from a fuller mutual understanding of how such novels represent both region and nation as inextricable from the capitalist world-system that, circa 1981 or so, we came to call "globalization."

NOTES

PREFACE

1. Bone, *The Postsouthern Sense of Place*, 253.
2. Baker and Nelson, "Preface," 231.
3. Jon Smith, "Toward a Post-postpolitical Southern Studies," 77–78.
4. Jon Smith, *Finding Purple America*, 3, 124.
5. Gross, "The Transnational Turn," 378. For an overview of the transnational turn that also signals its institutional ascendancy, see Shelley Fisher Fishkin, "Crossroads of Cultures" (the published version of Fishkin's 2004 American Studies Association presidential address).
6. Pfister, "Transnational American Studies for What?" 17, 18, 30.
7. Thompson, "Roundtable," 1083. Thompson rightly observes that too often transnationalism "keeps national contexts close to its heart," especially "by imagining a world whose globalization occurs in America's image" (1083). However, Jameson himself has argued that we need to remain alert to the ways in which "globalization" may sometimes be suspiciously similar to "Americanization," especially when it involves "the subordination of the other nation-states to American power." See Jameson, "Globalization and Political Strategy," 50, 53.
8. Lloyd, *Rooting Memory, Rooting Place*, 72, 137. (New) southern studies' hemispheric orientation was especially apparent in the mid-2000s, when I began this book; it continues with John Wharton Lowe's *Calypso Magnolia: The Crosscurrents of Caribbean and Southern Literature* (2016), published as I was completing this book.
9. Soja, *Postmodern Geographies*, 12; see also Bone, *The Postsouthern Sense of Place*, 47.
10. Giles, *Global Remapping*, 1. Giles draws on David Harvey's discussion of "historical-geographical materialism" (1) to critique the dematerialization and deterritorialization of money during economic globalization, a mechanism that tends to obscure the (related) "outsourcing and transnationalization" of labor (15).
11. Wallerstein, *Modern World-System*, 167.
12. Baker and Nelson, "Preface," 231.
13. Of course, for the Native victims of European settler colonialism, the continent that came to be named after Italian explorer Amerigo Vespucci was no "New World."

INTRODUCTION. The Transnational Turn in the South

1. "Guest Workers Tricked into Slavery," http://thecnnfreedomproject.blogs.cnn.com/2011/06/23/guest-workers-tricked-into-slavery (accessed January 5, 2017); "It Gets Even Worse," www.nytimes.com/2011/07/04/opinion/04mon1.html?_r=0 (accessed January 5, 2017)
2. Cobb and Stueck, "Introduction," 1; Peacock, Watson, and Matthews, "Introduction," 2.
3. Smith and Cohn, "Introduction," 2–3; McKee and Trefzer, "Preface," 680.

4. Tinsman and Shukla, "Introduction," 1.

5. Duck, "Space and Time," 710.

6. Eckes, "The South and Economic Globalization," 37; Watson, "Southern History, Southern Future," 279; Hopkins cited in Eckes, "The South and Economic Globalization," 36; Nonini, "Critique," 248–49.

7. Chu, *Race, Nationalism, and the State*, 9.

8. Guterl, *American Mediterranean*, 5, 11, 8, 20, 9.

9. Guterl, *American Mediterranean*, 7; Nwankwo, *Black Cosmopolitanism*, 13.

10. On the white southern rhetoric surrounding the Turner and Vesey plots as part of a "racial panic discourse" that frequently referenced Haiti, see Gabrial, "From Haiti to Nat Turner."

11. Guterl, *American Mediterranean*, 185, 165.

12. Coclanis, "Globalization before Globalization," 25.

13. Peacock, "The South and Grounded Globalism," 265.

14. Giles, *Global Remapping*, 189; Faust, *The Creation of Confederate Nationalism*.

15. Guterl, *American Mediterranean*, 54, 47, 48.

16. Reimers, "Asian Immigrants," 101.

17. Peacock, "The South and Grounded Globalism," 265.

18. Zink, *Mislaid*, 160.

19. Guterl, *American Mediterranean*, 148, 152, 156, 164–65, 173, 170, 173, 178, 179.

20. See Lichtenstein, *Twice the Work of Free Labor*, especially chapter 1.

21. Reimers, "Asian Immigrants," 100.

22. Regis, "Introduction," 2.

23. See Gregory, *The Southern Diaspora*.

24. Eckes, "The South and Economic Globalization," 38.

25. Kyriakoudes, "'Lookin' for Better All the Time,'" 10.

26. Reimers, "Asian Immigrants," 101.

27. Odem, "Latin American Immigration," 237.

28. Goldfield, "Unmelting the Ethnic South," 22.

29. Bourne, "Trans-national America," 2063, 2057; Mencken, "The Sahara of the Bozart," 136.

30. Bourne, "Trans-national America," 2064; Winders and Smith, "New Pasts," www.southernspaces.org/2010/new-pasts-historicizing-immigration-race-and-place-south (accessed January 5, 2017). Bourne believed that "America is a unique sociological fabric, and it bespeaks poverty of imagination not to be thrilled at the incalculable potentialities of so novel a union of men" (2059). Thus for Bourne the South was a warning and example: the backward space of "Anglo-Saxon" exception to this progressive *trans*national exceptionalism.

31. Reimers, "Asian Immigrants," 100.

32. Bankston, "The International Immigrants of Mississippi," 15; Walton, "Introduction," 4.

33. Loewen, *The Mississippi Chinese*, 4.

34. Bow, *Partly Colored*, 8, 9, 92.

35. Capote, "A Diamond Guitar," 125–26.

36. Rubin and Jacobs, "Introduction," 24.

37. See Silver, *Mississippi*.

38. Peacock, Watson, and Matthews, "Introduction," 2.

39. Nonini, "Critique," 249.

40. Berlin, *The Making of African America*, 205, 5; see also Nwankwo, *Black Cosmopolitanism*, 16–17.

41. See my "Narratives of African Immigration to the U.S. South," especially 65–67 and (on Eggers's *What Is the What*) 67–71.

42. Eckes, "The South and Economic Globalization," 42–43.

43. Mohl, "Globalization, Latinization, and the *Nuevo* New South," 71, 88.

44. DeGuzmán, "Four Contemporary Latino/a Writers," 455. Somewhat perversely, DeGuzmán does "not include Florida and Texas as part of my definition of the U.S. South" partly *because* of the deep Hispanic history in those states; this does, though, allow her to foreground Latino/a presences in, and writing about, "Georgia, North Carolina, and Tennessee" (458).

45. Odem, "Latin American Immigration," 242.

46. Barbara Smith, "Place and Past in the Global South," 694.

47. See my introduction to *Creating and Consuming the American South*, 3.

48. Nonini, "Critique," 249.

49. Kurotani, "The South Meets the East," 187. See also Guthrie-Shimizu, "From Southeast Asia to the American Southeast," 135–65.

50. Subramanian, "North Carolina's Indians," 192–93; Pfister, "Transnational American Studies for What?" 27–30.

51. Nonini, "Critique," 258; Rushing, *Memphis and the Paradox of Place*, 85.

52. Ward, "Caryl Phillips," 23.

53. Aboul-Ela, "Global South, Local South," 851. In the introduction to *Globalization and the American South*, Cobb and Stueck write: "If we reject globalization because it is exploitative, we reject the simple realities of capitalism, which, for all its manifold shortcomings, remains the only modern economic system that has demonstrated the capacity over time to improve the lot of those whom it exploits" (xv). By contrast, Aboul-Ela notes, *The American South in a Global World* begins with immigration and makes it more central to how "deterritorialization" is changing the South (852).

54. Wilson and Dissanayake, "Introduction," 2.

55. On "vulgar transnationalism," see my "The Transnational Turn in the South," 218–19. See also Robert Gross's more sanguine response to concerns that "enthusiasts of transnationalism" in American studies might be part of a "cosmopolitan elite" that is insufficiently critical of "[t]he intertwining of American and global interests." According to Gross, transnational American studies "retains the oppositional spirit that has animated American studies since the 1960s." Gross, "The Transnational Turn," 379–80.

56. Barbara Smith, "Place and Past," 694–95.

57. Hahamovitch, *No Man's Land*, 88, 73, 85.

58. Smith-Nonini, "Federally Sponsored Mexican Migrants," 61.

59. Bowe, *Nobodies*, 13, 39.

60. Giagnoni, *Fields of Resistance*, 43.

61. Ness, *Southern Insurgency*, 6, 33, 21, 20.

62. For Smith and Cohn, this status as "northern and southern (both in the global sense)" is one of the ways by which the U.S. South may yet remain "a space unique within modernity" ("Introduction," 9).

63. Ness, *Southern Insurgency*, 30, 31. Ness is rather dismissive about migrant workers' agency: following Raúl Delgado, he attributes "the vast majority of migration" within

and from the Global South to "an involuntary process brought about by the expansion of finance capital under contemporary neoliberal global capitalism" (63).

64. Cobb, "Beyond the 'Y'all Wall,'" 4.
65. Sassen, "Savage Sorting," 32.
66. Graham, "Free at Last," 604.
67. Flaherty, *Floodlines*, 215, 217–18; Graham, "Free at Last," 604. Bowe notes in *Nobodies* that "reconstruction efforts in Mississippi and Louisiana after Hurricane Katrina have generated numerous claims of forced labor from the immigrants doing the work" (xv).
68. See Caballero, "Alabama Brings Back Slavery," www.guardian.co.uk/commentisfree/cifamerica/2011/oct/12/alabama-slavery-latino-immigrants?intcmp=239 (accessed January 5, 2017).
69. Fink, *The Maya of Morganton*, 3; Levitt, *The Transnational Villagers*; Sassen, "Savage Sorting," 31; Beck, *The Cosmopolitan Vision*, 103; Arapoglou, Fodor, and Nyman, "Introduction," 3.
70. Striffler, "We're All Mexicans Here," 153, 164.
71. Tate, "The New Provincialism," 541, 535.
72. Castells, *The Informational City*, 310–11.
73. Giagnoni, *Fields of Resistance*, 17, 34.
74. "The New Southern Studies," http://southernlit.org/society-for-the-study-of-southern-literature-newsletter-47-1-spring-2013 (accessed January 5, 2017).
75. The quote is taken from David Davis's editorial introduction to the "New Southern Studies" issue of the SSSL newsletter cited in the previous note.
76. Baker and Nelson, "Preface," 235, 234. See also the issue's final essay, Ana Patricia Rodriguez's "Refugees of the South: Central Americans in the U.S. Latino Imaginary," which Baker and Nelson figure as "expand[ing] this issue's discussion of 'The South'" ("Preface," 241).
77. Baker, *Turning South Again*, 9, 85; see also my "The Transnational Turn," especially 195–96.
78. Richardson, "Southern Turns," 557–58.
79. Smith and Cohn, "Introduction," 13, 2.
80. McKee and Trefzer, "Preface," 678.
81. Ladd, "Literary Studies," 1634; see also Jon Smith, "The State," 549–50.
82. Peacock, "The South and Grounded Globalism," 269.
83. Martin and Martin, review of *Look Away!*, 239–40.
84. Aboul-Ela, "Global South, Local South," 855. In 2010 Richard H. King reiterated the point that "[m]ost of the contributors to the new Southern studies . . . are literary scholars" and proposed that "[t]o bring historians—of the U.S. South, of African America, of Latin America and the Caribbean, and of West Africa—into the deliberations might help to make the literary scholars more aware of historical complexities"—but, King added, this might "also teach the historians something too about taking interpretive chances" (King, "Allegories of Imperialism," 157). In 2014 Natalie Ring complained: "In the list of publications affiliated with the NSS project, historians are poorly represented," and contended that "scholars of the NSS often substitute reflexively the phrases 'New Southern Studies' and 'southern literature' for each other." Yet Ring acknowledges in a footnote that though her own first book had been slated for publication in the University of Georgia Press's New Southern Studies series, she took

the "judicious career move" to switch it to another series more likely to attract fellow historians (Ring, "An Irony of Ironies," 708–9).

85. Brian Ward, comment posted on February 5, 2010, and Karen Cox, comment posted on March 15, 2010, to the "Understanding the South, Understanding Modern America" discussion board, http://understandingthesouth.wordpress.com/discussion (accessed January 5, 2017).

86. O'Brien, "Epilogue," 274. For a critique of Louis D. Rubin's ahistorical "image" of the South, see my *Postsouthern Sense of Place*, 30–34.

87. O'Brien, "Epilogue," 276.

88. O'Brien, "Epilogue," 277.

89. King, "Allegories of Imperialism," 148.

90. Richardson, "The World and the U.S. South," 724; McPherson, "On Wal-Mart and Southern Studies," 696.

91. Baker, *I Don't Hate the South*, 95.

92. Adams, *Wounds of Returning*, 86–87.

93. Duck, "Plantation/Empire," 77.

94. McPherson, "Afterword," 320; Jon Smith, "Toward a Post-postpolitical Southern Studies," 84, 89.

95. Monteith and Yousaf, "Making an Impression," 214.

96. See Bone, *The Postsouthern Sense of Place*, 246–48 and 210–12.

97. Monteith, "Southern Like U.S.?" 71.

98. Peacock, *Grounded Globalism*, 171.

99. Melanie Benson Taylor, "Faulkner and Southern Studies," 127; Yaeger, *Dirt and Desire*, 34, 38.

100. McPherson, *Reconstructing Dixie*, 24–25.

101. Winders and Smith, "New Pasts," www.southernspaces.org/2010/new-pasts-historicizing-immigration-race-and-place-south (accessed January 5, 2017).

102. Bow, "Asian Americans," 493; McPherson, *Reconstructing Dixie*, 78

103. Bone, "The Transnational Turn" (2005), 192; Faulkner, *Absalom, Absalom!*, 289. For the coinage "Quentissential," see Michael Kreyling's *Inventing Southern Literature*, 110. More recently, Keith Cartwright has recast the key sentence "You would have to be born there" so that "there" refers throughout *Absalom, Absalom!* not just to "the South" but "a kind of intertidal zone of time/space fluidity" which encompasses "backwater routes of narration via harbors of creolization in Haiti, Martinique, and Louisiana." See Cartwright, *Sacral Grooves, Limbo Gateways*, 4.

104. Monteith and Yousaf, "Making an Impression," 217; Monteith, "Southern Like U.S.?" 68; Yousaf, "Immigrant Writers," 210.

105. Suzanne W. Jones, "Who Is a Southern Writer?" 725.

106. Giles, *Global Remapping*, 1, 12, 16.

107. Jon Smith, *Finding Purple America*, 124, 3.

108. Lassiter and Crespino, "Introduction," 13, 12.

109. Barbara Smith, "Place and Past," 693.

110. Jon Smith, "The U.S. South," 156; Jon Smith, "Toward a Post-postpolitical Southern Studies," 75; Duck, "Southern Nonidentity," 329.

111. Marston, Ward, and Jones, "Scale," 665.

112. Neil Smith, "Contours of a Spatialized Poetics," 73, 62, 60.

113. Dimock, "Planetary Time and Global Translation," 488–89, 507; see also Lukács,

"Specific Particularity." Dimock rejects the term "globalization" because she believes it privileges space over time and defines "planetary" as not only spatial but temporal: "nothing less than the full length and width of our human history and habitat" (489–90).

Neil Smith's "sequence of specific scales" and stress on a "spatialized poetics" can be usefully related to Lukács's earlier emphasis on the aesthetics of "particularity" as literature mediates between "individual" and "universal" dimensions of reality. For Lukács, a historical-materialist approach elucidates both "the social causes and the aesthetic manifestations" of historical (and geographical) change, while "[a]esthetic reflection" on the movement from and between individuality, particularity, and universality—at least loosely comparable to Smith's "sequence of scales" between the body and the global—allows literature "to grasp and reveal the totality of reality in all of its unfolded substantive and formal richness" (Lukács, "Specific Particularity," 220, 232, 221).

114. Tanoukhi, "The Scale of World Literature," 84–85, 79.
115. Ward, "Caryl Phillips," 30.
116. Giles, *Global Remapping*, 1, 16.
117. Wilson and Dissanayake, "Introduction," 5.
118. Stecopoulos, *Reconstructing the World*, 6–7. For Stecopoulos's emphasis on "a variety of geographic scales," see also 3, 35, 114, 170n10. Yaeger briefly addresses scale in *Dirt and Desire*, where she posits that "examining matters of scale and morphology will be crucial to rethinking southern literature." Yaeger's own examination focuses mostly on the scale of the body in the case of "gargantuan women" in southern women's writing (114; see also 240).
119. Giles, *Global Remapping*, 222.

CHAPTER 1. The Extended South of Black Folk

1. Hurston, "Florida's Migrant Farm Worker," typed and numbered pages 3, 5, 1.
2. Neil Smith, "Contours of a Spatialized Poetics," 73.
3. Alice Walker, "Zora Neale Hurston," 85.
4. Beebe, letter to Silver, July 9, 1958.
5. The papers rescued by neighbor Patrick DuVal were donated to the University of Florida libraries in 1961 by Margaret Silver. On Hurston's friendship with Silver, see Boyd, *Wrapped in Rainbows*, 428–29.
6. Giles, *Global Remapping*, 205. One might qualify that Hurston's "early work" is really her short stories and essays from the 1920s.
7. Thadious M. Davis, "Southern Standard Bearers," 305–7.
8. Cooper, "Zora Neale Hurston," 64.
9. Yaeger, *Dirt and Desire*, 34, 33; see also chapter 9.
10. See Trefzer, "Possessing the Self"; Henninger, "Zora Neale Hurston"; Duck, "'Rebirth of a Nation'"; and Lowe, "'Calypso Magnolia,'" especially 63–69.
11. Cartwright, *Sacral Grooves, Limbo Gateways*, 179.
12. Carby, "Politics of Fiction," 173.
13. Willis, *Specifying*, 48.
14. Carby, "Politics of Fiction," 181, 176. On *Their Eyes* as "highly romanticized," see "Ideologies of Black Folk," 148; for Carby's take on Willis's reading of Hurston, see "Reinventing History / Imagining the Future," 131–32.

15. Carby, "The Politics of Fiction," 182, and "Ideologies of Black Folk," 147.

16. Dubey, "Postmodern Geographies," 359; Baker, *Workings of the Spirit*, 88; Dubey, "Postmodern Geographies," 363–64 (on Baker's *Workings of the Spirit*, see also 360–61).

17. Cartwright, *Sacral Grooves, Limbo Gateways*, 160, 163.

18. Duck, *The Nation's Region*, 134.

19. Wright, "Between Laughter and Tears," http://people.virginia.edu/~sfr/enam358/wrightrev.html (accessed December 20, 2016).

20. Rosemary Hathaway, "The Unbearable Weight of Authenticity," 169, 171, 174. Hathaway details how Hurston's innovative deconstruction of the disciplinary distinction between ethnography and fiction—the way in which the novelistic use of folkloric materials usually goes "unsignified"—"both supports and resists a touristic reading of *Their Eyes*" (177).

21. Cartwright, *Sacral Grooves, Limbo Gateways*, 161.

22. Locke bemoaned Hurston's "entertaining pseudo-primitives," which, he claimed, "[p]rogressive southern fiction has already banished." The relevant excerpt of Locke's *Opportunity* review dated June 1, 1938, is available at http://people.virginia.edu/~sfr/enam358/wrightrev.html (accessed December 20, 2016).

23. Yaeger, *Dirt and Desire*, 35, 47.

24. Carby, "The Politics of Fiction," 181. Carby herself concentrates on Hurston's "discursive displacement" from *Mules and Men* (1935) to *Tell My Horse* (1938); hence, unlike Yaeger, she does not discuss how John moves "farther south" in *Jonah's Gourd Vine*.

25. Hurston, *Their Eyes Were Watching God*, 32. In this chapter, further references will be to this 2006 HarperPerennial Modern Classics edition and cited in the main text.

26. Hurston, *Jonah's Gourd Vine*, 103. In this chapter, further references will be to this 1990 Perennial Library edition and cited in the main text.

27. Hurt, "Introduction," 2, 3.

28. Kyriakoudes, "'Lookin' for Better All the Time,'" 10.

29. I do not mean to suggest that plantation labor is better than sharecropping but, rather, that John's life on the Pearson plantation is clearly preferable (to him) than being driven like a slave by his stepfather. He appreciates the sense of community and solidarity he shares with his fellow workers, but also, as Rita Dove has noted, "there is every indication that John is the illegitimate son" of Alf Pearson, which ensures that John receives preferential treatment from the plantation owner (Dove, "Foreword," *Jonah's Gourd Vine*, viii). John was born on the Pearson plantation; only subsequently did his mother, Amy, marry Ned Crittenden and move over the creek.

30. See Duck, *The Nation's Region*, 128.

31. Yaeger, *Dirt and Desire*, 35, 51.

32. John could have gone to a northern city and reestablished himself as a preacher with much the same congregation. When John muses that local preachers "don't know whether tuh g'wan North wid de biggest part of our churches or stay home wid de rest," Hambo replies: "Some of 'em done went. Know one man from Palatka done opened up uh church in Philadelphy and most of 'em is his ole congregation" (150).

33. Kyriakoudes, "'Lookin' for Better All the Time,'" 14.

34. Tolnay and Beck, "Racial Violence and Black Migration," 104. I am grateful to Nina Sokol for alerting me to this article while writing her University of Copenhagen MA dissertation on Hurston and Wright.

35. Zora Neale Hurston, *Mules and Men*, 1.

36. Carby, "The Politics of Fiction," 181.

37. Hahamovitch, *No Man's Land*, 25–26.

38. Nicholls, "Migrant Labor," 469, 470, 472. Nicholls is quoting Charlotte Todes's *Labor and Lumber* (1931). In *Mules and Men*, one migrant worker tells a tale about a junior supervisor "up in Middle Georgy"; another about a mean "road boss" on "de East Coast" (69); another offers a tall tale based on his experiences working "back in South Carolina" (112).

39. Hurston, *Mules and Men*, 60.

40. Duck, *The Nation's Region*, 127–28.

41. Sundquist, *The Hammers of Creation*, 53, 75–76, 53.

42. Richardson, "'A house set off,'" 127. Echoing Richardson, Eve Dunbar argues that Hurston's ethnographic focus on the South was an attempt to stress "*black rural modernity*": "her particular demand that the rural black South and its inhabitants be understood not only as the contemporaries of more northern metropolitan blacks but as modern subjects in their own right." Dunbar insists too that *Mules and Men*'s emphasis on the historical continuities "from work under slavery to black work postemancipation" provides "the very sort of social-racial critique that Hazel Carby suggests is lacking." However, Dunbar pays no sustained attention to the role of black southern or Caribbean migrant labor in Hurston's ethnographic writing and argues that Hurston privileges (African) American nationalism over and above black southern connections to the Caribbean. She mentions *Their Eyes* only in passing and *Jonah's Gourd Vine* not at all. See Dunbar, *Black Regions of the Imagination*, 30, 33, 46.

43. Yaeger, *Dirt and Desire*, 22.

44. Duck, *The Nation's Region*, 133.

45. Yaeger, *Dirt and Desire*, 274.

46. Cooper, "Zora Neale Hurston," 66.

47. Like Cooper, Weaks-Baxter emphasizes Janie's connection with "the southern soil" and renders the muck as a site of rural, agricultural community while downplaying the hurricane's impact: "in the Everglades," Janie "is *for a time* part of a community that sets her on equal terms with everyone else" (my emphasis). See Weaks-Baxter, *Reclaiming the American Farmer*, 100–101.

48. Yaeger, *Dirt and Desire*, 16–17.

49. Wright, "Down by the Riverside," 64, 123–24.

50. Yaeger, *Dirt and Desire*, 17.

51. Scheiber, "The Wrong They Could Not Bury," www.sptimes.com/News/022501/news_pf/Floridian/The_wrong_they_could_.shtml (accessed December 21, 2016).

52. Brochu, "Florida's Forgotten Storm," www.sun-sentinel.com/sfl-ahurricane14sep14-story.html (accessed December 21, 2016).

53. Mykle, *Killer 'Cane*, 208–9.

54. Scheiber, "The Wrong They Could Not Bury."

55. Mykle, *Killer 'Cane*, 6–7.

56. Kleinberg, *Black Cloud*, 14.

57. Howard Johnson, *The Bahamas*, 163.

58. Hahamovitch, *No Man's Land*, 33–34; see also 19.

59. Mykle, *Killer 'Cane*, 7.

60. Mykle, *Killer 'Cane*, 211.

61. October 28, 1928, edition of the Florida State Board of Health newsletter (quoted in Kleinberg, *Black Cloud*, 213).

62. Some of the Bahamian laborers caught up in the 1928 hurricane may have been illegal workers. After 1920, "[m]any Bahamians, who had worked as seasonal laborers on the farms in southern Florida, were prevented from returning to the United States by a law which made passing a literacy test a requirement for entry.... With the passing of the Johnson-Reed Act in 1924 the exclusion of Bahamians from the Florida labor market was complete" (Howard Johnson, *Bahamas*, 172). These immigration restrictions suggest that the Bahamian workers in the Everglades in 1928 were either relatively long-standing residents of the United States or migrated illegally after 1924.

63. Hicks, "Rethinking King Cotton," 81. Drawing on the new southern studies (65–66), Scott Hicks's ecocritical argument that Hurston's "novels celebrate migration between farms" and "depict African Americans engaged in diversified agriculture outside white surveillance" (78) downplays that white "bossmen" own the Everglades "muck." For Hicks, the muck is a utopian site where "Janie and Tea Cake find happiness ... a 'new' landscape, an ecological and social 'contact zone'" that, "despite its acquiescence to agribusiness, nonetheless presents a prototypical vision of Eden that includes, not excludes, persons of color" (79). Hicks's analysis excludes the Bahamian workers who most vividly embody (yet whose marginal status might complicate his reading of) "an alternative subjectivity via mobility and migrancy" in Hurston's work (83).

64. Carby, "The Politics of Fiction," 176, 181.

65. Pavlić, "'Papa Legba,'" 79. Pavlić's designation of a "diasporic community" is idealized: there is no textual evidence of communication between the Bahamians and Seminoles beyond the former group heeding the latter's storm warning. See too the ostensibly more nuanced model of muck community sketched by William Gleason: "Indiscriminately composed of African Americans, Native Americans, and 'Bahaman workers,' muck play ... creates and sustains a diverse community of autonomous subgroups, separate from the white 'bossman' but also, when the hurricane comes, ready to split back along its constituent cultural lines." This overlooks the African American workers' initial condescension toward the Bahamian immigrants and the native blacks' view that "Indians are dumb anyhow, always were" (*Their Eyes* 155). See Gleason, *Leisure Ethic*, 338.

66. Lamothe, "Vodou Imagery," 171.

67. Mykle, *Killer 'Cane*, 21.

68. Trefzer, "Possessing the Self," 309; Rowe, *Literary Culture and U.S. Imperialism*, 256. See also Pavlić, "'Papa Legba,'" 80–81.

69. Cartwright, *Sacral Grooves, Limbo Gateways*, 161. Cartwright makes this point partly in response to Carby. Lowe similarly notes Hurston's "firm belief that her native Florida ... was the heir of the African diaspora via the Caribbean" but emphasizes how this emerges in her Federal Writers' Project writings during the late 1930s ("Calypso Magnolia," 63).

70. Hurston, *Dust Tracks on a Road*, 140.

71. Hurston, letter to Langston Hughes, 149. In *Dust Tracks on a Road*, Hurston remarks that during this 1929 trip to Nassau she experienced a "terrible five-day hurricane. It was horrible in its intensity and duration. I saw dead people washing around on the streets when it was over" (142). Robert Hemenway comments that this experience "would become fiction in *Their Eyes Were Watching God*": see Hemenway, *Zora Neale Hurston*, 127. Similarly, Cartwright observes that Hurston's own "experience in 1929 of a powerful hurricane in Nassau" informed "the storm-swept hierophany of *Their*

Eyes Were Watching God'" (*Sacral Grooves, Limbo Gateways*, 159). The specific associations between novel and local history suggest that the 1928 Okeechobee hurricane was the primary "source"—albeit not experienced firsthand by Hurston—for the hurricane in *Their Eyes*.

72. Hurston, "Dance Songs," 300n1, 295.

73. Hurston, *Dust Tracks on a Road*, 141; Hurston, "Spirituals and Neo-Spirituals," 79–84; Carby, "The Politics of Fiction," 173.

74. Hurston, "Other Negro Folklore Influences," 90, 91.

75. This comment appears in Hurston's notes in the program for "The Fire Dance," adapted from *The Great Day* and performed in Orlando during January and February 1939. See "The Fire Dance, January 25, 1939—8pm." In the opening section of the script for "The Fire Dance" performance, Hurston writes: "There are thousands of Bahamians in south Florida, and nightly in the Everglades around the bean fields and sugar mills can be heard the pulsing of the dance drums. They are holding a 'jumping dance.' This is part of the dance cycle known as the Fire Dance. It is part of the celebration of New Year's from West Africa" (Hurston, "The Fire Dance," in *Go Gator*, 153).

76. Hurston, "Characteristics of Negro Expression," 56.

77. Hurston, "Florida's Migrant Farm Worker," typed and numbered page 5.

78. See Hahamovitch, *No Man's Land*, 85, 73, 82–83. The long-standing exploitation of black labor by U.S. Sugar led to the launch of an FBI investigation in 1942, after which the Justice Department indicted U.S. Sugar's labor camp managers for kidnapping, imprisoning, and shooting at employees. That such abuses made black southern migrant workers increasingly circumspect about going to south Florida was one of the main reasons for growers lobbying to bring in Bahamian guestworkers. See Hahamovitch, *No Man's Land*, 32–33.

79. Hurston, "Florida's Migrant Farm Worker," typed and numbered page 4.

80. Hurston, "Florida's Migrant Farm Worker," typed and numbered pages 1–2.

81. Hurston, "Florida's Migrant Farm Worker," typed and numbered pages 7, 8, 6.

82. Hahamovitch, *No Man's Land*, 102.

83. Duck, *The Nation's Region*, 143.

84. Hurston, "Court Order," 738. As Andrew Delbanco has noted, Hurston's insistence that blacks should be proud of their own (segregated) culture, and her resistance to "a certain kind of shame that takes root among people who have been trained in self-contempt," came across as "political naivete" in the context of *Brown v. Board of Education*. See Delbanco, "Political Incorrectness," 106.

85. Duck, *The Nation's Region*, 145. A typed outline shows that Hurston planned four sections or installments including a subsection focusing on "The coming of the Bahaman workers." See Hurston, "Florida's Migrant Farm Worker," front page outline.

86. Wallerstein, *Modern World-System*, 167. Wallerstein's work on this "extended Caribbean, stretching from northeast Brazil to Maryland," covers an earlier period when plantation slavery existed throughout the hemisphere.

87. Hahamovitch, *No Man's Land*, 6. The H-2 category was introduced in 1952.

88. Danticat, "Foreword," xvi.

89. "America's Sugar Daddies," www.nytimes.com/2003/11/29/opinion/america-s-sugar-daddies.html (accessed December 20, 2016); Lydersen, "Some Immigrants," http://newstandardnews.net/content/index.cfm/items/2410 (accessed December 20, 2016).

90. Hurston, "Folklore," numbered typed manuscript page 13. In this manuscript, Hurston specifically identifies the role of Cuban and Bahamian labor and culture (11–12).

CHAPTER 2. Transnational/Intertextual Migrations and U.S. Southern, Danish, and English "Folk" Identities in Nella Larsen's Fiction

1. Yaeger, *Dirt and Desire*, 51.
2. Baker, *Workings of the Spirit*, 23, 35, 22, 36, 88, 63.
3. Griffin, *"Who Set You Flowin'?"* 155, 160.
4. Favor, *Authentic Blackness*, 88, 86.
5. Dubey, "Postmodern Geographies," 360. As Dubey notes, "Baker explicitly feminizes the notion of a racially authentic culture, describing the rural South as the space of black mothers" (363).
6. Quoted in Thadious Davis, *Nella Larsen*, xviii, 67.
7. Charles Larson, *Invisible Darkness*, 189.
8. Thadious Davis, *Nella Larsen*, 68–69, 140–41.
9. Gilroy, *The Black Atlantic*, 18.
10. Hutchinson, "Nella Larsen," 339. For a more detailed account of Larsen's Afro-Danish family background, her claims to a Danish identity, and critics' skeptical readings of such claims, see my essays *"Den Sorte"* and "Teaching *Quicksand* in Denmark."
11. Carby, *Reconstructing Womanhood*, 166, 171–72. There are parallels here with Carby's contention that Hurston "displaced" the Great Migration by connecting black southern folklife to the Caribbean (see chapter 1). But much as Carby overlooked Hurston's representation of intraregional and transnational migration within the South itself, she fails to consider Larsen's depiction of Helga's life in Denmark's capital city on its own terms.
12. Quoted in Thadious Davis, *Nella Larsen*, 110.
13. Thadious Davis, *Nella Larsen*, 110.
14. Nella Larsen, *Quicksand*, 8. All subsequent references to *Quicksand* in this chapter will be to the 2002 Penguin Classics edition and incorporated into the main text.
15. Baker, *Turning South Again*, 56, 44, 56.
16. Griffin, *"Who Set You Flowin?"* 154, 155.
17. Baker, *Turning South Again*, 57, 58.
18. Baker, *Turning South Again*, 58.
19. Baker, *Turning South Again*, 34.
20. Baker, *I Don't Hate the South*, 70.
21. Baker, *Turning South Again*, 60, 61, 63.
22. Carby, *Reconstructing Womanhood*, 172.
23. F. James Davis, *Who Is Black?* 5, 58.
24. Wegmann-Sánchez, "Rewriting Race and Ethnicity," 143.
25. Thadious Davis, *Nella Larsen*, 229; Larsen's July 19, 1927, letter to Dorothy Peterson quoted on 228.
26. Gilroy, *The Black Atlantic*, 16.
27. The scene echoes Larsen's own experience aboard the S.S. *C. F. Tietgen* while traveling from Copenhagen to New York in 1909. Though Nella's nationality was listed

in the ship manifest as American, "the ship's surgeon, Dr C. A. Larsen, identified her 'race or people' as 'Scandinavian,' despite explicit instructions that anyone with a visible 'admixture of Negro blood' was to be listed as 'African (black).'" See Hutchinson, *In Search of Nella Larsen*, 66.

28. Thadious Davis, *Nella Larsen*, 266.
29. See Fjelstrup, "Jagten på rødderne," 1.
30. Lunde and Stenport, "Helga Crane's Copenhagen," 229.
31. Hutchinson, *In Search of Nella Larsen*, 69. See also Lunde and Stenport on how "*Quicksand*'s Copenhagen is thus temporally dislocated and projected back in time" ("Helga Crane's Copenhagen," 232).
32. Macherey, *A Theory of Literary Production*, 85–86.
33. For more on Danes' racialized treatment of Helga, see my "*Den Sorte*," 213–17.
34. Lunde and Stenport, "Helga Crane's Copenhagen," 236.
35. For more on Helga's interactions with working-class Danes, see my "*Den Sorte*," 217–18.
36. Hutchinson, *In Search of Nella Larsen*, 70.
37. W. Glyn Jones, *Denmark*, 76, 74.
38. Vorre, "The Market," 39–40.
39. Duck, *The Nation's Region*, 143.
40. W. Glyn Jones, *Denmark*, 76.
41. Willerslev, *Sådan boede vi*, 21. My translation from the Danish.
42. See Levine, *Poverty and Society*, 73–76; the passage from the June 1890 constitution is quoted on 73–74. As Daniel Levine notes, Denmark outlawed begging with the first national poor law of 1708 (74).
43. See the "African American Influences" and "Transatlantic Debate" pages at the website of the Dvořák American Heritage Association, www.dvoraknyc.org/african-american-influences and www.dvoraknyc.org/transatlantic-debate (accessed December 29, 2016).
44. Thadious Davis, *Nella Larsen*, 269; Hutchinson, "Subject to Disappearance," 188, 186.
45. Hurston, *Jonah's Gourd Vine*, 150.
46. Duck, *The Nation's Region*, 117–18, 122–23.
47. Griffin, *"Who Set You Flowin'?"* 159.
48. Thadious Davis, *Nella Larsen*, 280.
49. Debra Silverman notes that "Larsen's removal of Helga from the city into the rural space of the South is a journey to Hurston's folk" that "brings children instead of pleasure." See Silverman, "Nella Larsen's *Quicksand*," 612. Anna Brickhouse observes that *Quicksand* revises *Cane*'s "lyrical, fertile black South" by "[l]iteralizing Toomer's metaphor of the 'pregnant negress' . . . in a rural South where the very fertility Toomer celebrates will clearly prove fatal" to Helga. See Brickhouse, "Nella Larsen," 554–55.
50. Yaeger, *Dirt and Desire*, 16–17.
51. James Weldon Johnson, *Autobiography*, 154; Favor, *Authentic Blackness*, 90; see also 46. Johnson's novel anticipates Larsen's by stressing the problematic nature of its biracial protagonist's relationship to the rural southern folk: a relationship that is variously romantic, anthropological, class-inflected, and exploitative. Brickhouse usefully notes that *Quicksand* also "revises the terms of . . . birthright" in T. S. Stribling's

novel *Birthright* (1922), in which the biracial protagonist Peter Siner's "deepest heredity" is through his black southern mother, which means he remains "a negro." Brickhouse argues that "Helga's hidden but binding tie, by contrast, links her to the 'pale and powerful people' rather than the 'brown folk,'" and that it is "this birthright connecting her to the white world [that] has been 'stolen'" ("Intertextual Geography," 549). I would qualify that Helga's "birthright" is the connection to her white Danish family rather than the wider "white world." As Wegmann-Sánchez rightly remarks, "Helga never identifies with 'White' people per se, only with her Danish ethnic (not racial) heritage" on her mother's side ("Rewriting Race and Ethnicity," 142).

52. Jeffrey Gray states: "Criticism of *Quicksand* has seldom failed to mention the problem of its ending. The transformation of Helga from strong, independent, and charismatic world-traveler to born-again, rural, baby-making drudge is abrupt if not incredible." See Gray, "Essence and the Mulatto Traveler," 267.

53. Jackman quoted in Thadious Davis, *Nella Larsen*, 349.

54. Larsen's "The Author's Explanation" from *Forum*'s April 1930 issue is quoted in Thadious Davis, *Nella Larsen*, 352.

55. Dearborn, *Pocahontas's Daughters*, 57.

56. Wall, *Women of the Harlem Renaissance*, 134.

57. Miller, *Accented America*, 223.

58. Brickhouse, "Nella Larsen," 536; see also my "Intertextual Geographies of Migration." Dearborn argues that accusations of plagiarism have disproportionately plagued "ethnic female authorship" and points out that Hurston faced similar accusations (*Pocahontas's Daughters*, 56). Thadious Davis observes that Larsen previously "had contemplated how certain works treating white characters might be translated into 'Negro' material" (*Nella Larsen*, 351). Hutchinson asks: "Could Larsen have been toying with a sort of deconstruction of racial difference by making an 'English' tale into a 'Negro' one?" (*In Search of Nella Larsen*, 344). Miller suggests "that recontextualizing a tale of class tensions and involuntary violence from England as a story about black-on-black violence in the United States is not at all an insignificant artistic project" (*Accented America*, 224–25). However, that "Sanctuary" "tak[es] an English story and recasts it with American blacks" has also been read as another manifestation of Larsen's allegedly pathological relationship to her white mother. Beverly Haviland's psychobiographical analysis posits that "[i]f Larsen did plagiarize (as I believe she did), this act of theft from a white woman [Kaye Smith] who had an identity as an author can be understood as an act of aggression against her rejecting white mother." Haviland thus figures Larsen's relationship to her mother as so defining (and damaging) that even her most concentrated fictional representation of black southern life is read primarily as a reaction to that relationship. See Haviland, "Passing from Paranoia to Plagiarism," 296, 304.

A wider consideration of transnational intertextuality during the Harlem Renaissance might include Jon Woodson's argument that Hurston's *Their Eyes* is indebted via Larsen to Jens Peter Jacobsen's *Marie Grubbe*, published in Danish in 1876 and in translation in the United States in 1917. Woodson argues that Hurston read Jacobsen's novel after Larsen cited it in a 1926 letter to *Opportunity* defending Walter White's new novel *Flight*. See Woodson, "Zora Neale Hurston's *Their Eyes*." Lunde and Stenport offer brief observations regarding the connections between *Quicksand* and Jacobsen's 1880 novel

Niels Lyhne and mention the links between Helga and two Henrik Ibsen heroines: Nora Helmer (see also my reading of *Quicksand*'s final scene) and Hedda Gabbler ("Helga Crane's Copenhagen," 238–40).

59. Kaye-Smith, "Mrs Adis," 322, 321. Larsen could also have encountered the story in *Joanna Godden Married and Other Stories* (New York: Harper and Brothers, 1926).

60. Kelli A. Larson, "Surviving the Taint of Plagiarism," 88.

61. Kaye-Smith, "Mrs Adis," 323, 324, 326.

62. Larsen, "Sanctuary," 21, 22, 23.

63. Miller sharply observes that when Larsen "excises" from her adaptation Peter Crouch's expression of remorse over his accidental murder of Tom Adis, she "render[s] Jim Hammer a far less sympathetic figure and heighten[s] Annie's dislike of him" (*Accented America*, 225). It is notable too that Larsen also removes Kaye-Smith's reference to the possibility that Crouch "shall swing" for killing Tom. Larsen may have recognized that though the killing of a white man would leave a black man at the mercy of a lynch mob, white southerners would be rather less likely to mete out such rough justice in the case of a black-on-black killing.

64. Larsen, "Sanctuary," 27.

65. Chu, *Race, Nationalism, and the State*, 164–65.

CHAPTER 3. Downsouth, Upsouth, Global South

1. Gayle, "Foreword" to Killens, *Youngblood*, vii.
2. Killens, "Address," typed and numbered page 9.
3. Angelou, *The Heart of a Woman*, 33.
4. Killens, "Downsouth-Upsouth," 57.
5. Lassiter and Crespino, "Introduction," 7.
6. Baker and Nelson, "Violence, the Body, and 'the South,'" 231, 236.
7. Lassiter and Crespino, "Introduction," 7.
8. Killens quoted in Wald, *Trinity of Passion*, 62. On Wright's fiction as "sociological," see Hoffman, *The Art of Southern Fiction*, 165.
9. Each of the four parts of *Youngblood* features an epigram from a "Negro spiritual"; in part 3, "Jubilee," black schoolchildren learn about and pass on black southern history through a Jubilee Day performance of the spirituals.
10. Killens, "Introduction," in *Black Southern Voices*, 1, 3. Killens's continued marginalization from southern literary studies is encapsulated by the 2008 "Literature" volume of *The New Encyclopedia of Southern Culture*. M. Thomas Inge's introduction includes Killens in his "beginning list of other significant practitioners of short fiction and the novel among the second-generation renaissance writers." The double diminution ("other" and "second-generation") is compounded by the absence of an individual entry for Killens, despite the total number of entries being expanded fivefold from the original *Encyclopedia* to include over two hundred authors. Killens is only mentioned twice in the volume's five-hundred-plus pages: a single sentence in the entry on "African American Literature" and a mention of his teaching role at Fisk in the entry about Nikki Giovanni. See Inge, *New Encyclopedia*, 9: 13, 24, 286.
11. Stecopoulos, *Reconstructing the South*, 11.
12. Killens, *Youngblood*, 15–16. All subsequent page references in this chapter to

Youngblood will be to this 1982 University of Georgia Press edition and incorporated into the main text. On "narratives of ascent," see Robert Stepto's *From Behind the Veil*, especially 167.

13. Gilyard, *John Oliver Killens*, 8.
14. See Gilyard, *John Oliver Killens*, 11.
15. Gilyard, *John Oliver Killens*, 39.
16. Duck, *The Nation's Region*, 117–18.
17. Locke, "Harlem," http://xroads.virginia.edu/~drbr/locke_2.html (accessed January 3, 2017).
18. Duck, *The Nation's Region*, 119.
19. Wald, *Trinity of Passion*, 58; Jackson, *The Indignant Generation*, 406.
20. Jameson, *The Political Unconscious*, 79.
21. Bigsby, *The Second Black Renaissance*, 167.
22. Gilyard, *John Oliver Killens*, 29.
23. Killens, "Downsouth-Upsouth," 60–61.
24. Wald, *Trinity of Passion*, 56.
25. Wald, *Trinity of Passion*, 49–50.
26. Gilyard notes that the prototype for *Youngblood*, Killens's 1947 manuscript "Stony the Road We Trod," is even more focused on labor issues and is "a story of unqualified success, a good deal more than the CIO and its Operation Dixie actually achieved during the 1940s" (*John Oliver Killens*, 74).
27. Killens, "Downsouth-Upsouth," 93.
28. Gilyard, *John Oliver Killens*, 124.
29. Joseph Walker, "An American Author," 19.
30. Wald, *Trinity of Passion*, 55.
31. Killens's notebook with "story ideas, 1945," unpaginated, in the John Oliver Killens Papers at Emory University; see also the published version of this passage in "For National Freedom," 254. Killens pointed out that "World War II migrations were primarily from the plantations to cities within the South": thus the "liberal" belief that a "Mass Exodus" of rural southern blacks to the urban North would trump Jim Crow was "wishful thinking" ("For National Freedom," 250).
32. Killens, "For National Freedom," 256.
33. Wald, *Trinity of Passion*, 56. Haywood was not the originator of the Black Belt Nation thesis, adopted at the Sixth World Congress of the Soviet Comintern in 1928. Haywood was initially skeptical toward "the idea of a Black nation within U.S. boundaries," which he believed would hinder "unity of Black and white workers against the common enemy, U.S. capitalism." But by 1928 Haywood advocated the view that African American struggle must center on the "right of self-determination here in the Deep South." Rejecting his brother Otto's view that black nationalism was "a foreign importation artificially grafted onto the freedom movement of U.S. blacks by the West Indian nationalist, [Marcus] Garvey," Haywood insisted it was "an indigenous product, arising from the soil of Black super-exploitation and oppression in the United States. It expressed the yearnings of millions of blacks for a nation of their own." Haywood qualified that black nationalist self-determination in the South was not merely a racialized mystification of capitalism's economic base: it was "a special feature of the struggle for the emancipation of the whole American working class." See Haywood, *Black Bolshevik*,

219, 230, 228, 230, 279. *Black Bolshevik* mentions Killens in the acknowledgments, and a blurb from Killens appears on the back cover.

34. Killens, notebook with "story ideas."
35. "For National Freedom," 248; Killens's notebook with "story ideas."
36. Wald, *Trinity of Passion*, 56.
37. See Gilyard, *John Oliver Killens*, 78–79.
38. Hunton, "Why Worry About Africa?" 73.
39. Gilyard, *John Oliver Killens*, 103.
40. Higashida, *Black Internationalist Feminism*, 24. Higashida also points out that confining the "civil rights struggle to a domestic context" contributes to a perspective that "unhelpfully situates Old Left, civil rights, Black Power, and New Left movements in discrete periods or decades" (6)—precisely the kind of ideological segregation and periodization that has hampered understanding of Killens's work.
41. See Maxwell, *F. B. Eyes*, 17, 86. Killens's complete FBI file is available at the accompanying website: http://omeka.wustl.edu/omeka/exhibits/show/fbeyes/killens (accessed January 3, 2017).
42. Higashida, *Black Internationalist Feminism*, 3.
43. Killens, *Lower Than the Angels* manuscript, act 1, scene 1, typed and numbered page 6; act 2, scene 1, page 4. Gilyard remarks that "Killens had already drafted a play, *Lower Than the Angels*" by 1958 (*John Oliver Killens*, 137), but I am citing here the manuscript copy of the play cataloged as box 74, folder 4, and microfiche roll 23 in the Free Southern Theater (FST) records, 1963–1978, of the Amistad Research Center at Tulane University. This finished copy is dated November 1, 1960, as is another version in the John Oliver Killens Papers, Stuart A. Rose Manuscript, Archives, and Rare Book Library, Emory University (box 46, folders 11 and 12, and box 47, folder 1), archived alongside a 1965 "final script" (box 47, folder 3). My thanks to Elizabeth Rodriguez Fielder for finding the FST copy of *Angels* during her own research. The closest *Lower Than the Angels* came to a full theatrical performance was a "Rehearsed Reading" at New York's American Place Theatre in January 1965, the program for which can be found in the Killens Papers (box 47, folder 3).

Angels also facilitates a fuller assessment of how Killens's downsouth-upsouth dialectic developed. Jim Kilgrow Jr.—a black childhood friend of Oscar Jefferson who, in *Youngblood*, grows up to become union activist Jim Collins—is adamant about moving to New York, like his older brother Johnny. Yet Johnny's firsthand account of life in the urban North provides a sobering contrast to Jim Jr.'s idealized vision: "there are no penthouses on Lenox Avenue underneath the Harlem moon. Georgia is *down*-South and Harlem is *up*-South. That's about the only difference." Johnny's disillusionment with the northern promised land is compounded by his conviction that, with the emergence of the movement, the South is the crucible of a national struggle for black identity and liberty: "the Southern Negro should stay with the South, where the fight for his dignity has more meaning, since it is the scene of its greatest denial. I wish I were a Southern Negro, but I have become Northernized" (act 1, scene 1, page 6).

44. Killens, "Black Man's Burden," 154, 170. On Killens's trips to Africa, see also Gilyard, *John Oliver Killens*, 155–62.
45. Malcolm's *Pittsburgh Courier* letter is quoted in Marable, *Malcolm X*, 167.
46. Marable, *Malcolm X*, 159, 172–73. Killens recalled Castro's visit to Harlem in "The Myth of Non-Violence," 116.

47. Gilyard, *John Oliver Killens*, 168, 188. Malcolm insisted on numerous occasions that "When we say South ... we mean south of the Canadian border. America in its entirety is segregationist and is racist. It's more camouflaged in the north, but it's the same thing." This insistence was firmly rooted in Malcolm's own upbringing as a member of an itinerant family, headed by a black southern migrant and UNIA activist father, which moved from Nebraska via Wisconsin to Michigan until his father's death, likely at the hands of white racists, in 1931: "This wasn't in the South. This was in Michigan." See Glanville, "When the *NS* met Malcolm X," www.newstatesman.com/world-affairs/2013/04/when-ns-met-malcolm-x (accessed January 3, 2017).

48. Lehman, *Development of the Black Psyche*, 31. Lehman notes that Killens sought a "world perspective" but identifies it with a future, utopian stage. I am arguing that Killens's "world perspective" already emerged during World War II.

49. Bigsby, *Second Black Renaissance*, 166–67. Like Lehman, Bigsby adheres to a linear model but constructs a narrative of decline rather than development, so that in U.S. society broadly and Killens's writing specifically "[t]he optimism of the early 1950s gave way to an apocalypticism in the middle and late 1960s" (*Development of the Black Psyche*, 164).

50. Wald, *Trinity of Passion*, 62.

51. Jennifer C. James, *A Freedom Bought with Blood*, 264–65.

52. Killens, "The Black Psyche," 16; Killens, "The Half Ain't Never Been Told," quoted in Wald, *Trinity of Passion*, 53.

53. Killens's notebook with "story ideas, 1945."

54. Gilyard, *Liberation Memories*, 43–44. Killens's first published fiction, the short story "God Bless America" (1952), became a section of *Thunder*. Already in an October 19, 1954, letter to the *Pittsburgh Courier*, Killens wrote: "I am at presenting working on a novel dealing with World War II and the relationships between Negro and white soldiers in the South Pacific."

55. Killens, *And Then We Heard the Thunder*, 5. All further page references in this chapter to *And Then We Heard the Thunder* will be to this 1963 Alfred A. Knopf first edition and incorporated into the main text.

56. Quoted in Rawn James Jr., *The Double V*, 142.

57. Stecopoulos, *Reconstructing the South*, 107–9.

58. Duck, *The Nation's Region*, 3. James argues: "The kinship that Saunders feels for Scotty and Fannie Mae, both southerners, is hardly accidental. Killens also intends for Saunders's transition to mark the acceptance of a racial consciousness rooted in the South, black southern history, and the experience of slavery" (*Freedom Bought with Blood*, 268–69). My reading sees Solly disavowing Fannie Mae and the South as much as he accepts her and it.

59. Stecopoulos, *Reconstructing the South*, 108.

60. Gilyard, *Liberation Memories*, 48–49.

61. Hastie quoted in Rawn James Jr., *The Double V*, 144–45. The California sequence likely derives partly from Killens's own experiences with the 813th Amphibian Truck Company, which was trained on the Californian coast before shipping out for combat in the South Pacific at the end of 1943.

62. In a second typescript draft of the novel, already at the army camp in Georgia Solly begins to feel a connection with Asian struggles against colonialism. In that typescript, chapter 7 opens with Solly "reading an autobiographical book about a

colored man named Nehru, in a place thousands of miles away from Georgia, written while he languished in a British prison in his own and native land." Continuing to read the book—*Toward Freedom* (1936), by the first prime minister of India, Jawaharlal Nehru—Solly ponders how now "Nehru was free! They could not lock up his mind and spirit. But Solomon Saunder [*sic*] was not free. He was in a big vast prison in the foreign country of his birth." Killens, *Thunder*, typescript version 2.

63. Killens, "Battle of Brisbane." The Poston quote derives from his review of *Thunder* in the *New York Post* magazine, March 31, 1963, 13. This "Battle of Brisbane" between black and white troops over several days in March 1942 should not be confused with another "Battle of Brisbane" that took place on Thanksgiving Day (November 26) 1942. The latter was a showdown between Australian and American troops, against the backdrop of simmering tension about Australian women interacting with American soldiers (black and white).

64. Saunders, "In a Cloud of Lust," 187.

65. Stecopoulos, *Reconstructing the South*, 13.

66. Hurley quoted in Saunders, "In a Cloud of Lust," 180.

67. Saunders, "In a Cloud of Lust," 182, 184 (including army report and MacArthur quotes).

68. Stecopoulos, *Reconstructing the South*, 109.

69. Saunders, "In a Cloud of Lust," 180.

70. This sequence undermines reviewer William Pomeroy's puzzling claim that "[t]he Australians in general are presented as without racial prejudice, in contrast to white Americans, but Killens overlooks or ignores the significance of the 'white Australia' policy of excluding Asian peoples from that continent, which has always incensed the colored people of Asia." See Pomeroy, "Killens 'Thunders,'" 10.

71. Jennifer C. James, *Freedom Bought with Blood*, 269.

72. Bigsby, *Second Black Renaissance*, 168–69. Bigsby's reading is undermined by his belief that *Thunder* was published in 1968, an error that leads him to read *Thunder* as extending the apocalyptic tenor of Killens's third novel, *'Sippi* (1967).

73. Marable, *Malcolm X*, 271 and 407.

74. See Gilyard, *Liberation Memories*, 41.

75. Gilyard, *John Oliver Killens*, 167.

76. Marable, *Malcolm X*, 338.

77. Gilyard, *Liberation Memories*, 59–60; see also 61, 64–65.

78. Killens, "The Black Psyche," 10; "Black Man's Burden," 150, 158, 175.

79. Cruse, *The Crisis of the Negro Intellectual*, 197, 207; Killens, "Black Man's Burden," 175. Cruse witheringly observed: "In Harlem, back in the 1950s, the Killens group had always been in strong, silent favor of interracial unity"; for a black cultural nationalist like Cruse, this was suspiciously "in line with the Negro-white unity . . . theme of the radical leftwing" (212). Cruse's attack culminates when he ridicules Killens's declaration of support for Black Power circa 1966: "Never the originator of a single new concept, style, or exposition whether in literature or politics, Killens has been the neutralizing temporizer, the non-controversial, moderating lid-sitter par excellence" (561). Aside from the transparent personal bitterness dating back to Cruse's split from the Harlem Writers Guild and his founding of the Harlem Writers Club, Cruse never discusses Killens's fiction.

80. Killens, *'Sippi*, v. All subsequent references to *'Sippi* in this chapter will be to the 1967 Trident Press edition and incorporated into the main text.
81. Gilyard, *Liberation Memories*, 22.
82. Cruse, *The Crisis of the Negro Intellectual*, 383.
83. See the July 5, 1972, FBI document included in Killens's file at http://omeka.wustl.edu/omeka/exhibits/show/fbeyes/killens.
84. Killens, "Introduction," *Black Southern Voices*, 3–4.

CHAPTER 4. The North-South Axis of Race, Class, and Migration in Russell Banks's Fiction

1. Hutchison, "Representative Man," 67.
2. Wylie, "Reinventing Realism," 747.
3. "Transcript of Russell Banks Interview," http://pandora.cii.wwu.edu/banks/Banks_transcript.pdf (accessed January 6, 2017).
4. Davidson and Arroyo, "Finding the Melody," 60, 67, 68.
5. Fuentes, "Central and Eccentric Writing," 119.
6. Glissant, *Faulkner, Mississippi*, 163, and *Poetics of Relation*, 63. Glissant states: "The Caribbean ... may be held up as one of the places in the world where Relation presents itself most visibly" because it "has always been a place of encounter and connivance and, at the same time, a passageway toward the American continent." For Glissant, then, both Caribbean *and* U.S. literatures are characterized by creolization, a term that "approximates the idea of Relation for us as nearly as possible": indeed, he perceives "a total poetics of Relation" in Walt Whitman's poetry as well as Faulkner's fiction (*Poetics of Relation*, 33–34).
7. Adams, "Introduction," 3.
8. Banks, letter (with list of "Current Project and Proposals") to Ted Solotaroff, Banks Papers.
9. Dave Smith's blurb, only part of which was used on the dust jacket, began: "Russell Banks knows, as Melville and Faulkner knew, what happens when you cut loose and run, whatever the direction or the reason." Smith, letter to Ted Solotaroff, Banks Papers.
10. Roche, "Russell Banks, Toulouse 2006," 174.
11. Banks, "'H&I'," 56.
12. Banks quoted in Niemi, *Russell Banks*, 7.
13. "Transcript of Russell Banks Interview."
14. Banks quoted in Lee, "About Russell Banks," www.pshares.org/issues/winter-1993-94/about-russell-banks-profile (accessed January 6, 2017).
15. Trevitte, "An Interview with Russell Banks," 113, 111, 122–23 ("The Adjutant Bird" quoted at 122).
16. Davidson and Arroyo, "Finding the Melody," 68; Banks's 1991 *Boston Globe* interview quoted in Niemi, *Russell Banks*, 95.
17. Roche, "Russell Banks, Toulouse," 171; Farren and Munger, "Russell Banks," 76.
18. Roche, "Russell Banks, Toulouse"; Banks interview from August 1995 quoted in Niemi, *Russell Banks*, 105.
19. Banks taught at the real New England College in Henniker, New Hampshire, after returning from Jamaica.

20. Banks, *The Book of Jamaica*, 73. All subsequent references in this chapter to *The Book of Jamaica* will be to this 1996 HarperPerennial edition and incorporated into the main text.

21. Flynn starred in the Hollywood film *Captain Blood* (1935). Born in Australia, Flynn became an American citizen in 1942 and moved to Jamaica in the early 1950s. Rumors circulated that Flynn and his medical professor father were involved in the murder of a black Jamaican laundress whose headless body was discovered near Port Antonio in June 1952. See McNulty, *Errol Flynn*, 250.

22. Niemi, *Russell Banks*, 99–100.

23. Hurston, *Tell My Horse*, 3–4. All subsequent references in this chapter to *Tell My Horse* will be to this 1990 Perennial Library edition and incorporated into the main text.

24. Duck, "'Rebirth of a Nation,'" 135.

25. F. James Davis, *Who Is Black?* 5.

26. Rosemary Hathaway, "The Unbearable Weight of Authenticity," 169.

27. Lowe, "'Calypso Magnolia,'" 65.

28. Dunbar, *Black Regions of the Imagination*, 51, 47.

29. Muthyala, *Reworlding America*, 86.

30. Faulkner, "The Bear," 199.

31. As Duck notes, "*Tell My Horse* emphasizes cultural differences between the United States and the Caribbean, often favoring the former" ("'Rebirth of a Nation,'" 135). Trefzer argues: "On the one hand, Hurston (as a black woman) identifies with the plight and destiny of free maroon societies. On the other hand, she regards these communities from the standpoint of an American ethnographer who comments on their 'primitive' lifestyles.... This conflict between racial and national identification remains essentially unresolved throughout *Tell My Horse*" ("Possessing the Self," 308).

32. Hurston, *Mules and Men*, 1.

33. Kolodny, *The Lay of the Land*.

34. Niemi, *Russell Banks*, 103.

35. Rosemary Hathaway, "The Unbearable Weight of Authenticity," 169.

36. Hathaway, "The Unbearable Weight of Authenticity," 172. The postmodern turn in anthropology is itself inseparable from the parallel (or rather, overlapping) turn in literary studies. It can be dated back to the 1960s, but key texts were published in the years just before and after *The Book of Jamaica* appeared: for example, Clifford Geertz's *The Interpretations of Cultures* (1973), Edward Bruner's "Ethnography as Narrative" (1986), and James Clifford's *The Predicament of Culture* (1988).

37. Roche during his interview with Banks, "Russell Banks, Toulouse," 175.

38. Trefzer, "Possessing the Self," 306.

39. Niemi, *Russell Banks*, 98.

40. Faggen and Munger, "Russell Banks," 75–76.

41. Banks, October 19, 1981, diary entry in "Diary, handwritten notes."

42. Banks, October 21, 1981, diary entry in "Diary, handwritten notes"; Jaynes, "33 Haitians Drown," A1.

43. Banks's October 30, 1981, diary entry references *New York Times* reports about the April 1980 conviction on six counts of manslaughter of "boat captain" Jeffrey Hastings from Hypoluxo, Florida, and Bahamian deckhand James Knowles. After their boat was

tracked by the coast guard, Hastings pulled a gun on the Haitian mother and her five children, forcing them to jump overboard.

44. Muller, *New Strangers in Paradise*, 221.
45. Stuart Taylor Jr., "Deciding How to Stop Haitians," E4.
46. Stepick, "The Refugees Nobody Wants," 61.
47. Stuart Taylor Jr., "Deciding How to Stop Haitians," E4; Jaynes, "33 Haitians Drown," A1.
48. Stepick, "The Refugees Nobody Wants," 60, 64; Jaynes, "33 Haitians Drown," A1.
49. Crossette, "U.S. to Redesign," A1, A15. This and the other *New York Times* articles cited in this and the previous paragraph were all clipped by Banks and are among the "Research material (clippings)" in box 17, folder 1, Russell Banks Papers, Harry Ransom Center, University of Texas, Austin.
50. Banks, *Continental Drift*, 1–2. All subsequent page references in this chapter to *Continental Drift* will be to this 1985 Harper & Row first edition and incorporated into the main text. (I have chosen not to cite the more widely available 2007 Harper-Perennial Modern Classics paperback edition because a couple of pages are missing, apparently due to a typesetting error.)
51. Reeves, "The Search for Clarity," 22–23.
52. Maslin, "News Story Inspired Banks's 'Drift,'" www.nytimes.com/1985/04/29/books/news-story-inspired-banks-s-drift.html (accessed January 6, 2017).
53. Walker, "Beyond the Peacock," 52.
54. Glissant, *Faulkner, Mississippi*, 74, 65.
55. Faulkner, "A Letter to the Leaders in the Negro Race," 110. *Ebony* published the essay with the title "If I Were a Negro."
56. Wylie, "Reinventing Realism," 750.
57. Muller, *New Strangers in Paradise*, 220.
58. Leahy, "Seeking a Place," 8.
59. Reeves, "Search for Clarity," 17.
60. Kakutani, "Books of the Times," C20.
61. Gould and White, *Mental Maps*.
62. Pavlić, "'Papa Legba,'" 61; Hurston, *Their Eyes Were Watching God*, 88.
63. Komunyakaa, "Crossroads," quoted in Pavlić, "'Papa Legba,'" 65–66.
64. Pavlić, "'Papa Legba,'" 84; Hurston, *Their Eyes Were Watching God*, 167.
65. In an early outline archived in the Banks papers, Vanise's journey is explicitly compared to the slave trade: "The horror, as of the Middle Passage. Invisible chains binding Vanise and the others as tightly as slavery chains." See Banks, outline for "Grand Chemin" section.
66. Dayan quoted in Cartwright, *Sacral Grooves, Limbo Gateways*, 120.
67. Accilien, "Haitian Creole," 78.
68. Glissant, *Faulkner, Mississippi*, 115–16. Here Glissant is assessing, in Faulkner's Yoknapatawpha, white characters' fearful recognition that their supposedly pure culture is "inextricably bound up in Relation" and so "tend[s] to become composite" or mixed—not least due to whites' own role in racial miscegenation. Hence Faulkner's white characters long for the supposed legitimacy and homogeneity of "atavistic" origins.
69. Gilroy, *Postcolonial Melancholia*, 101.

70. In a draft for *The Trade* (the novel's original title), the Dubois family's fear that they are the true foreigners is overt: "It's Bob and his family who are the newcomers, the immigrants, the Johnny-Come-Lately's at the Florida trough." "Making a Killing" section, Banks Papers, page 11.

71. Muller, *New Strangers in Paradise*, 225.

72. Muthyala, *Reworlding America*, 90.

73. Recalling the Bahamian workers in *Their Eyes*, we learn how Tyrone too moved to and around south Florida: "As a teenager, Tyrone fled a migrant work camp in the cane fields west of Miami and drifted across the Everglades and down the Keys" (222). Much as Hurston depicts tensions as well as connections between diasporic blacks in Florida, Banks suggests the limits of circum-Caribbean solidarity when Tyrone "worked with [Haitians] in the cane fields in Florida as a youth" (288). Just as Janie was the first black American to watch the Bahamian dances, so Tyrone "alone among the Jamaican workers, would join in [with the Haitians' parties], and before long he learned to talk with them, not well but enough to enjoy their company" (288). But where Janie fostered transnational community, Tyrone maintained his belief that the Haitians were different, "innocent," and unreliable. Tyrone also demonstrates little interest in the African retentions of Haitian (or Jamaican) culture: "That particular aspect of the Haitians' voudon, possession, is also ordinary, common, to Tyrone, something for old women and drunken men—he's seen it in church, on dance floors, at feasts in the maroon towns in the Cockpit Country of west Jamaica" (293–94). Tyrone too is "possessed" by the spirit of capitalism: while taking the Haitians' money for the fateful boat trip to south Florida, he is twice told that his presence is anathema to their *voudon* ceremony: "This is Africa" (291; see also 296).

74. Adams, *Wounds of Returning*, 11.

75. Cartwright, *Sacral Grooves, Limbo Gateways*, 134.

76. Hurston, letter to Langston Hughes, 149.

77. Wylie, "Reinventing Realism," 751.

78. Trefzer, "Possessing the Self," 311.

79. Hurston, "The Sanctified Church," 104.

80. Roach, *Cities of the Dead*, 209.

81. Chu, *Race, Nationalism, and the State*, 24–25.

82. Trucks, "Interview," 95.

83. Locoge, "An Interview with Russell Banks," 152.

84. Banks, *Rule of the Bone*, 155–56. All further page references in this chapter to *Rule of the Bone* will be to this 1995 HarperCollins edition and incorporated into the main text.

85. Weitzmann, "Russell Banks," 140.

CHAPTER 5. Workings of the Spirit, Spirit of the Workers

1. Kutzinski, "Borders and Bodies," 70. Pinto suggests in *Difficult Diasporas* that *Louisiana* "nearly fictionalizes Hurston's ethnographic biography" (109).

2. Brodber, *Louisiana*, 3. All subsequent page references in this chapter to *Louisiana* will be from this 1997 University Press of Mississippi edition and incorporated into the main text.

3. Hurston, *Mules and Men*, 1.

4. Brodber briefly references *Tell My Horse* in a 1997 lecture: see *The Continent of Black Consciousness*, 145. The lecture's discussion of the links between Gullah South Carolina and the Caribbean island of Carriacou (part of Grenada) in Paule Marshall's *Praisesong for the Widow* (1983) can be read for insights into *Louisiana*: Brodber notes that *Praisesong* "is not . . . located within a national boundary: it is located in the Africa of the diaspora, and this, in its spiritual manifestation as well as its physical" (150).

5. Toland-Dix, "'This Is the Horse,'" 191.

6. Hurston, *Mules and Men*, 183.

7. Roach, *Cities of the Dead*, 34.

8. Hurston, *Tell My Horse*, 219.

9. Pinto, *Difficult Diasporas*, 116.

10. Toland-Dix, "'This Is the Horse,'" 205. Similarly, Joseph Roach notes that in New Orleans the popular acclaim of Marie Laveau and her daughter ("the Voodoo Queens") challenged the social, economic, and labor structures of nineteenth-century Louisiana: "The ethos of spirit-world possession pointedly focuses attention on the autonomy and ownership of living bodies, an attention most unwelcome to slaveholders in antebellum times as well as to their heirs in the era of Jim Crow" (*Cities of the Dead*, 208).

11. Pinto, *Difficult Diasporas*, 122.

12. Brodber writes briefly about the Jamaican Louisiana, once a coffee estate with 130 slaves, in *The Continent of Black Consciousness*, 174.

13. Apter, *Against World Literature*, 185.

14. Heather Hathaway, *Caribbean Waves*, 16. As Hathaway notes, black southern and Afro-Caribbean migrants "were drawn to urban centers in the [U.S.] north in search of the jobs and wealth resulting from the wartime economic boom," but because "both newcomers from the South and the islands competed with black New Yorkers for the same jobs, housing, and monetary rewards, considerable tensions arose" (16–17).

15. Khoker, "Dialoguing Borders," 38.

16. Hurston, "Dance Songs and Tales," 295; Cynthia James, "Gender and Hemispheric Shifts," http://english.chass.ncsu.edu/jouvert/v5i3/cyja.htm (accessed January 12, 2017). In *Mules and Men*, Hurston recounts how she "learned all of the Leveau routines" during her five months of study with a local hoodoo doctor (*Mules and Men*, 202).

17. Brodber, *The Continent of Black Consciousness*, 76.

18. Rodrigue, *Reconstruction in the Cane Fields*, 11.

19. Rodrigue, *Reconstruction in the Cane Fields*, 22, 150, 143.

20. On sugar workers moving to New Orleans, see Rodrigue, *Reconstruction in the Cane Fields*, 71; on "Kansas Fever," see Becnel, *Labor, Church, and the Sugar Establishment*, 5–6. In response, planters tried to import workers from other ethnic groups: Chinese, German, Scandinavian, Italian, Dutch, Irish, Spanish, and Portuguese immigrants were all encouraged to come to south Louisiana. See Rodrigue, *Reconstruction in the Cane Fields*, 136–37, and the introduction to this book.

21. Rodrigue, *Reconstruction in the Cane Fields*, 189.

22. Rodrigue, *Reconstruction in the Cane Fields*, 187, 190. *Louisiana* gestures to the difficulties faced by labor activists trying to penetrate the South in these years when Ella's partner Reuben Kohl is confused with Reuben Cole, a white labor organizer who was run out of St. Mary "ten or so years ago" (67).

23. Arnesen, *Waterfront Workers of New Orleans*, 91.

24. See Arnesen, *Waterfront Workers of New Orleans*, 44, 56–58; see also Northrup, "New Orleans Longshoremen," 527.

25. Arnesen, *Waterfront Workers of New Orleans*, 63, 64, 74, 164; see also Northrup, "New Orleans Longshoremen," 528–29.

26. Arnesen, *Waterfront Workers of New Orleans*, 160; Northrup, "New Orleans Longshoremen," 529.

27. Arnesen, *Waterfront Workers of New Orleans*, 220.

28. Hurston, *Jonah's Gourd Vine*, 151.

29. Carby, "The Politics of Fiction," 181.

30. Tony Martin, *Race First*, 9.

31. Killens, *Youngblood*, 126.

32. Abraham, "Erna Brodber," http://bombmagazine.org/article/2622/erna-brodber (accessed January 12, 2017).

33. Tony Martin, *Race First*, 15–16. Martin also notes that on Garvey's first speaking tour of the United States in 1916, his five-month agenda was "confined to black audiences mostly in the South" (7).

34. Brodber, *The Continent of Black Consciousness*, 83, 82.

35. Harold, "Reconfiguring," 207, 208, 213. Established New Orleans black labor activists like John B. Cary worked with and for local Garveyism (206–7), and UNIA officials forged alliances with the New Orleans National Association for the Advancement of Colored People (NAACP), despite the notorious conflict between Garvey and NAACP leader W. E. B. Du Bois (220).

36. Brodber, *The Continent of Black Consciousness*, 99–100.

37. Rolinson, *Grassroots Garveyism*, 20.

38. Harold, "Reconfiguring," 211.

39. Rolinson, *Grassroots Garveyism*, 20.

40. Harold, "Reconfiguring," 213, 211.

41. Rolinson, *Grassroots Garveyism*, 201; Tony Martin, *Race First*, 17. Rolinson shows that in the mid-1920s St. Mary parish alone had 834 UNIA members (198).

42. Pinto, *Difficult Diasporas*, 127.

43. Brodber, *The Continent of Black Consciousness*, 102.

44. Cynthia James, "Gender and Hemispheric Shifts."

45. Rolinson, *Grassroots Garveyism*, 1.

46. Harold, "Reconfiguring," 220. When I presented a very early version of part of this chapter at the 2007 "Southern Women, Southern Writing" conference at Berry College, New Orleans poet Brenda Marie Osbey shared some anecdotes about her own experience of the UNIA's legacy in the city.

47. Hahamovitch, *No Man's Land*, 54–55; see also 53. Brodber briefly discusses the development of the Jamaican "small settler" class, and their role in the development of a "peasant agriculture-cum-marking system [that] in time fed into the American fruit market," in *The Continent of Black Consciousness*, 54; on the expansion in St. Mary Parish of "banana-growing plantation style" for U.S. export, see 71–72.

48. Hahamovitch, *No Man's Land*, 57, 68, 72, 74.

49. Hahamovitch, *No Man's Land*, 2.

50. Pinto, *Difficult Diasporas*, 125.

51. In *Race Rebels* (1994), Kelley demonstrates that during the 1920s and 1930s "ethnic

nationalism [such as Garveyism] and [communist] internationalism were not mutually exclusive" (105)—a point that also helps contextualize the similar, supposedly irreconcilable mix of black leftism and internationalism in John Oliver Killens's life and work between the 1940s and 1960s (see chapter 3). Kelley points out that even before the Communist Party's Black Belt Thesis, the black nationalist African Blood Brotherhood (ABB) "was the first organization to demand self-determination for black Americans in the Southern United States" (106). The ABB was founded in 1918 and led by a Jamaican, Cyril Briggs, who was at different times a colleague and rival of Marcus Garvey; in 1925 the ABB was swallowed up by the CPUSA as its leaders acceded to the official Communist line that "an interracial proletarian party would be a more effective form of organization" (106). The CPUSA also tried to harness the UNIA's popular success among African Americans and considered the possibility of yoking together pan-Africanist black nationalism and proletarian internationalism. As I noted in chapter 3, come 1928 African American Communist Harry Haywood advocated the view that black struggle must center on the "right of self-determination here in the Deep South" (see chapter 3, note 33). For Briggs, Haywood, and others, black nationalist political struggles were compatible with the cross-racial, transnational cause of the proletariat. Nevertheless, throughout the 1920s Garvey and the UNIA maintained a tense distance from the CPUSA and interracial unions, and Garvey's emphasis on black economic independence appealed to the more bourgeois aspirations of many African Americans.

52. Harold, "Reconfiguring," 221.
53. Tony Martin, *Race First*, 17.
54. Haywood, *Black Bolshevik*, 230. See also chapter 3, note 33, and note 51 above.
55. Gilroy, *The Black Atlantic*, 15; on Gilroy's distinction between "roots" and "routes," see 19.
56. See Hurston, "Spirituals and Neo-Spirituals," 80, and *Dust Tracks on a Road*, 141.
57. Roach, *Cities of the Dead*, 66; Washburne, "The Clave of Jazz," 69. Washburne emphasizes that the migration of approximately three thousand free black refugees from Haiti to New Orleans between 1806 and 1810 (64) played a significant role in New Orleans's growth and "provides evidence in support of the Caribbean tie to the formative period of jazz" (59). In *Louisiana*, this history of "cultural mixing" through circum-Caribbean migration is echoed when Ella remarks that "the singing in my parlour of the U.S.–West Indian men has more than once been the inspiration for a jazz work" (130). My thanks to Anne Dvinge for directing me to Washburne's essay.
58. Gilroy, *The Black Atlantic*, 103.
59. Jameson, *The Political Unconscious*, 35.
60. Pinto, *Difficult Diasporas*, 129.
61. Pinto's discussion of *Tell My Horse* cites Jenny Sharpe's notion of "'history as spirit possession,' an epistemology animated by a few lingering traces, as well as the absence, of evidence surrounding displaced cultural identities" (114). This definition may apply even more aptly to *Louisiana*.
62. Roach, *Cities of the Dead*, 209.
63. Hurston, *Tell My Horse*, 220, 223.
64. Brodber, *Myal*, 37, 67.
65. Pinto, *Difficult Diasporas*, 132, 123, 108.
66. Banks, *Continental Drift*, 328.
67. Gaines, *The Autobiography of Miss Jane Pittman*, vi–vii.

68. Gaines's novel too was inspired by the WPA interviews of the 1930s: see Gaudet, "Miss Jane and Personal Experience Narrative," 30.

CHAPTER 6. Neoslavery, Immigrant Labor, and Casino Capitalism in Cynthia Shearer's *The Celestial Jukebox*

1. Guterl, *American Mediterranean*, 186.
2. Shearer, *The Celestial Jukebox*, 30. All subsequent page references in this chapter to *The Celestial Jukebox* will be to the 2005 Shoemaker & Hoard edition and incorporated into the main text.
3. Douglass quoted in Bow, *Partly Colored*, 34.
4. Loewen, *The Mississippi Chinese*, 23. See also Jung, *Coolies and Cane*.
5. Loewen, *The Mississippi Chinese*, 26–27.
6. Reimers, "Asian Immigrants in the South," 105; Loewen, *Mississippi Chinese*, 34.
7. Loewen, *The Mississippi Chinese*, 53, 4–5.
8. See Bone, *The Postsouthern Sense of Place*, 12–14.
9. Segars, "How to Be Chinese in Mississippi," 57.
10. Neil Smith, "Contours of a Spatialized Poetics," 60.
11. McPherson, *Reconstructing Dixie*, 12.
12. Nelson and Mason, "Mississippi," 40–41; von Herrmann, "The Casino Resort Solution," 5.
13. Trethewey, *Beyond Katrina*, 59–60. After the legalization of gambling in Mississippi, the state abruptly became the South's leading job creator. By 2002, Mississippi casinos were paying $327 million in taxes: approximately 10 percent of the state's annual budget. See Nelson and Mason, "The Politics of Casino Gambling," 34, 44.
14. Strange, *Casino Capitalism*, 1–2.
15. Warren, "Literature as a Symptom," 354.
16. See Strange, *Casino Capitalism*, 115–16. That time can seem to warp within the weirdly hermetic material spaces of Mississippian casino capitalism has also been noted by sociologist Dena C. Wittmann, who explores its effects on employees as well as customers. After the legalization of gambling in 1992, "a new class of service workers emerged as casinos require that workers be present on a rotating basis twenty-four hours a day, seven days a week, 365 days a year." Wittmann quotes a casino employee who remarks that the combination of sealed environment and shift work means that "there's no concept of time in the casino." See Wittmann, "A Day in the Night," 121, 128.
17. Romine, "Orphans All," 162, 180–81n7; Hannah, *Yonder Stands Your Orphan*, 229.
18. Strange, *Casino Capitalism*, 111, 116.
19. Strange, *Casino Capitalism*, 113; Jameson, "The Brick and the Balloon," 43. "A financial future is a promise to buy or sell a financial instrument like a bond, a currency or a basket of shares at a market-fixed price on a given delivery date" (*Casino Capitalism*, 120n6). While land is at one level an "old-fashioned" material commodity, unlike these abstract "financial futures" that Strange sees as prominent under casino capitalism, its "value" is likewise based on what Jameson calls "the expectation of future value." Jameson draws on David Harvey's insight that the value of land constitutes "fictitious capital" because it involves "a flow of money capital not backed by any commodity transaction." Hence "the value of land is revealed to be intimately related to the credit system, the stock market and finance capital generally" in that all such forms of

"fictitious capital" are (again quoting Harvey) "a claim upon future profits from the use of the land or, more directly, a claim upon future labor" ("The Brick and the Balloon," 43). Seen in this light, Futuristics' role in *The Celestial Jukebox* as an emblem of casino capitalism's focus on "financial futures" is redoubled: the firm gambles on future value through both land speculation *and* the construction and operation of casinos.

20. Strange points out that as well as being unwitting victims of globalized casino capitalism, U.S. farmers are willing participants in it: "Some of the volatility of the markets in grain, soybeans, pork bellies, frozen orange juice and 90 or so other commodities produced in the United States is undoubtedly due to the widespread participation in futures trading by the farmers themselves" (*Casino Capitalism*, 113). It is not clear whether Aubrey's online forays into the NASDAQ involve "gambling" in the very commodities he produces, but evidently Aubrey is speculating in some form of "futures trading."

21. McPherson, *Reconstructing Dixie*, 3, 40.
22. Romine, *The Real South*, 58.
23. Baudrillard, *Simulations*, 11. I am drawing here on Baudrillard's formulations for the first and third stages in "the successive phases of the image."
24. McPherson, *Reconstructing Dixie*, 13.
25. Adams, *Wounds of Returning*, 10, 54.
26. Adams, *Wounds of Returning*, 86–87.
27. Adams, *Wounds of Returning*, 8 (Marx's *Capital* quoted 163n27).
28. Roediger, *The Wages of Whiteness*, 66, 82.
29. Cobb, "Beyond the 'Y'all Wall,'" 4.
30. Smith-Nonini, "Federally Sponsored Mexican Migrants," 60.
31. Bow, *Partly Colored*, 96–97; Loewen, *The Mississippi Chinese*, 72, 2. In 1924 Chinese merchant Gong Lum challenged a ban preventing his daughter from attending a white public school in Rosedale, Mississippi. The state supreme court upheld the racial segregation of schools by citing the 1890 Mississippi Constitution to define the Chinese as part of the "colored races" rather than "white" (Loewen, *The Mississippi Chinese*, 67); this decision was reaffirmed in 1927 by the federal Supreme Court decision in *Rice v. Lum*, which cited 1896's *Plessy v. Ferguson* as a precedent. Many Chinese left the delta for Memphis and elsewhere after these verdicts, and "not until the 1930s and 1940s did the Chinese and their children become 'white,' or white enough to enroll in white schools and patronize white churches and public facilities" (Reimers, "Asian Immigrants in the South," 104).
32. Bow, *Partly Colored*, 9.
33. Segars, "How to Be Chinese," 61.
34. Bow, *Partly Colored*, 10.
35. Segars, "How to Be Chinese," 61.
36. Groom, "McDonald's Agrees to Pay More for Florida Tomatoes," www.reuters.com/article/consumerproducts-SP/idUSN0933192520070409 (accessed January 8, 2017); Bowe, *Nobodies*, 13.
37. Bowe, "Nobodies," www.newyorker.com/magazine/2003/04/21/nobodies (accessed January 8, 2017).
38. Bowe, *Nobodies*, 56. In the diluted version of the bill that was finally passed, "the penalties for involuntary servitude apply virtually only to labor contractors—the lowest rung of employers" (*Nobodies* 57).

39. Guterl, *American Mediterranean*, 188; "nobodies" alludes to Bowe's book of that name.

40. Baker, *I Don't Hate the South*, 95.

41. Goyal, *Romance, Diaspora, and Black Atlantic Literature*, 208.

42. Bibler, "The Flood Last Time," 509.

43. Karyn Anderson, "Dangerously Smooth Spaces," 211.

44. Bales, *Disposable People*, 81.

45. Bales, *Disposable People*, 83–84, 119.

46. Foner, *Give Me Liberty!* 385.

47. Jarmakani, *Imagining Arab Womanhood*, 143, 142, 152, 159.

48. Bales, *Disposable People*, 119. In 1960 the Islamic Republic of Mauritania gained independence from France. Slavery had been banned under French colonial law. The latest law criminalizing slavery passed in 2007, but estimates suggest 140,000 of the nation's approximately 3.8 million people remain enslaved. See Nossiter, "Mauritania Confronts Long Legacy of Slavery," www.nytimes.com/2013/11/12/world/africa/mauritania-confronts-long-legacy-of-slavery.html?pagewanted=all&_r=0 (accessed January 8, 2017).

49. Adorno, "On Popular Music," 308.

50. Gilroy, *The Black Atlantic*, 81.

51. Gilroy, *The Black Atlantic*, 88.

52. Rushing, *Memphis and the Paradox of Place*, 151; Gilroy, *The Black Atlantic*, 104.

53. On the tenuous basis that the owners of Chess Records (the leading label for blues artists such as Muddy Waters in the 1950s and 1960s) were Jews, the Wastrel extrapolates: "*Such sorrow is well rehearsed.... The Jews know a commodity when they see it*" (151).

54. Benson, *Disturbing Calculations*, 3; see also Romine, *The Real South*, 33.

55. Yaeger, *Dirt and Desire*, 17.

56. For Gilroy's notion of the "slave sublime," see *The Black Atlantic*, especially 131 and 187–223.

57. Karyn Anderson's take on the novel's "nearly utopian vision of cultural hybridity" and optimistic emphasis on immigrant characters' ability to negotiate "smooth spaces" are notably qualified when she turns to "the book's abrupt ending and dismantling of the rhizomatic" smooth spaces following the post-9/11 clampdown on immigrants like the Mauritanians in Madagascar. The shift is notable partly because Anderson fails to address other *pre*-9/11 forms of "oppression from within and without": casino capitalism and neoslavery labor relations. Anderson, "Dangerously Smooth Spaces," 201, 215, 214.

58. Rushing, *Memphis and the Paradox of Place*, 124.

59. Lytle, "The Hind Tit," 244.

60. Chappell, "Blue Dive," 94. Stovebolt comments that "these days now ... they've got them a record box where the customers have to pay for the music. But what I play, the way I play it, you can't get out of no machine" (83). At the Blue Dive, Stovebolt begins performing traditional blues as a way of "preventing the newcomers from playing the jukebox" (91), declaring that "machine music" is "purely hateful to me" (94). Ultimately he fails to convince Hawkins—the new northern, urban black owner of the Blue Dive—to hire him; Hawkins dismisses Stovebolt's traditional blues repertoire as "old-time nigger whining songs" (93).

61. Turner, *Africanisms in the Gullah Dialect*, 195.

62. In an interview after publication, Shearer remarked that "that there is actually some internet term 'celestial jukebox' that refers to projects that try to collect all known music in one place. And to charge a fee for it, of course!" See Robertson, "Interview with Cynthia Shearer," http://southernlitreview.com/authors/cynthia_shearer_interview.htm (accessed January 8, 2017).

63. Du Bois, *The Souls of Black Folk*, 10.

CHAPTER 7. Southern Transpacific

1. Wilson, "Tracking the 'China Peril,'" 168–69, 174.
2. Stecopoulos, *Reconstructing the World*, 9.
3. Harker, "Introduction," 2.
4. Bow, *Partly Colored*, 164.
5. Melanie Benson Taylor, "Faulkner and Southern Studies," 127.
6. Bow, "Asian Americans," 493.
7. Suzanne W. Jones, "Who Is a Southern Writer?" 725.
8. Bow, "Asian Americans," 496.
9. Reimers, "Asian Immigrants in the South," 107.
10. Faulkner, *Absalom, Absalom!* 289, 142.
11. Berlin, *The Making of African America*, 4–5.
12. Reimers, "Asian Immigrants in the South," 106.
13. Wilson, "Tracking the 'China Peril,'" 170.
14. See Ryan, "Outsiders with Insider Information," 244; Reimers, "Asian Immigrants in the South," 114.
15. Dao, "The Vietnamese in Mississippi," 272. Valerie Martin's fine novel *Trespass* (2007) features a Croatian immigrant fishing family in Louisiana headed by Branko Drago, "the Oyster King."
16. Cha, "Creating a Multiethnic Gulf South," 206.
17. Butler, "Relic," 139. I discuss two other stories from Butler's collection—"Crickets" and "Snow"—in my essay "You Don't Have to Be Born There," 484–85.
18. Dao, "Vietnamese in Mississippi," 276.
19. Trethewey, *Beyond Katrina*, 59–60.
20. Dao demonstrates that long before Katrina, the gaming industry had been encroaching on Biloxi's Vietnamese neighborhoods ("Vietnamese in Mississippi" 263–64).
21. Cha, "Creating a Multiethnic Gulf South," 203–5; see also Tang, "A Gulf Unites Us."
22. Kreyling, *Inventing Southern Literature*, 121.
23. Truong, "A Reader's Guide" in *Bitter in the Mouth*, 291. All further page references in this chapter to *Bitter in the Mouth* will be to the 2011 Random House paperback edition and included in the main text. In the "Reader's Guide," Truong remarks that "I must have found in Atticus's words and actions a primer for understanding why the children of my small town had taunted me for the color of my skin. Before I came to the United States, I didn't even know that my skin had a color, and I could have never imagined that the color would be 'yellow'" (290).
24. Truong quoted in Squint with Yousaf, "Both Souths That I've Known," 43.
25. Faulkner, *Absalom, Absalom!* 142.
26. Peacock, *Grounded Globalism*, 171.

27. Bow, *Partly Colored*, 5, 1, 5.

28. Bow, *Partly Colored*, 6, 92. Since I drafted this analysis of *Bitter in the Mouth*, Bow has published an essay partly focused on Truong's novel in which she stresses how "proximity to the black or white communities provides the only significant, if inadequate, reference point for locating . . . her [Linda's] visually differentiated body, the overdetermined surface of racial meaning." See Bow, "Asian Americans," 506–7.

29. McPherson, *Reconstructing Dixie*, 7.

30. Hutchinson, *In Search of Nella Larsen*, 295.

31. Sollors, *Neither White nor Black*, 250.

32. Bow notes "Truong's ability to convey by means other than visual markers or the texture and color provided by ethnic references." For example, *Bitter in the Mouth* "explore[s] the *emotional* substance of race" through the emphasis on Linda's audio-gustatory synesthesia: the "suggestive structural comparison" offers "a commentary on the limits of a visual epistemology in which 'yellow' fails to signify." See Bow, "Asian Americans," 505–6, 496.

33. Squint with Yousaf, "Both Souths That I've Known," 45; Price, "'The Void and the Missing,'" 64.

34. Price observes that Linda's adoption by the Hammericks in 1976 involves "'outsourcing' the labor of pregnancy and childbirth to the global South; it becomes a way to build a family through the channels of global capitalism" ("'The Void and the Missing'" 62).

35. Truong quoted in Squint with Yousaf, "Both Souths That I've Known," 44.

36. For my reading of *The Foreign Student*, see "You Don't Have to Be Born There," 477–79.

37. Monteith, "Southern Like U.S.?" 71.

38. Cao, *Monkey Bridge*, 30; Reimers, "Asian Immigrants in the South," 114. All subsequent page references in this chapter to *Monkey Bridge* will be to the 1997 Viking edition and incorporated into the main text.

39. Monteith and Yousaf, "Making an Impression," 220.

40. Faulkner, *Absalom, Absalom!* 7.

41. Jin, *The Writer as Migrant*, 5.

42. Ryan, "Outsiders with Insider Information," 237, 245.

43. Ryan, "Outsiders with Insider Information," 241, 244.

44. Monteith and Yousaf, "Making an Impression," 215, 223, 215.

45. Reimers, "Asian Immigrants in the South," 116.

46. Jin, *A Free Life*, 97, 252, 264. All subsequent page references in this chapter to *A Free Life* will be to the 2007 Pantheon edition and incorporated into the main text.

47. Jin, *The Writer as Migrant*, 23, 22.

48. Jin, *The Writer as Migrant*, 22, 63.

49. Jin, *The Writer as Migrant*, 66, 85.

50. Bow, *Partly Colored*, 127.

51. Cohn, "Southern Regionalism and U.S. Nationalism," 250; the Lawrence Schwartz quote is from Schwartz's book *Creating Faulkner's Reputation: The Politics of Modern Literary Criticism* (1988).

52. Bow, "Asian Americans," 496, 495.

53. Nonini, "Critique," 249; Kurotani, "The South Meets the East," 187; Nonini, "Critique," 258.

54. Sonnenberg, *Home Leave*, 43. All subsequent page references to *Home Leave* will be to the 2014 Grand Central edition and incorporated into the main text.

55. Chris Kriegstein's business-class white American privilege does not go unchallenged: in Bombay, a Singaporean businessman of Indian descent challenges his unthinking neo-imperial rubric: "America is a continent, my friend.... Do you mean the United States?" (Sonnenberg, *Home Leave*, 76).

EPILOGUE. Transnational American Studies with "the South"

1. Suzanne W. Jones, "Who Is a Southern Writer?" 725.
2. Jon Smith, *Finding Purple America*, 124.
3. Duck, "Plantation/Empire," 77.
4. Duvall, *Race and White Identity*, 158.
5. Thadious M. Davis, *Southscapes*, 36, 19. Davis qualifies that "I do not mean to suggest... that all black people in the United States are 'southerners.' Morrison is a midwesterner who until 1998 had never even visited her father's southern birthplace, Cartersville, Georgia" (36).
6. Lloyd, *Rooting Memory, Rooting Place*, 119, 121, 120, 126–27. In *Home*, Frank's ambivalence about returning to the South—which he does to rescue his sister from an abusive white doctor in Atlanta before bringing her back to Lotus to recover—is apparent in his "feeling of safety and goodwill [that], he knew, was exaggerated, but savoring it was real." Later, back in Lotus, "he could not believe how much he had once hated this place. Now it seemed both fresh and ancient, safe and demanding." Morrison, *Home*, 118, 132.
7. Morrison, *Tar Baby*, 166. All subsequent page references in this epilogue to *Tar Baby* will be to the 1981 Alfred A. Knopf edition and incorporated into the main text.
8. Glissant, *Faulkner, Mississippi*, 10.
9. Dubey, "Postmodern Geographies," 359; Baker, *Workings of the Spirit*, 36, 98, 136. Despite Dubey's skeptical observations on how "Morrison curiously claims to write 'village literature,'" she absolves Morrison of simple nostalgia for a black southern past by noting that *Song of Solomon* "celebrates a blatantly fictive South" rather than a real (and racially segregated) Jim Crow region ("Postmodern Geographies," 359, 366). In 1985 Morrison herself noted that critics trying "to show certain kinds of connections between myself and Zora Neale Hurston are always dismayed and disappointed in me because I hadn't read Zora Neale Hurston except for one little short story before I began to write." Morrison nevertheless insisted "the fact that I had never read Zora Neale Hurston and wrote *The Bluest Eye* and *Sula* anyway means that the tradition really exists... the world as perceived by black women at certain times does exist." See Naylor, "A Conversation," 214.
10. In a 1998 essay on the South and "southern ethos" in Morrison's fiction, Lucille P. Fultz discusses four out of five of Morrison's novels between *The Bluest Eye* and *Beloved*—the exception being *Tar Baby*, which is not even mentioned. See Fultz, "Southern Ethos / Black Ethics."
11. Larsen, *Quicksand*, 120.
12. In Paris, Jadine is simultaneously fascinated with and intimidated by the vision of an African "woman's woman—that mother / sister / she" (*Tar Baby* 46).
13. Morrison, *Home*, 119–20.

14. Goyal, "The Gender of Diaspora," 396, 412n15, 402.

15. Nwankwo, *Black Cosmopolitanism*, 13–14. Gideon has returned home to Dominique despite surrendering his hard-earned U.S. citizenship: "'The U.S. is a bad place to die in,' he said. He didn't regret it" (*Tar Baby* 154). Restricted access to citizenship, Social Security, or work permits severely constrains national affiliation for transnational migrant workers like Son and Gideon, yet as Goyal stresses, it is also "Son's 'restlessness' as an undocumented man [that] leads him to a strong critique of capitalism, colonialism, and racism" ("Gender of Diaspora," 403).

16. Giles, *Global Remapping*, 1, 12.

17. These quotes appear on the cover of and inside the Modern Library paperback edition of *Shadow Country*.

18. LeClair, "A History of Violence," www.nytimes.com/2008/04/27/books/review/LeClair-t.html (accessed January 1, 2017).

19. Matthiessen, *Shadow Country*, x. All subsequent page references in this epilogue to *Shadow Country* will be to the 2008 Modern Library edition and incorporated into the main text. *Shadow Country* is a condensed "new rendering" of Matthiessen's earlier trilogy of novels: *Killing Mr. Watson* (1990), *Lost Man's River* (1997), and *Bone by Bone* (1999).

20. Watson has considerable personal experience with convict labor. He was once a prisoner rented out by "a work gang captain at Little Rock" (611) and learns that his dissolute Confederate veteran father supervised black convict laborers in South Carolina: "Went through them niggers like goobers, worked 'em straight to death, ol' Ring-Eye did" (621).

21. See Woodward, *The Origins of the New South*, chapter 11 ("The Colonial Economy"); Handley, *Postslavery Literatures in the Americas*, 20.

22. Jameson, *Postmodernism*, 405.

23. Stecopoulos, *Reconstructing the World*, 26, 22.

24. Bowe, *Nobodies*, 13.

25. DeGravelles, "The Global Meets the Local," 139–40. On "New Orleans exceptionalism" and Katrina, see DeGravelles, "Global Meets the Local," 147–48; and Lightweis-Goff, "'Peculiar and Characteristic.'"

26. Greeson, *Our South*, 12.

27. DeGravelles, "Global Meets the Local," 147.

28. Greeson, *Our South*, 12; Stecopoulos, *Reconstructing the World*, 1.

29. See Helen Taylor, *Circling Dixie*, 98.

30. Eggers, "It Was Just Boys Talking," www.theguardian.com/books/2007/may/26/featuresreviews.guardianreview29 (accessed January 15, 2017); Eggers, *What Is the What*, 23. See also my essay "Narratives of African Immigration," especially 67–71.

31. Eggers, *Zeitoun*, 79. All subsequent references in this epilogue to *Zeitoun* will be to the 2010 Vintage paperback edition and incorporated into the main text.

32. The quote from A. J. Liebling's *The Earl of Louisiana* (1961) achieved renown as an epigram to John Kennedy Toole's novel *A Confederacy of Dunces* (1980).

33. Codrescu, "New Orleans or Baghdad?" 270.

34. Adams, *Wounds of Returning*, 138, 149.

35. Lloyd, *Rooting Memory, Rooting Place*, 66.

36. See Bush, "Address to a Joint Session of Congress," http://georgewbush-whitehouse.archives.gov/news/releases/2001/09/20010920-8.html (accessed January

1, 2017). Lloyd's otherwise illuminating reading of *Zeitoun* privileges "the Southern lens" over "more transnational frames" (68) and so does not discuss Eggers's considerable attention to Abdulrahman's life in Syria. Zeitoun was arrested in 2012 on charges of trying to murder his wife: though acquitted, he was arrested again in May 2014. Helen Taylor has suggested that Abdulrahman and Kathy "may well prove to be two of the highest-profile examples of post-Katrina trauma victims." See Taylor, "Recovering through a Cultural Economy," 197n28.

37. Eckes, "The South and Economic Globalization," 37; Watson, "Southern History, Southern Future," 279. See the introduction to this book.

38. Lalami, *The Moor's Account*, 5. All subsequent page references in this epilogue to *The Moor's Account* are to the 2014 Pantheon edition and will be incorporated into the main text.

39. Goodwin, *Crossing the Continent*, 48.

40. Goodwin argues that, though "[w]e know that he lived for a time at Azemmour," nevertheless "Esteban was almost certainly Negroid and of sub-Saharan ancestry" (*Crossing the Continent* 79, 83).

41. Lalami quotes this single reference in her acknowledgments (*The Moor's Account*, 323). Cabeza De Vaca's travelogue was published in Spanish in 1542 and in an expanded version in 1555; an English translation did not appear in the United States until 1851.

42. On the Native reception of Esteban and the Castilians as "Children of the Sun," see Goodwin, *Crossing the Continent*, 254.

43. Eric Gary Anderson, "Literary and Textual Histories," 18, 30, 17, 30. Anderson qualifies that we cannot fully know Native experiences and perspectives via "European writing and textuality" (20). Given that Lalami's novel is an imaginative attempt to reconstitute Esteban/Mustafa's African-Muslim experiences and perspectives, then we might qualify that he too could not always know Native experiences and perspectives, even though he learns various tribal languages, lives for long periods with various tribes, and marries Oyomasot of the Avavares. Still, as Anderson notes, "Native actors and actions, visible and audible in non-Native sources, leave their mark on, and take their place within, the textual and literary histories of the Native South" (21); we could say the same for Lalami's novel and the historical sources upon which she partly bases Mustafa's "account."

44. The historical fate of Esteban Dorantes is unknown: he was last seen by a Spaniard in March 1539, having been ordered to scout the northward route of this latest expedition. See Goodwin, *Crossing the Continent*, 335; like Lalami, Goodwin concludes that Esteban effectively became "a *cimarrón*, a runaway slave" (337).

45. Goodwin, *Crossing the Continent*, 12.

46. Goodwin, *Crossing the Continent*, 10–11; see also 79. Goodwin also notes that although Esteban's story presages this mass transportation via the Middle Passage of black African slaves, the slaves themselves "had no concept of being 'African' or 'black,'" which were European designations (80).

47. Jon Smith, "Toward a Post-postpolitical Southern Studies," 75; Kreyling, *The South That Wasn't There*.

48. Goodwin posits Esteban as "a postmodern man in an early modern world, an inhabitant of the global village before its foundations had been dug" (*Crossing the Continent*, 302).

WORKS CITED

Aboul-Ela, Hosam. "Global South, Local South: The New Postnationalism in U.S. Southern Studies." *American Literature* 78, no. 4 (December 2006): 847–58.

Abraham, Keshia. "Erna Brodber." *Bomb* 86 (Winter 2003–4). http://bombmagazine.org/article/2622/erna-brodber (accessed January 12, 2017).

Accilien, Cécile. "Haitian Creole in a Transnational Context." In *Just below South*, ed. Adams, Bibler, and Accilien, 76–94.

Adams, Jessica. "Introduction: Circum-Caribbean Performance, Language, History." In *Just below South*, ed. Adams, Bibler, and Accilien, 1–21.

———. *Wounds of Returning: Race, Memory, and Property on the Postslavery Plantation.* Chapel Hill: University of North Carolina Press, 2007.

Adams, Jessica, Michael P. Bibler, and Cécile Accilien, eds. *Just below South: Intercultural Performance in the Caribbean and the U.S. South.* Charlottesville: University of Virginia Press, 2007.

Adorno, Theodor. "On Popular Music." In *On Record: Rock, Pop, and the Written Word*, ed. Simon Frith and Andrew Goodwin. London: Routledge, 1990. 301–14.

"America's Sugar Daddies." *New York Times*, November 29, 2003. www.nytimes.com/2003/11/29/opinion/america-s-sugar-daddies.html (accessed December 20, 2016).

Anderson, Eric Gary. "Literary and Textual Histories of the Native South." In *The Oxford Handbook of the Literature of the U.S. South*, ed. Hobson and Ladd, 17–32.

Anderson, Karyn. "Dangerously Smooth Spaces in Cynthia Shearer's *The Celestial Jukebox*." *MELUS* 37, no. 1 (Spring 2012): 199–217.

Angelou, Maya. *The Heart of a Woman.* New York: Bantam, 1981.

Apter, Emily. *Against World Literature: On the Politics of Untranslatability.* New York: Verso, 2013.

Arapoglou, Eleftheria, Mónika Fodor, and Jopi Nyman. "Introduction." In *Mobile Narratives: Travel, Migration, and Transculturation*, ed. Arapoglou, Fodor, and Nyman. New York: Routledge, 2014. 1–12.

Arnesen, Eric. *Waterfront Workers of New Orleans: Race, Class and Politics, 1863–1923.* New York: Oxford University Press, 1991.

Baker, Houston A., Jr. *I Don't Hate the South: Reflections on Faulkner, Family, and the South.* New York: Oxford University Press, 2007.

———. *Turning South Again: Re-thinking Modernism / Re-reading Booker T.* Durham, N.C.: Duke University Press, 2001.

———. *Workings of the Spirit: The Poetics of Afro-American Women's Writing.* Chicago: University of Chicago Press, 1991.

Baker, Houston A., Jr., and Dana D. Nelson. "Preface: Violence, the Body and 'The South.'" *American Literature* 73, no. 2 (June 2001): 231–44.

Bales, Kevin. *Disposable People: New Slavery in the Global Economy.* Rev. ed. Berkeley: University of California Press, 2012.

Banks, Russell. *The Book of Jamaica*. New York: HarperPerennial, 1996.
———. *Continental Drift*. New York: Harper & Row, 1985.
———. "Diary, handwritten notes. 6 October 1981–1 January 1983." Box 72, folder 8, in Russell Banks Papers, Harry Ransom Center, University of Texas at Austin.
———. "'H&I': PEN/Hemingway Prize Speech, Presented at the John F. Kennedy Library, 4 April 2004." *The Hemingway Review* 24, no. 1 (Fall 2004): 53–60.
———. Letter (with list of "Current Project and Proposals") to Ted Solotaroff, October 4, 1984. Box 16, folder 5, Russell Banks Papers, Harry Ransom Center, University of Texas at Austin.
———. "Making a Killing" section typescript of *The Trade*, rough draft (1 of 3). Box 13, folder 3, Russell Banks Papers, Harry Ransom Center, University of Texas at Austin.
———. Outline for "Grand Chemin" section in *The Trade*, rough draft (3 of 3). Box 13, folder 5, Russell Banks Papers, Harry Ransom Center, University of Texas at Austin.
———. *Rule of the Bone*. New York: HarperCollins, 1995.
Bankston, Carl. "The International Immigrants of Mississippi: An Overview." In *Ethnic Heritage in Mississippi: The Twentieth Century*, ed. Walton and Carpenter, 15–31.
Baudrillard, Jean. *Simulations*. New York: Semiotext[e], 1983.
Beck, Ulrich. *The Cosmopolitan Vision*. Cambridge: Polity, 2006.
Becnel, Thomas. *Labor, Church, and the Sugar Establishment: Louisiana, 1887–1976*. Baton Rouge: Louisiana State University Press, 1981.
Beebe, George. Letter to Doug Silver, July 9, 1958. Correspondence box 1, folder 11, Zora Neale Hurston Papers, Special and Area Studies Collections, George A. Smathers Libraries, University of Florida, Gainesville.
Benson, Melanie R. *Disturbing Calculations: The Economics of Identity in Postcolonial Southern Literature, 1912–2002*. Athens: University of Georgia Press, 2008.
Berlin, Ira. *The Making of African America: The Four Great Migrations*. New York: Viking, 2010.
Bibler, Michael P. "The Flood Last Time: 'Muck' and the Uses of History in Kara Walker's 'Rumination' on Katrina." *Journal of American Studies* 44, no. 3 (August 2010): 503–18.
Bigsby, C. W. E. *The Second Black Renaissance: Essays in Black Literature*. Westport, Conn.: Greenwood Press, 1980.
Bone, Martyn. "*Den Sorte*: Nella Larsen and Denmark." In *Afro-Nordic Landscapes: Equality and Race in Northern Europe*, ed. Michael McEachrane. New York: Routledge, 2014. 208–26.
———. "Intertextual Geographies of Migration and Biracial Identity: *Light in August* and Nella Larsen's *Quicksand*." In *Faulkner and Formalism: Returns of the Text*, ed. Annette Trefzer and Ann Abadie. Jackson: University Press of Mississippi, 2012. 144–62.
———. "Introduction: Old / New / Post / Real / Global / No South: Paradigms and Scales." In *Creating and Consuming the American South*, ed. Bone, Ward, and Link, 1–23.
———. "Narratives of African Immigration to the U.S. South: Dave Eggers's *What Is the What* and Cynthia Shearer's *The Celestial Jukebox*." *CR: New Centennial Review* 10, no. 1 (Spring 2010): 65–76.
———. *The Postsouthern Sense of Place in Contemporary Fiction*. Baton Rouge: Louisiana State University Press, 2005.

———. "Teaching *Quicksand* in Denmark." In *Approaches to Teaching the Novels of Nella Larsen*, ed. Jacquelyn McLendon. New York: Modern Language Association, 2016. 169–76.
———. "The Transnational Turn, Houston Baker's New Southern Studies and Patrick Neate's *Twelve Bar Blues*." *Comparative American Studies* 3, no. 2 (June 2005): 189–211.
———. "The Transnational Turn in the South: Region, Nation, Globalization." In *Transnational America: Contours of Modern U.S. Culture*, ed. Russell Duncan and Clara Juncker. Copenhagen: Museum Tuscalanum, 2004. 217–35.
———. "You Don't Have to Be Born There: Immigration and Contemporary Fiction of the U.S. South." In *The Oxford Handbook of the Literature of the American South*, ed. Hobson and Ladd, 473–92.
Bone, Martyn, Brian Ward, and William A. Link, eds. *Creating and Consuming the American South*. Gainesville: University Press of Florida, 2015.
Bourne, Randolph. "Trans-national America." In *Heath Anthology of American Literature: Concise Edition*, ed. Paul Lauter et al. Boston: Houghton Mifflin, 2004. 2053–65.
Bow, Leslie. "Asian Americans, Racial Latency, Southern Traces." In *The Oxford Handbook of the Literature of the American South*, ed. Hobson and Ladd, 493–513.
———. *Partly Colored: Asian Americans and Racial Anomaly in the Segregated South*. New York: New York University Press, 2010.
Bowe, John. "Nobodies." *The New Yorker*, April 12, 2003. www.newyorker.com/magazine/2003/04/21/nobodies (accessed January 8, 2017).
———. *Nobodies: Modern American Slave Labor and the Dark Side of the New Global Economy*. New York: Random House, 2008.
Boyd, Valerie. *Wrapped in Rainbows: The Life of Zora Neale Hurston*. New York: Scribner, 2003.
Brickhouse, Anna. "Nella Larsen and the Intertextual Geography of *Quicksand*." *African American Review* 35, no. 4 (Winter 2001): 533–60.
Brochu, Nichole Sterghos. "Florida's Forgotten Storm: The Hurricane of 1928." *South Florida Sun Sentinel*, September 14, 2003. www.sun-sentinel.com/sfl-ahurricane14sep14-story.html (accessed December 21, 2016).
Brodber, Erna. *The Continent of Black Consciousness: On the History of the African Diaspora from Slavery to the Present Day*. London: New Beacon Books, 2003.
———. *Louisiana*. Jackson: University Press of Mississippi, 1997.
———. *Myal*. London: New Beacon, 1988.
Bush, George W. "Address to a Joint Session of Congress and the American People," September 20, 2001. http://georgewbush-whitehouse.archives.gov/news/releases/2001/09/20010920-8.html (accessed January 1, 2017).
Butler, Robert Olen. "Relic." In *A Good Scent from a Strange Mountain*. London: Minerva, 1993. 137–42.
Caballero, Alex. "Alabama Brings Back Slavery for Illegals." *The Guardian*, October 12, 2011. www.guardian.co.uk/commentisfree/cifamerica/2011/oct/12/alabama-slavery-latino-immigrants?intcmp=239 (accessed January 5, 2017).
Cao, Lan. *Monkey Bridge*. New York: Viking, 1997.
Capote, Truman. "A Diamond Guitar." In *Breakfast at Tiffany's*. Victoria: Penguin Australia, 2008. 125–38.
Carby, Hazel V. *Cultures in Babylon: Black Britain and African America*. London: Verso, 1999.

———. "Ideologies of Black Folk: The Historical Novel of Slavery." In *Cultures in Babylon*, 146–59.
———. "The Politics of Fiction, Anthropology, and the Folk: Zora Neale Hurston." In *Cultures in Babylon*, 168–85.
———. *Reconstructing Womanhood: The Emergence of the Afro-American Woman Novelist*. New York: Oxford University Press, 1987.
———. "Reinventing History / Imagining the Future." In *Cultures in Babylon*, 129–34.
Cartwright, Keith. *Sacral Grooves, Limbo Gateways: Travels in Deep Southern Time, Circum-Caribbean Space, Afro-Creole Authority*. Athens: University of Georgia Press, 2013.
Castells, Manuel. *The Informational City*. Oxford: Blackwell, 1989.
Cha, Frank. "Creating a Multiethnic Gulf South: Vietnamese American Cultural and Economic Visibility before and after Katrina." In *Creating and Consuming the American South*, ed. Bone, Ward, and Link, 203–25.
Chappell, Fred. "Blue Dive." In *Stories of the Modern South*, ed. Ben Forkner and Patrick Samway. New York: Penguin, 1986. 77–100.
Chu, Patricia E. *Race, Nationalism, and the State in British and American Modernism*. Cambridge: Cambridge University Press, 2006.
Cobb, James C. "Beyond the 'Y'all Wall': The American South Goes Global." In *Globalization and the American South*, ed. Cobb and Stueck, 1–18.
Cobb, James C., and William Stueck. *Globalization and the American South*. Athens: University of Georgia Press, 2005.
———. "Introduction." In *Globalization and the American South*, ed. Cobb and Stueck, xi–xvi.
Coclanis, Peter A. "Globalization before Globalization: The South and the World to 1950." In *Globalization and the American South*, ed. Cobb and Stueck, 19–35.
Codrescu, Andrei. "New Orleans or Baghdad?" In *New Orleans, Mon Amour: Twenty Years of Writings from the City*. Chapel Hill, N.C.: Algonquin, 2006. 269–70.
Cohn, Deborah. "Southern Regionalism and U.S. Nationalism in William Faulkner's State Department Travels." In *Creating and Consuming the American South*, ed. Bone, Ward, and Link, 248–67.
Cooper, Jan. "Zora Neale Hurston Was Always a Southerner Too." In *The Female Tradition in Southern Literature*, ed. Carol Manning. Urbana and Chicago: University of Illinois Press, 1993. 57–69.
Crossette, Barbara. "U.S. to Redesign Its Aid Program for Haiti Despite Rights Problem." *New York Times*, November 9, 1981, A1, A15.
Cruse, Harold. *The Crisis of the Negro Intellectual*. New York: Quill, 1984.
Danticat, Edwidge. Foreword to *Their Eyes Were Watching God*, by Zora Neale Hurston, ix–xviii.
Dao, Vy Thuc. "The Vietnamese in Mississippi." In *Ethnic Heritage in Mississippi*, ed. Walton and Carpenter, 263–83.
Davidson, Rob, and Fred Santiago Arroyo. "Finding the Melody: An Interview with Russell Banks (1996)." In *Conversations with Russell Banks*, ed. Roche, 48–70.
Davis, F. James. *Who Is Black? One Nation's Definition*. Philadelphia: Pennsylvania University Press, 1991.
Davis, Thadious M. *Nella Larsen, Novelist of the Harlem Renaissance: A Woman's Life Unveiled*. Baton Rouge: Louisiana State University Press, 1994.

———. "Southern Standard Bearers in the New Negro Renaissance." In *The History of Southern Literature*, ed. Louis D. Rubin et al. Baton Rouge: Louisiana State University Press, 1985. 291–313.

———. *Southscapes: Geographies of Race, Region, and Literature*. Chapel Hill: University of North Carolina Press, 2011.

Dearborn, Mary. *Pocahontas's Daughters: Gender and Ethnicity in American Culture*. New York: Oxford University Press, 1986.

deGravelles, Karin H. "The Global Meets the Local: The Third World-ing of New Orleans." *Journal of Curriculum and Pedagogy* 6, no. 1 (2009): 139–55.

DeGuzmán, María. "Four Contemporary Latino/a Writers Ghost the U.S. South." In *The Oxford Handbook of the Literature of the U.S. South*, ed. Hobson and Ladd, 454–72.

Delbanco, Andrew. "The Political Incorrectness of Zora Neale Hurston." *Journal of Blacks in Higher Education* 18 (Winter 1997–98): 103–8.

Dimock, Wai Chee. "Planetary Time and Global Translation: 'Context' in Literary Studies." *Common Knowledge* 9, no. 3 (2003): 488–507.

Dove, Rita. Foreword to *Jonah's Gourd Vine*, by Zora Neale Hurston, vii–xv.

Dubey, Madhu. "Postmodern Geographies of the U.S. South." *Nepantla: Views from the South* 3, no. 2 (2002): 351–71.

Du Bois, W. E. B. *The Souls of Black Folk*. Ed. Henry Louis Gates and Terri Hume Oliver. New York: W. W. Norton, 1999.

Duck, Leigh Anne. *The Nation's Region: Southern Modernism, Segregation, and U.S. Nationalism*. Athens: University of Georgia Press, 2006.

———: "Plantation/Empire." *CR: New Centennial Review* 10, no. 1 (Spring 2010): 77–87.

———. "'Rebirth of a Nation': Hurston in Haiti." *Journal of American Folklore* 117, no. 464 (Spring 2004): 127–46.

———. "Southern Nonidentity." *Safundi: The Journal of South African and American Studies* 9, no. 3 (July 2008): 319–30.

———. "Space and Time." *American Literature* 78, no. 4 (December 2006): 709–11.

Dunbar, Eve. *Black Regions of the Imagination: African American Writers between the Nation and the World*. Philadelphia: Temple University Press, 2013.

Duvall, John N. *Race and White Identity in Southern Fiction: From Faulkner to Morrison*. New York: Palgrave Macmillan, 2008.

Eckes, Alfred E. "The South and Economic Globalization, 1950 to the Future." In *Globalization and the American South*, ed. Cobb and Stueck, 36–65.

Eggers, Dave. "It Was Just Boys Talking." *The Guardian* (UK), May 26, 2007. www.theguardian.com/books/2007/may/26/featuresreviews.guardianreview29 (accessed January 15, 2017).

———. *What Is the What: The Autobiography of Valentino Achak Deng*. San Francisco: McSweeney's, 2006.

———. *Zeitoun*. New York: Vintage, 2010.

Farren, Robert, and Barry Munger. "Russell Banks: The Art of Fiction No. 152." In *Conversations with Russell Banks*, ed. Roche, 71–93.

Faulkner, William. *Absalom, Absalom!* New York: Vintage International, 1990.

———. "The Bear." In *Go Down, Moses*. New York: Vintage International, 1990. 181–315.

———. "A Letter to the Leaders in the Negro Race." In *Essays, Speeches, and Public Letters*, ed. James Meriwether. New York: The Modern Library, 2004. 107–12.

Faust, Drew Gilpin. *The Creation of Confederate Nationalism*. Baton Rouge: Louisiana State University Press, 1988.

Favor, J. Martin. *Authentic Blackness: The Folk in the New Negro Renaissance*. Durham, N.C.: Duke University Press, 1999.

Fink, Leon. *The Maya of Morganton: Work and Community in the Nuevo New South*. Chapel Hill: University of North Carolina Press, 2003.

Fishkin, Shelley Fisher. "Crossroads of Cultures: The Transnational Turn in American Studies." *American Quarterly* 57, no. 1 (2005): 17–57.

Fjelstrup, Libbie. "Jagten på rødderne." *Politiken*, "Kultur" section, January 9, 2005, 1.

Flaherty, Jordan. *Floodlines: Community and Resistance from Katrina to the Jena Six*. Chicago: Haymarket, 2010.

Foner, Eric. *Give Me Liberty! An American History*. 2nd Seagull ed. New York: W. W. Norton, 2009.

Fuentes, Carlos. "Central and Eccentric Writing." In *Lives on the Line: The Testimony of Contemporary Latin American Authors*, ed. Doris Meyer. Berkeley: University of California Press, 1988. 111–25.

Fultz, Lucille P. "Southern Ethos / Black Ethics in Toni Morrison's Fiction." *Studies in the Literary Imagination* 31, no. 2 (Fall 1998): 79–95.

Gabrial, Brian. "From Haiti to Nat Turner: Racial Panic Discourse during the Nineteenth Century Partisan Press Era." *American Journalism* 30, no. 3 (2013): 336–64.

Gaines, Ernest. *The Autobiography of Miss Jane Pittman*. New York: Bantam, 1972.

Gaudet, Marcia. "Miss Jane and Personal Experience Narrative: Ernest Gaines' *The Autobiography of Miss Jane Pittman*." *Western Folklore* 51, no. 1 (January 1992): 23–32.

Gayle, Addison. Foreword to *Youngblood*, by John Oliver Killens, vii–x.

Giagnoni, Silvia. *Fields of Resistance: The Struggle of Florida's Farmworkers for Justice*. Chicago: Haymarket, 2011.

Giles, Paul. *The Global Remapping of American Literature*. Princeton: Princeton University Press, 2011.

Gilroy, Paul. *The Black Atlantic: Modernity and Double Consciousness*. London: Verso, 1993.

———. *Postcolonial Melancholia*. New York: Columbia University Press, 2005.

Gilyard, Keith. *John Oliver Killens: A Life of Black Literary Activism*. Athens: University of Georgia Press, 2010.

———. *Liberation Memories: The Rhetoric and Poetics of John Oliver Killens*. Detroit: Wayne State University Press, 2003.

Glanville, Brian. "When the *NS* met Malcolm X." *New Statesman*, April 29, 2013. Interview conducted June 12, 1964. www.newstatesman.com/world-affairs/2013/04/when-ns-met-malcolm-x (accessed January 3, 2017).

Gleason, William. *The Leisure Ethic: Work and Play in American Literature, 1840–1940*. Stanford: Stanford University Press, 1999.

Glissant, Édouard. *Faulkner, Mississippi*. Chicago: University of Chicago Press, 2000.

———. *Poetics of Relation*. Ann Arbor: University of Michigan Press, 1997.

Goldfield, David. "Unmelting the Ethnic South: Changing Boundaries of Race and Ethnicity in the Modern South." In *The American South in the Twentieth Century*, ed. Craig S. Pascoe, Karen Trahan Leathem, and Andy Ambrose. Athens: University of Georgia Press, 2005. 19–38.

Goodwin, Robert. *Crossing the Continent, 1527–1540: The Story of the First African-American Explorer of the American South.* New York: Harper, 2008.

Gould, Peter, and Rodney White. *Mental Maps.* London: Routledge, 1986.

Goyal, Yogita. "The Gender of Diaspora in Toni Morrison's *Tar Baby*." *Modern Fiction Studies* 52, no. 2 (Summer 2006): 393–414.

———. *Romance, Diaspora, and Black Atlantic Literature.* New York: Cambridge University Press, 2010.

Graham, Allison. "Free at Last: Post-Katrina New Orleans and the Future of Conspiracy." *Journal of American Studies* 44, no. 3 (August 2010): 601–11.

Gray, Jeffrey. "Essence and the Mulatto Traveler: Europe as Embodiment in Nella Larsen's *Quicksand*." *Novel: A Forum on Fiction* 27, no. 3 (Spring 1994): 257–70.

Greeson, Jennifer Rae. *Our South: Geographic Fantasy and the Rise of National Literature.* Cambridge: Harvard University Press, 2010.

Gregory, James N. *The Southern Diaspora: How the Great Migrations of Black and White Southerners Transformed America.* Chapel Hill: University of North Carolina Press, 2005.

Griffin, Farah Jasmine. *"Who Set You Flowin'?" The African-American Migration Narrative.* New York: Oxford University Press, 1996.

Groom, Nichola. "McDonald's Agrees to Pay More for Florida Tomatoes." *Reuters,* April 9, 2007, www.reuters.com/article/consumerproducts-SP/idUSN0933192520070409 (accessed January 8, 2017).

Gross, Robert. "The Transnational Turn: Rediscovering American Studies in a Wider World." *Journal of American Studies* 34, no. 3 (December 2000): 373–93.

"Guest Workers Tricked into Slavery." CNN, June 26, 2011, http://thecnnfreedomproject.blogs.cnn.com/2011/06/23/guest-workers-tricked-into-slavery (accessed January 5, 2017).

Guterl, Matthew Pratt. *American Mediterranean: Southern Slaveholders in the Age of Emancipation.* Cambridge: Harvard University Press, 2008.

Guthrie-Shimizu, Sayuri. "From Southeast Asia to the American Southeast: Japanese Business Meets the Sun Belt South." In *Globalization and the American South,* ed. Cobb and Stueck, 135–63.

Hahamovitch, Cindy. *No Man's Land: Jamaican Guestworkers in America and the Global History of Deportable Labor.* Princeton: Princeton University Press, 2011.

Handley, George B. *Postslavery Literatures in the Americas: Family Portraits in Black and White.* Charlottesville: University Press of Virginia, 2000.

Hannah, Barry. *Yonder Stands Your Orphan.* London: Atlantic Books, 2001.

Harker, Jaime. "Introduction: Cavaliers in Paradise: The U.S. South and the Pacific Rim." *The Global South* 3, no. 2 (fall 2009): 1–13.

Harold, Claudrena. "Reconfiguring the Roots and Routes of New Negro Activism: The Garvey Movement in New Orleans." In *Escape from New York: The New Negro Renaissance Beyond Harlem,* ed. Davarian L. Baldwin and Minkah Makalani. Minneapolis: University of Minnesota Press, 2013.

Hathaway, Heather. *Caribbean Waves: Relocating Claude McKay and Paule Marshall.* Bloomington: Indiana University Press, 1991.

Hathaway, Rosemary. "The Unbearable Weight of Authenticity: Zora Neale Hurston's *Their Eyes Were Watching God* and a Theory of 'Touristic Reading.'" *Journal of American Folklore* 117, no. 464 (2004): 168–90.

Haviland, Beverly. "Passing from Paranoia to Plagiarism: The Abject Authorship of Nella Larsen." *Modern Fiction Studies* 43, no. 2 (1997): 295–318.

Haywood, Harry. *Black Bolshevik: Autobiography of an Afro-American Communist*. Chicago: Liberator, 1978.

Hemenway, Robert. *Zora Neale Hurston: A Literary Biography*. Urbana: University of Illinois Press, 1977.

Henninger, Katherine. "Zora Neale Hurston, Richard Wright, and the Postcolonial Gaze." *Mississippi Quarterly* 56, no. 4 (Fall 2003): 581–95.

Hicks, Scott. "Rethinking King Cotton: George W. Lee, Zora Neale Hurston, and Global/Local Revisions of the South and the Nation." *Arizona Quarterly* 65, no. 4 (Winter 2009): 63–91.

Higashida, Cheryl. *Black Internationalist Feminism: Women Writers of the Black Left, 1945–1995*. Urbana: University of Illinois Press, 2011.

Hobson, Fred, and Barbara Ladd, eds. *The Oxford Handbook of the Literature of the U.S. South*. New York: Oxford University Press, 2016.

Hoffman, Frederick. *The Art of Southern Fiction*. Carbondale: Southern Illinois University Press, 1967.

Hunton, Alphaeus. "Why Worry about Africa?" In *No Easy Victories: African Liberation and American Activists over a Half Century, 1950–2000*, ed. William Minter, Gail Hovey, and Charles Cobb. Trenton, N.J.: Africa World Press, 2007. 73.

Hurston, Zora Neale. "Characteristics of Negro Expression." In *The Sanctified Church*, 49–68.

———. "Court Order Can't Make Races Mix." *Orlando Sentinel*, August 11, 1955. In *Hurston: A Life in Letters*, ed. Kaplan, 738–40.

———. "Dance Songs and Tales from the Bahamas." *Journal of American Folklore* 43 (July–September 1930): 294–312.

———. *Dust Tracks on a Road*. New York: HarperPerennial, 1991.

———. "The Fire Dance." In *Go Gator and Muddy the Water*, 153–56.

———. "The Fire Dance, January 25, 1939—8pm." Box 13, folder 6, Zora Neale Hurston Papers, Special and Area Studies Collections, George A. Smathers Libraries, University of Florida, Gainesville.

———. "Florida's Migrant Farm Worker." Manuscript box 10, Zora Neale Hurston Papers, Special and Area Studies Collections, George A. Smathers Libraries, University of Florida, Gainesville.

———. "Folklore." Manuscript box 12, Zora Neale Hurston Papers, Special and Area Studies Collections, George A. Smathers Libraries, University of Florida, Gainesville.

———. *Go Gator and Muddy the Water: Writings by Zora Neale Hurston from the Federal Writers Project*, ed. Pamela Bordelon. New York: W. W. Norton, 1999.

———. *Jonah's Gourd Vine*. New York: Perennial Library, 1990.

———. Letter to Langston Hughes, October 15, 1929. In *Zora Neale Hurston: A Life in Letters*, ed. Kaplan, 148–49.

———. *Mules and Men*. New York: Perennial Library, 1990.

———. "Other Negro Folklore Influences." In *Go Gator and Muddy the Water*, 89–93.

———. "The Sanctified Church." In *The Sanctified Church*, 103–7.

———. *The Sanctified Church: The Folklore Writings of Zora Neale Hurston*. Berkeley: Turtle Island, 1981.

———. "Spirituals and Neo-Spirituals." In *The Sanctified Church*, 79–84.
———. *Tell My Horse: Voodoo and Life in Haiti and Jamaica*. New York: Perennial Library, 1990.
———. *Their Eyes Were Watching God*. New York: HarperPerennial Modern Classics, 2006.
———. *Zora Neale Hurston: A Life in Letters*, ed. Carla Kaplan. New York: Anchor, 2002.
Hurt, R. Douglas, ed. *African-American Life in the Rural South*. Columbia: University Press of Missouri, 2003.
———. "Introduction." In *African-American Life in the Rural South, 1900–1950*, ed. Hurt, 1–9.
Hutchinson, George B. *In Search of Nella Larsen: A Biography of the Color Line*. Cambridge: Belknap Press of Harvard University Press, 2006.
———. "Nella Larsen and the Veil of Race." *American Literary History* 9, no. 2 (Summer 1997): 329–49.
———. "Subject to Disappearance: Interracial Identity in Nella Larsen's *Quicksand*." In *Temples for Tomorrow: Looking Back at the Harlem Renaissance*, ed. Genevieve Fabre and Michel Feith. Bloomington: Indiana University Press, 2001. 177–92.
Hutchison, Anthony. "Representative Man: John Brown and the Politics of Redemption in Russell Banks's *Cloudsplitter*." *Journal of American Studies* 41, no. 1 (April 2007): 67–82.
Inge, Thomas, ed. *Literature*. Volume 9 of *The New Encyclopedia of Southern Culture*. Chapel Hill: University of North Carolina Press, 2008.
"It Gets Even Worse." *New York Times*, July 3, 2011, www.nytimes.com/2011/07/04/opinion/04mon1.html?_r=0 (accessed January 5, 2017).
Jackson, Lawrence. *The Indignant Generation: A Narrative History of African American Writers and Critics, 1934–1960*. Princeton: Princeton University Press, 2011.
James, Cynthia. "Gender and Hemispheric Shifts in the Caribbean Narrative in English at the Close of the 20th Century: A Study of Paule Marshall's *Daughters* and Erna Brodber's *Louisiana*." *Jouvert* 5, no. 3, http://english.chass.ncsu.edu/jouvert/v5i3/cyja.htm (accessed January 12, 2017).
James, Jennifer C. *A Freedom Bought with Blood: African American War Literature from the Civil War to World War II*. Chapel Hill: University of North Carolina Press, 2007.
James, Rawn, Jr. *The Double V: How Wars, Protest, and Harry Truman Desegregated America's Military*. New York: Bloomsbury, 2013.
Jameson, Fredric. "The Brick and the Balloon: Architecture, Idealism, and Land Speculation." *New Left Review* 228 (March/April 1998): 25–46.
———. "Globalization and Political Strategy." *New Left Review* 4 (July–August 2000): 49–68.
———. *The Political Unconscious: Narrative as a Socially Symbolic Act*. London: Methuen, 1981.
———. *Postmodernism, or, the Cultural Logic of Late Capitalism*. London: Verso, 1991.
Jarmakani, Amira. *Imagining Arab Womanhood: The Cultural Mythology of Veils, Harems, and Belly Dancers in the U.S.* New York: Palgrave Macmillan, 2008.
Jaynes, Gregory. "33 Haitians Drown as Boat Capsizes off Florida." *New York Times*, October 27, 1981, A1.
Jin, Ha. *A Free Life*. New York: Pantheon, 2007.
———. *The Writer as Migrant*. Chicago: University of Chicago Press, 2008.

Johnson, Howard. *The Bahamas in Slavery and Freedom*. Kingston, Jamaica: Ian Randle, 1991.

Johnson, James Weldon. *The Autobiography of an Ex-Colored Man*. New York: Penguin Classics, 1990.

Jones, Suzanne W. "Who Is a Southern Writer?" *American Literature* 78, no. 4 (August 2006): 725–27.

Jones, W. Glyn. *Denmark: A Modern History*. London: Croom Helm, 1986.

Jung, Moon Ho. *Coolies and Cane: Race, Labor, and Sugar in the Age of Emancipation*. Baltimore: Johns Hopkins University Press, 2006.

Kakutani, Michiko. "Books of the Times." Review of Russell Banks's *Continental Drift*. *New York Times*, February 27, 1985, late city final edition, C20.

Kaye-Smith, Sheila. "Mrs Adis." *The Century Magazine* 103, no. 3 (January 1922): 321–26.

Kelley, Robin D. G. *Race Rebels: Culture, Politics, and the Black Working Class*. New York: The Free Press, 1994.

Khokher, Reginald. "Dialoguing Borders: The African Diasporic Consciousness in Erna Brodber's *Louisiana*." *Canadian Woman Studies / Les Cahiers de la Femme* 23, no. 2 (Winter 2004): 38–42.

Killens, John Oliver. "Address to the Association for the Study of Negro Life and Culture [Montgomery, Alabama, 1957]." Box 52, folder 23, John Oliver Killens Papers, Stuart A. Rose Manuscript, Archives, and Rare Book Library, Emory University.

———. *And Then We Heard the Thunder*. New York: Alfred A. Knopf, 1963.

———. *And Then We Heard the Thunder*, typescript version 2. Box 27, folder 3, John Oliver Killens Papers, Stuart A. Rose Manuscript, Archives, and Rare Book Library, Emory University.

———. "Battle of Brisbane." Box 28, folder 4, John Oliver Killens Papers, Stuart A. Rose Manuscript, Archives, and Rare Book Library, Emory University.

———. "Black Man's Burden." In *Black Man's Burden*, 147–76.

———. *Black Man's Burden*. New York: Trident Press, 1965.

———. "The Black Psyche." In *Black Man's Burden*, 1–22.

———. "Downsouth-Upsouth." In *Black Man's Burden*, 55–96.

———. "For National Freedom." *New Foundations* 2, no. 4 (Summer 1949): 245–58.

———. "Introduction." In *Black Southern Voices: An Anthology of Fiction, Poetry, Drama, Nonfiction, and Critical Essays*, ed. Killens and Jerry Ward. New York: Meridian, 1992. 1–4.

———. Letter to *Pittsburgh Courier*, October 19, 1954. Box 20, folder 9, John Oliver Killens Papers, Stuart A. Rose Manuscript, Archives, and Rare Book Library, Emory University.

———. *Lower Than the Angels*. Unpublished play, 1960. Box 74, folder 4, and microfiche roll 23, Free Southern Theater records, 1963–1978, Amistad Research Center, Tulane University.

———. "The Myth of Non-Violence versus the Right of Self-Defense." In *Black Man's Burden*, 97–123.

———. Notebook with "story ideas, 1945." Box 55, folder 5, John Oliver Killens Papers, Stuart A. Rose Manuscript, Archives, and Rare Book Library, Emory University.

———. *'Sippi*. New York: Trident Press, 1967.

———. *Youngblood*. Athens: University of Georgia Press, 1982.

King, Richard H. "Allegories of Imperialism: Globalizing Southern Studies." *American Literary History* 23, no. 1 (2010): 148–58.

Kleinberg, Elliot. *Black Cloud: The Deadly Hurricane of 1928.* New York: Carroll and Graf, 2003.

Kolodny, Annette. *The Lay of the Land: Metaphor as Experience and History in American Life and Letters.* Chapel Hill: University of North Carolina Press, 1975.

Kreyling, Michael. *Inventing Southern Literature.* Jackson: University Press of Mississippi, 1998.

———. *The South That Wasn't There: Postsouthern Memory and History.* Baton Rouge: Louisiana State University Press, 2010.

Kurotani, Sawa. "The South Meets the East: Japanese Professionals in North Carolina's Research Triangle." In *The American South in a Global World*, ed. Peacock, Watson, and Matthews, 175–91.

Kutzinski, Vera. "Borders and Bodies: The United States, America, and the Caribbean." *CR: New Centennial Review* 1, no. 2 (2001): 55–88.

Kyriakoudes, Louis M. "'Lookin' for Better All the Time': Rural Migration and Urbanization in the South, 1900–1950." In *African-American Life in the Rural South*, ed. Hurt, 10–26.

Ladd, Barbara. "Literary Studies: The Southern United States, 2005." *PMLA* 120, no. 5 (October 2005): 1628–39.

Lalami, Laila. *The Moor's Account.* New York: Pantheon, 2014.

Lamothe, Daphne. "Vodou Imagery, African American Tradition and Cultural Transformation in Zora Neale Hurston's *Their Eyes Were Watching God*." *Callaloo* 22, no. 1 (1999): 157–75.

Larsen, Nella. *Quicksand.* Ed. Thadious M. Davis. New York: Penguin Classics, 2002.

———. "Sanctuary." In *An Intimation of Things Distant: The Collected Fiction of Nella Larsen.* New York: Anchor, 1992.

Larson, Charles. *Invisible Darkness: Jean Toomer and Nella Larsen.* Iowa City: University of Iowa Press, 1993.

Larson, Kelli A. "Surviving the Taint of Plagiarism: Nella Larsen's 'Sanctuary' and Sheila Kaye-Smith's 'Mrs Adis.'" *Journal of Modern Literature* 30, no. 4 (Summer 2007): 82–104.

Lassiter, Matthew, and Joseph D. Crespino. "Introduction: The End of Southern History." In *The Myth of Southern Exceptionalism*, ed. Lassiter and Crespino, 3–22.

———, eds. *The Myth of Southern Exceptionalism.* New York: Oxford University Press, 2010.

Leahy, John. "Seeking a Place in the Sun." Review of Russell Banks's *Continental Drift*. *San Francisco Examiner-Chronicle*, June 16, 1985, 8.

LeClair, Tom. "A History of Violence." Review of Peter Matthiessen's *Shadow Country*. *New York Times*, April 27, 2008, www.nytimes.com/2008/04/27/books/review/LeClair-t.html (accessed January 1, 2017).

Lee, Don. "About Russell Banks." *Ploughshares* 19, no. 4 (Winter 1993/1994), www.pshares.org/issues/winter-1993-94/about-russell-banks-profile (accessed January 6, 2017).

Lehman, Paul. *The Development of the Black Psyche in the Writings of John Oliver Killens, 1916–1987.* Lewiston, N.Y.: Edwin Mellen Press, 2003.

Levine, Daniel. *Poverty and Society: The Development of the American Welfare State in International Comparison*. New Brunswick, N.J.: Rutgers University Press, 1988.

Levitt, Peggy. *The Transnational Villagers*. Berkeley: University of California Press, 2001.

Lichtenstein, Alex. *Twice the Work of Free Labor: The Political Economy of Convict Labor in the New South*. London: Verso, 1996.

Lightweis-Goff, Jennie. "'Peculiar and Characteristic': New Orleans Exceptionalism from Olmsted to the Deluge." *American Literature* 86, no. 1 (June 2014): 147–69.

Link, William A., David Brown, Brian Ward, and Martyn Bone, eds. *Creating Citizenship in the Nineteenth-Century South*. Gainesville: University Press of Florida, 2013.

Lloyd, Christopher. *Rooting Memory, Rooting Place: Regionalism in the Twenty-First Century American South*. New York: Palgrave Macmillan, 2015.

Locke, Alain. "Harlem." *Survey Graphic* (March 1925). http://xroads.virginia.edu/~drbr/locke_2.html (accessed January 3, 2017).

Locoge, Valentin. "An Interview with Russell Banks." In *Conversations with Russell Banks*, ed. Roche, 152–62.

Loewen, James W. *The Mississippi Chinese: Between Black and White*. Cambridge, Mass.: Harvard University Press, 1971.

Lowe, John. "'Calypso Magnolia': The Caribbean Side of the South." *South Central Review* 22, no. 1 (Spring 2005): 54–80.

Lukács, Georg. "Specific Particularity as the Central Category of Aesthetics." In *The Continental Aesthetics Reader*, ed. Clive Cazeaux. London: Routledge, 2000. 220–33.

Lunde, Arne, and Anna Stenport. "Helga Crane's Copenhagen: Denmark, Colonialism, and Transnational Identity in Nella Larsen's *Quicksand*." *Comparative Literature* 60, no. 3 (2008): 228–43.

Lydersen, Kari. "Some Immigrants Suffer Doubly after Hurricane Katrina." *The New Standard*, September 28, 2005, http://newstandardnews.net/content/index.cfm/items/2410 (accessed December 20, 2016).

Lytle, Andrew. "The Hind Tit." In *I'll Take My Stand: The South and the Agrarian Tradition*, by Twelve Southerners. Baton Rouge: Louisiana State University Press, 1977. 201–45.

Macherey, Pierre. *A Theory of Literary Production*. London: Routledge and Kegan Paul, 1978.

Marable, Manning. *Malcolm X: A Life of Reinvention*. New York: Viking, 2011.

Marston, Sallie, Kevin Ward, and John Paul Jones. "Scale." In *The Dictionary of Human Geography*, 5th ed., ed. Derek Gregory et al. Oxford: Wiley-Blackwell, 2009. 664–66.

Martin, Cheryl English, and Charles H. Martin. Review of *Look Away! The U.S. South in New World Studies*. *Journal of Southern History* 72, no. 1 (February 2006): 238–40.

Martin, Tony. *Race First: The Ideological and Organization Struggles of Marcus Garvey and the Universal Negro Improvement Association*. Westport, Conn.: Greenwood Press, 1976.

Maslin, Janet. "News Story Inspired Banks's 'Drift.'" *New York Times*, April 29, 1985, www.nytimes.com/1985/04/29/books/news-story-inspired-banks-s-drift.html (accessed 6 January, 2017).

Matthiessen, Peter. *Shadow Country*. New York: Modern Library, 2008.

Maxwell, William J. *F. B. Eyes: How J. Edgar Hoover's Ghostreaders Framed African American Literature*. Princeton: Princeton University Press, 2015.

McKee, Kathryn, and Annette Trefzer. "Preface: Global Contexts, Local Literatures: The New Southern Studies." *American Literature* 78, no. 4 (December 2006): 677–90.

McNulty, Thomas. *Errol Flynn: The Life and Career.* Jefferson, N.C.: McFarland, 2004.

McPherson, Tara. "Afterword: After Authenticity." In *Creating and Consuming the American South*, ed. Bone, Ward, and Link, 309–23.

———. "On Wal-Mart and Southern Studies." *American Literature* 78, no. 4 (December 2006): 695–98.

———. *Reconstructing Dixie: Race, Gender, and Nostalgia in the Imagined South.* Durham, N.C.: Duke University Press, 2003.

Mencken, H. L. "The Sahara of the Bozart." In *Prejudices: Second Series*. New York: Alfred A. Knopf, 1920. 136–54.

Miller, Joshua L. *Accented America: The Cultural Politics of Multilingual Modernism.* New York: Oxford University Press, 2011.

Mohl, Raymond. "Globalization, Latinization, and the *Nuevo* New South." In *Globalization and the American South*, ed. Cobb and Stueck, 66–99.

Monteith, Sharon. "Southern Like U.S.?" *The Global South* 1, no. 1 (Winter 2007): 66–74.

Monteith, Sharon, and Nahem Yousaf. "Making an Impression: New Immigrant Fiction in the Contemporary South." *Forum for Modern Language Studies* 40, no. 2 (2004): 214–24.

Morrison, Toni. *Home.* New York: Alfred A. Knopf, 2012.

———. *Tar Baby.* New York: Alfred A. Knopf, 1981.

Muller, Gilbert H. *New Strangers in Paradise: The Immigrant Experience and Contemporary American Fiction.* Lexington: University Press of Kentucky, 1999.

Muthyala, John. *Reworlding America: Myth, History, and Narrative.* Athens: Ohio University Press, 2006.

Mykle, Robert. *Killer 'Cane: The Deadly Hurricane of 1928.* New York: Cooper Square Press, 2003.

Naylor, Gloria. "A Conversation: Gloria Naylor and Toni Morrison." In *Conversations with Toni Morrison*, ed. Danille Taylor-Guthrie. Jackson: University Press of Mississippi, 1994. 188–217.

Nelson, Michael, and John Lyman Mason. "Mississippi: The Politics of Casino Gambling." In *Resorting to Casinos*, ed. von Herrmann, 26–46.

Ness, Immanuel. *Southern Insurgency: The Coming of the Global Working Class.* London: Pluto Press, 2016.

"The New Southern Studies: An Interview with Jon Smith and Deborah Cohn." *Society for the Study of Southern Literature Newsletter* 47, no. 1 (Spring 2013), http://southernlit.org/society-for-the-study-of-southern-literature-newsletter-47-1-spring-2013 (accessed January 5, 2017).

Nicholls, David G. "Migrant Labor, Folklore, and Resistance in Hurston's Polk County: Reframing *Mules and Men*." *African American Review* 33, no. 3 (Autumn 1999): 467–79.

Niemi, Robert. *Russell Banks.* New York: Twayne, 1997.

Nonini, Donald M. "Critique: Creating the Transnational South." In *The American South in a Global World*, ed. Peacock, Watson, and Matthews, 247–64.

Northrup, Herbert R. "The New Orleans Longshoremen." *Political Science Quarterly* 57, no. 4 (December 1942): 526–44.

Nossiter, Adam. "Mauritania Confronts Long Legacy of Slavery." *New York Times*, November 11, 2013, www.nytimes.com/2013/11/12/world/africa/mauritania

-confronts-long-legacy-of-slavery.html?pagewanted=all&_r=0 (accessed January 8, 2017).

Nwankwo, Ifeoma. *Black Cosmopolitanism: Racial Consciousness and Transnational Identity in the Nineteenth-Century Americas*. Philadelphia: University of Pennsylvania Press, 2005.

O'Brien, Michael. "Epilogue: Place as Everywhere." In *Creating Citizenship in the Nineteenth-Century South*, ed. Link, Brown, Ward, and Bone, 271–89.

Odem, Mary E. "Latin American Immigration and the New Multiethnic South." In *The Myth of Southern Exceptionalism*, ed. Lassiter and Crespino, 234–60.

Pavlić, Edward M. "'Papa Legba, Ouvrier Barriere por Moi Passer': Esu in *Their Eyes* and Zora Neale Hurston's Diasporic Modernism." *African American Review* 38, no. 1 (Spring 2004): 61–85.

Peacock, James L. *Grounded Globalism: How the U.S. South Embraces the World*. Athens: University of Georgia Press, 2010.

———. "The South and Grounded Globalism." In *The American South in a Global World*, ed. Peacock, Watson, and Matthews, 265–76.

Peacock, James L., Harry L. Watson, and Carrie R. Matthews, eds. *The American South in a Global World*. Chapel Hill: University of North Carolina Press, 2005.

———. "Introduction: Globalization with a Southern Face." In *The American South in a Global World*, ed. Peacock, Watson, and Matthews, 1–5.

Pfister, Joel. "Transnational American Studies for What?" *Comparative American Studies* 6, no. 1 (2008): 13–36.

Pinto, Samantha. *Difficult Diasporas: The Transnational Feminist Aesthetic of the Black Atlantic*. New York: New York University Press, 2013.

Pomeroy, William. "Killens 'Thunders.'" Review of *And Then We Heard the Thunder*, by John Oliver Killens. *National Guardian*, May 9, 1963, 10.

Price, Rachael. "'The Void and the Missing': History, Mystery, and Throwaway Bodies in Monique Truong's *Bitter in the Mouth*." *North Carolina Literary Review* 24 (2015): 50–64.

Reeves, Trish. "The Search for Clarity: An Interview with Russell Banks." In *Conversations with Russell Banks*, ed. Roche, 15–25.

Regis, Helen A. "Introduction." In *Caribbean and Southern: Transnational Perspectives on the U.S. South*, ed. Regis. Athens: University of Georgia Press, 2006. 1–6.

Reimers, David M. "Asian Immigrants in the South." In *Globalization and the American South*, ed. Cobb and Stueck, 100–134.

Richardson, Riché. "'A house set off from the rest': Ralph Ellison's Rural Geography." *Forum for Modern Language Studies* 40, no. 2 (2004): 126–44.

———. "Southern Turns." *Mississippi Quarterly* 56, no. 4 (Fall 2003): 555–79.

———. "The World and the U.S. South." *American Literature* 78, no. 4 (December 2006): 722–24.

Ring, Natalie. "An Irony of Ironies: The Discipline of History in the New Southern Studies." *Journal of American Studies* 48, no. 3 (August 2014): 706–12.

Roach, Joseph. *Cities of the Dead: Circum-Atlantic Performance*. New York: Columbia University Press, 1996.

Robertson, J. C. "Interview with Cynthia Shearer." *Southern Literary Review*, May 7, 2009, http://southernlitreview.com/authors/cynthia_shearer_interview.htm (accessed January 8, 2017).

Roche, David, ed. *Conversations with Russell Banks*. Jackson: University Press of Mississippi, 2010.

———. "Russell Banks, Toulouse 2006." In *Conversations with Russell Banks*, ed. Roche, 163–81.

Rodrigue, John C. *Reconstruction in the Cane Fields: From Slavery to Free Labor in Louisiana's Sugar Parishes, 1862–1880*. Baton Rouge: Louisiana State University Press, 2001.

Roediger, David R. *The Wages of Whiteness: Race and the Making of the American Working Class*. 3rd ed. New York: Verso, 2006.

Rolinson, Mary G. *Grassroots Garveyism: The Universal Negro Improvement Association in the Rural South, 1920–1927*. Chapel Hill: University of North Carolina Press, 2007.

Romine, Scott. "Orphans All: Reality Homesickness in *Yonder Stands Your Orphan*." In *Perspectives on Barry Hannah*, ed. Martyn Bone. Jackson: University Press of Mississippi, 2007. 161–82.

———. *The Real South: Southern Narrative in the Age of Cultural Reproduction*. Baton Rouge: Louisiana State University Press, 2008.

Rowe, John Carlos. *Literary Culture and U.S. Imperialism: From the Revolution to World War II*. Oxford: Oxford University Press, 2000.

Rubin, Louis D., and Robert D. Jacobs. "Introduction: Southern Writing and the Changing South." In *South: Modern Southern Literature in Its Cultural Setting*, ed. Rubin and Jacobs. Garden City, N.Y.: Doubleday, 1961. 11–25.

Rushing, Wanda. *Memphis and the Paradox of Place: Globalization in the American South*. Chapel Hill: University of North Carolina Press, 2009.

Ryan, Maureen. "Outsiders with Insider Information: The Vietnamese in the Fiction of the Contemporary American South." In *South to a New Place: Region, Literature, Culture*, ed. Suzanne W. Jones and Sharon Monteith. Baton Rouge: Louisiana State University Press, 2002. 235–52.

Sassen, Saskia. "A Savage Sorting of Winners and Losers: Contemporary Versions of Primitive Accumulation." *Globalizations* 7, nos. 1–2 (March–June 2010): 23–50.

Saunders, Kay. "In a Cloud of Lust: Black GIs and Sex in World War II." In *Gender and War: Australians at War in the Twentieth Century*, ed. Joy Damousi and Marilyn Lake. Cambridge: Cambridge University Press, 1995. 178–90.

Scheiber, Dave. "The Wrong They Could Not Bury." *St. Petersburg (Florida) Times*, February 25, 2001, www.sptimes.com/News/022501/news_pf/Floridian/The_wrong_they_could_.shtml (accessed December 21, 2016).

Segars, Neil. "How to Be Chinese in Mississippi: Representations of a Chinese Grocer in Cynthia Shearer's *The Celestial Jukebox*." *The Global South* 3, no. 2 (Fall 2009): 50–63.

Shearer, Cynthia. *The Celestial Jukebox*. Washington, D.C.: Shoemaker & Hoard, 2005.

Silver, James W. *Mississippi: The Closed Society*. New York: Harcourt, Brace and World, 1964.

Silverman, Debra. "Nella Larsen's *Quicksand*: Untangling the Webs of Exoticism." *African American Review* 27, no. 4 (Winter 1993): 599–614.

Smith, Barbara Ellen. "Place and Past in the Global South." *American Literature* 78, no. 4 (December 2006): 693–95.

Smith, Dave. Letter to Ted Solotaroff, November 2, 1984. Box 16, folder 5, Russell Banks Papers, Harry Ransom Center, University of Texas at Austin.

Smith, Jon. *Finding Purple America: The South and the Future of American Cultural Studies*. Athens: University of Georgia Press, 2013.

———. "The State of United States Southern Literary Studies." *PMLA* 121, no. 2 (2006): 549–50.

———. "Toward a Post-postpolitical Southern Studies: On the Limits of the 'Creating and Consuming' Paradigm." In *Creating and Consuming the American South*, ed. Bone, Ward, and Link, 72–94.

———. "The U.S. South and the Future of the Postcolonial." *The Global South* 1, no. 1 (Winter 2007): 153–58.

Smith, Jon, and Deborah Cohn. "Introduction: Uncanny Hybridities." In *Look Away! The U.S. South and New World Studies*, ed. Smith and Cohn. Durham, N.C.: Duke University Press, 2004. 1–19.

Smith, Neil. "Contours of a Spatialized Poetics: Homeless Vehicles and the Production of Geographical Scale." *Social Text* 33 (1992): 54–81.

Smith-Nonini, Sandy. "Federally Sponsored Mexican Migrants in the Transnational South." In *The American South in a Global World*, ed. Peacock, Watson, and Matthews, 59–79.

Soja, Edward, *Postmodern Geographies: The Reassertion of Space in Critical Social Theory*. London: Verso, 1989.

Sollors, Werner. *Neither White nor Black Yet Both: Thematic Explorations of Interracial Literature*. Cambridge, Mass.: Harvard University Press, 1997.

Sonnenberg, Brittani. *Home Leave*. New York: Grand Central, 2014.

Squint, Kirstin, with Nahem Yousaf. "Both Souths That I've Known: An Interview with Monique Truong." *North Carolina Literary Review* 24 (2015): 38–49.

Stecopoulos, Harilaos. *Reconstructing the World: Southern Fictions and U.S. Imperialisms, 1898–1976*. Ithaca, N.Y.: Cornell University Press, 2008.

Stepick, Alex, III. "The Refugees Nobody Wants: Haitians in Miami." In *Miami Now! Immigration, Ethnicity, and Social Change*, ed. Guillermo J. Grenier and Alex Stepick III. Gainesville: University Press of Florida, 1992. 57–82.

Stepto, Robert. *From Behind the Veil: A Study of Afro-American Narrative*. Urbana: University of Illinois Press, 1979.

Strange, Susan. *Casino Capitalism*. Manchester: Manchester University Press, 1997.

Striffler, Steve. "We're All Mexicans Here: Poultry Processing, Latino Migration, and the Transformation of Class in the South." In *The American South in a Global World*, ed. Peacock, Watson, and Matthews, 152–71.

Subramanian, Ajantha. "North Carolina's Indians: Erasing Race to Make the Citizen." In *The American South in a Global World*, ed. Peacock, Watson, and Matthews, 192–201.

Sundquist, Eric J. *The Hammers of Creation: Folk Culture in Modern African-American Fiction*. Athens: University of Georgia Press, 1992.

Tang, Eric. "A Gulf Unites Us: The Vietnamese Americans of Black New Orleans East." *American Quarterly* 63, no. 1 (March 2011): 117–49.

Tanoukhi, Nirvana. "The Scale of World Literature." In *Immanuel Wallerstein and the Problem of the World: System, Scale, Culture*, ed. David Palumbo-Liu, Bruce Robbins, and Nirvana Tanoukhi. Durham, N.C.: Duke University Press, 2011. 78–98.

Tate, Allen. "The New Provincialism: With an Epilogue on the Southern Novel." In *Essays of Four Decades*. Chicago: Swallow, 1968. 535–46.

Taylor, Helen. *Circling Dixie: Contemporary Southern Culture through a Transatlantic Lens*. New Brunswick, N.J.: Rutgers University Press, 2001.

———. "Recovering through a Cultural Economy: New Orleans from Katrina to Deepwater Horizon." In *Creating and Consuming the American South*, ed. Bone, Ward, and Link, 178–99.

Taylor, Melanie Benson. "Faulkner and Southern Studies." In *The New Cambridge Companion to William Faulkner*, ed. John T. Matthews. New York: Cambridge University Press, 2015. 119–33.

Taylor, Stuart, Jr. "Deciding How to Stop Haitians—And Why." *New York Times*, November 1, 1981, E4.

Thompson, Graham. "Roundtable." *Journal of American Studies* 48, no. 4 (November 2014): 1082–86.

Tinsman, Heidi, and Sandhya Shukla. "Introduction: Across the Americas." In *Imagining Our Americas: Toward a Transnational Frame*, ed. Tinsman and Shukla. Durham, N.C.: Duke University Press, 2007. 1–33.

Toland-Dix, Shirley. "'This Is the Horse. Will You Ride?' Zora Neale Hurston, Erna Brodber, and Rituals of Spirit Possession." In *Just Below South*, ed. Adams, Bibler, and Accilien, 199–210.

Tolnay, Stewart E., and E. M. Beck. "Racial Violence and Black Migration in the American South, 1910 to 1930." *American Sociological Review* 57, no. 1 (February 1992): 103–16.

"Transcript of Russell Banks Interview Talk Show." October 15, 2003, Western Washington University. http://pandora.cii.wwu.edu/banks/Banks_transcript.pdf (accessed January 6, 2017).

Trefzer, Annette. "Possessing the Self: Caribbean Identities in Zora Neale Hurston's *Tell My Horse*." *African American Review* 34, no. 2 (Summer 2000): 299–312.

Trethewey, Natasha. *Beyond Katrina: A Meditation on the Mississippi Gulf Coast*. Athens: University of Georgia Press, 2010.

Trevitte, Chad. "An Interview with Russell Banks (2000)." In *Conversations with Russell Banks*, ed. Roche, 109–30.

Trucks, Rob. "Interview (1999)." In *Conversations with Russell Banks*, ed. Roche, 94–108.

Truong, Monique. *Bitter in the Mouth*. New York: Random House, 2011.

Turner, Lorenzo Dow. *Africanisms in the Gullah Dialect*. Chicago: University of Chicago Press, 1949.

von Herrmann, Denise. "The Casino Resort Solution to Mississippi's Problems: An Introduction." In *Resorting to Casinos*, ed. von Herrmann, 3–10.

———, ed. *Resorting to Casinos: The Mississippi Gambling Industry*. Jackson: University Press of Mississippi, 2006.

Vorre, Birgit. "The Market as a Place of Work: A Study of the Fishwives' Trade at 'Gammel Strand' in Copenhagen." *Ethnologia Scandinavica: A Journal for Nordic Ethnology* 7 (1977): 12–45.

Wald, Alan. *Trinity of Passion: The Literary Left and the Antifascist Crusade*. Chapel Hill: University of North Carolina Press, 2007.

Walker, Alice. "Beyond the Peacock: The Reconstruction of Flannery O'Connor." In *In Search of Our Mothers' Gardens*. 42–59.

———. *In Search of Our Mothers' Gardens: Womanist Prose*. London: The Women's Press, 1984.

———. "Zora Neale Hurston—A Cautionary Tale and a Partisan View." In *In Search of Our Mothers' Gardens*. 83–92.

Walker, Joseph. "An American Author's Views on Freedom: Says Negroes Pushing for the Right to Fight Back." *Muhammad Speaks*, March 3, 1963, 19.

Wall, Cheryl A. *Women of the Harlem Renaissance*. Bloomington: Indiana University Press, 1995.

Wallerstein, Immanuel. *The Modern World-System: Mercantilism and the Consolidation of the European World-Economy, 1600–1750*. San Diego: Academic Press, 1980.

Walton, Shana. "Introduction: Ethnicity in Mississippi: Stories Worth Telling." In *Ethnic Heritage in Mississippi*, ed. Walton and Carpenter, 3–11.

Walton, Shana, and Barbara Carpenter, eds. *Ethnic Heritage in Mississippi: The Twentieth Century*. Jackson: University Press of Mississippi, 2012.

Ward, Brian. "Caryl Phillips, David Armitage, and the Place of the American South in Atlantic and Other Worlds." In *The American South and the Atlantic World*, ed. Ward, Bone, and Link, 8–44.

Ward, Brian, Martyn Bone, and William Link, eds. *The American South and the Atlantic World*. Gainesville: University Press of Florida, 2013.

Warren, Robert Penn. "Literature as a Symptom." In *Who Owns America? A New Declaration of Independence*, ed. Herbert Agar and Allen Tate. Wilmington, Del.: ISI Books, 1999. 343–62.

Washburne, Christopher. "The Clave of Jazz: A Caribbean Contribution to the Rhythmic Foundation of an African-American Music." *Black Music Research Journal* 17, no. 1 (spring 1997): 59–80.

Watson, Harry L. "Southern History, Southern Future: Some Reflections and a Cautious Forecast." In *The American South in a Global World*, ed. Peacock, Watson, and Matthews, 1–5.

Weaks-Baxter, Mary. *Reclaiming the American Farmer: The Reinvention of a Regional Mythology in Twentieth-Century Southern Writing*. Baton Rouge: Louisiana State University Press, 2006.

Wegmann-Sánchez, Jessica. "Rewriting Race and Ethnicity across the Border: Mairuth Sarsfield's *No Crystal Chair* and Nella Larsen's *Quicksand* and *Passing*." *Essays on Canadian Writing* 74 (Fall 2001): 136–65.

Weitzmann, Marc. "Russell Banks: Views from the American Crossroads." In *Conversations with Russell Banks*, ed. Roche, 136–41.

Willerslev, Rich. *Sådan boede vi: Arbejdernes boligforhold i København omkring 1880*. Copenhagen: Akademisk Forlag, 1979.

Willis, Susan. *Specifying: Black Women Writing the American Experience*. Madison: University of Wisconsin Press, 1987.

Wilson, Rob. "Tracking the 'China Peril' along the U.S. Pacific Rim." In *Imagining Our Americas*, ed. Shukla and Tinsman, 168–89.

Wilson, Rob, and Wimal Dissanayake. "Introduction: Tracking the Global/Local." In *Global/Local: Cultural Production and the Transnational Imaginary*, ed. Wilson and Dissanayake. Durham, N.C.: Duke University Press, 1996. 1–18.

Winders, Jamie, and Barbara Smith. "New Pasts: Historicizing Immigration, Race and Place in the South." *Southern Spaces*, November 4, 2010, www.southernspaces.org/2010/new-pasts-historicizing-immigration-race-and-place-south (accessed January 5, 2017).

Wittmann, Dena C. "A Day in the Night of a Casino Worker: Shift Work Culture of Mississippi Dockside Gaming Employees." In *Resorting to Casinos*, ed. von Herrmann, 121–42.

Woodson, Jon. "Zora Neale Hurston's *Their Eyes Were Watching God* and the Influence of Jens Peter Jacobsen's *Marie Grubbe*." *African American Review* 26, no. 4 (Winter 1992): 619–35.

Woodward, C. Vann. *The Origins of the New South, 1877–1913*. Baton Rouge: Louisiana State University Press, 1951.

Wright, Richard. "Between Laughter and Tears." Review of *Their Eyes Were Watching God*, by Zora Neale Hurston. *New Masses*, October 5, 1937, http://people.virginia.edu/~sfr/enam358/wrightrev.html (accessed December 20, 2016).

———. "Down by the Riverside." In *Uncle Tom's Children*. New York: HarperPerennial, 1993. 62–124.

Wylie, J. J. "Reinventing Realism: An Interview with Russell Banks." *Michigan Quarterly Review* 39, no. 4 (Fall 2000): 737–53.

Yaeger, Patricia. *Dirt and Desire: Reconstructing Southern Women's Writing, 1930–1990*. Chicago: University of Chicago Press, 2000.

Yousaf, Nahem. "Immigrant Writers: Transnational Stories of a 'Worlded' South." In *The Cambridge Companion to Literature of the American South*, ed. Sharon Monteith. Cambridge: Cambridge University Press, 2013. 204–19.

Zink, Nell. *Mislaid*. London: Fourth Estate, 2015.

INDEX

Abernathy, Ralph, 91
Aboul-Ela, Hosam, 11, 19, 217n53
Absalom, Absalom! (Faulkner), 22, 185, 199, 203, 219n103
Accilien, Cécile, 126; *Just Below South* (ed. with Adams and Bibler), 107
Adams, Jessica, 129, 162–63, 210; *Just Below South* (ed. with Accilien and Bibler), 107; *Wounds of Returning*, 20
"Adjutant Bird, The" (Banks), 109
Adorno, Theodor, 171
Affliction (Banks), 106
African Blood Brotherhood (ABB), 238–39n51
Agrarians, ix, 109, 158; neo-Agrarianism, 9, 18, 26–27, 30, 39, 79
Alabama, 78, 212; convict labor, 12; HB56 law, 14; in Hurston's *Jonah's Gourd Vine*, 33–35; in Killens' *Youngblood*, 82, 84; in Larsen's *Quicksand*, 55, 70–74, 77; Tuskegee Institute, 56; in world-system, 24
American exceptionalism, 7, 79, 96
American Literature (journal), 2, 16, 17, 79
American Mediterranean (Guterl), 3
American South and the Atlantic World, The (ed. Ward, Bone, and Link), 25
American South in a Global World, The (ed. Peacock, Watson, and Matthews), 1, 19, 217n53
American studies, ix–x, xi, 29, 214; region and, 2–3, 25–26; scale and, 25–26, 214; transnational turn and, ix–x, xvii, 7, 16–17, 23, 176, 196, 214, 217n55; transpacific turn and, xvi, 176
Anderson, Eric Gary, 212, 247n43
Anderson, Karyn H., 170, 242n57
And Then We Heard the Thunder (Killens), xiv, xviii, 81, 84, 88, 92–105, 231n54, 232n72
Angelou, Maya, 78–79, 84
Apter, Emily, 138
Arizona, 1
Arkansas, 7, 15, 161, 185, 186
Arnesen, Eric, 143, 149
Atlanta, Ga., xvii, 9, 55, 58, 77, 85, 126, 207, 208; as "international city," 21, 24, 194; in Jin's *A Free Life*, 178, 188–93; in Sonnenberg's *Home Leave*, 193–94
Australia, xiv, 90, 193, 234n21; Killens in, 98; in Killens's *And Then We Heard the Thunder*, 93, 98–102, 232n70; White Australia policy, 100–102, 232n70; in World War II, 98–100
Authentic Blackness (Favor), 54
Autobiography of an Ex-Colored Man, The (Johnson), 74
Autobiography of Miss Jane Pittman, The (Gaines), 153

Bahamas, 41, 42, 118, 128, 136, 150, 177; Bahamian immigrants in Hurston's *Their Eyes Were Watching God*, xiii, 32, 42–52 passim, 150–51, 236n73; Bahamian immigrants in U.S. South, 32, 42–43, 128, 130, 223nn62–63, 223n65, 224n75, 224n85; in Banks's fiction, 119, 124–25; Hurston and, 46
Baker, Houston, 56–60, 137, 169; new southern studies and, ix–x, xiv, 16–17; southern folk aesthetics and, 31, 53–54, 79, 80, 199, 225n5
—works of: *I Don't Hate the South*, 60; *Modernism and the Harlem Renaissance*, 56; *Turning South Again*, 16–17, 56–59; *Workings of the Spirit*, 31, 53–54, 56
Baldwin, James, 78
Bales, Kevin, 170
Banks, Russell, xi, xiv–xv, 106–34 passim, 152, 162, 184, 191; in Florida, 108; Hurston and, 108, 124–26; in Jamaica, 109, 233n19; "north-south axis" and, 107, 122, 134; at University of North Carolina, 108
—works of: "The Adjutant Bird," 109; *Affliction*, 106; *The Book of Jamaica*, xiv, xv, 108, 109–11, 113–18, 126, 129, 133; *Continental Drift*, xv, 107–8, 118–34 passim, 137, 148, 152, 153, 162, 171, 191; *The Darling*, 106; *Hamilton Stark*, 109; *Lost Memory of Skin*, 133; *Rule of the Bone*, 132–33, 184; *The Sweet Hereafter*, 106
Bañuelos Brothers, 175
Bates, Daisy, 91

Baudelaire, Charles, 60
Baudrillard, Jean, 162, 241n23
"Bear, The" (Faulkner), 113
Beck, E. M., 37
Beck, Ulrich, 15
Becnel, Thomas, 140
Beebe, George, 28, 51
Beloved (Morrison), 198, 245n10
Benson, Melanie, 173
Berlin, Germany, 194
Berlin, Ira, 178; *The Making of African America*, 9
Bibler, Michael P., 169; *Just Below South* (ed. with Adams and Accilien), 107
Bigsby, Christopher, 87, 92, 101, 231n49, 232n72
Birthright (Stribling), 226–27n51
Bitter in the Mouth (Truong), xvii, 177–78, 180–85 passim, 188, 192, 244n28, 244n32
Black Atlantic, 17, 63, 156, 171, 174, 197, 201
Black Atlantic, The (Gilroy), 54, 171–72
Black Bolshevik (Haywood), 229–30n33
Black Boy (Wright), 84
Black Internationalist Feminism (Higashida), 90
Black Liberation (Haywood), 88
Black Man's Burden (Killens), 79, 103
Black Southern Voices (ed. Killens and Ward), 105
Blake, William, 25
"Blue Dive" (Chappell), 174
Boas, Franz, 37, 113, 116
Book of Jamaica, The (Banks), xiv, xv, 108, 109–11, 113–18, 126, 129, 133
Boston, 108; in Jin's *A Free Life*, 178, 189, 190
Bourne, Randolph, 7, 216n30
Bow, Leslie, 8, 22, 167, 176–77, 181, 182, 190, 244n28, 244n32; *Partly Colored*, 176
Bowe, John, 19; *Nobodies*, 12, 218n67
Brickhouse, Anna, 75, 226n49, 226–27n51
Briggs, Cyril, 238–39n51
Brodber, Erna, xi, xv, xviii, 135–54 passim, 176, 177, 196, 237n4; Hurston and, 135–37, 236n1; Jamaica and, 138, 237n12, 238n47
—works of: *The Continent of Black Consciousness*, 145, 237n4, 238n47; *Louisiana*, xv, 135–54 passim, 236n1, 237n4, 237n22, 239n57, 239n61; *Myal*, 152–53
Broward, Napoleon, 204, 205
Brown v. Board of Education, 51, 86, 88, 103, 105, 154, 193, 224n84

Bruner, Edward, 116, 234n36
Burleigh, Harry T., 69
Bush, George H. W., 129
Bush, George W., 209–10
Butler, Benjamin, 140, 142
Butler, Robert Olen, 243n17; *A Good Scent from a Strange Mountain*, 179

Cabeza de Vaca, Álvar Núñez, 211, 247n41
Caicos Islands, 119, 123, 124
California, 78–79, 81; in Killens's *And Then We Heard the Thunder*, 93, 96, 98; as "up-South," 79
Cane (Toomer), 73, 95, 226n49
Cao, Lan, xi, xvi, xviii, 177, 189; *Monkey Bridge*, xvi–xvii, 177–78, 185–88, 192, 196, 214
Capital (Marx), 163
Capitalism, 137, 158, 202, 203–5; "casino capitalism," xvi, 156, 160–64, 175, 240–41n16, 240n19, 241n20; globalization and, 3–4, 10–13, 23, 26; neoliberalism and, 11–13, 164; scale and, 24; slavery and, 3, 204; spirit possession / zombification and, 118–19, 124, 129–32, 137, 152–53, 171, 191, 236n73; as world system, xvii, 24, 214
Capote, Truman, 21, 180; "A Diamond Guitar," 8; *Other Voices, Other Rooms*, 180–81
Carby, Hazel, 42, 61, 78, 225n11; Caribbean and, 97, 137; Caribbean immigrants in U.S. South and, 6, 8, 12, 42–52 passim, 136, 137, 147–49, 157, 169, 206, 222n42; extended Caribbean and, xi, 25, 52, 80, 107, 224n86; on Hurston's "discursive displacement" of Great Migration, xiii, 30–31, 33, 35, 43, 52, 144; in Morrison's *Tar Baby*, 198–202; New World slavery and, 3, 198; *Reconstructing Womanhood*, 55; U.S. South and, 4–5, 9, 107, 144, 147, 154, 176
Carpentier, Alejo, 107
Cartwright, Keith, 30, 32, 46, 129, 223n69, 223n71
Cash, Johnny, 171, 175
Casino Capitalism (Strange), 160, 240n19, 241n20
Castells, Manuel, 15
Castro, Fidel, 91, 108, 119, 230n46
Celestial Jukebox, The (Shearer), xvi, 9, 16, 155–75 passim, 207; casino capitalism and, 156, 160–62, 240–41nn19–20; Chinese immigrants in, 156–58, 166; Honduran

immigrants in, 155, 161, 165; Mauritanian immigrants in, 156, 160, 163–65
Cha, Frank, 179–80
Chapel Hill: Banks and, 108–9; in Truong's *Bitter in the Mouth*, 181
Chappell, Fred, 174
Chicago: in Brodber's *Louisiana*, 143, 144, 147; in Larsen's *Quicksand*, 58, 60–61, 64, 69, 71, 72; in Larsen's *Passing*, 74
Chicago Defender, 99
China, 6, 176; Chinese Exclusion Act, 157, 178; Chinese immigrants in Shearer's *The Celestial Jukebox*, 156–58, 166–67; Chinese immigrants in U.S. South, 4, 5, 6, 7, 156–58, 166–67, 177–78; "coolie" labor, 5, 12, 157, 169, 178, 204; in Jin's *A Free Life*, 185–88; second Sino-Japanese war, 157; in Sonnenberg's *Home Leave*, 193–94
Chiweshe, Stella, 172
Choi, Susan, 176, 191; *The Foreign Student*, 184
Chronicle of the Narváez Expedition (Cabeza de Vaca), 211, 247n41
Chu, Patricia, 3, 77, 132
Civil Rights movement, 51, 137, 178, 230n40; Banks's exposure to, 108–9; in Brodber's *Louisiana*, 153–54; Killens's take on white massive resistance to, 79, 80, 89; Killens's *Youngblood* and, 78, 86–88; in Shearer's *The Celestial Jukebox*, 165, 167–68
Civil War, 143, 163, 180, 185, 187
Clarksdale, Miss., 172, 173
Clifford, James, 116, 234n36
CNN (Cable News Network), 1, 11
Coalition of Immokalee Workers, 15–16, 168
Cobb, James, 14; *Globalization and the American South* (ed. with Stueck), 1, 11, 19, 217n53
Coclanis, Peter, 4
Codrescu, Andrei, 209
Cohn, Deborah, 2, 16, 192, 217n62; *History and Memory in the Two Souths*, 17; *Look Away!* (ed. with Smith), 17
Columbus, Christopher, 123, 129
"Communication" (Hurston), 46
Confederate States of America, 5, 157, 171, 185, 205
Congo (country), 150, 154
Congress of Industrial Organizations (CIO), 87–88, 229n26
Continental Drift (Banks), xv, 107–8, 118–34 passim, 137, 148, 152, 153, 162, 171, 191

Continent of Black Consciousness, The (Brodber), 145, 237n4, 238n47
Cooper, Jan, 39, 44, 222n47
Copenhagen, 54, 184, 225–26n27; Danish migration to, 66–68; in Larsen's *Quicksand*, 55, 63–70 passim, 71, 72
Cordill, C. C., 143
Cortés, Hernán, 213
Cosmopolitanism, 4, 6, 11, 208; from below, 4, 15, 202, 211
Cotillion, The (Killens), 105
"Court Order Can't Make Races Mix" (Hurston), 51
Creating and Consuming the American South (ed. Bone, Ward, Link), 20
Crespino, Joseph, 79; *The Myth of Southern Exceptionalism* (ed. with Lassiter), 23
Crisis of the Negro Intellectual, The (Cruse), 103
Crossing the Continent (Goodwin), 213
"Crossroads" (Komunyakaa), 124
Cruse, Harold, 104, 232n79; *The Crisis of the Negro Intellectual*, 103
Cuba, 108; Cuban immigrants in U.S. South, 6, 8, 119, 126, 224n90; Guantánamo Bay, 210; Spanish-American War, 204–5
Cullen, Countee, 75

"Dance Songs and Tales in the Bahamas" (Hurston), 46
Danish West Indies, 4, 54, 64–65; sale to United States, 65; slavery in, 64–65
Danticat, Edwidge, 52
Dao, Vy Thuc, 179–80, 243n20
Darling, The (Banks), 106
Davidson, Rob, 107
Davis, David, 218n75
Davis, F. James, 61
Davis, Thadious M., 30, 60, 62, 64, 70, 72, 227n58, 245n5; *Nella Larsen, Novelist of the Harlem Renaissance*, 54; *Southscapes*, 198
Dayan, Joan, 124, 132
Dearborn, Mary, 227n58; *Pocahontas's Daughters*, 75
deGravelles, Karin H., 206–7
DeGuzmán, María, 10, 217n44
Delbanco, Andrew, 224n84
Denmark: as colonial and slave-trading power, 64–65; Larsen in, 54; in Larsen's *Quicksand*, 63–70 passim, 72; welfare state and, 69
"Diamond Guitar, A" (Capote), 8
Dimock, Wai Chee, 25, 220n113

Dinesen, Isak (Karen Blixen), 115
Dirt and Desire (Yaeger), 21, 30, 33, 53
"Displaced Person, The" (O'Connor), 8
Disposable People (Bales), 170
Dissanayake, Wimal, 26; *Global/Local* (ed. with Wilson), 11
Dixon, Thomas, 205
Doll's House, A (Ibsen), 74
Dorantes, Esteban, 211, 247n40, 247n44, 247n46, 247n48; in Lalami's *The Moor's Account*, 211–14
Double V for Victory campaign, 94–95
Douglass, Frederick, 102, 157
Dove, Rita, 221n29
"Down by the Riverside" (Wright), 41
"Downsouth-Upsouth" (Killens), 79, 87
Dubey, Madhu, 31, 54, 199, 225n5, 245n9
Du Bois, W. E. B., 59, 238n35
Duck, Leigh Anne, 3, 20, 32, 38, 39, 42, 51, 68, 71, 95, 111, 196, 233n31; *The Nation's Region*, 16, 38, 84; "southern studies without 'the South,'" xvii, 24, 196
Dunbar, Eve, 112, 222n42
Dust Tracks on a Road (Hurston), 29, 46, 223n71
Duvalier, François ("Papa Doc"), 119
Duvalier, Jean-Claude ("Bébé Doc"), 119
Duvall, John, 197
Dvořák, Antonín, 69–70

Eatonville, Fla., 33, 39, 113
Eckes, Alfred E., 3, 6
Eggers, Dave: *What Is the What*, 9, 207–8; *Zeitoun*, xvii, 197, 206–10, 247n36
Ellison, Ralph, 56, 78, 84
Emergency Wartime Labor Program, 48, 148
England, in Kaye-Smith's "Mrs. Adis," 76–77, 227n58
Ethnic Heritage in Mississippi (ed. Walton and Carpenter), 7
Everglades (Fla.), 37, 54, 119; in Hurston's *Their Eyes Were Watching God*, xiii, 30–31, 38–43 passim, 222n47; Lake Okeechobee hurricane, 41–43, 223n62; in Matthiessen's *Shadow Country*, 205–6
Every Tongue Got to Confess (Hurston), 52

Faulkner, Mississippi (Glissant), 138
Faulkner, William, 8, 75, 88, 113, 120–21, 187, 235n68; Banks and, 106–8, 134, 233n9; Jin's *A Free Life* and, 191–92; Killens and, 88; Matthiessen's *Shadow Country* and, 203, 205; Morrison and, 198–99; "Quintessential fallacy" and, 22
—works of: *Absalom, Absalom!*, 22, 185, 199, 203, 219n103; "The Bear," 113; "If I Were a Negro," 121; *Intruder in the Dust*, 180; *Knight's Gambit*, 8; *Light in August*, 8, 75; *The Sound and the Fury*, 121, 196
Faust, Drew Gilpin, 5
Favor, J. Martin, 74; *Authentic Blackness*, 54
F. B. Eyes (Maxwell), 90
Federal Bureau of Investigation (FBI), 90, 105, 224n78
Federal Writers' Project, 34, 47, 48, 52, 223n69
Fields of Resistance (Giagnoni), 12
Fighting Maroons, The (Robinson), 114
Finding Purple America (J. Smith), ix
Fink, Leon, 15, 19
Fisk Normal School, 54, 55, 56
Fitzhugh, George, 164
Flagler, Henry, 205
Flaherty, Jordan, 14, 19
Florida, 12, 15–16, 28–52 passim, 168; Bahamian immigrants in, 30, 32, 223n62, 224n78; in Banks's fiction, 106–7, 118–34 passim, 148; Caribbean migrant workers in, 6, 8, 28, 32, 42–52; Cuban immigrants in, 7, 30; French and Spanish colonization of, 203–4; Haitian immigrants in, 30, 119–20; in Hurston's writing, 28–52 passim; Jamaican immigrants in, 48, 51; in Lalami's *The Moor's Account*, 211; in Matthiessen's *Shadow Country*, 203–6; in Morrison's *Tar Baby*, 198–202; Native peoples and, 45, 203–5, 211–12
"Florida's Migrant Farm Worker" (Hurston), 28–29, 48–52
Flynn, Errol, 110, 117–18, 233n21
Foner, Eric, 170
Foreign Student, The (Choi), 184
Forster, E. M., 115; *A Passage to India*, 194
Forum (magazine), 74–75, 227n54
Frazier, E. Franklin, 83
Free Life, A (Jin), xvi–xvii, 177–78, 188–93, 195, 196, 208, 214
Fuentes, Carlos, 107

Gaines, Ernest, 154, 240n68; *The Autobiography of Miss Jane Pittman*, 153
Garvey, Marcus, 97, 144–47, 149–50, 229n33, 238n33; "grassroots Garveyism," xvi, 144–

47, 149–50, 238–39n51; "local Garveyism," 146, 238n35
Gates, Henry Louis, 31
Gayle, Addison, 78
Geertz, Clifford, 116, 234n36
Georgia: Great Migration and, 37; in Jin's *A Free Life*, 185–88, 196; in Killens's *And Then We Heard the Thunder*, 93–96, 98, 100, 231–32n62; in Killens's *Youngblood*, 80, 81–88; in Sonnenberg's *Home Leave*, 193–94; Vietnamese immigrants in, 179, 196
Germany, 5; Nazism and, 94–95; in Sonnenberg's *Home Leave*, 193–94
Giagnoni, Silvia, 13, 19; *Fields of Resistance*, 12
Giles, Paul, 5, 23, 26, 29, 202, 215n10; *The Global Remapping of American Literature*, x
Gilroy, Paul, 17, 63, 126, 151, 171, 173, 201, 242n56; *The Black Atlantic*, 54, 171–72
Gilyard, Keith, 81, 91, 96, 102, 103, 229n26, 230n43
Giovanni, Nikki, 103
Gleason, William, 223n65
Glissant, Édouard, 107, 120–21, 126, 138, 199; *Faulkner, Mississippi*, 138; "poetics of relation" and, 107–8, 233n6, 235n68
Globalization, x–xi, 2, 4, 18–20, 23, 202; capitalism and, 3–4, 10–14, 23, 163, 214; immigration and, 1–2, 8, 11, 19–20, 23, 26, 177, 179; labor and, 11, 15–16, 19–20, 163, 169, 194, 202, 215n10; neoliberalism and, 11–12, 19, 197; region and, 2–3; of U.S. South, xii, 1, 9, 10–11, 23, 26–27, 155, 169, 175
Globalization and the American South (ed. Cobb and Stueck), 1, 11, 19, 217n53
Global/Local (ed. Wilson and Dissanayake), 11
Global Remapping of American Literature, The (Giles), x
Global South, 4, 12–16, 137, 158, 164, 217–18n63; in Killens's writing, 92, 103, 105; labor exploitation and, 13–16; new southern studies and, 17, 150; scale and, 25, 137; in Truong's *Bitter in the Mouth*, 183–84; and U.S. South, 12–16, 19, 183–84, 207
"God Bless America" (Killens), 231n54
Go Gator and Muddy the Water (Hurston), 52
Goldfield, David, 7
Goodman, Benny, 174
Good Scent from a Strange Mountain, A (R. O. Butler), 179

Goodwin, Robert, 211, 213–14, 247n40, 247n44, 247n46, 247n48; *Crossing the Continent*, 213
Go Tell It on the Mountain (Baldwin), 78
Gould, Peter, 123
Goyal, Yogita, 169, 201, 246n15
Graham, Allison, 14
Gray, Jeffrey, 227n52
Great Black Russian (Killens), 105
Great Day, The (Hurston), 47, 224n75
Great Depression, 36–38, 87, 88, 148
Great Gittin' Up Mornin' (Killens), 105
Great Migration, 6, 78, 88, 164, 199, 225n11; in Brodber's *Louisiana*, 137, 138, 142, 143; in Hurston's writing, 31–38 passim, 43, 45; in Larsen's *Quicksand*, 60, 62, 70–71
Greeson, Jennifer, 19, 207; *Our South*, 16
Gregory, James N., 6
Griffin, Farah Jasmine, 57, 62, 72; *"Who Set You Flowin'?,"* 54
Gross, Robert, x, 217n55
Grounded Globalism (Peacock), 19
Guatemalan immigrants in U.S. South, 15, 16
Guevara, Che, 108
Guterl, Matthew Pratt, 3–4, 5, 19, 155, 169; *American Mediterranean*, 3
Guthrie-Shimizu, Sayuri, 10, 193
Gyasi, Yaa, 9

Hahamovitch, Cindy, 12, 19, 37, 48, 51, 52, 148
Hair, William, 140
Haiti, xiv, xv, 4, 26, 45, 46, 136, 140, 177, 199, 219n103; in Banks's fiction, 106–7, 118–24 passim, 127–32 passim, 134, 148; Duvalier regimes, 119–20; Haitian immigrants in U.S. South, 15, 118–20, 130, 239n57; Haitian revolution, 4, 138–39, 216n10; in Hurston's *Tell My Horse*, 112–13, 116, 136; U.S. military occupation of, 112
Hamilton Stark (Banks), 109
Handley, George, 204
Hannah, Barry, 180, 186; *Ray*, 185; *Yonder Stands Your Orphan*, 160
Hansen, Mary, 54
Hardt, Michael, 24
Hardy Drew and the Nancy Boys, 79
Harker, Jaime, 176
Harlem, 55, 89, 145; in Killens's *And Then We Heard the Thunder*, 93; in Killens's *Youngblood*, 86; in Larsen's *Passing*, 74; in Larsen's *Quicksand*, 61–63, 64, 68, 70–71, 72

Harlem Renaissance, xiii, 53, 84, 227n58
Harlem Writers Guild, xiv, 90
Harold, Claudrena, 145, 146, 147, 149–50
Harpo, Slim, 175
Hart-Celler Immigration and Nationality Act, xvi, 9, 178, 180, 188
Harvey, David, x, 215n10, 240–41n19
Hastie, William, 96
Hathaway, Heather, 138, 237n14
Hathaway, Rosemary, 32, 112, 114, 122, 221n20
Haviland, Beverly, 227n58
Hawthorne, Nathaniel, 118
Hayes, Rutherford B., 141
Haywood, Harry, 80, 88–89, 150; Black Belt Nation thesis, 88–89, 150, 229–30n33, 238–39n51; *Black Bolshevik*, 229–30n33; *Black Liberation*, 88
Heart Is a Lonely Hunter, The (McCullers), 8
Hemenway, Robert, 223n71
Henninger, Katherine, 30
Herskovits, Melville, 116
Hicks, Scott, 223n63
Higashida, Cheryl, 230n40; *Black Internationalist Feminism*, 90
History and Memory in the Two Souths (Cohn), 17
History of Southern Literature, The (ed. Rubin et al.), 30
Hitler, Adolf, 93, 96
Home (Morrison), 198, 200, 245n6
Homegoing (Gyasi), 9
Home Leave (Sonnenberg), xvii, 193–95
Honduras, 155; Honduran immigrants in Shearer's *The Celestial Jukebox*, 155, 166, 168–69
"Hoodoo in America" (Hurston), 136
Hooker, John Lee, 172
House for Mr. Biswas, A (Naipaul), 191
Hughes, Langston, 46, 130
Hunton, Alphaeus, 90
Hurley, Patrick J., 100
Hurston, Zora Neale, xiii, 8, 28–52 passim, 111–18 passim, 143–44, 150, 221n22, 223n71, 223n75, 237n16; Banks and, xiv, 108, 124–26; Brodber and, xv, 135–38, 152, 236n1; Caribbean and, 30–33, 138; in Haiti, 45; Larsen and, 53–56, 68, 75; migrant labor and, 28–52 passim, 149; southern folk aesthetics and, 31–33, 53, 199; southern literary canon and, 30, 196
—works of: "Communication," 46; "Court Order Can't Make Races Mix," 51; "Dance Songs and Tales in the Bahamas," 46; *Dust Tracks on a Road*, 29, 46, 223n71; *Every Tongue Got to Confess*, 52; "Florida's Migrant Farm Worker," 28–29, 48–52; *Go Gator and Muddy the Water*, 52; *The Great Day*, 47, 224n75; "Hoodoo in America," 136; *Jonah's Gourd Vine*, xiii, 31, 32, 33–38 passim, 71, 137, 143, 221n24, 222n42; "The Migrant Worker in Florida," 28; *Mules and Men*, 29, 37–38, 45–46, 54, 113, 116, 126, 136, 221n24, 222n38, 222n42; "Other Negro Folk Influences," 47; *Seraph on the Suwanee*, 29. See also *Tell My Horse*; *Their Eyes Were Watching God*
Hurt, R. Douglas, 34
Hussein, Saddam, 210
Hutchinson, George B., 55, 65, 183, 227n58
Hutchison, Anthony, 106

Ibsen, Henrik, 73, 228n58; *A Doll's House*, 74
I Don't Hate the South (Baker), 60
"If I Were a Negro" (Faulkner), 121
I'll Take My Stand (Twelve Southerners), 174
Imagining Our Americas (ed. Tinsman and Shukla), 2
Immigration: class and, 10–11; globalization and, 1–2, 8, 11, 19–20, 23, 26, 177, 179; after Hart-Celler Act (1965), 8, 10; U.S. Cold War foreign policy and, 119; U.S. South and, 5, 7, 9–10, 19–20
In Country (Mason), 186
Inge, M. Thomas, 228n10
Intruder in the Dust (Faulkner), 180
Invisible Darkness (Larson), 54
Invisible Man (Ellison), 56, 78, 84
Iraq, 208–9

Jackman, Harold, 75
Jackson, Lawrence, 84
Jacobsen, Jens Peter, 227n58
Jamaica, 145–46; Banks in, 109; in Banks's fiction, 106–7, 109–11, 113–18, 122, 132–34; British colonial rule of, 110–11; in Brodber's fiction, 135, 138, 147–49, 152–54; in Hurston's *Tell My Horse*, 44, 111–13, 116–18; Jamaican immigrants in U.S. South, 48, 51, 136, 137, 147–49; and Maroons, 111–17, 133; U.S. power in, 110–12
James, Cynthia, 139, 147

James, Jennifer C., 92, 93, 101, 231n58
Jameson, Fredric, x, 87, 161, 205, 215n7, 240–41n19; *The Political Unconscious*, 151
Japan: Japanese immigrants in U.S. South, 10–11; second Sino-Japanese war, 157, 166; in World War II, 93–94, 96–97, 99
Jarmakani, Amira, 170–71
Jim Crow (segregation), 6, 8, 73, 148; in Hurston's *Their Eyes Were Watching God*, 39–41; "Juan Crow," 14; in Larsen's *Quicksand*, 64, 73; in U.S. Army during World War II, 92–102 passim
Jin, Ha, xvi, 177, 196; *A Free Life*, xvi–xvii, 177–78, 188–93, 195, 196, 208, 214; *The Writer as Migrant*, 185, 188, 190
Johnson, James Weldon, 226n51; *The Autobiography of an Ex-Colored Man*, 74
Jonah's Gourd Vine (Hurston), xiii, 31, 32, 33–38 passim, 71, 137, 143, 221n24, 222n42
Jones, Suzanne, 22, 197
Jones, W. Glyn, 66
Jung, Moon Ho, 157
Just Below South (ed. Adams, Accilien, and Bibler), 107

Kakutani, Michiko, 123
Kansas Fever, 6, 141, 157
Katrina (hurricane), xi, 14, 52, 179–80, 206–10, 218n67
Kaye-Smith, Sheila, 75–77, 227n58, 228n63; "Mrs. Adis," xiii, 74–77
Keita, Salif, 172
Kelley, Robin D. G., 149; *Race Rebels*, 238–39n51
Kentucky, 21, 97, 186
Khokher, Reginald, 139
Killens, John Oliver, xiv, 78–105 passim, 228n10, 231n54; in Africa, 91, 98, 145, 154, 229n26, 229n31, 230n33, 230n40; black nationalism/internationalism and, 80, 88–93, 98, 102, 103, 105; childhood of, in Macon, 79, 81–82, 87; Downsouth-Upsouth dialectic and, 78–81, 103–5, 230n43; FBI file on, 90, 105, 230n41; postcolonialism and, 80, 89–91, 98, 103, 105, 154; socialism and, 87, 89, 98, 102; in U.S. Army during World War II, 80, 81, 92–93, 231n61
—works of: *And Then We Heard the Thunder*, xiv, xviii, 81, 84, 88, 92–105, 231n54; 232n72; *Black Man's Burden*, 79, 103; *Black Southern Voices* (ed. with Ward), 105; *The Cotillion*, 105; "Downsouth-Upsouth," 79, 87; "God Bless America," 231n54; *Great Black Russian*, 105; *Great Gittin' Up Mornin'*, 105; *Lower Than the Angels*, 79, 91, 104; *A Man Ain't Nothing But a Man*, 105; 'Sippi, xiv, 103–5, 232n72; *Youngblood*, xiv, 78–88, 91, 94, 101, 103, 104, 105, 145, 154, 228n9, 230n43
King, B. B., 171
King, Martin Luther, 91, 102, 104–5; assassination of, 105, 175
King, Richard H., 19, 218n84
Kingsolver, Barbara, 21
Knight's Gambit (Faulkner), 8
Knights of Labor, 141–42
Kolodny, Annette, 114
Komunyakaa, Yusef, 124
Kreyling, Michael, 180, 214, 219n103
Krupa, Gene, 174
Kurotani, Sawa, 10, 193
Kutzinski, Vera, 135, 144, 152
Kyriakoudes, Louis M., 6, 34

Labor exploitation in U.S. South, 1–2, 6, 7, 11–16, 203, 218n67, 224n78
Ladd, Barbara, 17
Lake Okeechobee hurricane, 41–46 passim, 223n62, 223–24n71
Lalami, Laila, xi, xvii, 247nn43–44; *The Moor's Account*, xxvii, 197, 210–14, 247n41
Lamothe, Daphne, 44
Larsen, Nella, xiii–xiv, 53–77 passim, 166, 183, 228n63; Denmark and, 54–55, 225n10, 225–26n27; Hurston and, 53–56; plagiarism scandal, 74–75, 77, 227n54, 227n58, 228n59; representation of black southern folk, 53–56, 59–60, 70–77, 226n49, 226n51; representation of Danish folk, 66–69
—works of: *Passing*, 53, 74, 183; *Quicksand*, xiii, 53–77 passim, 84, 166, 227–28n58; "Sanctuary," xiii, 74–77
Larson, Charles, 54
Larson, Kelli A., 76
Lassiter, Matthew, 79; *The Myth of Southern Exceptionalism* (ed. with Crespino), 23
Laveau, Marie, 139, 237n10, 237n16
Leahy, John, 121
Lee, Harper, 180–81; *To Kill a Mockingbird*, 181, 184
Lee, Robert E., 185
Lehman, Paul R., 92, 231n48

Lewitt, Peggy, 15
Lichtenstein, Alex, 6
Liebling, A. J., 208, 246n32
Light in August (Faulkner), 8, 75
Link, William: *The American South and the Atlantic World* (ed. with Ward and Bone), 25; *Creating and Consuming the American South* (ed. with Bone and Ward), 20
Lloyd, Christopher, x, 198, 210, 247n36
Locke, Alain, 33, 51, 84, 221n22
Loewen, James W., 157–58, 167
Look Away! (ed. Smith and Cohn), 17
Lost Memory of Skin (Banks), 133
Louisiana, xvi, 105, 218n67, 219n103, 237n20; in Brodber's *Louisiana*, 135–54 passim; in Eggers's *Zeitoun*, 206–10; Jamaican immigrants in, 148; Reconstruction in, 137
Louisiana (Brodber), xv, 135–54 passim, 236n1, 237n4, 237n22, 239n57, 239n61
L'Ouverture, Touissant, 46, 139
Lowe, John, 30, 112, 215n8, 223n69
Lower Than the Angels (Killens), 79, 91, 104
Lukács, Georg, 25, 219–20n113
Lum v. Rice, 167, 241n31
Lunde, Arne, 65, 226n31, 227n58
Lytle, Andrew, 174

MacArthur, Douglas, 100
Macherey, Pierre, 65
Macon, xiv, 88; in Banks's *Continental Drift*, 126–27; Killens's childhood in, 79, 81–82, 87, 105; Killens's *Youngblood* and, 81–82
Making of African America, The (Berlin), 9
Malcolm X, 79, 91, 98, 102, 103, 104–5, 231n47; Killens and, xiv, 103
Man Ain't Nothing But a Man, A (Killens), 105
Man in Full, A (Wolfe), 21
Manley, Michael, 110
Marable, Manning, 102
Maroons (of Jamaica), xv, 148; in Banks's fiction, 110–11, 113–18, 133; in Hurston's *Tell My Horse*, 111–18; resistance to British colonialism and, 110, 117
Márquez, Gabriel García, 107
Marshall, Paule, 237n4
Martí, José, 3, 176
Martin, Tony, 238n33; *Race First*, 145
Martin, Valerie, 243n15
Martinique, 194, 199, 219n103
Marx, Karl, 152, 163–64; *Capital*, 163
Mason, Bobbie Ann, 180; *In Country*, 186

Massachusetts, 211; as Banks's birthplace, 106–7; in Hurston's writing, 112–13, 123; in Jin's *A Free Life*, 192
Matthews, Carrie, 2; *The American South in a Global World* (ed. with Peacock and Watson), 1, 19, 217n53
Matthiessen, Peter, xi, 12; *Shadow Country*, xvii, 197, 203–6, 214
Mauritania, 13, 26, 165; French colonialism and, 171, 242n48; in Shearer's *The Celestial Jukebox*, 155–56, 170–71, 242n57; slavery in, 156, 170–71, 242n48
Maxwell, William, 90
Mayfield, Julian, 91
McCullers, Carson, 21, 94; *The Heart Is a Lonely Hunter*, 8; *The Member of the Wedding*, 180
McKay, Claude, 90
McKee, Kathryn, 2, 17
McPherson, Tara, 20, 159, 162, 182; *Reconstructing Dixie*, 21
Member of the Wedding, The (McCullers), 180
Memphis, 11, 157, 172; in Shearer's *The Celestial Jukebox*, 164, 174–75
Mencken, H. L., 7
Mendoza, Lydia, 175
Mexico: *bracero* program and, 12, 20, 48; in Lalami's *The Moor's Account*, 213–14; Mexican immigrants in U.S. South, 14, 15, 20, 42, 165; Spanish colonialism in, 211–14
Miami, 9, 107, 119; in Banks's fiction, 107, 117–18, 130
Miami Herald, 28–29, 50, 51, 52, 203
"Migrant Worker in Florida, The" (Hurston), 28
Miller, Joshua L., 75, 227n58, 228n63
Mislaid (Zink), 5
Mississippi: Chinese immigrants in, 7–8; as "closed society," 9; Great Migration and, 37, 142; in Killens's *'Sippi*, 103–5; in Shearer's *The Celestial Jukebox*, 155–75; in Sonnenberg's *Home Leave*, 193–94
Modernism and the Harlem Renaissance (Baker), 56
Monkey Bridge (Cao), xvi–xvii, 177–78, 185–88, 192, 196, 214
Monteith, Sharon, 20–21, 22, 184, 185, 188
Moody, Ann, 181
Moor's Account, The (Lalami), xxvii, 197, 210–14, 247n41
Morocco, 103; in Lalami's *The Moor's Account*, 211–12
Morrison, Toni, xi, xvii, 107, 134, 197–202, 208;

Hurston and, 245n9; southern literature and, 197–98; U.S. South and, 199, 245n6, 245nn9–10
—works of: *Beloved*, 198, 245n10; *Home*, 198, 200, 245n6; *Song of Solomon*, 198, 245n9; *Tar Baby*, xvii, 197–202, 203, 206, 245n10, 246n15
"Mrs. Adis" (Kaye-Smith), xiii, 74–77
Muhammad Speaks (newspaper), 88
Mules and Men (Hurston), 29, 37–38, 45–46, 54, 113, 116, 126, 136, 221n24, 222n38, 222n42
Muller, Gilbert, 119, 121
Myal (Brodber), 152–53
Mykle, Robert, 41, 42
Myth of Southern Exceptionalism, The (ed. Lassiter and Crespino), 23

Nagin, Ray, 14, 209
Naipaul, V. S., 176; *A House for Mr. Biswas*, 191; *A Turn in the South*, 17
Narváez, Panfilo, 211
Nashville, 54, 55, 56
National Association for the Advancement of Colored People (NAACP), 85, 86, 238n35
National Labor Relations Board, 83, 90
Nation of Islam, 91, 102, 103
Nation's Region, The (Duck), 16, 38, 84
Native South, 212–14, 247n43
Negri, Antonio, 24
Nehru, Jawaharlal, 231–32n62
Nella Larsen, Novelist of the Harlem Renaissance (T. M. Davis), 54
Nelson, Dana, ix, x, xiv, 16, 17, 79, 80, 218n76
Neoliberalism, 11–13, 19, 24; globalization and, 11–13, 19, 197; new southern studies and, 19; U.S. South and, xii
Ness, Immanuel, 13–14, 217n63; *Southern Insurgency*, 13
New Encyclopedia of Southern Culture, 228n10
New Hampshire, in Banks's fiction, 107, 113, 121, 125–27, 128, 129, 132, 134
New Orleans, 7, 14–15, 140; in Brodber's *Louisiana*, 136, 137, 138, 141, 142, 144, 147, 151; in Eggers's *Zeitoun*, 206–10; exceptionalism of, 206; Haitian immigrants in, 46, 139, 239n57; Hurricane Katrina and, xvii, 14, 25, 52, 206–10; in Hurston's writing, 136; Jamaican immigrants in, 147–49, 154; labor struggles in, 137, 142–43; "Third Worlding" of, 206–10; United Negro Improvement Association and, 145–47, 238n35, 238n46; voodoo/hoodoo and, 136, 151
New Orleans Picayune, 143
New southern studies, ix–x, xii, 16–20, 22, 79, 218n84; black-white binary and, 21; Global South and, 17, 176; hemispheric/New World studies and, 17, 176, 215n8; neoliberalism and, 19; new labor history and, 149–50; Pacific Rim and, 176; transnationalism and, 16–20, 197, 214
New Southern Studies (University of Georgia Press book series), ix, 19, 218n84
New World Symphony (Dvořák), 69–70
New York: in Banks's fiction, 132–34; in Brodber's *Louisiana*, 138; in Jin's *A Free Life*, 178, 189, 192; in Killens's *And Then We Heard the Thunder*, 93, 95, 97; in Killens's *'Sippi*, 104; in Killens's *Youngblood*, 82–83, 85–86; in Larsen's *Quicksand*, 61–63, 64, 71, 72; in Morrison's *Tar Baby*, 199–201; in Truong's *Bitter in the Mouth*, 182; as "upsouth," 78–79, 83, 105
New York Post, 98
New York Review of Books, 203
New York Times, 1, 11, 118, 123, 234n43, 235n49
Nicholls, David G., 37
Niemi, Robert, 110, 114
Nobodies (Bowe), 12, 218n67
Nonini, Donald M., 9, 11, 193
North Carolina, 11, 15, 108–9, 145, 193; in Truong's *Bitter in the Mouth*, 180–85
Nwankwo, Ifeoma, 4, 15, 202

O'Brien, Michael, 17–20
O'Connor, Flannery, 120; "The Displaced Person," 8
Odem, Mary, 6
Operation Dixie, 87–88, 89, 229n26
Organization of Afro-American Unity (OAAU), 103
Orlando Sentinel, 51
Orpheus Descending (T. Williams), 8
"Other Negro Folk Influences" (Hurston), 47
Other Voices, Other Rooms (Capote), 180–81
Our South (Greeson), 16

Paris, in Morrison's *Tar Baby*, xvii, 198, 200
Partly Colored (Bow), 176
Passage to India, A (Forster), 194
Passing (Larsen), 53, 74, 183
Pavlić, Edward, 44, 46, 124, 223n65

Peacock, James, 4, 21, 182; *The American South in a Global World* (ed. with Watson and Matthews), 1, 19, 217n53; *Grounded Globalism*, 19
Perkins, Carl, 175
Peterson, Dorothy, 62
Pfister, Joel, x, 11
Philippines, in Killens's *And Then We Heard the Thunder*, xiv, 81, 93, 96–97, 98
Pickett, Wilson, 175
Pierce, Franklin, 118
Pinto, Samantha, 135, 136, 149, 152–53, 236n1, 239n61
Pittsburgh Courier, 91, 94, 231n54
Plessy v. Ferguson, 241n31
PMLA, 17
Pocahontas's Daughters (Dearborn), 75
Political Unconscious, The (Jameson), 151
Pomeroy, William, 232n70
Ponce de León, Juan, 123, 204, 212
Pope, Alexander, 191
Poston, Ted, 98
Praisesong for the Widow (Marshall), 237n4
Price, Rachael, 184, 244n34
Prodigal Summer (Kingsolver), 21
Publishers Weekly, 203
Pushkin, Alexander, 105

Quan, Robert Seto, 167
Quicksand (Larsen), xiii, 53–77 passim, 84, 166, 227–28n58

Race Against Empire (von Eschen), 90
Race and White Identity in Southern Fiction (Duvall), 197
Race First (T. Martin), 145
Race Rebels (Kelley), 238–39n51
Raisin in the Sun, A (Hansberry), 194
Ray (Hannah), 185
Reagan, Ronald, 119, 129–30
Reconstructing Dixie (McPherson), 21
Reconstructing the South (Stecopoulos), 26
Reconstructing Womanhood (Carby), 55
Reconstruction, xi, 6, 27, 137, 140–42, 165
Reconstruction in the Cane Fields (Rodrigue), 140
Redding, Otis, 175
Regis, Helen A., 6
Reimers, David, 6, 157, 188
"Relic" (R. O. Butler), 179
Richardson, Riché, 17, 38, 222n42

Ring, Natalie, 218n84
Roach, Joseph, 132, 136, 152, 153, 237n10
Robinson, Carey, 114
Roche, David, 117
Rockefeller, John D., 205
Rodrigue, John C., 142; *Reconstruction in the Cane Fields*, 140
Roediger, David, 164
Rolinson, Mary, 146, 147, 238n41
Romine, Scott, 16, 160, 162
Rooting Memory, Rooting Place (Lloyd), x, 198
Rowe, John Carlos, 46
Rule of the Bone (Banks), 132–33, 184
Rushdie, Salman, 189
Rushing, Wanda, 11, 172
Ryan, Maureen, 187–88

Salaam, Kalamu ya, 147
"Sanctuary" (Larsen), xiii, 74–77; and plagiarism scandal, 74–75, 77
Sassen, Saskia, 14, 15
Saunders, Kay, 98, 100
Scale, x–xi, 28, 193, 196–97; capitalism and, 24; "jumping" scales, 137, 155, 159; literary studies and, 24–27, 219–20n113; new southern studies and, 23–26, 214, 220n118; region and, 24, 28, 77, 103; U.S. South and, 23–27, 79, 133–34, 177–78, 192, 214; world-system theory and, 24, 25, 214
Schwartz, Lawrence, 192, 244n51
Segars, Neil, 158, 167–68
Seminoles, 30, 45
September 11, 2001, terrorist attacks, 174–75, 207–10, 242n57
Seraph on the Suwanee (Hurston), 29
Shadow Country (Matthiessen), xvii, 197, 203–6, 214
Shearer, Cynthia, xi, xvi, xviii, 9, 12, 16, 155–75, 176, 196, 243n62. See also *Celestial Jukebox, The*
Shukla, Sandha, 2–3; *Imagining Our Americas* (ed. with Tinsman), 2
Shuttleworth, Fred, 91
Silver, Doug, 28, 51
Silver, Margaret, 28, 220n5
Silverman, Debra, 226n49
Singapore, 194
'Sippi (Killens), xiv, 103–5, 232n72
Slavery, 3, 132, 152–53, 173, 176, 197, 208, 211, 214; heritage tourism and, 162–63; in Jamaica, 110, 112, 118, 152, 172; in Mauri-

tania, 170–71, 242n48; Middle Passage, 3, 124, 235n65, 247n46; neoslavery, 6, 12, 149, 157, 162–69, 205; New World and, 3–4, 198, 210–14, 224n86; U.S. South and, xii, 3–4, 12, 14, 19, 95–96, 155, 157, 203, 214
Smith, Barbara, 7, 10, 19, 21, 24
Smith, Dave, 107–8, 233n9
Smith, Jon, 2, 16, 20, 24, 214, 217n62; *Finding Purple America*, ix; *Look Away!* (ed. with Cohn), 17
Smith, Neil, 24, 28, 159, 220n113
Smith-Irvin, Jennifer, 145
Smith-Nonini, Sandy, 165
Soja, Edward, x
Song of Solomon (Morrison), 198, 245n9
Sonnenberg, Brittani, 196; *Home Leave*, xvii, 193–95
Sound and the Fury, The (Faulkner), 121, 196
South Africa, 90, 97
South Carolina, 14, 141
Southern exceptionalism, 7, 8, 23, 79
Southern Insurgency (Ness), 13
Southern literary studies, xii, xiv, 2, 20–23, 176, 181, 196–97; black-white binary and, 21–22, 177; representation of immigrants and, 8, 20–23, 176–77
Southern Poverty Law Center, 12; Immigrant Justice Project, 12
Southern Renaissance, xii, 8, 30, 53, 196
Southern Shrimp Alliance, 179, 187
South Korea, and the Korean War, 184
Southscapes (T. M. Davis), 198
Spain, 211; Spanish colonialism in New World, 204–5, 211–14
Spanish-American War, 204–5
Specifying (Willis), 30
Stecopoulos, Harilaos, 81, 94, 100, 176, 205, 220n118; *Reconstructing the South*, 26
Stenport, Anna, 65, 226n31, 227n58
Stepick, Alex, 119
Stimson, Henry, 96
Strange, Susan, 160–62, 240n16; *Casino Capitalism*, 160, 240n19, 241n20
Stribling, T. S., 226–27n51
Striffler, Steve, 15
Stueck, William, 1, 217n53
Sudan, 207–8
Sundquist, Eric J., 38
Sweet Hereafter, The (Banks), 106
Sydney Sun, 99

Syria: in Eggers's *Zeitoun*, 208–9, 247n36; Syrian immigration to U.S. South, 7

Talmadge, Eugene, 94
Tang, Eric, 180
Tanoukhi, Nirvana, 25
Tar Baby (Morrison), xvii, 197–202, 203, 206, 245n10, 246n15
Tate, Allen, 15, 187
Taylor, Helen, 247n36
Taylor, Melanie Benson, 21, 177
Tell My Horse (Hurston), xiv–xv, 44, 111–13, 116–18, 124, 131, 234n31; Brodber's *Louisiana* and, 136, 138, 239n61
Texas, 211–12
Their Eyes Were Watching God (Hurston), xiii, 29–33, 206, 223–24n71, 227n58; Banks's *Continental Drift* and, 124, 126, 236n73; Brodber's *Louisiana* and, 150–51; Larsen's *Quicksand* and, 68, 73
Thieu, Nguyen Van, 182
Thompson, Graham, x, 215n7
Tinsman, Heidi, 2–3; *Imagining Our Americas* (ed. with Shukla), 2
Tojo, Hideki, 93–94
To Kill a Mockingbird (H. Lee), 181, 184
Toland-Dix, Shirley, 135, 136, 137, 144, 145
Tolnay, Stewart, 37
Toomer, Jean, 73, 95, 226n49
Transnationalism, ix, x, xvii, 176; American studies and, ix–x, xvii, 7, 10–17 passim, 23, 176, 196, 214, 217n55; modernist studies and, 77; regionalism and, 23–27; scale and, 25–27; southern studies and, 16–20; transpacific turn and, 176
Trefzer, Annette, 2, 17, 30, 45–46, 117, 131, 233n31
Trethewey, Natasha, 160, 179–80
Truong, Monique, xi, xviii, 180–85, 191, 196, 243n23; *Bitter in the Mouth*, xvii, 177–78, 180–85 passim, 188, 192, 244n28, 244n32
Tubman, Harriet, 95
Turner, Frederick Jackson, 203
Turner, Lorenzo Dow, 175
Turner, Nat, 4, 216n10
Turning South Again (Baker), 16–17, 56–59
Turn in the South, A (Naipaul), 17
Tuskegee Institute, 56–58, 60; as Naxos in Larsen's *Quicksand*, 56–59
Tyner, Ernie, 50

INDEX 279

Uncle Tom's Children (Wright), 41, 79
United Fruit Company, 118, 147–49, 204
United Negro Improvement Association (UNIA), 97, 144–47, 149–51, 153, 231n47, 238n35, 238n41, 238n46, 238–39n51
U.S. Army, 84, 92–93, 148; in Australia during World War II, 98–102; Jim Crow segregation and, 92, 94, 96, 98; Killens in, 80, 92–93; in Killens's *And Then We Heard the Thunder*, 93–105
U.S. Sugar, 48, 148, 204, 224n78
U.S. Virgin Islands, 54

Vesey, Denmark, 4, 105, 216n10
Vietnam: in Cao's *Monkey Bridge*, 185–88; in Truong's *Bitter in the Mouth*, 180–84; U.S. war in, xvi, 105, 167, 179, 180, 181, 183, 201; Vietnamese immigrants in U.S. South, 177, 179–80, 207, 243n20
Virginia, 4, 145, 211; in Cao's *Monkey Bridge*, 185–88, 196; Vietnamese immigrants in, 185
Voices from the Storm, 207
von Eschen, Penny, 90
"Voodoo economics," 129–30, 132, 152
Vorre, Birgit, 66–67
Voting Rights Act, 9
Voudon/voodoo: in Banks's fiction, 120, 124, 129–32, 236n73; in Brodber's fiction, 136; in Haiti, 120, 136; in Hurston's writing, 124, 131, 136, 237n16; in New Orleans, 136, 151

Wald, Alan, 84, 87, 92
Walker, Alice, 28, 107, 120, 181
Walker, Joseph, 88
Walker, Peter, 54
Wall, Cheryl, 75
Wallace, Henry, 89
Wallerstein, Immanuel, xi, 24, 25, 52, 224n86
Walton, Shana, 7
Ward, Brian, 11; *The American South and the Atlantic World* (ed. with Bone and Link), 25; *Creating and Consuming the American South* (ed. with Bone and Link), 20
Ward, Jerry, 105
Warren, Robert Penn, 160
Washburne, Christopher, 151, 239n57
Washington, Booker T., 56–57, 59
Washington, D.C., in Killens's *Youngblood*, 82–85

Waters, Muddy, 172, 242n53
Watson, Harry L., 2, 3; *The American South in a Global World* (ed. with Peacock and Matthews), 1, 19, 217n53
Weaks-Baxter, Mary, 39, 44, 222n47
Wegmann-Sánchez, Jessica, 62, 227n51
What Is the What (Eggers), 9, 207–8
"Whirlwind Storm Warning UNIA" (Salaam), 147
White, Rodney, 123
"Who Set You Flowin'?" (Griffin), 54
Willerslev, Rich, 68
Williams, Robert, 91
Williams, Tennessee, 8
Willis, Susan, 30–31, 220n14; *Specifying*, 30
Wilson, Rob, 26, 176; *Global/Local* (ed. with Dissanayake), 11
Winders, Jamie, 7, 21, 22
Wittmann, Dena C., 240n16
Wolfe, Thomas, 189
Wolfe, Tom, 21
Woodward, C. Vann, 204
Workings of the Spirit (Baker), 31, 53–54, 56
Works Progress Administration (WPA), 135, 136, 139, 144, 149, 151, 153, 154, 240n68
World War I, 35, 82, 143
World War II, 12, 48, 90, 147, 157; in Killens's *And Then We Heard the Thunder*, 92–102 passim, 231n54; Killens's participation in, 80, 81, 92–93
Wounds of Returning (Adams), 20
Wright, Richard, 31, 32, 33, 42, 51, 78, 90, 228n8; *Black Boy*, 84; "Down by the Riverside," 41; *Uncle Tom's Children*, 41, 79
Writer as Migrant, The (Jin), 185, 188, 190
Wylie, J. J., 106

Yaeger, Patricia, 38–39, 41, 73, 77, 173, 220n118; *Dirt and Desire*, 21, 30, 33, 53; "reverse autochthony" and, 41, 73, 173
Yonder Stands Your Orphan (Hannah), 160
Youngblood (Killens), xiv, 78–88, 91, 94, 101, 103, 104, 105, 145, 154, 228n9, 230n43
Yousaf, Nahem, 20, 22, 185, 188

Zeitoun (Eggers), xvii, 197, 206–10, 247n36
Zink, Nell, 5

The New Southern Studies

The Nation's Region: Southern Modernism, Segregation, and U.S. Nationalism
BY LEIGH ANNE DUCK

Black Masculinity and the U.S. South: From Uncle Tom to Gangsta
BY RICHÉ RICHARDSON

Grounded Globalism: How the U.S. South Embraces the World
BY JAMES L. PEACOCK

Disturbing Calculations: The Economics of Identity in Postcolonial Southern Literature, 1912–2002
BY MELANIE R. BENSON

American Cinema and the Southern Imaginary
EDITED BY DEBORAH E. BARKER AND KATHRYN MCKEE

Southern Civil Religions: Imagining the Good Society in the Post-Reconstruction Era
BY ARTHUR REMILLARD

Reconstructing the Native South: American Indian Literature and the Lost Cause
BY MELANIE BENSON TAYLOR

Apples and Ashes: Literature, Nationalism, and the Confederate States of America
BY COLEMAN HUTCHISON

Reading for the Body: The Recalcitrant Materiality of Southern Fiction, 1893–1985
BY JAY WATSON

Latining America: Black-Brown Passages and the Coloring of Latino/a Studies
BY CLAUDIA MILIAN

Finding Purple America: The South and the Future of American Cultural Studies
BY JON SMITH

The Signifying Eye: Seeing Faulkner's Art
BY CANDACE WAID

Sacral Grooves, Limbo Gateways: Travels in Deep Southern Time, Circum-Caribbean Space, Afro-creole Authority
BY KEITH CARTWRIGHT

Jim Crow, Literature, and the Legacy of Sutton E. Griggs
EDITED BY TESS CHAKKALAKAL AND KENNETH W. WARREN

Sounding the Color Line: Music and Race in the Southern Imagination
BY ERICH NUNN

Borges's Poe: The Influence and Reinvention of Edgar Allan Poe in Spanish America
BY EMRON ESPLIN

Eudora Welty's Fiction and Photography: The Body of the Other Woman
BY HARRIET POLLACK

Keywords for Southern Studies
EDITED BY SCOTT ROMINE AND JENNIFER RAE GREESON

The Southern Hospitality Myth: Ethics, Politics, Race, and American Memory
BY ANTHONY SZCZESIUL

Navigating Souths: Transdisciplinary Explorations of a U.S. Region
EDITED BY MICHELE GRIGSBY COFFEY AND JODI SKIPPER

Where the New World Is: Literature about the U.S. South at Global Scales
BY MARTYN BONE

Red States: Indigeneity, Settler Colonialism, and Southern Studies
BY GINA CAISON

The Whole Machinery: The Rural Modern in Cultures of the U.S. South, 1890–1946
BY BENJAMIN S. CHILD